GLORY
IN
OUR
MIDST

A BIBLICAL-THEOLOGICAL READING OF
ZECHARIAH'S NIGHT VISIONS

Meredith G. Kline

Wipf and Stock Publishers
150 West Broadway • Eugene OR 97401
2001

Glory In Our Midst

By Kline, Meredith G.

Copyright©2001 by Kline, Meredith G.

ISBN: 1-57910-599-8

Printed by *Wipf and Stock Publishers*
150 West Broadway • Eugene OR 97401

to Geerhardus Vos
(1862-1949)

pioneer of the biblical theology way

PREFACE

The present publication is a reproduction, with minor revisions, of a series of articles that appeared in the journal *Kerux* in fourteen installments over seven years beginning with the September 1990 issue. Included also as an appendix is my essay, "The Structure of the Book of Zechariah," first published in *JETS* 34,2 (1991) 179-193. I have not tried to eliminate entirely the repetition found in the original *Kerux* series, due there to brief recapitulations provided from time to time for the sake especially of new readers not familiar with earlier articles. Whether originally due to that purpose or simply to my preoccupation with certain biblical-theological concepts, whatever of repetition remains here will, it is hoped, prove helpful even to those who now have the whole thing before them at once.

In keeping with the nature of *Kerux* as "A Journal of Biblical Theological Preaching," the studies that comprise this book were designed to serve quite directly the purposes of those preaching on Zechariah's night visions. More broadly, however, our intention has been to cultivate among all the Lord's people an appreciation of the biblical-theological approach in the exploration of the treasures of God's saving truth in the Scriptures. What is presented here is then a biblical-theological reading of the prophetic visions of Zechariah 1-6. We try to grasp the significance of these visions in the light of their identity as part of the overall eschatological drama of the kingdom of God from creation to consummation, that eschatological reality on which they, in turn, are themselves a window. Though differing somewhat in form from the usual verse-by-verse commentary, this biblical-theological study is still presented as a work of rigorous exegesis, with fresh solutions suggested for the interpretation of some of the key exegetical puzzles with which the enigmatic but not unfathomable symbolism of these visions confronts us.

Featured throughout the night visions is a remarkably rich revelation of the Messiah. Reflecting that, each of our chapters is entitled in terms of the office or redemptive act of Christ that is highlighted in the vision in view. Also conspicuous is the role of the Spirit in relation to the messianic mission, particularly in his identity as the theophanic Glory, the Glory-Spirit. This Glory of the heavenly Presence of the triune God is indeed the dominant reality in Zechariah's visionary world. And central in the message of the night visions is the gospel promise that this Glory-Presence is vouchsafed to God's people, at last in eschatological fullness. Hence the title: *Glory in Our Midst.*

The gratitude of all devotees of biblical theology in the tradition of Geerhardus Vos is due to James T. Dennison, Jr. for his labors as the editor of *Kerux*. I wish here to express my appreciation for his ever-accommodating spirit in arranging for the appearance of my Zechariah series in *Kerux* and for his readiness to facilitate the publication of these studies in their present form. I would also thank the editor of the *Journal of the Evangelical Theological Society* for his kind permission to reproduce in this work the article mentioned above. And I gratefully acknowledge that it is thanks to my son Meredith M. and to his son Jonathan that I have gotten through the technological mysteries of the editing process.

Quotations from the Bible, unless AV or otherwise noted, are my own, whether eclectic blendings or more distinctly independent renderings.

M.G.K.

CONTENTS

Vision One (1:7-17)

GOVERNOR OF THE NATIONS

I. THE THREE PRINCIPALS IN THE COSMIC TABLEAU (1:8)

The symbolic scene depicted in Zech 1:8 contains the essence of the prophet's night visions and, indeed, of his entire prophecy. His overall theme, developed in visions, oracles, symbolic actions, sermons, and "burdens", is the restoration and consummation of God's kingdom. Analysis of the structure of the book shows it to be unified by a repeating sequence of three main topics. First and primary is the return and presence of God's Glory in the midst of his people as their strength and salvation. The other two are the promised consequences of the first: the second in the triadic pattern is the elimination of evil, the evil of oppression from without and perversion within; and the third is the redemptive establishment of the Zion community as an expression and embodiment of God's universal sovereignty.

Involved as principals in this historical drama are the Glory-Presence of the Lord, the satanic world, and the redeemed covenant community. These three appear in Zech 1:8 in the symbolic guise of the rider of the red horse, the deep, and the myrtles, respectively. Each of these becomes the focus in one of the three following interpretive sections of the first night vision: the deep, in the report of the horsemen (1:9-11); the myrtles, in the Angel's intercession (1:12); and the Glory-Presence, in the Lord's response (1:13-17).

A. *The Rider of the Red Horse:*

1. *Messianic Angel of the Presence:* When the apostle John received his apocalyptic vision on Patmos, the opening revelation confronted him with the figure of the Son of Man in the transfigured brilliance of heaven's glory (Rev 1:13-16). Similarly, Zechariah in his opening vision beheld the commanding presence of a man riding a red horse, a man who was the Angel of the Lord, the pre-incarnate revelation of the coming Christ. That this man and the messianic Angel are in fact one and the same individual is brought out clearly by the pointed identification of the "the Angel of Yahweh" in v. 11 as "the one stationed among the myrtles," the phrase already used twice to describe the man-figure (vv. 8 and 10). Moreover, like this man, the Angel is the one with immediate authority over the other horsemen.

A second angel appears in this and subsequent visions, repeatedly described by Zechariah as "the angel who was talking with me" (1:9,13,14,etc.). Such an interpreting angel was also sent to other recipients of apocalyptic visions (cf., e.g., Dan 8:16ff.; Rev 22:8ff.). But the Angel of the Lord is unique among the angels. He is the Lord of angels. In the course of Zechariah's visions we find the same evidence of this Angel's divine attributes and prerogatives that appears elsewhere in the Scriptures and has led to the general recognition of this figure as a form of theophany, more specifically, as a manifestation of the second person of the Trinity. One such indication of the divine identity of the Angel of Yahweh in the present context is the reference to him in verse 13 as simply "Yahweh".

In this man-Angel the coming Messiah-Lord was revealing at the very outset of these visions his immediate presence with his people. He was there with them in their historical struggle, exercising his sovereign power in their behalf (cf. Isa 63:9 and 43:2). That personal presence of the Lord of Glory in the midst of the covenant community on earth was the all-important reality. To make known the meaning of the presence and mission of this messianic Angel is what Zechariah's visions are all about. They are an unveiling of the secret of the covenant, an apocalypse of the mystery of the divine Presence.

2. *Mounted Warrior:* The appearance of the divine Angel to Zechariah in this opening vision recalls his appearance to Joshua near Jericho at the beginning of the conquest of Canaan. Even in their literary form the accounts of the two appearances (Josh 5:13 and Zech 1:8) correspond closely, with similarities both in sentence structure and vocabulary. Like Zechariah, Joshua looks, and behold a man, standing over against him. The martial purpose of his presence, indicated by the drawn sword in his hand, was confirmed by his self-identification as commander of the army of Yahweh. His deity was revealed in his declaration that the place was sanctified by his presence (vv. 14,15; cf. Exod 3:5). Similarly, the divine man-Angel who confronted Zechariah was readily identifiable as an agent of God engaged in a military undertaking, mounted as he was on a red horse among the other supernatural world-traversing horsemen. He was the commander of these heavenly troops. It was to him they reported after their reconnoitering of the nations prior to a campaign of judgment (Zech 1:11; cf. the spying out of Canaan in Josh 2:1ff. and 7:2ff.). Zechariah's subsequent visions would develop the theme, but already in the first vision it was evident from the mode of the initial appearance of the man-Angel that his mission was one of bringing God's judgment on the hostile world powers and so making a place for the kingdom of the saints of the Most

High—precisely as was the case when he appeared to Joshua at the launching of the holy war to take possession of Canaan.

We should at least mention in this connection two other episodes involving the Angel of Yahweh with drawn sword in hand for possible further illumination of his appearance in Zechariah's first vision. Num 22:22ff. tells how shortly before the appearance to Joshua, before Israel had crossed the Jordan, the Angel took his stand opposing Balaam on his way to curse Israel. And 1 Chron 21:16 (cf. 2 Sam 24:16ff.) relates that David looked and saw the Angel of Yahweh, standing between heaven and earth, his drawn sword stretched out over Jerusalem, which he was in the process of destroying with the plague. Background for these angel-and-sword episodes is found in the cherubim associated with the flaming sword assigned to guard the original holy land of Eden from profanation (Gen 3:24; cf. Job 37:11,12).

It is not only in Zechariah's opening vision that the Scriptures represent the Messiah as a mounted figure. Closest of the other instances to the imagery of Zech 1:8ff. is the representation of Christ as rider on a white horse in Rev 19:11ff. (cf. Rev 6:2). There too Christ, the richly diademed King of kings, commands other horsemen, the armies of heaven, as he proceeds to judgment-battle against the beast, false prophet, and kings of the earth. Blended there with the mounted warrior symbolism of Zechariah 1 is the man-and-sword imagery of Joshua 5, for out of the rider's mouth issues a sharp sword with which to strike down the nations (v. 15). Different historical hours are in view in the two passages, Revelation 19 envisaging the final eschatological conflict and Zechariah 1 an earlier stage, but the warrior-judge role of the messianic horseman is the same in both.

Of a piece with the representation of the mounted Messiah is the portrayal of Yahweh, the divine warrior, driving his victorious horses and chariots (Hab 3:8). "The One mounted (or riding) on the clouds" is an epithet of Yahweh (Ps 68:4 [5]; cf. Isa 19:1), as it was of the Canaanite storm god Baal. Yahweh is also depicted as riding or mounted on the cherub (Ps 18:10 [11]) and on the heavens (Deut 33:26; Ps 68:33 [34]).

Later in the book of Zechariah the messianic king once again appears as a mounted figure.[1] This time, however, he rides a donkey rather than a horse (Zech 9:9). Resumed there is the patriarch Jacob's testamentary blessing on Judah (Gen 49:8-12), in which Shiloh, the coming one, tethers his donkey to the vine. A special designation for the donkey, shared by these two passages alone in the Old Testament, has been found to refer to a particular kind of animal that was used in the death-ritual by which ancient covenants were ratified.[2] Accordingly, in the fulfillment of the prophecy of Zechariah 9 at the triumphal entry of Jesus into Jerusalem (Matt 21:4,5), the donkey on which the Lord rode presaged the cross and the shedding of the blood of the new covenant. This donkey colt identified the lion of Judah as the lamb of God. Summed up in the two images of the mounted Messiah in Zechariah 1 and 9, the rider of the red horse and the rider of the donkey colt, is the dual status of Jesus as covenant Lord and covenant Servant; his double advent for sacrificial atonement and judicial conquest; his two-stage career of humiliation and exalted glory.

3. *Heaven's Legions:* With the mounted man-Angel were other horse(men). Represented by this equine symbolism here, and again in the seventh vision (Zech 6:1-8), are contingents of celestial beings. These heavenly hosts, who are seen surrounding the throne of God in visions of the divine court, take part in the deliberative assembly there, but they are also pictured as accompanying the King of Glory when he goes forth to battle on a day of the Lord. (Similarly, the members of the divine council in Canaanite mythology have a dual role, constituting an army when occasion requires.)

Such attendant heavenly forces are mentioned in those passages where we have found Yahweh depicted as a mounted warrior. For example, at the beginning of the blessings of Moses in Deuteronomy 33, the Lord is said to have come with an army of myriads of holy ones as he advanced from Sinai to Canaan in his warfare in behalf of Israel (v. 2). Celebrating the same occasion, Psalm 68 numbers in the thousands of thousands the chariotry forces among whom the One of Sinai proceeded (v. 17 [18]). Zechariah himself, echoing this opening vision at the close of his book, foretells the final advent of the Lord God in judgment with all the holy ones (14:5). Again, with specific reference to the Parousia of Christ, biblical prophecy portrays the final judgment event as a coming of the Son of Man in the glory of the Father with all the holy angels (e.g., Matt 16:27; 25:31; Mark 8:38; Luke 9:26; cf. Jude 14,15). As in Zechariah 1 and 6, equine imagery is used at times for these angelic forces elsewhere in the Bible. It may be merely implicit in references to chariotry or it may be explicit, as in the familiar episodes in the careers of Elijah and Elisha recorded in 2 Kings 2 and 6.

What Zechariah saw was a symbolic representation or actualizing of the divine epithet "Yahweh of hosts", which is used repeatedly in the context of these night visions. The rider of the red horse was a personal manifestation of Yahweh in angelic mode and the horsemen belonged to the hosts of Yahweh's angel legions (cf. Matt 25:31; Rev 12:7). The prevalent military connotation of the "Yahweh of hosts" title is not lost in this symbolic restatement, even though the mission of the horsemen is not one of battle. They are in fact engaged in world reconnaissance and it is likely the speed with which they executed their mission that is particularly emphasized by the imagery of horses. In Zechariah's day, the far-flung Persian government was noted for its rapid communications via a system of horsemen stationed along the roads of the empire. Nevertheless, the role of the horsemen of Zechariah 1 is not just that of general government administration, for their rapid gathering of information concerning the nations was part of a judicial process to assess the ripeness of the world for judgment and to determine the hour for the Lord of hosts to go forth to war.

Three (or perhaps only two) groups of horses are mentioned, distinguished from each other by different colors. The size of each group is not indicated. One group is chestnut-red, like the mount of the Angel of Yahweh. Another group is white. The other color-term, the second in the sequence of three, is usually thought to denote a lighter red and is rendered "bay" or "sorrel". These are all natural colors for horses and there are no convincing grounds for regarding these colors in themselves as symbols for specific, different destinations or missions; indeed, they all shared the same task of world surveillance. It may well be, however, that the palette selection of red(s) and white was designed to create the impression of flames and light. A desire to produce such a bright, fiery image would then explain why black horses, which are found in the seventh vision, are absent from this first one. Also, the second color-term, *šĕruqqîm*, evidently derives from a verbal root that is used for the shining of the sun. Now this term is possibly to be construed as in apposition to the first color. (Similarly, the term *ʾămuṣṣîm*, "strong ones", is annexed to the four color-terms used for the chariot horses in Zech 6:2,3). But whether it designates a distinct color group of horses separate from the other two or whether it is appositional to the first color and defines the red hue more precisely, it would highlight the fiery, brightly luminous appearance of these horses. This imagery would thus be an equivalent in prophetic vision for the fiery horses with the chariots of fire which were seen in similar yet distinctive visionary mode at Elijah's ascent into heaven (2 Kgs 2:11) and again later by Elisha and his servant when the forces of the king of Aram menaced Dothan (2 Kgs 6:17). This would not be the only place in biblical revelation where a bright hued color scheme was employed to produce the impression of flames of fire. Flame colored linen was used for the inside covering of the tabernacle (cf.

Exod 26:1,31,36). There too it was a matter of giving visual expression to the Name of God, Yahweh of hosts, in an earthly replica of the Glory-court of heaven, where the heavenly hosts were represented by cherubim figures, portrayed in the fiery curtains as well as in gleaming golden sculptured form above the ark. In the imagery of his first vision, Zechariah saw the same reality that was found in the tabernacle, that reproduction of the Glory-Spirit realm where Yahweh reigns on chariot throne as a flaming fire, amid ten thousand times ten thousand of holy ones (cf. Ezek 1:4,13; Dan 7:9,10).

Conveyed to Zechariah in this vision of the man-Angel with the other supernatural horse(men) was, therefore, the assurance of the earthly presence of the heavenly reality in its full panoply of power. The divine Presence, which Israel had in the past experienced as the visible Glory-epiphany, though not outwardly observable in Zechariah's day, was nevertheless really present—the Lord of angels and his holy retinue. Zechariah beheld this Presence in the Spirit.

B. The Deep:
1. *Background of Imagery of the Divine Warrior and the Deep:* If we follow the Masoretic tradition for the vocalization of the noun *mṣlh* in Zech 1:8, there is no reason to translate it "ravine" or otherwise to depart from the regular meaning of *mĕṣûlâ* or *mĕṣôlâ* (cf. *ṣûlâ* Isa 44:27), namely, the depths of the sea, the watery deep. This is the meaning it has, for example, later in the Book of Zechariah itself (see 10:11, where the plural *mĕṣûlôt* is used) and Ps 68:22 (23), the context of which is similar to Zechariah 1 in that it portrays the Lord as a riding figure (v. 5 [6]) accompanied by a myriad of forces (v. 17 [18]) For the rendering of the preposition (*beth*) as "by" in connection with a body of water, see, e.g., 1 Sam 29:1 ("by the spring") and Ezek 10:15,20 ("by the river"), the latter being of special interest because there too we find the motif of a Glory-theophany by the waters. The LXX rendering of *mṣlh*, "(the mountains) of the shadows," would reflect a reading *mĕṣillâ*, from a root meaning "be dark". If this reading were being considered, one might note the Accadian term *maṣallu*, used for the canopied area of a royal garden, a baldachin, and translate "the myrtles which serve as [*beth essentiae*] a canopy-shade." But the clearly attested *mĕṣûlâ* of the Masoretic tradition is to be preferred over other possibilities not attested elsewhere in biblical Hebrew. Zechariah saw the Lord of the angels of heaven standing between (or among) the myrtles by the deep. God's message of comfort and hope for his faithful was distilled in that cryptic, symbolic scene.

To unfold that message we examine first the association of the Glory-theophany of the divine horseman with the watery deep. The significance of this imagery may be determined by tracing it to its sources in earlier biblical revelation. Immediately obvious is the connection with the exodus event. There we find all the elements of Zechariah's scene, the equine figures as well as the Glory-theophany of God's cloud-chariot and, of course, the sea. The very term *měṣôlâ* is used in the Exodus 15 hymnic celebration of the victory of Yahweh, the divine warrior, who triumphed over the horse and rider and all the military might of Egypt. Yahweh hurled pharoah's horses and chariots into the sea, the depths covered them, they descended into the deeps (*měṣôlôt*) like a stone (v. 5). *Měṣûlâ* (or equivalents) is also found in later reminiscences of the Lord's salvation triumph at the Egyptian sea (Neh 9:11; cf. Ps 68:22 [23]). It is also used for the watery depths when exodus imagery is applied to a later exodus-like redemptive event, as in the reference to "all the depths of the Nile (or river)" in Zech 10:11.

Closely linked to Israel's passage through the Egyptian sea was their crossing of the Jordan. These twin episodes under the leadership of Moses and his successor Joshua (Josh 4:23) are blended in passages like Exod 15:13-17; Ps 114:3-5; and Hab 3:8. We have cited the appearance of the man to Joshua (Josh 5:13-15) as part of the tradition of Angel of the Lord theophanies that illuminates the significance of the Angel-rider figure in Zechariah 1. Now we note another point of connection between that episode and Zechariah's vision in the fact that the depths of the Jordan just traversed by Israel (Joshua 3 and 4) formed the backdrop for the theophany of the commander of the Lord's hosts to Joshua (Josh 4:19; 5:10).

Zechariah's imagery finds its explanation then in the exodus event and the exodus-like passage of the Jordan, each involving a theophany by the watery depths. The meaning of these events can in turn be more fully uncovered and thereby a more complete explanation of Zechariah's symbolism secured if we take the phenomenon of the Glory-theophany by the deep back beyond the exodus to the earliest instance of it, and then follow the development of this revelational motif forward in history to the exodus and on to Zechariah's era.

2. *The Deep in Creation:* Glory-theophany over the deep is first encountered in the creation record. After the declaration of the absolute beginning of the invisible heaven and the visible world in Gen 1:1, the narrative focuses in v. 2 on the earth at an unstructured stage of unbounded deep and darkness and reveals there, hovering eagle-like above,

the reality of the Glory of heaven's King, the Lord of heavenly hosts. This Glory-Presence is here called the Spirit of God, an identification attested elsewhere as well (cf., e.g., Gen 3:8; Neh 9:19,20; Isa 63:11-14; Hag 2:5). By virtue of the presence of this Glory-Spirit the darkness and deep would become bounded and formed into ordered realms (the theme of the first three days of the creation account), and those realms would abound with creatures who were to rule over them (the theme of the second three days, which are arranged in matching sequence to the first triad of days, so that rulers occur parallel to their realms).

Acted upon by the Spirit of life (cf. Ps 104:30, Ezek 37:1-14), the lifeless primeval deep would become a double source of life, the fructifying rain reservoirs above (Ps 104:13ff.) and the enlivening waters of springs and rivers below (Gen 2:6; Ps 104:10ff.). They would become the seas teeming with creatures (Ps 104:25,26). In Eden the dark, dead deep would be transformed into the river that watered the garden of God and the tree of life, the primal typological reality behind the biblical image of the river of life that flows from the throne of God (Ezek 47:1ff.; Rev 22:1,2).

Hence the presence of the King of Glory above the waters was a preindication that the dark deep would be subdued and filled, that the kingdom of God would emerge with royal earthlings made in the image of God and reigning in his name, commissioned, in imitation of their Creator, to the continuance of the kingdom program of subduing and filling the earth (Gen 1:26-28). Moreover, because the Glory constituted a Spirit-temple and functioned as a heavenly paradigm as well as a divine power in creation, the presence of this Glory gave promise that an ectypal likeness of the archetypal sanctuary would be reproduced in the visible world. Inchoate deep and darkness would be transformed into a cosmic temple for the enthronement-revelation of the divine Glory-light. More than that, a living temple of God-like spirits would be brought forth and fashioned into a holy habitation of the Lord of hosts. In short then, the Glory-Spirit over the waters was a revelation of the absolute sovereignty of the Creator-King, a guarantee that whatever the conditions that seemed unruly and contrary, they would be overcome and God's kingdom would be established and consummated in the form of a living and everlasting temple, the Omega-likeness of the Alpha Glory-Spirit.

3. *The Deep in the Deluge:* At the Noahic flood we once again find the theophanic Spirit present over the deep in a creation or, more specifically, a re-creation event. The narrative of the episode in Genesis 6-8 is so constructed that it reflects in various ways the form of the creation record

in Gen 1:1-2:3, so inviting the reader to see the Flood as another creation episode—as Peter did and so expounded it in 2 Pet 3:5-7.³ Strikingly reproduced in the physical phenomena of the Flood was the process of the original creation. There was a return to the deep-and-darkness of Gen 1:2 in the Flood's reversal of the separation and bounding of the waters above and below, described in day two of Genesis 1 (cf. Gen 7:11f.). Then followed a recapitulation of the creation sequence of the abatement and bounding of the waters; the reappearance of the dry land and vegetation; and the ultimate re-emergence of animals and mankind in the re-created world, the heavens and earth that now are, as Peter calls it (2 Pet 3:7). It is of particular interest that the biblical account of this re-creation event narrates it in a way that recalls the Spirit (rûaḥ) of Gen 1:2. Gen 8:1 marks the turning point between the watery chaos produced by the flood and the reconstruction of the cosmos by observing that rûaḥ (wind) was sent from God over the flooded earth. The theophanic presence of the Creator-Spirit of Gen 1:2 suggested by the word play on rûaḥ in Gen 8:1 is also disclosed by the episode of God's sealing the remnant in the ark (Gen 7:16). This presence of the Spirit over the waters in the re-creation event of the Flood signified his lordship over the waters (cf. Ps 29:10) and announced that he was ready to bring forth the new world-order out of chaos.

Further, re-creation since the Fall is necessarily by means of redemptive judgment; a work of destruction must clear the way for redemptive reconstruction. Re-creation involves de-creation (cf., e.g., Isa 65:17; Dan 7:11-14; Rev 20:11-21:1; 21:4,5). Hence, in the re-creation event of the Flood, the deluge waters from which God brought forth the new world were first employed by him for the de-creation of the old world.

The flood depths, though a return to the dark deep of Gen 1:2, had additional symbolic nuances. The primeval deep was dead in the sense of without life forms, but the deluge deep was not just devoid of life, it was the destroyer of life. It was the realm of the dead. For those in the ark the flood experience was a death passage, a death and burial. Hence God's mighty act with respect to the Flood waters may be construed not simply in terms of re-creation but of resurrection. In subsequent biblical revelation the deep is a familiar synonym for death and Sheol. (A reflex of this in Canaanite mythology is the confusingly similar roles of the gods Death and Sea as adversaries of the hero-god Baal.) Pss 18:4 [5] and 69:1,2,14,15 [2,3,15,16] contain pleas for deliverance from death-Sheol envisaged as the breakers, torrents, and miry depths of the sea (cf. also Pss 42:7 [8]; 88:6 [7]). In the New Testament application of Psalm 69 to Jesus, the overwhelming waters become a figure for Messiah's death-sufferings. Psalm 18 is especially relevant to the Zech 1:8 imagery because in response to the prayer of the psalmist for salvation from the breakers of death, Yahweh appears in Glory-theophany as a mounted warrior and snatches the suppliant from the deep waters (vv. 8-19 [9-20]). Again in the psalm of Jonah (Jon 2:2ff. [3ff.]) the prophet's descent into the heart of the seas is described as an experience of Sheol, so that the Lord's deliverance of him was a bringing him up from the underworld. Accordingly, the New Testament applies this (as it did Psalm 69) to the death-burial-resurrection of Christ (Matt 12:40). In the resurrection scene in Rev 20:13, the sea is paralleled by death and Hades—each giving up the dead that were in it. And in the vision of the new heaven and earth in Rev 21:1ff. this parallelism recurs: the sea is no more (v. 1) and death shall be no more (v. 4). Present in Revelation 20 and 21 is the theophany of the Glory of the God of the great white throne (Rev 20:11) and heavenly sanctuary (Rev 21:1-5,11). Manifesting himself as the re-creator of the new heaven and earth, he shows himself, over against the sea of death, to be the God of resurrection power, who can break open the bars of the deep and swallow up the watery depths of death in victory.

The waters of the flood also functioned as God's instrument for the destruction of rebellious mankind and thereby for the deliverance of the covenant remnant from the oppression of the wicked. The mighty waters were the servant of the almighty Lord in his execution of redemptive judgment. In terms of judicial procedure, they were the ordeal waters by which a verdict of justification was rendered for the godly remnant and condemnation was declared and punishment executed against the ungodly. Accordingly, the theophanic Spirit over these waters was a revelation that the King of Glory was in sovereign control over the threatening situation, even making the destructive deep itself serve to accomplish his will as he took action in remembrance of his covenant promise (Gen 8:1a). The heavenly Presence over the Flood waters proclaimed that the Creator was also the sovereign Judge of all the earth and the faithful Redeemer of his people.

Elsewhere in biblical revelation envisaging the final judgment ordeal by fire (2 Pet 3:6,7) the baptismal ordeal-waters of the Deluge (cf. 1 Pet 3:20,21) become an ordeal stream of fire (Dan 7:9-11). Like the river of life, the river of fire flows from God's throne, for the Glory-Spirit is the executor of the dual sanctions of the covenant, of both the blessing and the curse potential of the baptismal judgment ordeal (cf. Matt 3:11). In the eschaton, the stream of fire, the ordeal instrument, becomes the lake of fire, the realm of perdition, the second death (Rev 20:14; 21:8). Thus the story of the appearance of the Glory-Spirit over the primeval waters leads in the course of biblical symbolism to a double eschatological reality, to both a river of life and fiery lake of death.

4. *The Deep in the Exodus:* This brings us back to Israel's exodus from Egypt, which, we may now observe, was a creation event, a redemptive re-creation, like the Flood. We can now appreciate the significance of the fact that it was at this historical juncture that the Glory-Spirit reappeared (cf. Exod 14:21,22), to be in this new age a continuing visible divine presence in the midst of the covenant people. By thus manifesting himself in this Glory-Spirit theophany at the sea, the Lord identified himself as the God of the original creation—and of the diluvian re-creation—and gave notice that his present intention was to accomplish a kingdom-inaugurating re-creation.

Such is the reading of the situation in Deut 32:10,11. In this song Moses interprets the exodus as a redemptive recapitulation of Genesis 1, and he does so precisely in terms of the presence of the Shekinah-Glory in the exodus history. For he employs the key features of Gen 1:2 to describe Israel in the wilderness by the sea, under the ruling, guiding Glory-cloud. The intention to portray the exodus history as a replay of Gen 1:2 is made clear by the use in Deut 32:10,11 of two rare words (the noun *tōhû* and the verb *rḥp*), found in the Pentateuch only in these two passages. In the Song of Moses, the wilderness becomes the new *tōhû*, the waste land, equivalent to the primeval deep-and-darkness, and it is the Shekinah-cloud that is referred to as hovering (the verb *rḥp*) over Israel in the wilderness-*tōhû*. (This corroborates our understanding of Spirit in Gen 1:2 as one of the instances where it denotes the heavenly Glory.)

As in the Flood narrative, so in the Exodus account we read of the *rûaḥ* (wind, breath, spirit) as God's agent in dealing with the deep (Exod 14:21; 15:8), again evoking the *rûaḥ* (Spirit) of the original creation (Gen 1:2). Once more there is a dividing of the waters so that the dry land appears, and once again there is the fashioning of a kingdom people who are established in a paradise land under a covenant of works. With respect to this divine work of redeeming Israel from Egypt and forming them into his holy kingdom, the Lord is subsequently identified in Scripture as Israel's Creator (Isa 43:15) or Maker (Isa 45:11; cf. Gen 2:7).

Like the Deluge waters, the sea of the exodus was not only to undergo a creational kind of division and bounding, but was to be wielded by the Lord as an agent of judicial ordeal, as a weapon in an overwhelming judgment on the Egyptians. The Parousia of God in the Glory-cloud over that sea heralded, therefore, a work of destruction as well as of re-creation. It proclaimed the advent of a day of the Lord.

An additional turn is given to the meaning of the Egyptian sea in some biblical allusions to the exodus in that rather than viewing the waters as a means of judgment, as the waters of a baptismal ordeal, they use the sea as a figure for the objects of judgment. The sea, in the guise of a monster of the deep, is made to represent the forces of Satan, pharaoh and his army, the enemy power that is vanquished by Yahweh. Appearing in his storm chariot of Glory to perform miracles of redemptive judgment for the salvation of his people, the divine warrior slays the dragon, Sea. "It was you [O God] who split open the sea by your power, you broke the heads of the monster in the waters. It was you who crushed the heads of Leviathan" (Ps 74:13,14a [NIV]). "Was it not you who cut Rahab to pieces, who pierced that monster through? Was it not you who dried up the sea, the waters of the great deep, who made a road in the depths of the sea so that the redeemed might cross over?" (Isa 51:9b, 10 [NIV]).

In explanation of this development in the symbolism of the sea, there is the fact that at the exodus the sea stood as an obstacle in the way, threatening the existence of the fleeing Israelites. But it is also evident that the biblical authors are adapting the ancient mythological drama of a hero-god who vanquishes an evil deity depicted as draconic sea, and in the process creating the world or at least establishing world order and his own preeminence in the council of gods. Pagan myth thus commingled and perverted the truths of God's creation of the world and his subsequent overcoming of evil. When the biblical authors draw upon this imagery, they empty it of its mythological substance, employing it simply as a literary figure to portray the realities of God's warfare against Satan and his earthly allies in the course of redemptive history. Most familiar is the use of this imagery in the Book of Revelation to portray the conflict of Christ and Satan. Applying this dragon-sea figure to Egypt and its king exposes the satanic dimension of their hostility to the covenant people, while the imagery of Yahweh slaying the Leviathan suggests the re-creation aspect of the exodus event.

In tracing the complex development of the biblical symbolism of the deep, it has been found that the sea represents both death and the draconic adversary, Satan. This combination is understandable for there is a close connection between the devil and death. Scripture applies the same name, Belial, to both (cf. Ps 18:4 [5] and 2 Cor 6:15) and refers to both as enemies of the Lord's people and as devourers of their victims. Satan is indeed said to be the one who has the power of death (Heb 2:14).[4]

Summing up thus far, revelation of Yahweh in Glory-theophany by or over the sea proclaims him creator and re-creator, judge of the world, victor over Satan, and redeemer of his people. Such a Parousia-epiphany heralds a day of the Lord, the manifestation of God's supreme sovereignty over everything in heaven and earth, and the coming of his kingdom, crowned by his royal house and holy temple.

5. *Exile Visions of Theophany by the Deep:* These conclusions will find further substantiation as our attention is called to the fact that Zechariah's vision of theophany by the deep belongs to a cluster of such prophetic visions, all from the sixth century B.C. Zechariah's vision, received soon after the restoration began, was preceded by similar visions seen by Ezekiel and Daniel in the midst of exile. It was in his opening vision by the Kebar River, where Israelite exiles had been settled in the land of the Babylonians, that Ezekiel beheld the fiery, whirlwind coming of the chariot-enthroned Glory (Ezek 1:1ff.). By waters in the land of exile, Daniel too had visions of the divine Presence—by the Ulai near Susa (Dan 8:2,16ff.) and on the bank of the Tigris (Dan 10:4ff.; 12:5ff.).

This was a time when the world power dominated the covenant people, having attacked and overcome them and brought to an end the theocratic dynasty and kingdom. Israel's political status had in effect reverted to the situation when the Egyptians oppressed the Hebrews, before the establishment of the theocratic kingdom and the emergence of the messianic dynasty of David. It was natural that in this period of exile the symbolism of the sea as a figure for the contemporary kingdoms dominating the covenant community should come to the fore again in the imagery of prophetic vision. These kingdoms were viewed as monsters of the stormy deep, like leviathan Egypt of old. Such was the form they assumed in Daniel's night vision (Dan 7:2ff.). In this vision (read in the light of its interpretive restatement in Rev. 13:1ff.) the world kingdom enterprise takes on the character of a satanic counterfeit creation. Standing by the waters, like the Glory-Spirit over the deep in Genesis 1, Satan summons from the chaotic sea of the nations monstrous world kingdoms fashioned in his draconic likeness. The waters thus symbolize the satanic source of evil powers, hostile to the God of heaven and his people.

In this historical and literary context, the Kebar and Ulai and Tigris, the sites of the visions of Glory-theophany seen by Ezekiel and Daniel, are to be recognized as representing the kingdoms through which they flowed, those ungodly world powers that held sway over God's covenant land and people. And as for the appearance of the theophanic Glory above these waters of exile, it sealed the promise of a new exodus deliverance and triumph like that achieved by the Shekinah-Presence at the waters of the Egyptian sea. The presence of Israel's God in majestic splendor above these foreign waters gave reassurance that he was King of kings, ruler of all nations, and that the proud world kingdoms would therefore be brought down under his judgment, while his redemptive kingdom, though now lowly, would surely gain the upper hand and be exalted at last.

Zechariah's vision of theophany by the deep is to be understood as of a piece with those seen by Ezekiel and Daniel shortly before. To a limited extent restoration from exile had taken place in Zechariah's day, but the political conditions were not fundamentally changed. Persia, the second beast power from the deep in Daniel 7, still ruled over the heritage of covenant promise. In addition to the shared imagery of theophany by the waters and the basic similarity of the historical situation, there are other correspondences between Zechariah's vision and those of Ezekiel and especially of Daniel, particularly the visions recorded in Dan 10:4ff. and resumed in 12:5ff.

Some of those correspondences between the Zechariah and Daniel passages are matters of details in literary form, others concern the essential message. A date formula of similar construction introduces both visions (Zech 1:7; Dan 10:1,4; cf. 8:1). Note also the more than minimal identification of the seers, and the reference to them by the rare pronoun *hallāz* (Zech 2:4 [8]; Dan 8:16). (Common to both is a revelatory process in which an interpreting angel assists the human recipient in the understanding of the vision [Zech 1:9,13,14; Dan 10:l0ff.; cf. 8:16]. Compare too the similar affects of the visionary experience on the recipients [Zech 4:1; Dan 10:9,10].) Of larger import, each theophany vision begins with the statement that the seer looked, and behold a man (Zech 1:8; Dan 10:5; cf. Ezek 1:26,27). And that man in both cases is a manifestation of the divine Presence. In Daniel, the man is identifiable with the figure called Michael your prince (Dan 10:21) and Prince of the host, or Prince of princes (Dan 8:11,25), the same Prince of the host whose appearance to Joshua (Josh 5:14) served as a model for the appearance to Zechariah of the man, the mounted leader of the celestial contingent. Moreover, in both visions this messianic Angel-Prince figure is involved in military engagement with the world kingdoms, in particular with Persia (Zech 1:7,11; Dan 10:13,20). Further, the correspondence extends to the central burden of these visions, namely, their concern with the delay of God's decisive redemptive intervention. That eschatological concern, already intimated by the symbolic imagery of Zechariah's vision (particularly, the myrtles by the sea), is clearly voiced in the report of the horsemen and the intercession of the Angel (Zech 1:11ff.), pointedly so in the plea, "How long?" (v. 12). Precisely this same concern over the duration of the world's oppression of the covenant community is sounded in Daniel's parallel vision, there again expressed in the plaintive "How long?" (Dan 12:6).

It would be in the Lord's response to the Angel-rider's intercession at the end of Zechariah's first night vision that the ultimate triumph over the oppressive world power was reassuringly proclaimed. But the very presence of the messianic warrior by the sea, revealed in the opening symbolism of Zech 1:8, was already a sure token of the coming deliverance and victory.

C. The Myrtles: In our previous comments on the symbolism of Zech 1:8, we have treated the deep in connection with the figure of the rider of the red horse. In the text, it is the myrtles that are explicitly identified as being by the deep. The Angel-rider is by the deep because he comes and takes up a position in the midst of the myrtles. And that is the main point of this symbolic disclosure. While his people are in the world wilderness facing the satanic deep, while they are in the throes of their historic earthly struggle, Immanuel, mighty God, is present with them.

1. *Myrtles as Paradise Trees in the Wilderness:* Though a shrub, myrtles are sometimes listed in the Bible with trees. (Facilitating this is the fact the Hebrew ꜥēṣ signifies wood as well as tree.) Myrtles grow to some nine feet and as seen here probably stood at the height of the mounted horseman. With their delicate, star-like, white flowers and fragrant, bright green leaves the hardy evergreen myrtle naturally appears in idyllic pictures of the fertility and luxuriance of the earth in the messianic age (cf. Isa 41:18,19a; 55:13). Also suggesting that the myrtles by the deep are a paradisaical image is the fact that paradise by the deep is a feature of those historical episodes of creation, exodus, and Jordan crossing which we have noted as the background for understanding the symbolism of theophany by the deep.

At creation, the Glory-Spirit brought forth paradise out of the primordial deep and darkness to be mankind's dwelling place. The dead deep itself was transformed into the river of Eden that watered the garden with its trees, including the very tree of life, beneath the mountain of the Glory-theophany. From the beginning, luxuriant trees, in association with theophany by waters, are a conspicuous feature of paradise, and trees of life, flourishing on either side of a river of life, appear in apocalyptic visions of Eden's paradise at last redemptively restored and perfected (Ezek 47:12; Rev 22:1,2).

Paradise by the deep is also found to be an element of the exodus re-creation event. After recording the song of Yahweh's triumph over the deep (Exod 15:1-21), the narrative hastens to tell of Israel under the directing hand of the Glory-theophany coming to Elim and encamping there by the twelve springs of water among the seventy palm trees (Exod 15:27). As part of the larger Mosaic context in which the exodus wilderness experience is represented as a creation event, and in particular the wilderness is identified with the tōhû-deep (cf. Deut 32:10,11), the description of the Elim oasis in Exod 15:27 at once evokes the paradisaical waters and trees of the garden of Eden. Also suggestive of Elim's equivalency to Eden is the linkage with the mountain of theophany of the covenant Lord (cf. Exod 16:1).

Glory-theophany over Jordan's flooding deep in the days of Joshua was again the prelude to paradise, the paradise of the promised land flowing with milk and honey (cf. Josh 5:6), with the oasis of Jericho and its perennial spring, the city of palm trees (Deut 34:3), as an identification sign at the border. In the passage of Jordan's deep, Israel moved from the sphere of wilderness into a paradise realm (cf. Josh 5:12).

It thus appears that the myrtles by the deep in Zech 1:8 reinforce the other creation and exodus motifs already observed in the imagery of this vision. They do so by adding the element of the paradise land which the Creator-Redeemer provides as the dwelling for his people and as the site of his theophanic Presence. In his lordship over the deep the Lord God transforms it into a fructifying source for the arboreal blessings of his holy garden, the homeland of his people.

More particularly, the myrtle trees point to Eden's tree of life. Being evergreens, the myrtles were a natural symbol of everlasting life. Moreover, since the eternal paradisaical life they represent is a life which in redemptive re-creation the Lord brings forth from the sea of death, the myrtles represent life from the grave, resurrection.

As to the precise picture in Zech 1:8, it is difficult to determine whether the Angel-rider stands between two myrtles or in the midst of a larger group. Eden contained two special trees and paired trees of life flank the river of life in prophetic pictures of paradise restored. Also, visions corresponding to the first vision of Zechariah in the literary arrangement of the night visions contain symbolic pairs. In the seventh vision, the agents of Glory emerge from between two mountains (which evidently led the LXX translators to read "between the mountains" [instead of myrtles] in Zech 1:8). And in Zech 4:2,3, we read of the lampstand (*měnôrâ*) with an olive tree on either side. Further, a deity standing between two trees is a common Near Eastern image. It may well be then that the Zech 1:8 imagery is that of the Glory-theophany flanked by two paradise trees of life. The messianic Glory-Angel would thereby be identified as the Resurrection and the Life, as the divine Savior of Psalm 18, who raises up his suppliant people from death's deep waters.

If the myrtles between which the messianic Angel stands allude specifically to the original two special trees of Eden in their two distinct identities, then Zechariah's imagery would be informed not only by the tree of life symbolism but by the significance of the tree of judicial discerning between good and evil (cf. Gen 2:9). That tree represented the dominical authority with which man was invested as image of the sovereign Glory-Spirit. A claim was made by the Son of Man to what both the trees of Eden symbolized when he said that it was given to him by the Father to have life in himself and authority to execute judgment (John 5:26,27). This twofold messianic endowment with life and judicial authority was also represented by the two symbolic items associated with the two tables of the covenant in the ark of the covenant—the manna, heavenly bread of everlasting life (cf. John 6:32ff.), and the budded rod of Aaron, the sign of his authority in God's courts (cf. Zech 3:7; Heb 9:4; Num 17:10). Significantly, these symbols were located within the paradisaical decor of the holy of holies, beneath the Glory, flanked by cherubim, themselves peculiarly identified with life and holy authority.

Of the several instances of paradise by the deep that we have cited as background for the symbolism of Zech 1:8, Israel's encampment at the Elim oasis brings out most vividly the truth that the presence of God's Glory, the source and provider of the life and beatitude of holy paradise, may be enjoyed by his people while they are still in the wilderness, not yet arrived at their promised inheritance. The wilderness setting is mentioned just before and just after the Elim episode (Exod 15:27). From the sea of the exodus salvation to Elim was the journey through the wilderness of Shur (Exod 15:22-26). Then leading from Elim to Sinai was the journey through the wilderness of Sin (Exod 16:1ff.). Likewise in Zech 1:8, the wilderness is the setting of the myrtles of paradise and the Angel-rider's appearance there. This becomes evident when it is recognized that in the figure of the myrtles there is an allusion to the Feast of Tabernacles, or Booths, that graphic memorial of Israel's life in the wilderness. We shall trace the intricate web of this myrtles-Tabernacles connection, observing in advance that the wilderness, the common context of the Elim paradise, the Tabernacles experience, and the myrtles by the deep in Zech 1:8, is an appropriate metaphor for the political-eschatological situation confronting not only Zechariah but the church to the end of this present world.

2. *Myrtles and Tabernacles—Consummation Glory:* When the Feast of Tabernacles was celebrated in the days of Israel's return from exile, myrtles were designated along with olive and palm trees as meeting the requirement written in the Law of Moses for the construction of the shelters in which the people lived during the week of celebration (Neh 8:14ff., esp. 15; cf. Lev 23:39ff., esp. 40). One criterion in the Law for the selection of trees for this purpose was their practical suitability for constructing the huts; with this in view, trees with broad fronds of leafy branches were specified. The second criterion was ornamental appearance indicated by the phrase, "trees of *hādār* (glory or beauty)." Of the several designated trees, the flowered myrtle would best serve this function. The choice of the myrtle for the Zechariah 1 imagery might then be to direct attention primarily to the glory aspect of the tabernacles, while their protective function remained secondary. Highlighting this connection and further prompting the selection of the myrtles here would be a word play that obtains between *hādār* (glory) and *hădas* (myrtle).

To catch the full force of the myrtles image in Zechariah 1, we must then inquire into the typological meaning of the Feast of Tabernacles. It was celebrated at the close of the agricultural year when all the fruit of the land had been harvested and it was accordingly called the Feast of Ingathering (Exod 23:16; 34:22). Its date in the seventh month and its seven day duration, initiated and concluded (on a crowning eighth day) with days of solemn rest, emphasized its sabbatical-consummatory significance. Tabernacles was thus a typological prophecy of the completion of God's kingdom through the final universal ingathering of the elect of all nations to worship the Lord with joy as the King over all the earth, the Lord of hosts. Agreeably, Zechariah at the close of the book, returning to this theme of his opening vision, declares that in the eternal day the redeemed remnant of all the national families of the earth will from year to year come before God's throne to keep the Feast of Tabernacles (Zech 14:16). Employing the customary prophetic idiom of Old Testament typology, he thus indicated that beyond the final eschatological conflict (Zech 14:1ff.)

what Tabernacles had adumbrated will be realized. This would also be the fulfillment of the prophecy of Zechariah's contemporary, Haggai, dated on the last day of the most recent Tabernacles feast, shortly before Zechariah's visions (cf. Hag 2:1; Zech 1:7), declaring that the Lord would bring the glory of the nations into his house (Hag 2:6-9). Similarly, the apostle John saw the universal harvest of the worshippers of the Lamb (cf. Rev 14:14-16), an innumerable multitude out of every people and nation, with palms in hand engaged in Tabernacles celebration before God's throne (Rev 7:9), covered there by the tabernacle of God (Rev 7:15). The three annual festivals all featured pilgrimage of God's people to his house, but the connection of Tabernacles with the final completion of harvest made the Tabernacles pilgrimage to Jerusalem the premier sign of the final universal pilgrimage and permanent assembling of the covenant people of all ages at the heavenly Zion.

3. *Myrtles and Tabernacles—Present Glory in the Wilderness:* A curious feature of the Feast of Tabernacles is that while its place in the annual and agricultural calendars made it a sign of the consummation of the kingdom, the situation to which it pointed as a historical memorial and which it dramatized by the peculiar manner of its observance identified it with an earlier, emphatically preconsummation stage in the redemptive process. This intriguing combination of contrasting concepts finds expression in the two names of the festival—Ingathering and Booths. The former, as we have seen, speaks of the final harvesting into the heavenly assembly (cf. Rev 14:14-16). The latter refers to the preconsummation condition of God's people. The name Booths reflects of course the requirement that during the festival the pilgrims were to dwell in structures of leafy branches in imitation of the Israelites' mode of life while they were on the move in the wilderness between the salvation event at the Egyptian sea and their entrance into Canaan, the prototype of the sabbath-paradise to come (Lev 23:43). The rough simplicity of the booths underscored the unsettled, impermanent character of the wilderness situation. The huts occupied during the Tabernacles festival were only a temporary arrangement, like the booths that used to be set up in the fields by harvesters. This comparison suggests the possibility that an original connection of the two names, Ingathering and Booths, is to be found in some old harvest festival celebrated in such temporary shelters in the field. If the Mosaic ordinance of the Feast of Tabernacles is an adaptation of such a harvest festival, it has invested the old form with a totally new, redemptive-historical significance.

The transient nature of Israel's experience in the wilderness was further reflected in the kind of dwelling the Lord prescribed for himself at Sinai. As a gracious expression of his Immanuel-Presence with his people, the Lord adopted a form of residence similar to their own. The temporary nature of even this more elaborate tabernacle of the Lord is emphasized in the narrative of David's proposal to build a permanent house for the ark of God (2 Sam 7:1ff.). From what the Lord says on that occasion about his continuing use of the tabernacle-form of sanctuary, it is evident that the transitory character of Israel's existence extended beyond the wilderness journeying into the tumultuous days of their penetration of the land and the troubled period of the judges, down to the emergence of the Davidic dynasty and the obtaining of rest from all the enemies round about. A wilderness-like, impermanent state of affairs continued all the while God's dwelling place retained its temporary tent-form, until that very time when the Lord was arranging through covenant with David for the constructing of a temple-house by David's son (2 Sam 7:13).

Of course even under Israel's theocratic kings the kingdom of God did not yet attain its true permanence. After all, Canaan was not the true Sabbath land but only a prototype, and Jerusalem was not the heavenly city but only a foreshadowing of it. Celebrating the Feast of Tabernacles in those days would have been a reminder of this. There in Jerusalem, on the roofs and in the open court of the city of the Great King, the Israelites had to set up and reside in the temporary booths—a declaration that this was not the eternal city itself and this was not the time or place for the saints' everlasting mansions of glory. Did not the (apparent) preservation of the portable wilderness tabernacle within Solomon's temple (cf. 1 Kgs 8:4) serve as a similar reminder, as a sign that even this more durable structure on fixed foundations was only a typological prefiguration of the truly permanent temple to be built by the greater than Solomon? Though Israel enjoyed a privileged position in the typological order of things they were not thereby prematurely transported out of the basic circumstances of this present world. From the Fall until the inauguration of the world to come at the Consummation, life for the people of God is always a pilgrim journey through an alien wilderness under the shadow of death. So it was in Zechariah's day. So it is in ours.

Two different moments in the redemptive journey are symbolized in the Feast of Tabernacles, signified by the two names, Booths and Ingathering. It reminded God's people that they were pilgrims and aliens in this world (Booths) and simultaneously promised them that they were the heirs of heaven (Ingathering). But the symbolism of this festival was even more richly complex in its portrayal of the eschatological nature of the existence of God's people in this world. It did not simply declare that the promised goal of the consummation of redemption would at last be reached; it said something too about a present realization of that eschatological hope.

The actual character of the process of redemptive eschatology is such that heaven breaks into the history of this world beforehand, particularly in the reality of the presence of the Spirit, re-creatively fashioning God's people in the image of his Glory. It is especially (though not for the first time) in the present age of the church that this semi-eschatological situation obtains, the Consummation being already experienced in the inner glory of the supernatural presence and renewing power of the Spirit, even while the Consummation in its external dimensions of glory is not yet attained. And this realized eschatology of the inner glory of the Spirit, experienced even in the time of our tabernacling in the wilderness of this present age, we find to have had a place in the rich symbolism of the Feast of Tabernacles. (Of interest here is the way Paul combines the teaching of the gift of the Spirit as a present earnest of glorification with the representation of our temporal, mortal condition by the figure of a tabernacle [2 Cor 5:1-5; cf. 2 Pet 1:13,14].) To see how it was that the Feast of Tabernacles signified this additional feature of a present participation in the promised future glory, we must explore further the symbolism of the booths. In the process, we will also discover further confirmation of our interpretation of the myrtles in Zechariah 1 as containing an allusion to these booths.

4. *Myrtles and Tabernacles—Replicas of the Glory-Spirit:* Crude in form, hastily set up, and thus apt symbols of the impermanence of the wilderness era, the booths were nevertheless designed to be replicas of the theophanic Glory itself. Materials prescribed for construction of the booths are described in Lev 23:40-42 (cf. Neh 8:15) by terms that call attention to their likeness to the Glory-cloud. As we have noted, trees of splendor (*hādār*) were to be used and the term *hādār* is a synonym of *kābôd*, "glory", repeatedly serving as its poetic parallel in descriptions of the majestic radiance and beauty of the theophanic appearance of the heavenly King (cf. Pss 90:16; 96:6; 104:1; 145:5; Isa 2:10,19,21; 35:2). God's kingship over all the earth is dominant in these contexts. Of special interest in connection with the symbolism of Zech 1:8 is Ps 104:1, where the *hādār* is identified with the theophanic light of the Lord (v. 2), who is pictured as riding on his cloud chariot (v. 3). Other than Lev 23:40, *hādār* is applied to trees only in Isa 35:2. There it refers to the splendor of Carmel's wooded range and Sharon's dense vegetation, in parallelism with the *kābôd* of Lebanon's majestic cedars. And significantly the verse concludes by paralleling this *kābôd* and *hādār* of majestic trees to the *kābôd* and *hādār* of Yahweh, our

God. It is in the wilderness that this divine glory and arboreal splendor are said to appear. This forecast of the renewal of paradise in the wilderness is also found in Isa 41:19, which mentions the myrtle along with the cedar and other trees that will characterize the once dry wilderness now turned into springs and pools of water (v. 18) by the Lord's re-creating hand (v. 20, cf. *br²*). Such, we have seen, was the promise of the imagery of the myrtles by the deep in Zech 1:8, another link in the connection between these myrtles and the booths of Lev 23:40-42 (cf. Neh 8:15).

In light of this usage of *hādār,* the requirement that the booths of the Tabernacles festival be made of trees of *hādār* apparently had in view their serving as symbolic images of the Glory-Spirit. To the same effect is the stipulation in Lev 23:40 that the wood for the booths be selected from leafy trees, trees of densely interwoven foliage (*ʿābôt*). Here again, this time more subtly through the device of paronomasia, a connection is made with the Glory-cloud. For *ʿābôt* also appears as the plural of *ʿāb* ("dark cloud mass," also a "wood thicket"), which is the term found in Exod 19:9 for the theophanic cloud of Sinai. It is similarly used elsewhere, and in particular for the clouds as the chariot on which the Lord rides (Job 22:14; Ps 18:11,12 [12,13]; 104:3; Isa 19:1). The Psalm 18 example is of special importance because of its close relationship to the Zech 1:8 imagery of the mounted divine warrior who comes to deliver his people from the deep (cf. Ps 18:10,16 [11,17]).

The connection between the booths of glory-wood and the Glory theophany is also made from the other side. That is, not only are the booths described in Glory-cloud terms, but the Glory theophany is referred to as a booth (*sukkâ* the plural of which, *sukkôt*, is the name of the festival). One instance is the very verse (v. 11 [12]) in Psalm 18 just cited in illustration of the usage of *ʿāb* ("thick cloud"). Here God's *sukkâ* ("covert," cf. the parallel *sēter* "hiding place") is in fact identified as those dark water-clouds of the sky (cf. Job 36:29). Ps 31:20 (21) extols the Lord whose Presence is the hiding place (*sēter*), the *sukkâ* for those who take refuge in him (v. 20 [21]). In the preview of the day of Zion's consummation in Isa 4:2-6 it is said that when Yahweh engages anew in creation (cf. *bārāʾ, v.* 5) the Shekinah pillar of cloud and fire (v. 5), the Spirit (cf. *rûah,* v. 4) of the original creation, will overshadow the mountain of God and the assembly of the redeemed. Over everything the Glory (*kābôd*) will be a canopy (v. 5) and a covert (*sukkâ,* v. 6).

We can further demonstrate the identification of the shelters of the Tabernacles festival as replicas of the Glory theophany and at the same time clarify the choice of the myrtle in Zech 1:8 as a symbolic cipher for these booths by tracing the matter to its ultimate roots. Hovering over the mountain of God in Eden, the Glory-cloud was a shelter, a shade by day and light by night, a roof and a lamp. God was man's original dwelling place. This is the picture that informs prophetic views of the paradise of the new creation (Isa 4:5,6; Rev 22:5). A natural replica of this supernatural shelter was at hand in the trees the Lord made and among which he placed man in the garden. Trees, especially those with dense foliage, afforded a covering, a lodging place protected from the elements, a shade from the heat and a covert in the storm (cf. the cosmic tree of Dan 4:10-12, a dwelling place for all the creatures of the earth). And trees in their kindled state provided the light and warmth of fire, the benefits of the sun captured from the air and embodied in the living tree and then released into the air again in the tree sacrificed in the flames. Like the luminous, overshadowing Glory-cloud, trees were a house, a protecting roof and an illuminating torch-lamp. In other respects too there was likeness. Like the Glory-theophany in its majestic beauty, the trees were a delight to the eyes. Like the Glory-Spirit, the source of life, the trees provided the fruit of life; they were good for food. Indeed God invested one tree with special symbolic meaning as a tree of life, and another tree with the significance of the judgment tree, reflecting the judicial dominion of the Glory-Spirit. These two trees were sacramental means facilitating the full development of man as the image of God, the likeness of the Glory-Spirit.

The character of trees as natural poetic images of the Glory-canopy may explain the significance of the frequent appearance of trees as cultic objects at places of worship. But here we want to note that what the Lord prescribed by way of dwellings en route to the promised land and in the commemoration of this in the Feast of Booths was essentially an adaptation of the native role and simile-value of trees.

The tents in which the Lord and the Israelites tabernacled in the wilderness and the huts provided for the Feast of Booths are structurally quite similar. They are alike impermanent, wooden frame construction with non-rigid coverings. In so far as the tent coverings were made of cotton or linen cloth, as in the case of the inner curtains of the Lord's tabernacle, they were like the booths of the festival in having coverings of plant material. The wood and foliage of the trees were incorporated in ruder form in the huts, while the tree and other plant products used as material in the tents underwent more processing by the artisans. But that difference is simply disregarded as insignificant when booths are appointed for the Feast as equivalents of the tent-dwellings occupied by God's people in the wilderness (Lev 23:40). The booths and tents were much the same, and both were in form and material essentially modified tree shelters. That being so, the myrtle trees of the Zech 1:8 vision were all the more a natural symbol to evoke the Feast of Tabernacles and in particular the booths, revealing behind them a more fundamental level of symbolism in the trees of Eden and so illuminating their nature as replicas of the divine Glory, for such were the trees of the garden of God.

Moreover, the fundamental structural equivalency of the booths and the particular tent that the Lord prescribed as his own dwelling in the midst of the tents of Israel brings into still clearer focus the nature of the booths as replicas of the Glory-canopy. For the holy tabernacle was precisely and on a most elaborate scale the ectypal earthly replica of the archetypal heavenly Glory-temple that appeared on the mountain of God. It was the Council Tent (ʾohel môʿēd), so named as symbolic copy of the heavenly council (môʿēd) of the Lord of hosts. Because of the presence of this divine council on the mountain (har) of God, the latter was called har môʿēd (cf. harmagedōn), Council Mountain. Har Magedon is the mountain of God's enthronement and the mountain of judgment. The likeness of the booths of the Tabernacles festival to the holy tabernacle, therefore, reinforces the evidence previously presented identifying the booths as symbolic replications of the Glory-Spirit (namely, the shared designations of the booths and the Glory-theophany as alike canopies of royal beauty and their common relation to the trees of Eden). The picture that emerges in the Tabernacles festival is then one of the Glory-Spirit re-creatively overshadowing the redeemed Israelite community in the wilderness, fashioning them in his own glory-likeness. Consequently, the exodus typology depicts the mission of the coming Christ as a work of new creation, especially the creation of the new humanity in the image of God, a transformation perfected at last in their glorification and reception into the heavenly tabernacle.

5. *Myrtles and Tabernacles—Transfiguration and Tabernacles:* A foretaste of the ultimate restoration of the Glory-image and at the same time a dramatic exposition of the meaning of the Tabernacles festival along these lines was given in the episode of our Lord's Transfiguration. Various features of the Transfiguration relate that event to the Feast of Tabernacles, even while others identify it as a messianic counterpart to the encounter of Moses with the Glory theophany on Sinai. The Transfiguration was a wilderness event, apart on a high mountain. Redolent of the wilderness too were both the visitors seen with Jesus, Moses and Elijah. Also, there is the possibility that the introductory time detail, "after six days" (Matt 17:1; Mark 9:2; cf. Luke

9:28, "about 8 days"), refers to the time leading from the Day of Atonement to the Feast of Tabernacles. The exodus context of Tabernacles is echoed in the topic of conversation, the *exodos* ("decease" or "departure") about to be accomplished by Jesus (Luke 9:31). Above all, the mention of the booths, which Peter suggested be constructed for Jesus, Moses, and Elijah, recalls the wilderness shelters of the Israelites and the imitative reconstructions thereof prescribed in the Feast of Tabernacles. (On the rendering of *skēnē* as "booths", cf. the LXX use of it for *sukkâ* in Lev 23:42f. and the LXX use of *skēnopēgia* to designate the Feast of Tabernacles, e.g., in Zech 14:16.) Significant for the understanding of the festival booths as images of the Glory-cloud is the way the booths and the overshadowing cloud are brought together in the Transfiguration narrative. Peter's suggestion about the booths was made as Moses and Elijah were departing (Luke 9:33a). So far as it made sense at all (cf. Mark 9:6; Luke 9:33c), the idea apparently was that these two might be persuaded to stay on, continuing this "good" arrangement. As specifically stated in Matt 17:5 and Luke 9:34, it was while Peter was proposing the man-made shelters that the theophanic cloud, the divine covering, overshadowed the scene. In this combination of earthly booths and heavenly cloud the Transfiguration answers to the Israelite booths and the Glory-cloud in the wilderness and to the imitative commemoration of that wilderness situation in the Feast of Tabernacles.

That the Transfiguration was indeed antitypal to the Tabernacles symbolism becomes plain once we have recognized that the festival booths were designed to be images of the Glory-canopy, for the Transfiguration itself consists in precisely such a replication of the divine Glory. The physical glorification of Jesus was a fashioning in the likeness of the bright theophanic cloud (cf. Matt 17:5) that overarched the holy mountain. This majesty of Jesus was a revelation of him as the Son, the image-likeness of the Father, as the voice from the majestic Glory declared (cf. 2 Pet 1:16,17). In the case of the first Adam, likeness to the Glory-Spirit was never completed, the component of physical glory not having been attained. But the glory-image is perfected in the second Adam, as the firstfruits of a new humanity, and that ultimate consummating of the reproduction of the divine image in man was anticipated in the Transfiguration.

Additionally, the theme of renewal in the image of Glory is associated with both of those who appeared with Jesus in glory at the Transfiguration. As a result of his approach to the overshadowing Glory on Sinai, the countenance of Moses was transfigured. And Elijah, who had his own close encounter with the Glory on the mountain of God, also experienced a remarkable foretaste of physical glorification in his deathless exodus, borne aloft by the fiery chariots and horses of Glory. These two who participated in the Transfiguration with Jesus were the only two in the history of Israel qualified by both these credentials of theophanic encounter and physical transformation for appearance at this antitypal event of Glory replication.

So Peter spoke better than he knew in introducing the Tabernacles motif of the booths into the Transfiguration episode. Of course, the Son from heaven was here and it was therefore not a time for earthly symbols but for the heavenly reality. Nevertheless the Transfiguration was indeed a new covenant counterpart to Tabernacles. Hence in the antitypal Transfiguration event the image-relationship of the Tabernacles booths to the Glory as replicas to a divine paradigm received the bright illumination of historical fulfillment.

6. *Glory-Presence in the Midst of the Myrtles by the Deep:* We have found that the Feast of Tabernacles as a harvest festival was a promise of the final ingathering, the hope of ultimate glorification, and that its requirement to live in rustic booths simultaneously reminded worshippers of the wilderness-like, not-yet-arrived nature of their life in the present world. These very same booths were designed, however, to be replicas of the theophanic Glory and so were affirmations of the Creator's redemptive renewal of his people in his image, a re-creation that begins here and now during the wilderness journey, even if the perfecting of the Glory-likeness awaits arrival at the heavenly destination. The booths thus portray the complex eschatological character of the present existence of the saints as both already and not yet. By symbolizing the believers' present participation in the heavenly glory in the Spirit, the booths indicate that their life on earth, awaiting the future consummation of glory, is already in measure one of realized eschatology.

What is true of the Tabernacles booth will also be true of the imagery of the myrtles in Zech 1:8. The myrtles by the deep recall the Elim oasis in the wilderness and like it give promise of the glorious paradise inheritance at the end of the journey. As a promissory sign of the restoration of paradise at the Consummation, they correspond to the prophetic ingathering aspect of the Feast of Tabernacles. But they also correspond to the booths as symbolic replicas of the Glory- covering. When we were tracing a common rootage for the symbolism of the booths and the myrtles in the trees of the garden of Eden, we reflected on the character of these trees as natural images (and, in the case of the two special trees, as sacramental images) of the Glory-canopy over paradise. So perceived, the myrtles by the deep emerge as signs of God's redemptive re-creating of his image in the new humanity. Like the booths of Tabernacles, the myrtles teach an already/not yet eschatology of the anticipation of heaven in the course of the earthly pilgrimage of the redeemed, a realized eschatology of the Spirit's renewing of the glory within before the Parousia of the Glory without. They tell of a glory experienced by God's children even while laboring on through the wilderness over against the deep.

By portraying the replication of the divine image in the symbolism of the booths, the Feast of Tabernacles was a reminder of the presence of the Glory-Spirit himself, the archetypal Shekinah-shelter which hovered above the community in the wilderness. Tabernacles was thus a celebration of God's presence in the midst of his people. In the case of the equivalent symbolism of the myrtles in Zech 1:8, that reality of the divine presence took visible form in the appearance of the Lord of Glory in the figure of the Angel of the Presence, the rider of the red horse, seen by Zechariah as accompanied by the other agents of the divine council and stationed in the midst of the myrtles. This presence of the Lord himself among his myrtle-people is the glory of the covenant, the secret of all life and beatitude, a guarantee that the Glory within will be followed by the Glory without. For the people of God, the bearers of the Father's image, this Presence is an earnest of the transfiguration change awaiting them in the Sabbath-land beyond the wilderness at the Parousia-revelation of God's Glory.

7. *Glory-Angel in the Midst of the Myrtles and the Burning Bush:* Zechariah's opening vision answers in its imagery and message to the inaugural revelation of the old covenant order by which Moses was called to lead Israel out of Egypt, through the wilderness, to its promised inheritance (Exodus 3). Zechariah saw the Angel of the Lord, commander of the fiery heavenly beings, in the midst of the myrtle shrubs by the deep. Moses saw the theophanic fire, identified with the Angel of the Lord, in the midst of the desert shrub in the wilderness over against the Egyptian sea. These two episodes are linked through their mutual relationship to the appearance of the Angel to Joshua near Jericho, recounted in Joshua 5. We have observed above the interrelation of the Zechariah 1 and Joshua 5 appearances. The connection between the encounters of Moses and Joshua with the divine Angel is strengthened by the common feature of the divine command to each man to remove his footwear because the site of the Angel's presence was holy (Exod 3:5; Josh 5:15). A closer look at the theophany of Exodus 3 should open another window on the message of the vision of Zech 1:8.

Clear direction for understanding the significance of the theophany of the burning-but-unconsumed bush emerges from a comparison of that event (narrated in Exodus 3) and the Sinai theophany witnessed by Israel (as reviewed in Deuteronomy 4 and 5). Both events involve a fiery theophany and both transpire at Horeb, the mountain of God (Exod 3:1; Deut 4:10; 5:23). Possibly there is a word play on Sinai in the term *sĕneh,* "bush," in Exodus 3. In any case, both the bush and Sinai are described by the same phrase, "burning with fire" (Exod 3:2; Deut 4:11; 5:23), and both passages speak of people "approaching" (Exod 3:5; Deut 5:23) to "this great sight/fire" (Exod 3:3; Deut 5:25; 18:16). Certainly, then, the fire in the burning bush is not symbolic of the fiery trials of oppressed Israel, but is the manifestation of the presence of the Lord, who is a consuming fire (Exod 19:18; 24:17; Deut 4:24; cf. Deut 33:16). This is stated explicitly in Exod 3:2 if we translate: "The Angel of Yahweh appeared to him as [*beth essentiae*] a flame of fire." And this leads to the meaning of the bush and the wonder of its not being consumed. At Sinai a covenant was established between Yahweh and Israel as a nation, a covenant that brought the consuming fiery Presence of the Lord of Glory into the midst of the covenant community. In the Exodus 3 anticipation of Sinai, the bush in which the flaming theophany appears must then represent God's people. What depicts the afflicted condition of the Israelites is not the fire in the bush, but the nature of the bush itself: a lowly desert shrub. If, as often conjectured, it is a thorny type of bush, that fact and its wilderness location might be suggestive of the sin cursed world outside Eden, in which God's people, along with all the rest of mankind, have their existence until the end of the days (cf. Gen 3:17-19,23,24).

But the key question of interpretation concerns the great wonder that the bush is aflame, yet not consumed by the flames. It is the meaning of this, in particular, that is clearly explained by the comparison of Exodus 3 and the Deuteronomy 4 and 5 account of Sinai. It turns out that the main problem was not how the Israelites could manage to endure in the face of the world tyrant. Rather, the fundamental issue was the ultimate religious question of how sinners can survive in the Parousia-Glory presence of God and his consuming holiness. Israel's election to privileged covenant relationship, by bringing the Glory of the Lord into their very midst, seemed to threaten them with fiery destruction. Yet they were not consumed. That was the wonder, a mystery of redeeming love and grace. They expressed it in fearful amazement: "Behold, Yahweh our God has showed us his Glory and his Greatness and we have heard his voice from the midst of the fire. We have seen today that God can speak with man and he can still live!" (Deut 5:24). The Glory-flame descends upon the bush but does not consume it. The bush still lives. This miracle of grace was not to be presumed upon as a covenant guarantee regardless of Israel's covenant keeping or covenant breaking. Alert to the continuing threat of the holy Presence, the Israelites hasten to request some distancing of themselves from it through the provision of a mediator. They plead: "Why should we die? This great fire will consume us" (Deut 5:25).

After Israel's rebellion in the matter of the golden calf, the Lord expressed a reluctance to expose Israel to this danger inherent in the presence of his Glory-theophany in their midst. He proposed instead to send with them his Angel unattended by the Glory (Exod 33:2,3). For if God were to go with them in the Shekinah Glory, he might destroy them (v. 5). At the intercession of Moses, the Lord relented and promised: "My Presence will go with you" (Exod 33:14). However, precisely what Israel feared and God warned would happen did happen. One such divine judgment came in response to Israel's further rebellion against the covenant on their departure from Sinai, an episode that was memorialized by naming the site Taberah ("consuming," a designation that embodies the verbal root $b^c r$, used for the burning bush in Exod 3:2,3). The blessing of the covenant, the wonder of grace, is that the bush burns ($b^c r$), but is not consumed or devoured ($^{\gamma}kl$). Describing the curse of the covenant against repudiators of grace at Taberah, the biblical narrative employs the terminology of Exod 3:2 in an ironic reversal. Num 11:1 relates that fire from the Lord burned ($b^c r$) among the Israelites and devoured ($^{\gamma}kl$) some of them.

The old covenant canon closes not long after Zechariah's night visions with this theme of the crisis of the divine fire in the thorn bush. Malachi predicts the advent of the Angel of the covenant as a refiner's fire, a day that burns ($b^c r$) like a furnace, and raises again the ancient, cardinal question facing the sinner: Who can survive at his fiery Parousia (Mal 3:1,2; 4:1 [3:19])? As for the arrogant who do not fear the Lord, the prophet warns the fire will totally consume them (4:1 [3:19]). But he knows that the fiery Glory-Spirit is the executor of the blessings as well as the curses of the covenant. He has not forgotten the sign at the inauguration of the old covenant, the miracle of the Glory-flame in the bush that still lived. Accordingly he likens the Parousia-Glory not only to the burning furnace but to the sun of righteousness which rises with healing in its wings for those who fear God's name (4:2 [3:20]). The imagery of the winged sun-disc belongs to an ancient iconographic tradition that represented the majesty of the divine presence as a luminous glory between winged or other objects. It is a prominent motif in the symbolism of Zechariah's night visions, with a form of it, as noted above, possibly in the opening vision of the Glory Angel between the myrtles.

Present in the midst of the myrtles, the Angel-Commander of the fiery horses of heaven promises life and peace, vindication over against the satanic forces of the deep, and exaltation from wilderness existence into the glory of the consummated city of God. Like the burning bush, these myrtles are aflame with the presence of the divine Glory, but they are not consumed. This wonder seen by Zechariah is a sign confirming God's faithfulness to his covenant with Abraham and his seed, the covenant of promise not disannulled by the Law (Gal 3:17). It speaks of the Immanuel mystery, which is most fully revealed in the new covenant, whose mediator is the Glory-Angel become God-man, the incarnate rider on the red horse.

John, the seer of the New Testament Apocalypse, also saw a version of the sign of the burning bush (Rev 1:12-20), a version adapted from another Zecharian form of it (cf. Zechariah 4)—the transfigured-glorified Jesus, the light of the world, standing among the seven lamps, burning but not consumed, symbol of the church renewed in the luminous image of Christ, blessed by the presence of Glory within even during its present existence in the wilderness, bound for the Glory of the New Jerusalem. The Angel of fire in the bush, the Angel-rider in the midst of the myrtles, the glorified Christ in the midst of the lampstands—each represents the already/not yet stage in the process of the formation of the eternal temple-city, the stage of the covenant people's life in the present world wilderness.

II. STATE OF THE WORLD REPORT (1:9-11)

Confronted with the tableau of the rider on the red horse in the midst of the myrtles by the deep (Zech 1:8), Zechariah requests an explanation (v. 9). It is given by the Angel-rider himself. In particular, he identifies the horsemen (v. 10), whose report on their world mission (v. 11) prompts his intercession in behalf of Jerusalem (v. 12). The response of the Lord of hosts to this is then disclosed by the divine Angel to Zechariah through the interpreting angel (vv. 13-17). In the successive steps of this explanatory process each of the elements of the symbolic scene is in turn illuminated: the deep in the present section (vv. 9-11), and then the myrtles in v. 12, and the Glory-Presence in vv. 13-17.

A. *Jurisdiction over the Deep:* We have found that the sea symbolized the mighty forces of disorder and satanic hostility which the Lord overcomes in working out his creative kingdom purposes in the history of his covenant people. In Zechariah's vision, the deep represented the world power which had subjugated Israel and terminated the Davidic dynasty. Dispatched to this deep of the nations, the heavenly horsemen were to discover whether the imperial powers were now in compliance with the rule of Yahweh as sovereign of heaven and earth; more specifically, whether they were assuming a proper stance with respect to the nation of Israel, at that time God's kingdom on earth.

Indicative of the judicial character of the horsemen's mission is the verb used for their ranging over the earth (*Hithpael* of *hlk*). Zechariah employs it again for the world traversing heavenly chariots in the parallel seventh vision (Zech 6:7). Its first appearance in Scripture is in Gen 3:8, where it denotes the advent of God for judgment at the Fall of man. A judicial connotation may be present in the following passages, in all of which the Lord is the subject of this verb: Lev 26:12; Deut 23:14; 2 Sam 7:6; and Job 22:14. Used with reference to Enoch (Gen 5:22,24) and Noah (Gen 6:9), it signifies their involvement in the judicial council of the Lord of hosts, the heavenly experience that later characterized the true prophet in Israel. Similarly, the judicial oversight of Israel by the prophet-judge Samuel is summed up by this verb in 1 Sam 12:2, where it is also used for the king. In Psalm 82 (whose setting—God standing for judgment in the midst of the Elohim-beings of the divine council—is not unlike that in Zechariah's first vision), this verb describes the activity of the earthly judges who are the objects of the divine condemnation (v. 5). In Job 1:7 and 2:2 it refers to Satan's malicious scrutiny of men as he goes about like a lion (cf. Ezek 19:6) securing evidence for his accusations.

In the Job passages just cited a parallel verb is *šûṭ*, which is used in 2 Chr 16:9 for the eyes of the omniscient Lord judicially surveying the earth. The Lord's eyes are a figure for the divine agents of world serveillance, the same reality that is symbolized by the horsemen in Zechariah's first vision. Indeed, Zechariah himself employs the imagery of the seven eyes of the Lord in 3:9 and 4:10, making much the same point as 2 Chr 16:9, viz., Yahweh is Judge of all the earth. A prominent element throughout Zechariah's prophecy, the theme of the sovereignty of Israel's Lord over all the nations emerges in his opening vision. The scope of the heavenly horsemen's reconnaissance "to and fro through the earth" (1:10) which is reflected in their earth encompassing report (1:11) manifests the universal authority of him who sent them on their judicial mission.

B. *Eschatological Delay:* At the same time, however, the horsemen's report gives rise to an urgent theological question which becomes the central issue of this vision. It concerns the perplexing absence of penal enforcement of God's holy will against those who scorn his claim to universal sovereignty. For the scoffer this provides an occasion to call that claim in doubt. For the people of God this translates into a soul-trying postponement in the realization of the promised goal of their salvation, the coming of the kingdom in glory. In all ages until the end of their pilgrimage through this fallen world, eschatological delay places the patience of the faithful under severe strain. This is a theological issue that cannot be raised with theoretical detachment; it is profoundly existential and emotive. When the report of the horsemen brought this matter into focus, the divine Angel was at once stirred up to pastoral intercession, pleading, "How long?"

According to their report all the earth was living quietly at rest (*šqṭ*). That verb describes regions and peoples experiencing prosperous security, free from civil strife and warfare. It is used for the intermittent periods of relief from the succession of foreign oppressors during the time of the judges (Judg 3:11,30; 5:31; 8:28) and for times of quiet after conflict during the monarchy (e.g., 2 Chr 14:6 [5]; 20:30; 23:21). More to the point, in God's promises to his people this word depicts the happy conditions they would enjoy when he brought them home from exile (Jer 30:10; 46:27) and the peace of the messianic era (Isa 14:7; 32:17). It is precisely in connection with these cherished prospects that the report of the horsemen posed a problem. Their reconnaissance disclosed that what had been promised to God's people as distinctly their blessed future was being enjoyed instead by the other nations, the nations symbolized by the deep. Is not the sea supposed to be restless? Isaiah had described it as that which cannot rest (*šqṭ*). He used the turbulent waters of the deep as a simile for the wicked who are not supposed to have peace (Isa 57:20; cf. Jer 49:23). But strangely, according to the findings of the heavenly patrol, it was not the land of Israel but the sea of the wicked nations that was peacefully calm. In contradiction of the hope of Israel, the deep was undisturbed.

This peace predicated of the world in Zech 1:11 is sometimes interpreted narrowly of the political fortunes of the Persian empire. It is then disputed whether the tranquility reported in v. 11 harmonizes with the date formula in v. 7, since there is a question whether the disturbances that marred the beginning of the reign of Darius had completely subsided by his second year. But though the Persian empire was of central interest, the mission of the horsemen was of global scope and their report was not restricted to the state of Darius' reign. More importantly, such a narrow interpretation is out of touch with the redemptive-historical realities and concerns of the canonical context of Zechariah's visions.

The focus of concern is the myrtles by the deep—God's covenant people in relation to the world. In the history of the redemptive program Israel had been established as God's own nation, a unique holy kingdom of priests set apart from the common nations. This intrusion of a theocracy into world history produced for the contemporary surrounding nations a special situation, imposing on them peculiar obligations with respect to the cult and community of the Lord God thus kingdomized in their midst. It is the demands of this special historical-redemptive situation that are in view in the horsemen's scrutiny of the nations.

Specifically, their world reconnaissance was to discover what the world powers were doing in the second year of Darius by way of helping or hindering the Israelites in their efforts to reestablish themselves in their land and to restore the temple-cult of Yahweh in Jerusalem. Measured in terms of their special obligations in this typological situation, the nations were found wanting. They showed no inclination to fulfill the commitments that had been made by Cyrus to provide subsidies from the Persian treasury for restoring the Jerusalem temple (Ezra 1:1ff. and 6:1ff.). Opposition to the restoration of Jerusalem from various quarters had brought initial efforts to rebuild the temple to a halt (Ezra 4; cf. Hag 1:2) and in the interval the Persian officials had in fact become ignorant of the very existence of the earlier grants (Ezra 5). Moreover, whatever aid of this sort Persia rendered at one time or another, their imperial dominion over the Lord's covenant community was not relinquished. Any attempt to restore the Davidic dynasty and independent sovereignty would have been totally unacceptable to the Persian overlord.

The point of the patrol's report was not that there was a lull in the incessant international strife and warfare but rather that the world powers were manifesting their defiant indifference to the God of heaven and earth by failing to assist his covenant people in their struggle to recover from the devastation of the Babylonian exile and to rebuild the sanctuary where he placed his name. This indictment of the nations as guilty of hostile disregard for the honor of God's name and for the plight of his people is repeated in the Lord's own description of them as "at ease" (ša'ănān, v. 15). The overtones of scornful complacency, insolence and hateful arrogance attaching to this term are plain in the plea of the oppressed saints in Psalm 123. They cry to the Lord for mercy, lamenting that they have experienced their fill of "the scorn of those at ease and the contempt of the arrogant" (v. 4; cf. Isa 32:9,11,18; 37:29; Amos 6:1). What was disclosed by the horsemen's survey of the deep corroborated the portrayal of the great sea in Daniel's night vision. It was the spawning place of beast kingdoms, hostile to the kingdom of the Son of Man, animated by the spirit of antichrist (Daniel 7; for symbols of Persia see 7:5 and 8:3,4,20). Not only were the nations arrogantly ignoring their obligations to Israel and Israel's God, they were doing so with apparent impunity. The proverbially restless sea was at rest.

C. *Antitypical Dimension:* Another vital factor in interpreting the horsemen's state of the world report is the typological character of the prophetic idiom. In the divine structuring of redemptive history the old covenant was designed to relate to the new covenant as anticipatory prototype to the later ultimate reality. Israel's restoration from Babylonian exile is an instance of this. Like their exodus from Egypt, it was arranged by the Lord of history and redemptive revelation as an instructive model of the messianic salvation. Reflecting this typological structure of the history, the language of prophecy portrayed the coming new covenant salvation history under the figure of its old covenant prototypes. The prophets spoke of the messianic kingdom in parables, parables drawn from the Lord's grand historical parable, which was old covenant Israel.

In keeping with this parabolic idiom of prophecy, the reference of the horsemen's report is not limited to the immediate typal situation but carries a level of meaning pertaining to the messianic age. It has a more ultimately eschatological dimension. Hence the assessment of the nations as at rest is to be understood according to the standard of the ultimate kingdom hope of the redemptive covenant. A promissory forecast of that was made by Zechariah's fellow prophet Haggai four months earlier (Hag 2:6-9, cf. v. 1) and repeated just two months before (Hag 2:21-23, cf. v. 20). Haggai foretold a total reversal of the present subservience of God's people under the world power. As divine warrior the Lord would launch holy war against the enemy nations. They would be overthrown (*hpk*) amid cosmic convulsions and their treasures would be appropriated as battle spoils to adorn God's temple. Here again the prophecy was cast in the prophetic idiom, pointing beyond the typal level to the messianic antitype. Certainly no such total reversal of positions occurred before the new covenant order replaced the old. Moreover, the shaking of the nations prophesied in Hag 2:6 is interpreted in Heb 12:26-29 in terms of the kingdom inheritance still anticipated by believers under the new covenant. Isaiah had also foretold this ultimate spoiling of the world power in a declaration that combined the verb of overturning or reversal (*hpk*) echoed by Haggai and the image of the sea for the nations found in Zech 1:8. "The abundance of the sea will be overturned on you; the wealth of the nations will come to you" (Isa 60:5; cf. Zech 2:8,9 [12,13]; 14:14; Rev 21:26).

The condition of the nations discovered by the agents of the Angel-rider was in stark contrast to that eschatological hope. Seismic upheavals overturning the nations and emptying out the glory of their treasures into the holy city were nowhere to be detected. Not a tremor registered on the seismograph of heaven. All the earth was at rest. The great deep was calm. "Here is the patience and the faith of the saints" (Rev 13:10; cf. 14:12).

III. ADVOCACY OF THE ANGEL (1:12)

Here the focus moves from the deep to the myrtles. The depressed condition of the covenant nation was the correlate of the ease of the dominant world nations reported by the horsemen. Upon receiving that report, therefore, the Angel of the Lord was constrained to make intercession for Jerusalem and the cities of Judah (v. 12).

A. *Completed Retribution:* As the basis for his petition Israel's advocate referred to a completed period of seventy years. This was an allusion to an earlier divine promise given through Jeremiah. The Angel was thus appealing to the integrity of the Lord of the covenant as he sought prompt action on behalf of Judah.

Some two decades earlier Daniel, still in exile, had made a remarkably similar prayer-claim (see Daniel 9). It was the first year of Darius the Mede (that is, Cyrus),[5] the year the Medo-Persian empire had overthrown Babylon (Dan 9:1). Study of two prophecies of Jeremiah concerning a seventy year period of exile (viz., Jer 25:9-14 and 29:10-14) had convinced Daniel that the time for restoration had arrived (Dan 9:2). The first passage dated to 605 B.C. (cf. Jer 25:1), the year Jerusalem's captivity began and Daniel himself was taken to Babylon by Nebuchadnezzar (Dan 1:1). In it Jeremiah indicated that the end of the seventy years appointed for subservience to the king of Babylon (25:11) would be marked by the fall of Babylon (25:12). Implicit in Jeremiah 25 was the promise of the return of the captives at the completion of the seventy years and that promise became explicit in the second passage (see Jer 29:10). Having witnessed the fulfillment of Jeremiah 25 in the fall of Babylon to Cyrus, Daniel proceeded in the first year of Cyrus (538 B.C.) to plead for the fulfillment of Jeremiah 29. His prayer-claim was that the promised restoration of the holy city and temple had been joined to Babylon's fall as a twin indicator of the end of the allotted seventy years (Dan 9:3-19; cf. 2 Chr 36:22) and should, therefore, shortly come to pass.

Of course, the Lord was going to honor his prophetic promise and in the vision of the seventy weeks (Dan 9:24-27) he assured Daniel that restoration of the typological cultic order would begin at once and be satisfactorily completed, in spite of certain difficulties (v. 25). That very year Cyrus issued a decree authorizing the return (2 Chr 36:22,23; Ezra 1:1-5) and the Israelites soon were availing themselves of the privilege. However, the troublous times of which the Lord forewarned had followed (cf. Ezra 4). Indeed, the restoration of Jerusalem and its temple progressed so slowly and relationships with the world powers remained so little improved that twenty years later (in 520 B.C.) the Angel of the Lord, as seen in Zechariah's vision, had to reiterate the plea of Daniel. He appealed to the fact that the returned captives were the ones "against whom you had indignation those seventy years," that is, the period of exile predicted by Jeremiah.[6] The debt to divine justice had been fully met (such is the significance of the seventy years, as we shall see), and surely now, these twenty years later, it was time for a more conspicuous display of God's restoring mercies. This was the contention of the Angel advocate.

As interpreted above the seventy years were a literal, if slightly rounded, number for the critical period of captivity (605-538).[7] In the biblical context it appears that "seventy years" carries additional symbolic overtones. It amounts to ten sabbatical periods. Such a sabbatical significance of the seventy years exile is brought out in the Chronicler's account of it as a fulfillment of Jeremiah's prophecy. From the perspective of the land of Israel the time of exile was one of Sabbath rest in which it made up for (rṣh) the Sabbath years in which it should have lain fallow but had been worked by the covenant-breaking Israelites (2 Chr 36:21). According to the Chronicler each of the seventy years of exile was in effect a sabbatical year, and seven years were then equivalent to forty-nine years, a jubilee period, and thus the seventy years were tantamount not just to ten sabbatical periods but to ten jubilee periods (or seventy weeks of years).[8]

By virtue of these sabbatical-jubilee overtones, the seventy years of Zech 1:12 suggest a period that entails the full completion of a work, the consummating of a divine purpose. The specific divine purpose, as the Angel's plea indicates, was that of manifesting God's indignation against the violation of his covenant. Isaiah 10 is the main source of this indignation terminology.[9] Isaiah prophesied that the nation God employed as the instrument of his indignation against his disobedient vassal people Israel (Isa 10:5; cf. Ezek 21:31 [36]) would itself succumb to another world-power, also serving as the weapon of Yahweh's indignation (Isa 10:26; 13:5; cf. Jer 50:25). This event was coordinated in Isaiah's prediction, as in

Jeremiah's prophecy of the seventy years exile, with the completing of God's indignation against his own people (Isa 10:25).

When the Babylonian captivity of Israel is perceived as a combination of the Lord's indignation and of the seventy years understood as signifying the completion of divine action, it emerges as a parable of the eternal perdition of hell, as a punishment that constituted at a temporal-typological level a consummate divine retribution, a full satisfaction of divine justice. Such significance had been assigned to this ultimate covenant curse of exile by Moses in his prophetic overview of the course of old covenant history in Leviticus 26. This passage depicts the exile as an extended Sabbath for the land (the idea echoed in 2 Chr 36:21) and it contains the motif of sevenfold (i.e., complete) punishment for sin (vv. 18,21,24, and 28). Most to the point, it states that the exiles' experience of misery and anguish would make up for (*rṣh*) their iniquity (v. 41). This verb is used in v. 34 to express the land's making up for its missed Sabbaths during the exile (again cf. 2 Chr 36:21). These two ideas are indeed conjoined in v. 43, with *rṣh* used for both: "The land will make up for its Sabbaths while it lies desolate without them and they will make up for their iniquity."[10]

Israel in exile received a full equivalence in penal recompense for her sins. Those sufferings were not a sacrificial atonement akin to the propitiatory achievement of the Cross. Captive Israel was not the suffering Servant heralded by Isaiah, the vicariously suffering Servant stricken of God for the transgressions of others. Her sufferings were rather the kind of reparations paid by those condemned to hell. However, unlike the doom of the lake of fire, God's judicial response at the ultimate eschatological level of radical religious reality to reprobate individuals, the sentence of Babylonian exile dealt with Israel at the typological level of the provisional Mosaic economy. At the level of the second death retribution is unending; at the typological level a finite period of retribution, the seventy years, sufficed as a complete payment, a making good in full for national Israel's transgressions.

B. *Poignant Appeal:* That is the point being made by the Angel advocate in Zech 1:12. Israel had met in full the curse-debt of the broken covenant. The allotted seventy years indignation had been completed some twenty years ago. But how disappointingly slow had been the progress in restoring the theocratic community and its temple. Still scarred by ruins, Jerusalem remained without walls for defense. Scarcely any headway had been made on the temple since the original efforts had been interrupted by vociferous foes. The land was unproductive. Recovery of independent national self-rule and reinstituting of the Davidic dynasty were nowhere in sight. How long was this to continue? Had not the Lord promised in a prophecy of Haggai just two months before Zechariah's night visions that from that day onward, the day of the community's taking up afresh the task of building God's house, he would bless them (Hag 2:19)?

"How long?"—the cry of the Angel—is a familiar introduction to prayers that lament intolerable circumstances and express yearning for relief. They are characterized by calls for divine mercy and deliverance from adversaries. Most poignant is the lament that longs for a cessation of what is perceived as the displeasure of the Lord himself (see, e.g., Pss 6:3 [4]; 80:4 [5]; 90:13; cf. 79:5). Some Psalms where the "how long?" appears reflect situations like that in Zech 1:12 and indicate more explicitly the kind of divine action the Angel would have been requesting. Ps 74:10 asks how long the enemy will continue to reproach and blaspheme God's name. Adversaries have devastated God's sanctuary, profaning his name (vv. 3-8). The psalmist laments that God has cast off his congregation in anger forever (vv. 1,2) but appeals to him as the Creator (vv. 16,17), the God of the exodus who overcame the sea and the sea-monsters (vv. 13-15). In remembrance of his covenant (vv. 2,20) let him achieve victory in the midst of the earth (v. 12). Ps 80:4 (5) asks how long the Lord, the God of hosts, would be angry against his people, beset by derisive foes (vv. 6,12,13 [7,13,14]). God is identified in terms of the Glory enthroned above the cherubim, which he is requested to manifest in power, shining forth for the salvation of his people (vv. 1-3,7,19 [2-4,8,20]). Ps 94:3 asks how long the arrogant defiance of the wicked will continue. They have crushed the Lord's people and afflicted his heritage, as though divine justice were blind (vv. 4-7). As judge of all the earth, the God of vengeance, the Lord is petitioned to shine forth, rising up in judgment to render to the proud their deserts (vv. 1,2).

C. *Sojourning Saints:* While the Angel's plea for such divine intervention in Zech 1:12 does take account of the immediate situation and though it is couched in the typological terms of that stage of redemptive history, the horizon of his concern extends far beyond into the antitypical age of the new covenant. This perspective is required by the context. When dealing with God's response to the Angel (vv. 13-17) we shall see that it contains promises clearly pertaining to the messianic age. Here we want to observe that the wilderness situation of the faithful portrayed in the symbolism of the myrtles by the deep (v. 8), the situation that evoked the Angel's intercession, continued throughout the remainder of old covenant times, into the new covenant age, and indeed obtains until the Final

Judgment.[11] If so, then the rectifying of that situation sought by the Angel must also ultimately be the final, eschatological deliverance.

The Angel's advocacy was not without more immediate results at the typological level. For the rebuilding of the temple and Jerusalem with its environs did move forward decisively, even though the city walls were not finished for many years (cf. Neh 7:4; 11:1). Nevertheless, in fundamental respects the existence of the covenant community continued to be a wilderness experience. Restoration of the temple did not end the domination of the temple-community by the kingdoms of the earth. The succession of world beast-powers surveyed in Daniel 7 continued in the state of defiant ease reported by the horsemen to the Angel of the Lord for centuries longer. That would at last be changed by the cataclysmic judgment predicted by Haggai (Hag 2:6,7,21,22), but nothing of the sort accompanied the limited restoration after the Babylonian exile. David's fallen tabernacle remained in ruins, not to be raised up within Old Testament times.

Why was restoration of the kingdom in its typological form so limited? In particular, why was the Davidic throne not restored and another glory age enjoyed in those postexilic centuries? For one thing, although Israel had, at the typological level, fully paid for its past offences by the seventy years exile, that payment did not earn future blessings. Israel's restoration to the land, like their original reception of it after the exodus, was a gift of grace. Moreover, in the postexilic phase of the old covenant as in the preexilic a principle of works was operating in the sense that retention of the typological kingdom blessings had to be earned by demonstrated covenant obedience, with the measure of such blessings fluctuating with Israel's erratic faithfulness (cf. Rom 10:5,6; Gal 3:12). Further, since it was a major purpose of the Mosaic economy to prepare an appropriate historical setting for the advent of the Messiah and since he must appear in a state of humiliation to fulfill his mission as the suffering Servant, the covenant community could hardly have been in a state of glorious power with a representative of David's dynasty on the throne when Jesus Christ was born.

Wilderness status still characterizes God's people in the present new covenant era. To be sure, the Lord, true to the Davidic Covenant and in fulfillment of specific promise, has raised up the tabernacle of David (Amos 9:11,12; Acts 15:16-18), and that not merely on the level of the typal throne in old Jerusalem but on the antitypal plane of the heavenly reign of Jesus. Nevertheless, the New Testament portrays the church on earth as a sojourning pilgrim people, as a church in the wilderness (cf., e.g., Heb 3:7-

4:11; 1 Pet 1:17; 2:11; Rev 12:14).[12] Satan's agent, the Beast power from the deep, still wars against the saints and is yet to come up out of the abyss for his hour of apparent triumph over them before he goes into perdition (Rev 11:7; 13:1ff.; 16:13-16; 17:10-13; 19:19; 20:7-9).

The purview of the whole context before and after the Angel's intercession in Zech 1:12 thus includes the future of the covenant people down to the consummation of the messianic age and this clearly determines the eschatological horizon of that intercession. Such a long-range concern is only what would be expected on the part of this Angel. The "how long?" question he raises in Zech 1:12 had been put to him not long before. The occasion was the vision described in Daniel 12, one that resembles Zechariah's first vision in several respects. It contains a theophany by the waters; it deals with a situation fraught with peril for the saints; and it envisages the church age, including the final antichrist crisis (cf. Dan 11:36ff.; 2 Thess 2:3,4). At that time, the "how long?" was voiced by one of the heavenly beings who accompanied the Glory-Angel (Dan 12:6). By way of answer the theophanic Angel spoke of the three and a half times (v. 7), the symbol in the books of Daniel and Revelation for the preconsummation history of the church of the new covenant, the time of the church in the wilderness (Rev 12:6,14; cf. Rev 13:5; Dan 9:27). Only after this period would deliverance come to the people of Michael-Messiah (cf. Dan 12:1-3). Whether answering or asking the "how long?" of eschatological hope, the messianic Angel could not but have in view those new covenant developments that would be set in motion by his own entrance into history as the Messiah, the son of David. When he cries "how long?" he is expressing the eagerness of the Son for the arrival of the hour when the Father will send him to earth on his covenanted mission to make an atonement for his people, to bring in everlasting righteousness, and to anoint the eternal temple. His cry of longing reveals the passionate love of the savior-shepherd for the flock he hastens in spirit to seek and find and bring home.

D. *Christ—Judge and Advocate:* In the opening night vision of Zechariah the messianic Angel is cast in the dual role of judge of the nations and advocate of the Israel of God. Remarkably, this portraiture of Christ in his royal-priestly office is found again at each main juncture in the structure of Zechariah: in the central, fourth member (3:1-10) of the seven night visions; in the central hinge section (6:9-15) of the overall diptych form of the book; and in the central unit (11:1-17) of the burdens that comprise the second half of the prophecy. Most like the first vision is Zechariah 3, where the Angel of the Lord is again present, presiding as

Judge, yet simultaneously advocating the cause of Joshua the high priest, Satan-accused but chosen of God.

The Christian readily recognizes his savior-shepherd as the subject of this priest-king portrait. Jesus is the Angel of the Lord, now come in the flesh. To him all authority in heaven and earth has been given and in the day of his Parousia he will judge all the nations in righteousness. Until that day he intercedes in the court of heaven for his afflicted flock in the wilderness. His claim before the ancient of days is that the "seventy years" curse of divine wrath has been fully accomplished for his redeemed. That eternal wrath of God against them was compressed into the hours of his once-for-all sufferings on the Cross. Hence, the accuser of the brethren is rebuked (cf. Zech 3:2). They overcome him because of the blood of the Lamb (Rev 12:11). Beyond his passive obedience in his enduring of the "seventy years," our advocate at the right hand of the Father presents in our behalf the claim of his active obedience, the fulfillment of the covenant probation, and that merit imputed to us is the ground of our inheritance of the heavenly Jerusalem. The advocacy of our ever-living heavenly priest is not in vain. It prevails to bring the longed for response of favor and blessing from the Lord of hosts (cf. Zech 1:13-17). He is the true Servant of the Lord, able to save to the uttermost them that draw near unto God through him (Isa 53:12; Rom 8:34; Heb 7:28).

IV. ORACLE OF HOPE (1:13-17)

In the Angel's intercession (v. 12), the focus moved from the deep to the myrtles (cf. vv. 8-11); in this closing oracle (vv. 13-17), the focus is on the Glory Presence or, in terms of the symbolism of this first night vision, on the rider of the red horse.

A. *Introduction.*

1. *Literary Structure:* The oracular response of Yahweh of hosts to the Angel of Yahweh is communicated by this divine Angel (denoted in v. 13 simply as "Yahweh") to the interpreting angel and then relayed by the latter to Zechariah to be proclaimed to God's people. Though the act of response is not explicitly narrated, the ultimate divine speaker of the oracular message handed along in this complex transmission chain is made clear by the interpreting angel's fourfold repetition of the formula, "thus says Yahweh of hosts," within vv. 14-17. That the contents of vv. 14-17 are to be understood as the expected divine response to the Angel's plea in v. 12 is further indicated by their general appropriateness as a reassuring answer to the concerns expressed by the Angel. Also, like v. 12, they refer

to both Jerusalem and the cities of Judah (called "my cities" in v. 17). Standing as the link between the petition of v. 12 and the response of vv. 14-17, the statement in v. 13 is plainly intended as an introductory summary of the response. Confirming this is the appearance of the verb "comfort" (*nḥm*) in the latter (cf. v. 17), echoing the description of the Angel's words in the former as "comforting" (*niḥūmîm*).[13]

Zechariah receives the oracle in the form of a charge to proclaim it. This charge, expressed by the verb *qrʾ*, "cry,"[14] plus the messenger formula, "thus says Yahweh of hosts," frames and thus unifies the oracle, for the interpreting angel begins with this commissioning of Zechariah to prophetic activity (v. 14) and concludes with a repetition of it (v. 17).

In v. 16a, the word of solemn verification, *lākēn* ("verily"), with the messenger formula introduces the central, utterly crucial affirmation of God's presence. The preceding part of the oracle (vv. 14,15) relates directly to the report of the horsemen about the oppressor nations (v. 11), and the following part (vv. 16b,17) deals with the mercies which God purposes to bestow on Jerusalem. As the Angel's intercession showed (v. 12), the disheartening status of the covenant community was implicit in the reported contemptuous ease of the dominant nations and accordingly there is already a reflection on this in the reference to Jerusalem and Zion in the first part of the Lord's response concerning the nations (cf. v. 14). But in the concluding part of the oracle, the plight of the covenant people is addressed directly as the Lord promises them a future of blessing that will spell the end of the world power's dominance over them. Prospects for the temple and city are presented in v. 16b and then restated in v. 17, with reversed sequence (i.e., city and temple). The mention of Zion and Jerusalem at the close (v. 17) forms an inclusio echoing (again in chiastic arrangement) the reference to Jerusalem and Zion at the beginning (v. 14), and is thus an additional unifying feature of the oracle as a whole.

2. Covenantal-Typological Context: What we shall find to be the sum and substance of this oracle is the promise of a restoration that would, in effect, bring to consummate form the holy kingdom covenanted from the beginning in Eden. At its origination the kingdom in the garden had as its cultic focus the mountain of God's Glory-council. There the heavenly King was present, the protector and provider of his priestly family on earth. Set before mankind was an historical mission, the global propagation of the human family and expansion of their delegated dominion over creation. They were to develop the kingdom city from its original cultic focus to its cultural fullness, to a predestined *pleroma*. The cultural task would be cult-oriented for the kingdom-city at its fullness would still retain its cultic focus; it would be a temple-city, the city of the great King. Moreover, the *pleroma* of mankind would itself be God's temple, destined for incorporation into the heavenly temple of the Glory-Spirit.

This original goal of the Covenant of Creation was resumed as the *telos* of the program of redemptive restoration after the Fall. The heavenly temple-city became the ultimate kingdom hope to be achieved through the coming One, the promised Messiah. In premessianic times the heavenly inheritance of the redeemed humanity in Christ was symbolically modelled in the form of the kingdom bestowed on Israel in Canaan, a provisional pointer to the true fulfillment of kingdom promise to be attained under the new and better covenant ratified by the sacrifice of the God-man mediator. In Israel's paradise in Canaan, the type of heaven, a cultic focus was established, Zion the mountain of God, crowned by the temple-city of Jerusalem. It was set in the center of the kingdom fullness defined by the stipulated bounds of the promised land. Henceforth in biblical revelation particular features of the typological kingdom of Israel would serve in prophetic parlance as designations for their counterparts in the messianic kingdom. In this idiom, Zion and Jerusalem signify the true heavenly mountain and temple-city of the world to come.

Also portrayed in Israel's typological history was the fact that the eternal city would be secured as an act of gracious restoration of blessings forfeited in the Fall. Like man under the Covenant of Creation, Israel broke a covenant of works (the principle operative in the typological kingdom dimension of the Mosaic economy), lost its covenant status and was exiled as Lo-Ammi, Not-My-People, from its holy paradise. However, in a display of divine grace, Israel was regathered from Babylonian exile to the land of promise and that was, of course, the immediate historical context of the prophets Haggai and Zechariah. While this typological restoration of Jerusalem, the temple, and the cities of Judah is indeed addressed in the Lord's response in Zech 1:13-17, the oracle looks beyond to a greater restoration of which the typological history becomes a figurative image. It serves as a symbolic medium in which the Lord expresses the promise of a future restoration of the kingdom of God, a restoration not realized in Old Testament times, a messianic restoration not fully realized until the end of this present world.

B. *Return of the Lord of Glory:* In our treatment of the particulars of the Lord's response (1:14-17) we will begin with the heart of the matter, which is stated in the middle of the oracle (v. 16a). "Truly, thus says

Yahweh, I am returned to Jerusalem with mercies." The verb return (*šûb*) is used in the opening exhortation in 1:1-6 to sum up both the covenant obligation of the people to commit themselves anew to their holy calling and the covenant blessings which the Lord promises to bestow on them: "return unto me...and I will return unto you" (v. 3).

The personal presence of the One who covenants with us to be our God is the preeminent reality of biblical religion. "Whom have I in heaven but you? And there is none on earth that I desire besides you" (Ps 73:25). In Ezekiel's visions the essence of exile-judgment is captured in the scene of the departure of the Glory of Yahweh from the temple-mount (Ezek 10:18,19; 11:23) and, correspondingly, the epitome of restoration is represented as the return of that Glory from the east and its presence once more, filling again the temple in Jerusalem (Ezek 43:2-5). Apart from God's Presence there is no restoration, no holy land, no holy city, no holy temple, for it is this Presence alone that sanctifies. Nor is there paradise land of life, for the Glory-Spirit is the life-giving Spirit. He is the One from whom all blessings flow, the fount of all covenant beatitude.

Agreeably, "with mercies" is appended to the promised return of the Lord (1:16a). The reference is to the benefits that will accompany his presence, the benefits of vindication (1:14,15), sanctification and exaltation (1:16b,17). God's mercies or compassions (*rahămîm*) are often mentioned in the context of prayer (cf., e.g., Neh 9:27; Dan 9:18; Zech 10:6). In the oracle of Zech 1:14-17 the promise of mercies is in response to the plea of the Angel that the Lord show mercy (the verb *rḥm*) to his people (v. 12). Deut 30:3; Isa 14:1; 49:10,13; 54:8; Jer 33:6; Ezek 39:25; and Hos 2:19 (21) are other passages where either the verb or noun in question is used with reference to restoration from a state of exile. All of these are prophecies of new covenant restoration (some of them so interpreted in specific New Testament citations), reminding us that the Zechariah 1 oracle also has this antitypical dimension.

Supreme among, as well as source of, all the other promised blessings is God's own Presence, granted in grace. In the development of the theme of the rebuilding of Jerusalem in Zechariah's third vision, the thought of God as the all in all is expressed by the picture of his Glory as an all-encompassing and all-filling presence in the temple-city: "For I, saith Yahweh, will be unto her a wall of fire round about, and I will be the glory in the midst of her" (Zech 2:5[9]; cf. the original paradise-sanctuary in Eden).

Insofar as the return of God's Presence affirmed in Zech 1:16 had reference to the prophet's own day it had to be accepted by the Israelites on faith on the basis of God's word, because to ordinary mortal eyes it was not a visible presence (cf. 2 Kgs 6:17). Only the prophet-seer himself, in the Spirit, saw the Presence. The Lord's declaration, "I am returned," was simply a verbalizing of the reality symbolized in the vision of the rider on the red horse, present in the midst of the myrtles. The divine Presence was present in the person of this divine Angel-rider, Lord of angels, judge of the nations, advocate of God's elect, making intercession for the myrtle community in the wilderness by the deep.

A new stage in the history of God's presence begins with the advent recorded in the Gospels. Christian hearts rejoice in the incarnation-presence of the messianic Angel, Immanuel his name, who declares that he who has seen him has seen the Father (John 14:9). In him the Lord of mercies has returned to mankind in their exile from Eden, dispersed in the wilderness of the fallen world. Though in these post-ascension, preconsummation days the divine presence is again not visible, the Son having gone to the Father, we bear witness to God's presence in the Spirit. In joyful faith we say: Let the Feast of Tabernacles be celebrated. The Lord is present, tabernacling in the midst of his people here and now in the Spirit, forming us anew in his image as his spiritual temple. The re-creation has begun within, an invisible token of the future return of Glory (a kind of inside-out sacrament). In the Spirit's presence we have the foretaste of the new heavens and new earth and its temple-city, New Jerusalem, the kingdom inheritance of the saints in the consummate, eternal age of creation's history.

The Angel whose appearance in Zechariah's vision manifests the return of God to his people is the Angel of the Presence. He is the agent of the Glory-Spirit, the One who is executor of the covenant's dual sanctions of blessing and curse. Such was the twofold office of God's Presence in the redemptive judgments of the flood and exodus. He shielded and guided the people of God (Exod 13:21; 14:19,20), but discomfited and destroyed their foes and persecutors (Exod 14:24). Consonant with that, the assurance of God's return in the Angel of the Presence in Zech 1:16 is attended by the declaration that the Lord will both comfort Jerusalem and deal in anger with the nations. The threat of wrath comes first in the divine oracle (vv. 14,15), then the promise of blessings (vv. 16,17).

C. *Jealous Wrath against the Nations:* Beginning with an announcement of what the Lord's return portends for the nations, the oracle speaks of his "great jealousy" and "great wrath." In intensity of feeling this response matches the importunate intercession of the Angel. The Lord of hosts displays as much zeal for granting salvation in fulfillment of his covenant as did the advocate of his people in requesting it. His great jealousy and wrath here are complementary aspects of his attitude towards one and the same object. This combination is found again in an elaboration of this theme in Zech 8:2, where the Lord says he is "jealous with great anger."[15]

Most frequently in the Old Testament God's angry jealousy is his response to Israel for disloyalty to him in favor of other gods. So, for example, the identification of Yahweh as a jealous God in the curse sanction attached to the second stipulation of the Decalogue-covenant (Exod 20:5; Deut 5:9) threatens judgment on those who violate their sworn commitment by worshipping some creature-thing, not the Creator Lord himself. Such jealousy is a matter of offended honor and outraged majesty. Another notable instance of God's jealousy directed against Israel is found in the judicial witness song of Deuteronomy 32. Here Moses warns that when Israel, prosperously ensconced in Canaan, provokes God to jealousy with their no-gods and to anger with their vain idols, he will respond by applying the *lex talionis*, provoking them to jealous anger with a no-people (vv. 16-21).

But the situation in Zech 1:14,15 is of a different sort. Here it is the nations of the deep, not the covenant people, who have incited the angry jealousy of Yahweh. The fact that his jealousy is said to be "for Jerusalem and for Zion" (v. 14; cf. 8:2) has misled some into separating the jealousy from the anger against the nations and viewing the former as a solicitous jealousy for Israel's welfare, a zeal to prosper them. Actually, the phrase "for Jerusalem and Zion" goes with the anger as much as with the jealousy and indicates the area with respect to which the nations have offended the Lord God and made him angrily jealous against them. The point is that Jerusalem-Zion represents the people whom Yahweh had claimed as his own servants, bringing them under his suzerainty by covenant; Israel was his own vassal people. They were his private, personal possession, the portion he set aside as his royal inheritance long ago when he was distributing the people of the earth among the sons of El (Deut 32:8,9).[16] And Yahweh's prerogatives as suzerain over the Israelites had been challenged by the great kings of the earth who took them into captivity. These usurpers were exacting from Yahweh's vassals the tributary allegiance which belonged to him. His great name was being scoffed at among the nations by reason of Israel's inglorious state. It was, therefore, out of concern for his own name and sovereign claims that the Lord was jealously furious with these rival suzerains, these antichrists who would grasp his domain and spoil him of his own with respect to Jerusalem and Zion. This jealous concern for the reclaiming and repossessing of what was rightfully his finds further expression, as the oracle continues, in the repeated possessive pronouns: "my house...my cities" (1:16,17).

Joel 2:18 also speaks of Yahweh's jealousy in a context of threats to drive off the aggressor nations that brought reproach on Israel and scorn on the name of their God (2:17,19,20). There too Yahweh's concern for his own prerogative and property surfaces in the possessive pronouns: he "was jealous for his land and had pity on his people." Once more in Ezek 39:25, another passage that mentions the divine jealousy in a restoration context, the jealousy is for God's own honor. Dispersal of his people from their land had resulted in defamation of God's name among the nations and he states specifically that it is out of jealousy "for my holy name" that he will take action to sanctify his name and glorify himself in the eyes of his people and of all the nations (Ezek 38:16,23; 39:6,7,21,22,27,28). Back of all these prophetic passages lies the Mosaic witness song of Deuteronomy 32. We noted above that the situation in Zech 1:14,15 is to be distinguished from that in Deut 32:21, where the divine jealousy is provoked by Israel and is manifested in the infliction of the covenant curses through the agency of the foreign nations. But later in this song a subsequent situation of a different kind is addressed. As a sequel to the exile of Israel, it is related that the nations God employed to execute his threatened curse-sanction would misunderstand this event and exalt themselves, discounting the God of captive Israel. Thereupon, out of concern for his maligned name, the Lord would bring vengeance on those nations and restore his covenant people (Deut 32:26-43; cf. Heb 10:30,31). This later situation is the one that is in view in Zech 1:14,15.

Such is the understanding of this jealous fury of God indicated by the reason assigned for it: "Because I was angry [only] for a little while, but they [the nations at ease] helped for evil" (Zech 1:15). God had indeed been angry (cf. "very angry," Zech 1:2) with Israel, as Moses had warned (Deut 32:19-25), but his ultimate plans for his covenant people in Christ, in faithfulness to his promises to Abraham, were for shalom, "not for evil" (Jer 29:11). Through Isaiah the Lord declares: "For a brief moment I forsook you, but with great mercies I will regather you. In overflowing wrath I hid my face from you for a moment, but with everlasting kindness I will show mercy to you, says Yahweh your Redeemer" (Isa 54:7,8). Though the Lord would cast off Israel for breaking the Mosaic covenant of works, he would remember his covenant of grace with Abraham (continuous through the Mosaic economy and foundational thereto) and fulfill its promises. Beyond Israel's fall, and even through it, God purposed to bring about the fullness of Israel in Christ (cf. Isa 27:7-13; Rom 11:11-32). This divine purposing of good beyond the evil of the covenant curse came to expression in the Babylonian exile of Israel in the limitation of seventy years set on the judgment with a view to the subsequent restoration of the typological order. And that restoration was designed in God's master plan of salvation to tide things over until Christ, the promised seed of Abraham, came as a covenant of the people, to speak peace unto the nations.

Blind, however, to God's purpose and power, the nations used by him to accomplish his righteous will upon Israel misconstrued their role (as Moses also foretold, Deut 32:26-43) and "helped for evil" (Zech 1:15).[17] That is, they performed their appointed historical function, but, if not in ignorance, certainly with malicious motives and in a manner subversive of God's glory and his intentions for his people's future hope and peace. It is against this perversity that Zech 1:14,15 registers the Lord's jealous indignation.

Zechariah was resuming a theme found in Isaiah 47. There, Babylon is contemplated, prophetically, as guilty of cruelty to the people of God, who were delivered by him into her hands (v. 6). Thereby Babylon displayed contempt for the name of Yahweh of hosts, the holy Redeemer of Israel (v. 4), boasting that she would be "mistress of kingdoms...forever" (vv. 5,7). For this offense Babylon is threatened with God's judgment of sudden desolation (vv. 1ff., 11).

As we have previously observed, the nations would persist in provoking this jealous wrath of the Lord, already incurred by their treatment of captive Israel, throughout the history of the typological kingdom. Whatever degree of restoration occurred at that old typological level, there was not a basic change in the relation of the world power to the covenant community. Beyond that, suppression of the community of faith continued on into the new covenant era. Even though in this new age the promised return of the Lord to his people has taken the form of the divine Angel in Jesus Christ, the beast-powers (as they are symbolically represented in the books of Daniel and Revelation) still oppress and persecute the saints. Also, the Scriptures foretell a climactic manifestation of the antichrist spirit of the nations "at ease" that will provoke God's final fury, bringing to an end at last the tensions of prolonged eschatological delay, voiced in the poignant cry, "How long?"

One prophecy of this final crisis is found in the section of the Book of Ezekiel to which we pointed for a case of God's jealousy against the nations, parallel to that in Zech 1:14,15 (cf. Ezek 39:25). Ezekiel describes the advent of Gog, head of the hordes of hostile forces. At the end of the years he comes from Zaphon, the pseudomountain of God, to attack Zion, the true mountain of divine assembly (Har Magedon), and so presents himself as a rival claimant to Yahweh's lordship over the world (Ezek 38:2ff.). Challenged by antichrist-Gog, Yahweh, in wrathful jealousy for his name, pours out fiery doom, delivering his besieged people and destroying forever the power of the satanic enemies (Ezek 38:18ff.; cf. Rev 6:12-17; 11:11-18; 16:17-21; 17:14b; 19:17,18,20,21; 20:9b,10). So at last God's jealous wrath is completely satisfied and his name everlastingly glorified among the nations (Ezek 38:16,23; 39:6,7,21-29).

D. _Renewal on Zion:_ Moving on from the ominous consequences of God's return (v. 16a) for the nations of the deep (vv. 14,15), the oracular response announces the blessings that must follow from the divine presence in the midst of the myrtles (vv. 16b, 17). These mercies were the implicit corollary of God's judgment on the hostile world and that means that they, like the threatened judgment, span the entire future of redemptive history and indeed concern especially the new covenant order, including its consummate stage. Chiastically arranged, this section opens (v. 16b) and closes (v. 17c) with the promise of the rebuilding of the temple, while the middle part deals with the restoration of the rest of the theocratic community (vv. 16c and v. 17b, with a renewal of the prophetic charge to Zechariah in the center, v. 17a).

Return of the holy Presence of the Lord to dwell among his kingdom people in Jerusalem calls for the reconstruction of his royal temple-residence there. Hence the assurance, "I am returned," is at once followed by the promise, "my house shall be built in it" (v. 16b). This promise is reiterated in the closing declaration that Yahweh "will again choose Jerusalem" (v. 17b; cf. 2:12 [16]; 3:2). Jerusalem's election was anticipated in the repeated references in the Deuteronomic covenant to the place that the Lord would choose to put his name (Deut 12:5,21; 14:24) or cause his name to dwell (Deut 12:11; 14:23; 16:2,6,11; 26:2). God's name is his theophanic Glory. He would select a site in the promised land as a permanent dwelling and place of enthronement for his Glory-Presence, and that would then also be the location of the central altar. In due course Jerusalem was designated as the site of God's Name and the temple was constructed there. That the choosing of Jerusalem refers specifically to the building of God's house there is also evidenced in the pairing of the two in

Solomon's prayer of temple dedication: "the city you have chosen and the temple I have built for your name" (1 Kgs 8:44,48; cf. 1 Kgs 11:36).

Rebuilding of the temple was naturally, indeed necessarily, attended by the reconstruction of the city of Jerusalem, the place chosen as its site. Hence, immediately following the promise of the former (Zech 1:16b) is the statement: "a line shall be stretched over Jerusalem" (v. 16c). In view here is the builder's marking out the planned perimeters of the city with a cord. Job 38:5 attributes to God the performance of this particular task in the constructing of the earth at creation. Somewhat earlier than Zechariah, Jeremiah had used the same imagery of the measuring line when he too was portraying the rebuilding of Jerusalem (Jer 31:39) and the context makes clear that the line was being employed to establish the contemplated boundaries of the city (cf. Jer 31:38-40).

Significantly, the setting of this parallel picture of the restoration of Jerusalem in Jeremiah is his classic prophecy of the new covenant age (cf. Jer 31:31ff.). The new Jerusalem he speaks of is a messianic product, the eternal holy city of God's Glory-Presence provided in the cosmic re-creation at the consummation of the ages. Just as it was the Lord God who stretched the line over the earth in the beginning, so it is he who does so again as he builds the New Jerusalem in his creating of the new heaven and new earth, the event which Jeremiah, and Zechariah following him, prophesied. This heavenly city is the sum of the inheritance promised in the Abrahamic Covenant to the patriarch and his seed, and God is its architect and artisan (cf. Heb 11:10). Agreeably, when Zechariah in his third vision resumes the theme of the rebuilding of Jerusalem, it is the divine Angel who is engaged in a related function involving a measuring line (2:1 [5]). Christ, the Angel incarnate, is the builder of the new temple city, for in the new covenant the city and temple coalesce, and Christ is the one who, with his body the church, is the temple and builds the temple.

According to the original commission given man in Eden, the kingdom city was to expand from its cultic focus at the mountain of God outward to a global fullness So again in the symbolic re-establishment of the Edenic order in Israel, God's kingdom reaches out from Jerusalem, the temple-city focus, and embraces the full promised land with all the satellite cities in orbit around Zion. Employing this typological symbolism to picture the restoration of the kingdom, Zechariah's vision does not stop, therefore, with the rebuilding of the temple and Jerusalem but includes the renewal of the total theocratic domain. "Thus says Yahweh of hosts: My cities shall yet overflow[18] with prosperity" (1:17b). Like the other promised mercies associated with it in the oracle, this outward felicity of the kingdom envisages more than the reconstruction of the cities of Judah in Zechariah's days; it too looks ahead to the new covenant and the new heaven and earth.

Between the reference in 1:17b to the prosperity of the other theocratic cities and the closing declaration concerning the choice of Jerusalem (v. 17c) comes the promise: "Yahweh shall yet comfort Zion." Does this promise connect with the former and pertain to relief from political-economic distress through a revival of paradise-like conditions, or is it linked with the latter and thus have to do with the temple? Favoring the first option is the similar prophecy of Isa 51:3, where Yahweh's comforting of Zion is explained as his having compassion on her ruins and turning her wilderness into a luxuriant, joyful garden of Eden. However, the second option is favored by the structural parallelism of the last two clauses in Zech 1:17. If so, then Mount Zion is used here as a synonym for the city located on it, chosen to be the site of God's Presence and sanctuary-residence. Mount Zion is thus promised that it will again enjoy the status of mountain of God, seat of God's enthronement between the cherubim, assembly place of the heavenly council. Like the similar prospect in Isa 51:3, this promise to comfort Zion will then signify a restoration of the arrangements found in Eden, but particularly its cultic focus. It is a prophecy of the re-creation event, when Eden is not simply restored but consummated, when the mandated kingdom fullness has been realized, when indeed the cultic focus has expanded and become co-extensive with the kingdom fullness in a cosmic temple-city on the heavenly mountain of God.

At the beginning of the oracle (Zech 1:14) and again in the midst of the announcement of blessings (v. 17a), the Angel of the Lord (through the interpreting angel) charges Zechariah to proclaim (qr^3) God's words of comfort (cf. v. 13). A comparable charge to proclaim comfort (same terminology) is found in Isa 40:1,2. There too the leading thought is the advent of the divine Glory with recompense for his people (Isa 40:5,9-11). This divine advent is to be heralded by a voice crying (qr^3) in the wilderness[19] to prepare the processional way of the Lord (Isa 40:3), a voice identified in the Gospels with John, the forerunner of Jesus (Matt 3:3; Mark 1:3; Luke 3:4; John 1:23). Bringing together Isaiah 40 and Malachi's prophecy of the advent, Jesus identified John with the "Elijah the prophet" who was to prepare the way for the messianic "Angel of the covenant" in his appearing for judgment and salvation (Mal 3:1ff.; 4:5 [3:23]; Matt 11:10; Luke 7:27). And the Angel of the covenant is, of course, Jesus himself.[20]

Reflecting on the message of comfort in Zech 1:14-17 in the light of its relationship to Isaiah 40 and Malachi 3 and 4 we become more distinctly aware that the giving of a charge by the Angel of the Lord to Zechariah to proclaim that message was an act of the pre-incarnate Son, commissioning a herald of his own future advent. It was a charge to the prophet of the myrtles community in the wilderness by the deep to be a precursor of the later voice crying in the wilderness by the Jordan.

E. *Persevering in Hope:* That the eschatological range of Zechariah's first vision extends into our new covenant age is confirmed (as has been previously intimated) by the remainder of his prophecy. Preliminary to noting some of the salient evidence, a reminder of a couple of features of the literary structure of the book. The seven night visions are arranged in two triads around the central, fourth vision. The unitary nature of the first three visions is attested by the way the second and third visions develop in turn the two themes of the divine oracle in the opening vision, namely, God's wrath against the nations and his restorative mercies for Jerusalem and the temple. Also, the Book of Zechariah overall is a diptych, the seven visions of 1:7-6:8 being balanced by the "burdens" of 9:1-14:21, which are an apocalyptic recasting of the visions, arranged in parallel sequence. In this pattern, the first vision is paralleled by 9:1-17.

God's choice of Jerusalem as the place of his Presence, the main affirmation of the oracle in vision one, is again the major theme in vision three (2:1-13 [2:5-17]). There, Jerusalem's election as the temple site, with the concomitant restoration of the city, is portrayed as a rebuilding of Jerusalem, expanded to unprecedented dimensions (2:4 [8]), and this symbolism is interpreted in terms of an ingathering of converted Gentiles, a distinctive feature of the church age: "Many nations will join themselves to Yahweh in that day and will be my people" (2:11 [15]). Associated with this development is the total reversal in the power relationship of "Jerusalem" and "Babylon" (2:8 [13]) that does not occur until the Final Judgment. Moreover, all of this is said to serve as validation of the divine authorization of the mission of Messiah: "You will know that Yahweh of hosts has sent me unto you" (2:9,11 [13,15]).

Once more we encounter the main themes of the first vision in 9:1-17, its parallel in the "burdens": God's presence and the promise to restore his house, proclamation of glad tidings to Jerusalem, and prosperous prospects for all the covenant community around Zion. The new covenant age is again the eschatological setting. God's presence takes the form of the advent of the messianic king, come to speak God's reconciling peace to the nations and to exercise his universal sovereignty (9:9,10). And the prosperity of the covenant kingdom is achieved through a final divine conquest of the hostile world, which introduces the time of sabbatical peace that knows no interruption (9:8).

Zechariah's opening vision is then to be understood as prophetic of the perfecting of the kingdom under the new covenant with its better promises and better country. Not that it failed to address the typological realities of Zechariah's day. The promised mercies of Zech 1:16,17 were experienced at that level of the Mosaic Covenant in the completion of the temple, the rebuilding of Jerusalem and its walls, the resettlement of other cities and the general re-establishment of the theocratic order under the Law. But what we want to reflect on in closing is how this vision speaks to us upon whom the ends of the ages are come and particularly on the relevance for us of the central issue of the eschatological "How long?" of the messianic Advocate (1:12).

Our present church age is the time of the missionary harvesting of the nations that results in the swelling of "Jerusalem" into "a city inhabited as villages without walls" (2:4 [9]; cf. 1:6). Not yet, however, has the hour of Final Judgment struck when the world is shaken to its foundations, the worldly powers become a spoil to the saints, and all the habitations of God's people henceforth overflow with the prosperity of heaven's eternal glory (1:17).

As disclosed in Rev 6:10, Christian martyrs are still raising the cry of Zech 1:12 during this church age: "How long, O Sovereign holy and true, do you not judge and avenge our blood on those who dwell on the earth?" And the divine response is that they must wait in their intermediate state of rest while the number of the martyr-witnesses is being filled up in the course of church history on earth (Rev 6:11). Such is again the characterization of this age of the great commission in Revelation 20, there symbolized as a thousand years. The millennium is a time when believers are being beheaded for the testimony of Jesus (Rev 20:4)[21] as they advance the gospel witness out from Jerusalem into all those nations hitherto in the darkness of satanic deception, but no longer so because Christ has bound the devil for these thousand years (Rev 20:1-3).

Revelation 20 knows nothing of a political dominion of the church over the earth during this millennial age of the great commission. That expectation is a delusion of the prophets of theonomic postmillennialism, who, in their impatience with the way through the wilderness, have succumbed to carnal cravings for worldly power. It is revealing that in order to defend their false forecasts they find it necessary to scorn as losers those whom the Scriptures honor as overcomers, indeed as "more than conquerors" (cf. Rom 8:35-37), the martyr-witnesses who overcome Satan "because of the blood of the Lamb, and because of the word of their testimony, and they loved not their life unto death" (Rev 12:11). One cannot but be appalled at the railing of certain of these reconstructionist postmillenarians against the Holy Spirit's soteric ministry thus far in the church age. What has been in the eyes of heaven a triumphant working of the Spirit of Christ, effecting the salvation of all God's elect in every nation and every generation without fail, a sovereign fulfilling of the good pleasure of God's will to the praise of his grace—this is dismissed by the pundits of this postmillennialist cult as dismal failure and a history of defeat. Nothing betrays more clearly than this blasphemous contempt for the gospel triumphs of the Spirit how alien to biblical Christianity is the ideology of theonomic reconstructionism.

Psalm and prophecy foretell a time when the conspiring nations gathered by antichrist-Gog will rage against the Lord God and his Christ, and the Almighty will vent the jealous fury of his wrath on them (Ps 2:1ff.; Rev 11:17,18). Meanwhile the saints witness and wait. They watch and pray, confident that their prayers ascend through their Advocate to the heavenly throne (Rev 8:3) and evoke divine judgments that culminate at the seventh trumpet in the finishing of the mystery of God (Rev 10:7). But until that final trumpet sounds and there is "delay no longer" (Rev 10:6) and the time has arrived for the dead to be judged and the saints to be vindicated (Rev 11:18), the cry "How long?," will continue to be wrung from the soul of the church. Until he who promises, "Yea, I come quickly," does come, the church in the wilderness by the demonic deep will be pleading out of the depths of its great tribulation (Rev 7:14; cf. 1:9), "Amen: come Lord Jesus" (Rev 22:20).

Unseen, the rider of the red horse is present in the midst of the myrtles. The Lord who is to come is the one who was and who is, who is with us now, within us now. He is within us now by the Holy Spirit of promise, who seals us in Christ and is the earnest guaranteeing our inheritance, hoped for but not yet seen (Eph 1:13,14). We persevere in hope, persuaded that the momentary, light affliction of this age works for us a far greater, eternal weight of glory (2 Cor 4:17). Through Christ's holy Presence within we are strengthened with all power by his glorious might so that we may have great endurance and patience, joyfully giving thanks to the Father, who has qualified us to share in the inheritance of the saints in the kingdom of light (cf. Col 1:11,12), "to the praise of his glory" (Eph 1:14).

---

1 The literary-thematic pattern of the night visions is repeated in the "burdens" (Zechariah 9-14), the overall structure thus being a diptych. The two passages portraying Messiah as a mounted figure (1:8 and 9:9) occupy corresponding positions in this parallelism.

2 See *Archives royales de Mari* II, No. 37:5-14. An English translation of the text is available in J. B. Pritchard, ed., *Ancient Near Eastern Texts Relating to the Old Testament* (1969), 482c.

3 For a full discussion of this, see my *Kingdom Prologue* (privately published, 1993) 136-139.

4 See further my "Death, Leviathan, and the Martyrs: Isaiah 24:1-27:1," in *A Tribute to Gleason Archer*, ed. W. C. Kaiser and R. F. Younglood (Chicago, 1986) 235-6.

5 Cf. Dan 6:28, translating: "even in the reign of Cyrus the Persian."

6 Note the correspondences of Zech 1:1-6 to the Jeremiah 25 context, especially vv. 3-9.

7 The seventy years have also been understood as a conventional expression for a full span of divine displeasure (cf. Isa 23:15). Others see a reference to the period from the fall of Jerusalem in 587 to the time of Zechariah's night visions (520), or to the revelation he received two years later (and thus almost exactly seventy years after 587), in which "these seventy years" are again mentioned (Zech 7:5).

8 This symbolism was then used again in the prophetic vision of Dan 9:24-27, given in response to the prayer of Daniel, itself prompted by reflection on Jeremiah's seventy years prophecy.

9 Isaiah 10 lies behind the passages in Jeremiah and Daniel that were the literary background of Zech 1:12 (cf., e.g., Isa 10:22,23 with Dan 9:26,27).

10 For *rṣh* in the sense of make good, make up for, receive one's due (whether compensation or retribution) see Job 14:6, where it refers to the hired laborer working off his contracted day, and Job 20:10, where it means to indemnify in a case of ill-gotten gain. In Isa 40:2 this verb refers, as in Lev 26:41, to making up for sin. It is reinforced there by statements that the allotted years of the sentence have been completed and that God's people have received from the Lord's hand the full equivalent (not "double") for all their sins.

11 The wilderness image in the above analogy is simply the area outside the promised paradise land through which the saints make their pilgrim journey. It does not entail the notion of exile-like banishment to wanderings under the sentence of divine wrath. The redeemed travel a processional highway home through this wilderness (cf. Isa 11:16; 35:8-10; 40:3; 49:11,12).

12 Cf. Richard B. Gaffin, Jr., "Theonomy and Eschatology: Reflections on Postmillennialism," in *Theonomy: A Reformed Critique*, eds. W. S. Barker and W. R. Godfrey (Grand Rapids, 1990) 197-224.

13 These interrelationships between the several sections of vv. 12-17 argue against the critical denial of the oracle's integral connection with the first vision.

14 The same verb is used in summarizing the paraenesis of the pre-exilic prophets in Zech 1:4.

15 Note also the parallelism of God's jealousy and wrath, both directed against the same offender, in Deut 32:21 and Ps 78:58.

16 On this passage, see my *Kingdom Prologue* 195-96.

17 Various alternative renderings have been suggested for the verb (^{c}zr) in this phrase, explaining it on the basis of alleged Arabic or Ugaritic equivalents or through emendation. The most plausible of these would result in the idea of multiplying or prolonging the evil. This would provide a more precise contrast to the temporal aspect expressed by *mĕ^{c}aṭ*, "a little while."

18 For this meaning of *pûṣ*, cf. 2 Sam 18:8; Job 40:11; Prov 5:16. That the preposition *min* here means "(overflow) because of" not "(be scattered) from lack of" is clear from its use in the related picture of urban expansion in Zech 2:4(8).

19 Incidentally, the phrase "in the wilderness" is to be taken both with what precedes, viz., the voice crying, as in LXX and NT quotes, and with what follows, viz., the preparation of the way, as is required by the parallelism with "in the desert." This is a recognized poetic device, employed elsewhere by Isaiah himself (cf., e.g., "in warfare" in Isa 27:4).

20 In Israel's exodus march to Zion, the Angel of the covenant or Presence proceeded as king at the head of the processional way (Exod 23:20). In the new exodus there is again the royal procession, the way prepared by prophets (and disciples, cf. the triumphal entry into Jerusalem), and it is again the Angel of the Lord, now the Lord incarnate, who is the royal leader.

21 The state of the martyrs during the millennium is depicted here as one of royal-priestly rest (v. 4), as in Rev 6:11. Clearly, both passages deal with the same epoch.

AVENGER OF THE AFFLICTED

In Zechariah's first vision the messianic angel appeared as a warrior mounted on a red horse, present in the midst of God's people (the myrtles). Under his command stood a squadron of supernal agents (the flame-colored horses), ready to execute the judgment which the Lord threatened against the evil world-empire (the deep), usurper of dominion over mount Zion. Here was a predisclosure that when Christ was manifested, it would be to "destroy the works of the devil" (1 John 3:8), to cast Satan down from heaven to hell (Luke 10:18; Rev 12:10; 20:10), and so fulfill the primeval decree that God's champion should crush the draconic head lifted up against the holy mount in Eden (Gen 3:15).

This theme of the ultimate divine avenging of Zion against her enemies is taken up again in Zechariah's second vision (1:18-21 [2:1-4 in Hebrew]).[1] The hostile nations are symbolized here by four horns and the inflicters of divine judgment by four specialist workmen.

I. ASSAULTERS OF ZION

The interpreting angel describes the horn-nations as having lifted up the horn against Judah, Israel, and Jerusalem, scattering them so that they could no longer lift up the head (1:18,21 [2:1,4]). This language confronts us again with prophetic idiom: the prophets employed the typological situation of their time to represent the antitypical realities of the coming messianic age. Through Zechariah, the Spirit of prophecy speaks beforehand of Christ's church (cf. 1 Pet 1:10-12) under the form of the restored covenant community of Judah, centering in Jerusalem on the temple mount.[2]

The offense of the horn-nations consisted both in putting down the chosen folk and in exalting themselves against the Lord God. Translated into the terms of John's portrayal of the horned beast in the Apocalypse: they made war against the saints and they blasphemed the name of God (Rev 13:6,7). We will analyze in turn these two dimensions of their assault on Zion.

A. *Enmity Against the Saints:* Though the symbol of the four horns appears to be polyvalent, contextual indications suggest that the primary image evoked is simply that of horns borne by animals. Conjured up by the aggressive lifting of the horns (v. 21 [2:4]) is an attacking bull, lowering its head and then thrusting its lethal horns upward. The verb used in v. 21 [2:4] for frightening away the horns (ḥrd) is elsewhere used for scaring off birds of prey, lions, and other animals (cf. e.g., Deut 28:26; Nah 2:12). Also, the horns are equated with imperial powers hostile to Israel and the metaphor of monstrous beasts, like the multiheaded leviathan, is often applied to such nations in Scripture (cf. e.g., Ps 74:13,14; Isa 27:1; Ezek 29:3).

Comparison with similar symbolism in the book of Daniel confirms the primarily bestial nature of the image of the four horns. In Daniel 7 and 8 the horns of various animals figure conspicuously in the depiction of empires ascendant over the realm covenanted to David. Medo-Persia is symbolized in Daniel 8 by a ram with two horns and Greece by a goat, which begins as a unicorn, then has four horns, one of which sprouts the little horn whose career of antagonism against Zion is an Old Testament adumbration of the final antichrist episode. Daniel 7 presents a series of four bizarre beasts, the last of which, the terrible destroyer whose career terminates in the final judgment, has ten horns plus an eleventh, the little horn that symbolizes the antichrist spirit and program throughout church history. Marking the connection between Zechariah's horn-nations and the nations represented by the horned animals in Daniel 7 is their common place of origin. It is from the great stormy deep that the four beasts of Daniel 7 emerge (vv. 2,3). And if we appreciate the relationship of the second vision to the first within the unity of Zechariah's opening triad, we will recognize that the spawning place of the four horn-nations of vision two is the deep, which symbolizes the hostile world in vision one.[3]

In the first instance then, the horns of Zechariah's second vision are to be seen as belonging to animals. Indeed, the animal motif apparently extends to the picturing of God's people, the victims of the horns' attack, as a flock, a favorite image later in Zechariah (cf. 9:16; 10:2,3; 11:3-17; 13:7). For zrh, the verb denoting the dispersing of Judah (vv. 19,21 [2:2,4]), is used for the scattering of sheep (cf. Ps 44:11 [12]; Jer 31:10). It is noteworthy that the theme of the dispersed flock is found in Zech 10:1-4, the section on the second side of the over-all diptych structure of the book that corresponds to the second vision on the first side.[4] Moreover, the afflicters of the flock are there also animals, goats (10:3), and once again, as in vision two, the Lord in his anger against the animal-powers provides deliverance for his flock (10:3,4).

By itself the image of exalting the horn signifies simply the exertion of power and achievement of success or attainment of glory, while the cutting off and casting down of one's horn symbolizes defeat and impotence. An equivalent image is that of lifting up the head (bearer of the horns), with its opposite, being unable to lift up the head. Combining the two forms of the metaphor, Zechariah introduces into the meaning of lifting up the horns the specific connotation of ferocity, hostility and tyranny by qualifying the action as an animal-like attack against Judah that devastated it and rendered it helpless. Such then was the offense of the horn-nations: their exaltation involved a malicious trampling of the covenant people into the ground. Coming up from the dark deep at the devil's instigation, the bestial horn-nations exhibited satanic enmity against the saints.

B. *Blasphemy Against the Most High:* Inasmuch as the bull-like assault of the nations was directed against Judah, the lifting *up* of their horns becomes an image of persecuting the godly. But to attack Judah is also to defy the heavenly Protector to whom Judah cried, "How long"? Indeed to march against Jerusalem-Zion (Zech 1:19 [2:2]) is to storm the very mountain stronghold where the holy Lord is enthroned. Hence, the act becomes one of blasphemy against the God of Zion, a lifting up of the horn (or head) in vainglorious challenge to the Most High, an Har Magedon event.[5]

Psalm 74 emphasizes this blasphemous dimension of attacking the Lord's heritage. The situation is much like that in Zechariah's vision. God's people, pictured as his flock (vv. 1,2), appeal to him, the one who broke the heads of the leviathan monster (vv. 13,14), to raise them from the ruins wrought by their adversaries (v. 3), who are referred to as animals (vv. 4,19). They lament that the foes "burned your sanctuary to the ground; they defiled the dwelling place of your Name" (v. 7) and they plead, "How long will the enemy mock you, O God?" (v. 10). "Rise up O God, and defend your cause" (v. 22). And in Psalm 75 such defiance of the God of heaven is described by the horn metaphor: "To the arrogant I say, 'Boast no more,' and to the wicked, 'Do not lift up your horns. Do not lift your horns against heaven'" (vv. 4,5a [5,6a]).

In the animal-horn symbolism in the Danielic background of Zechariah's visions the blasphemy aspect is again prominent. The little horn of the goat in Daniel 8 (representing Antiochus Epiphanes) magnifies himself to the hosts of heaven, even to the prince of the host (vv. 10,11,24,25). And the little horn of the fourth beast in Daniel 7 has facial features, eyes and mouth—it is a combined horn-head, and it is lifted up in defiance of heaven, for the mouth spoke great words against the Most High (vv. 8,20,25).

Within Zechariah's second vision itself the titanic, heaven- challenging stance of the nations comes to expression in a second image of lifting up the head-horn, an image evoked by the symbol of the four horns that is different from the one so far considered. In this image the horns no longer rise from the heads or backs of beasts but project upwards from the corners of an altar. This altar image urges itself upon us compellingly for it is the four-horned altar that is usually in view when four horns are mentioned in the Bible (cf., e.g., Exod 27:2; 30:2; 1 Kgs 1:50). It accounts at once for the number four. If the symbol is interpreted simply as animal horns, the four can indeed be readily understood as signifying universality, as in the case of the four winds of heaven (Zech 2:6 [10]) or the four chariot-spirits of heaven (Zech 6:5). But the design of the altar provides a more immediate, concrete explanation of the number four. Also, while we have observed that certain details of the second vision are congruous in an animal scenario, the identification of God's counteragents against the horns as ḥārāšîm points naturally (though not necessarily) to a fabricated object like an altar, since that term is most often used for craftsmen of some sort.[6] Moreover, as we shall be discussing at length, the four-horned altar structure constituted a lifting up of the head, the action attributed to the horns in Zechariah's second vision. Interpreters need not choose between the two meanings of the four-horn symbolism. We may simply recognize that certain overtones are added to the basic animal-horn significance of this polyvalent metaphor by the import of the specific image of four animal horns crowning an altar.

Exploration of the symbolism of lifting up the head (horns) leads along a fascinating trail of altars and idols and ziggurats and mountains.[7] We start by returning to the roots of Zechariah in the Book of Daniel, focusing now on the vision of the world kingdom in the form of the colossus in Daniel 2. Here was a lifting up of the head, the head of gold at the top of the image, representing Nebuchadnezzar and his Babylon in the land of Shinar (vv. 37,38). Manifestations abound of the idolatrous spirit of this head of gold, exalting itself against the Lord God. Dan 1:2 records that Nebuchadnezzar had carried off to Babylon the captives of Judah and treasures and furnishings of the house of God, which he relocated in the temple of his god. Daniel 3 tells of the gigantic golden idol, with dimensions according to the number of man, whose worship the bestial monarch and his false prophets demanded. Daniel 4 describes the self-glorying of

Nebuchadnezzar as alpha and omega of the Babylonian kingdom (vv. 29,30) and portrays the king as a cosmic tree with its top reaching unto heaven (vv. 11,20). Daniel 5 narrates the judgment on Belshazzar for lifting himself up against the Lord of heaven and promoting the praise of idols (v. 23).

This was a revival of the lifting up of the head (horns) that occurred at Babylon's beginnings in the land of Shinar (Gen 11:1-9; cf. Dan 1:2; Zech 5:11). Acutely aware of the loss of the original Har Magedon, the mountain of God in Eden, the cultic focus that gave coherence to the mandated kingdom fullness,[8] the ancient Babelites tried to regain humanity's lost ecumenicity by themselves erecting a cosmic mountain focus in the form of a tower that reached unto heaven.[9] The ideology of the Babel enterprise is illuminated by Mesopotamian mythology. The *Enuma Elish* epic[10] attributes the origins of Babylon to the gods at the founding of the world order. In honor of Marduk, their champion, they constructed his temple with its tiered tower, named Esagila. That name is of special interest to our present investigations for it means "the house of the lifting up of the head." Punning on that name, the text says that after a year of making the bricks for it (cf. Gen 11:3) "they raised the head of Esagila on high" (*Enuma Elish*, VI, 62). Also of particular interest for our immediate purposes, the text notes that once Marduk was enthroned there, "they looked up to its horns" (*Enuma Elish*, VI, 66). The temple tower was crowned with horns. Similarly, ziggurats as later depicted in inscription and bas-relief have horns on the summit. Symbolized by such a crown of horns was the divine power and glory of the resident deities. Elsewhere in iconographic representations of gods they appear with headpieces composed of paired horns, some with four or more horns. One wonders whether such multitiered crowns tapering toward the top imitate ziggurat form. Certainly, like the horns on the ziggurat, they symbolize divine might and majesty, the ultimate lifting up of the head.

Viewed as a whole, a ziggurat represented a mountain. The term[11] was used for the summit of a mountain as well as a staged tower. Individual ziggurats had names that identified them more specifically as the cosmic mountain, the axis or access between earth and heaven: house of the mountain, house of the mountain of the universe, house of the link between heaven and earth, and (so the ziggurat at Babylon) house of the foundation of heaven and earth.[12] Ziggurats were then gigantic models of a terraced mountain, the mountain of the gods. By their tiered form with staircase ascents they were intended to serve as a way of ascent and descent between earth and heaven for men and deities. To aspire to fellowship with the living God, to seek access to him in worship and communion, is to appreciate the *summum bonum* of human existence. In the beginning the Creator provided for such sacramental divine presence and human approach in the mountain of God in Eden and after the Fall he restores this redemptively (cf. Jacob's staircase to heaven, Sinai, and Zion). But the Babel-tower tradition did not express a longing of the soul for the living and true God and his heaven. It was rather a rebellious attempt of fallen mankind, rejecting in unbelief God's redemptive offer of restoration, to regain heaven by human works. As a substitute for true religion it was an idolatrous venture, an antichrist affront to the true Har Magedon. It was from Nimrod to Nebuchadnezzar[13] a lifting up of the head-horns against the Lord God.

The roots of Zechariah's symbolism in Daniel reach back to Babel, and this Daniel-Babel source lends support to our seeing an allusion to an altar in the image of the four horns. For there are strong points of correspondence between the altar and the temple-tower or ziggurat-mountain phenomenon that looms so large in this Daniel-Babel tradition drawn on by Zechariah.

Most obvious is the fact that the altar in Israel's cult and the ziggurats are alike in being capped by four horns, bronze in each case, which are symbolic of divine power. This correspondence has prompted the inverse identification of the ziggurats as colossal altars.

Secondly, there is evidence that the altar form was a stylized stepped mountain. Thus, in Ezekiel's prophetic description of the antitypical restoration of the temple on the top of the mountain, the altar is depicted as a tiered structure, the topmost stage having four horn projections (43:13-17). Besides this ziggurat shape of the altar, certain terms in Ezekiel's description are evocative of the mountainous nature of ziggurats; namely, "the bosom of the earth" (with reference to the bottom of the altar) and "mountain of God" (with particular reference to the top with its four horns), if that is the proper understanding of *har'ēl* and *'ărî'ēl*.

This mountain motif is also associated with the particular four- horned altar alluded to in Zechariah's second vision, which is, of course, not God's altar but rather one that symbolizes the lifting up of the head by the hostile world power. For Zechariah employs the image of a mountain for that imperial opposition to the restoration of God's temple (Zech 4:7; cf. 6:2), identifying it, moreover, in Genesis 11 terms with the land of Shinar (5:11).

We shall also see that the fate of the four horns in Zechariah's vision is reminiscent of that of Babel's mountain-tower.

The Daniel-Babel connection of Zechariah is clear and it confirms the reference of the symbol of the four horns to an altar, in this case an altar erected by the pagan powers. Illuminated by the Daniel-Babel data, Zechariah's symbolism is seen to capture the ideological essence of the beast-kingdom in its antichrist, self-deifying defiance of the Lord's Anointed who reigns on the true Har Magedon. It was a lifting up of the horn-head in enmity against God's people and in blasphemous idolatry against God himself.

II. AGENTS OF VENGEANCE

According to Jeremiah's reading of the situation, the horn- nations had interpreted perversely their defeat of the covenant people and their dominion over them. Exploiting the fact that Israel and Judah deserved the punishment of exile because they had violated the Lord's covenant, the captor-nations declared themselves innocent, the instruments of divine justice (Jer 50:7). Yet in their hearts they were maliciously glad that the Lord's heritage was destroyed (Jer 50:11). For this evil God would send destroyers and spoilers against them (Jer 50:2ff.,9f.,12ff.). In Psalm 75 God declares concerning those who lifted up their horns against heaven (v. 5 [6]): "I will cut off the horns of all the wicked" (v. 10 [11]).

A. *Dragon Slayers:* At his disposal the Lord had counteragents to dispatch against the smugly triumphant horn-nations (cf. Zech 1:15). Zechariah saw them coming forth in the form of four *ḥārāšîm*. As previously noted, these are craftsmen with various specialties, often smiths or carpenters. But here they are specialists in dealing with horns, experts in executing judgment—like those called "skillful to destroy" (lit. "craftsmen of destruction"), into whose hands the Lord threatened to deliver the Ammonites (Ezek 21:31 [36]).

The theme of expert artisans in the service of gods is attested in ancient mythology. For example, in the Ugaritic epics, Kothar-and-Hasis (Skilled and Cunning) is the divine craftsman who fashioned two clubs by which Baal overcame adversary Yamm (Sea) and to whose workshop messengers were sent when a house was to be constructed for the victorious deity.

Likewise in the Bible, when God is creating his royal cosmic house, his own divine wisdom is portrayed as the expert builder who designs and superintends the construction (Prov 8:22ff.). And when, following the Lord's triumph over the leviathan sea-dragon of Egypt, the tabernacle is being erected as a replica of his creation-palace, God's Spirit qualifies Bezalel and Oholiab as experts in all kinds of craftsmanship for the enterprise.[14] But talents for destruction as well as construction are imparted by the Lord. The psalmist says God had trained his hands for battle (Ps 18:34 [35]) and the judges were gifted by the Spirit to be superheroes, experts at driving the oppressors of Israel from the land (cf. Heb 11:32-34). Zechariah himself prophesies how God will turn his scorned people into mighty warriors who will trample their enemies (10:5), the feeble becoming like David in battle (12:8).

Other reminders are found in Zechariah that the resources for vengeance and deliverance must and do come from the Lord. In the final night vision it is from the two mountains of bronze, the Zion command-post of the Glory-Spirit, that the four chariots advance towards all points of the compass with judgment against the nations (6:1,5). Zech 10:1-4 (the section of the "burdens" that parallels the second vision) directs the flock unto the Lord as the source from whom comes corner, peg, battlebow, and leadership for the battle against the foe. From his limitless resources he supplies forces competent to meet and match the enemy and prevail. If there are four horn powers lifted up, there are four counteragents sent, expert at terrifying and casting down (1:21 [2:4]). If Babylon lifts up her head (horn) to heaven, yet from the Lord shall come spoilers with judgment that reaches unto heaven (see Jer 51:9,53).

God's judgments feature the total reversal, the bringing low of what was high—as prelude to lifting the lowly up on high. Dramatic instances are contained in the Daniel-Babel background of Zechariah's imagery of lifting up the head (horns). As a result of the descent of the divine Angel and his angelic troops, the Babel project was turned upside down. Instead of the ecumenical coherence they coveted they were cursed with linguistic bewilderment and an intensification of the fracturing and scattering of their society. Where Esagila had raised its head majestically on high, only truncated ruins remained. Likewise in Daniel 2, the impressive colossus with head of gold lifted up in pride to heaven, being smitten by the messianic stone from the mountain, collapsed into dust and disappeared, dispersed by the winds of God. And in Daniel 4, the cosmic tree grown unto heaven, image of Nebuchadnezzar's greatness, was felled at the command of the holy watchers come down from heaven (vv. 14,22,23; cf. Gen 11:5,7; 18:21). God's visitation reduced deified human glory to bestial grovelling. Total reversal.

The actions of God's experts in Zechariah's second vision radically reversed the condition of the horn-nations in two respects. As reported by the surveillance troop those nations were at rest, arrogantly secure (Zech 1:11,15), but the coming of God's avengers filled them with alarm and scattered them in a panic of terror.[15] Second, the heavenly agents cast down the horns that had been raised high against the residents of Zion, and against its divine Resident. Though the verb for "cast down" is not well attested[16] and various emendations have been suggested, the immediate context and the sources behind this vision call for the idea of bringing low the lofty and accordingly most of the suggested textual changes involve verbs for cutting down and the like. Jeremiah uses this image: "the horn of Moab is cut off" (Jer 48:25). A more complete parallel is the Lord's threat through Amos: "On the day I visit the altars of Bethel with judgment, the horns of the altar will be cut off and fall to the ground" (3:14). This motif of reversing the enemy's dominant status reappears repeatedly in Zechariah. Instances within the visions are 2:9 (13), where Babylon, spoiler of Zion, becomes a spoil to its former victims, and 4:7, where the great mountain of the hostile world lifted up to heaven is levelled into a plain.

The judicial act of the artisans has been interpreted in a somewhat different way, one that fits in with the satanic aspect of the horn powers.[17] The verb we have rendered "cast down" is taken as equivalent to the Ugaritic verb *ydy*, which is found in magical spells with the meaning "cast out". Among the objects expelled are snake venom, disease, sea monsters, and demons. And significantly these acts of expulsion are attributed to artisans, who are regarded as skillful in incantations. According to this view the imagery of Zechariah's second vision would be that of a divinely wrought exorcism. It would portray God, through his artisan agents, delivering his holy land from the presence of the demonic imperial agents of Satan who were oppressing the covenant people.[18] This would be an overthrowing that was a dispossessing of the horns, a casting down that was a casting out.

The horn-nations missed the message that Israel's destruction held for them: "Behold, I begin to work evil at the city which is called by my name; and will you go utterly unpunished? You will not go unpunished, for I will summon a sword upon the inhabitants of the earth, declares Yahweh of hosts" (Jer 25:29; cf. 1 Pet 4:17). In the design of the ages, Israel under its covenant of works brought into focus the picture of all mankind in Adam under the original covenant of works. Let the nations of the ungodly consider the fate of Israel and see in Jerusalem's desolation the divine vengeance that will inevitably overtake them all as covenant-breakers in Adam, except they repent.

Through their own role of inflicting divine judgment on Israel, God was warning the horn-nations of their own impending doom. Why the Mosaic economy? Why Israel? Part of the answer is that old covenant history, especially its termination in the destruction of Jerusalem, was calculated to sound an alarm in a world oblivious to the wrath to come, and so capture the attention of the Gentiles for the church's witness to Jesus Christ and the way of escape offered in the gospel. Let them know that the fall of Jerusalem is, typologically, the beginning of the end of the world. Let them be advised that the anointed prince who sent his armies and destroyed the holy city and temple (Dan 9:26) is the one by whom God will judge the world in righteousness on the day he has appointed (Acts 17:30,31).

Zechariah's four experts at executing judgment (vision two) act as the agents of the messianic rider of the red horse (vision one). Their mission of casting down or casting out the horns symbolically portrays the mission of Christ as the great dragon slayer. He comes to destroy the devil, the monstrous red dragon having seven crowned heads and ten horns (Heb 2:14,15; Rev 12:3). Already Christ with his angel army has prevailed, driving the dragon out of heaven (Rev 12:7-11) and binding him in the bottomless pit for a season (Rev 20:1-3; cf. Luke 11:29; Isa 49:24,25). And on the coming day of the Son of Man he will consummate his work of vengeance against the dragon and the beast-powers (they too with heads and horns lifted up against heaven and the saints), hurling them down into the sea of fire forever (Rev 20:10; cf. 19:20).

B. *Precursors of Zion's Glory:* After the threat, "I will cut off the horns of all the wicked," Psalm 75 closes with the promise, "but the horns of the righteous will be lifted up" (v. 10 [11]). The great redemptive reversal goes beyond the destruction of the currently exalted world power. Daniel 2 does not stop with the collapse of the colossus. It goes on to tell how, after demolishing the great image, the small stone from mount Zion is transformed into an exceedingly great mountain, the eschatological Zion, a cosmic mountain with which earthly empires can no longer co-exist. Isaiah foretold the same: at the end of the days, when the Lord has put an end to nations lifting up swords against nations, the mountain of the house of God will be established as the highest of all, the focus of global pilgrimage (2:2-4).

This sequel to the avenging action against the horn-nations is not presented within Zechariah's second vision, but in vision three. There the rebuilding of Jerusalem on a universal scale is prophesied.[19] Vision two presents the necessary precursor: the elimination of the nations occupying Israel's territory.

Like vision two, vision six (its parallel in the structural chiasm) focuses on the holy land and portrays the clearing away of the unclean (5:1-11), the prelude to the perfecting of God's holy reign (vision seven). Similarly, Zech 13:2-9 (the corresponding passage to vision six in the "burdens") deals with the removal of impurity from the land preliminary to the inauguration of the eternal theocratic order (Zechariah 14). The scope of vision five is broader, it presents not just the prelude judgment but the whole reversal pattern of heads cast down and heads lifted up. It declares that the lofty world-mountain's fate is to be flattened into a plain (4:7a) then immediately adds the victorious announcement that the messiah-figure (Zerubbabel) will bring forth the capstone in completion of God's house of glory (4:7b). Satan's Esagila-Olympus will fall and the true Har Magedon of the Lord's Anointed will lift up its head. Messiah's hands lay the foundations of the temple and, after he overthrows the dragon, his hands finish the holy construction (4:10). Then the triumphant cry sounds at the gates of the holy city: "Lift up your heads that the king of glory may come in." Hail Zion's royal architect and artisan, its divine author and finisher!

The mission of the four expert exterminators is the first act in the Parousia of the rider on the red horse, precursor of God's taking up his permanent dwelling in the midst of his people gathered out of all the nations into their restored heritage. The Lord Jesus shall be revealed from heaven with his mighty angels in flaming fire taking vengeance on them that know not God and obey not the gospel, who shall suffer eternal destruction when he comes to be glorified in his saints (cf. 2 Thess 1:7-10).

The saints praise God as the One who lifts up their head-horn. "My horn is exalted in the Lord" (1 Sam 2:1). "You, O Lord … are the lifter up of my head" (Ps 3:3 [4]). "You [O Lord] have lifted up my horn like that of the wild ox" (Ps 92:10 [11]).

God is also praised as the one who exalts the horn of the Messiah. "[The Lord] will give strength to his king; he will lift up the horn of his anointed" (1 Sam 2:10; cf. Pss 89:17,18 [18,19]; 148:14). Psalm 110 celebrates this eschatological event. It is Messiah's head that is exalted in victory (v. 7b), whether we understand the subject of the action to be Yahweh, swearer of the oath (vv. 1,4) or Messiah himself, David's Lord (v. 1), recipient of the sworn appointment as priest-king forever. And either way it is the Lord who lifts up the head. This psalm displays the full pattern of the great reversal, for the Lord's striking down heads in his wrath against the nations (v. 6) is the precursor to the lifting up of his own head in glory (v. 7).

Referring to Jesus, Zechariah (father of John) blesses God because "he has raised up a horn of salvation for us in the house of his servant David" (Luke 1:68,69). Christ Jesus *is* the lifting up of the head-horn; it is in him, its head, that the church's horn is exalted. He is the original that was counterfeited in Babel's Esagila ziggurat (cf. Deut 30:12,13; Rom 10:6,7). He is the true mountain stairway to God and gate of heaven (cf. Gen 28:12-17; John 1:51), the true altar and tabernacle, the true and only way to the heavenly Father. Jesus *is* the head lifted up. For God "raised him from the dead and set him at his own right hand in the heavenly places, far above all principality and power and might and dominion, and every name that is named, not only in this age but also in that which is to come; and hath put all things under his feet and gave him to be the head over all things to the church, which is his body, the fullness of him that filleth all in all" (Eph 1:20-23).

---

1 The third vision (2:1-13 [5-17]) resumes the other theme found in the closing oracle of vision one, namely, the restoration and perfecting of God's kingdom under the new covenant.

2 The additional term "Israel" in v. 19 [2:2] may identify post-exilic Judah as the continuation of the ancient nation of God. Otherwise, it broadens the historical range of the typological allusion to include the subjugation of the northern kingdom.

3 In our discussion of the deep in vision one we noted that the imagery of the rising of the draconic beasts from the sea in Daniel 7 and Revelation 13 signified the demonic character of the bestial world powers as products of a satanic counterfeit creation.

4 The correspondences noted here corroborate the analysis presented in the Appendix.

5 Perhaps there is a deliberate ambiguity in the use of *ʾel* (1:21[2:4]), which can mean "unto a limit" as well as "against", thus allowing the idea that the upward thrust of the horn-nations was unto the mountainous heights of Judah, and even up to Zion's peak.

6 R. M. Good ("Zechariah's Second Night Vision [Zech 2:1-4]", *Biblica* 63:1 [1982], 56-59) grants that the altar belongs to the implicative field of the four-horns metaphor, but perceiving the bucolic setting as primary, he interprets *ḥārāšîm* (on the basis of a different parsing) as ploughmen, who chase the horned animals back to their folds (*lydwt* being treated as preposition plus plural of *yad*, used for animal folds). He is obliged, however, to reject as a mistaken interpretive gloss all the rest of v. 21[2:4] after *lydwt*.

7 A mere sketch of all this as I presently perceive it must do, with acknowledgment of the lack of consensus on many a detail.

8 Cf. the discussion of this theme in our comments on vision one.

9 The continuity of the Daniel 2 and Genesis 11 situations is further evidenced in the coherence ideal by which the kingdoms are evaluated in Daniel 2.

10 Cf. A. Heidel, The *Babylonian Genesis: the Story of* the *Creation* (Chicago, 1963). On ziggurats, cf. A. Parrot, *The Tower of Babel* (New York, 1955).

11 It comes from *zaqāru*, "be high", "raised up".

12 Agreeably, the Babylonian-Sumerian name of the city meant "gate of god".

13 Accenting the revival of Babel in the kingdom of Nebuchadnezzar is Jeremiah's identification of Babylon in ziggurat mountain terms as a "destroying mountain" that "mounts up to heaven" (51:25,53).

14 See Exod 35:30ff. Cf. my *The Structure of Biblical Authority* (Grand Rapids, 1975) 86-87. The tabernacle belongs with the altar and ziggurat in the series of reproductions of the cosmic mountain of God. It was a portable Sinai, with the three vertical zones of base, mid-mountain, and summit (accessible respectively to the people, elders-priests, and Moses [cf. Exod 24:1,2]) laid horizontal (with court open to the people, holy place to the priests, and holy of holies to the high priest). Cf. my *Images of the Spirit* (Grand Rapids, 1980) 37-41. Noah's ark is another mountain-house of God structure with the vertical sectioning of the latter replicated in the three-story design of this cosmic house. Cf. my *Kingdom Prologue*, 139-40.

15 See comments above on the use of *ḥrd* for scaring away predatory animals.

16 In Lam 3:53 it is used for casting down stones from above on Jeremiah in the pit below.

17 For this view see E.J.C. Tigchelaar, *Prophets of Old and the Day of the End* (Leiden, 1996) 47-55.

18 The incantational curse becomes then one of the points of parallelism between visions two and six. Tigchelaar would distinguish the horns from the nations and identify them as the demonic beings in charge of the nations.

19 Cf. the comments on the unity of the first three visions in the introduction to this chapter. Perhaps *ḥārāš* with its common meaning "craftsman" was selected for the agents of judgment in vision two in anticipation of the imagery of the measurer-builder in vision three.

BUILDER OF GOD'S CITY

"In other generations [the mystery of Christ] was not made known to the sons of men, as it has now been revealed unto his holy apostles and prophets in the Spirit" (Eph 3:5). It was, for one thing, the typological idiom used by the Old Testament prophets that kept their disclosures concerning the new covenant community from being as perspicuous as the revelation of the church given in the New Testament. This relative lack of clarity was especially the case with respect to the reception of the Gentiles as fellow-heirs, fellow members of the body, fellow partakers of the promise in Christ (Eph 3:6). Nevertheless, as the comparison in Eph 3:5 implies and as Paul states explicitly in Rom 16:25,26, this mystery of divine wisdom, hidden from human discovery (cf. Eph 3:9; Col 1:26) but unveiled by divine revelation, had already been manifested in "the scriptures of the prophets." In the concatenation of quotations in Rom 15:9-12, Paul appeals to statements in all three sections of the Old Testament canon—the law (v. 10: cf. Deut 32:43), the prophets (v. 12; cf. Isa 11:10), and the writings (vv. 9 and 11; cf. Ps 18:49 and Ps 117:1)—to substantiate the truth that in Christ the Gentiles find acceptance along with Jews in God's kingdom.

One notable example of an Old Testament prophecy of the church is Zechariah's third vision, with its symbolic portrayal of the future inclusion of a *pleroma* (fullness) of the Gentiles in the true Israel of God. This vision consists of imagery (2:1-5 [5-9]), which unfolds in two scenes (2:1,2 [5,6] and 2:3-5 [7-9]), followed by a kerygma (proclamation) section (2:6-13 [10-17]). Visions one, three, five, and seven all contain a kerygmatic oracle that makes interpretive application of the preceding imagery. This distribution underscores the structural pattern of the seven visions. For in the arrangement of them into two triads around a central fourth vision, each triad having a concentric (ABA) form, the visions with the imagery-kerygma format coincide with the four A-visions.[1]

That the oracular kerygma is an integral part of the third vision, though often disputed, is evidenced in the way the rationale given for the exhortations in 2:6-13 (10-17) in every case resumes and develops one, or both, of the themes introduced by the speaker in 2:3-5 (7-9), namely, the presence of the divine Glory and the future expansion of Jerusalem. Indeed, the kerygma is a continuation of the words of that speaker and thus the second scene of the symbolic drama (2:3-5 [7-9]) interlocks the kerygma with the imagery section.

I. IMAGERY: MESSIAH AND METAPOLIS

A. *The Messianic Measurer.* Sorting out the *dramatis personae* in vision three is a more complex matter than usual. Things fall in place, however, as we trace the identity of the main speaker, observing how it remains constant throughout the vision.

In scene one, Zechariah, entering into the vision, queries the man with the measuring line concerning the goal of his mission (v. 2a [6a]) and the latter responds (v. 2b [6b]). There is no warrant for injecting the figure of the interpreting angel as a mediator of the response. It is the measurer who addresses Zechariah directly, and we shall find that from this point on all the first-person speeches are to be attributed (ultimately) to him.

In scene two the familiar interpreting angel makes his appearance and with him appears "another angel," (v. 3 [7]). One of these speaks, sending the second to "this young man" with an announcement, which actually furthers the account of the symbolic imagery by its picturing of the future Jerusalem (v. 4 [8]). The speaker cannot be the interpreting angel, for his role is never that of controlling the visionary action, as would be the case if he were viewed as sending the other angel to the measurer with directions of some sort (for example, to desist from his supposedly impossible task). Neither would the interpreting angel send another angel to Zechariah (if he is seen as "this young man") to perform what was his own peculiar responsibility of interpreting the visions to the prophet. Hence, the speaker in vv. 4,5 (8,9) is the "other angel." Further, since the results of the measuring mission which he announces would naturally be disclosed by the measurer himself, this "other angel" is, if not the measurer, at least an angel-messenger come from the measurer and speaking in his name. The measurer is thus the (ultimate) speaker in vv. 4,5 (8,9), his further communication here being an up-dating of his reply to Zechariah's earlier question (v. 2 [6]). And Zechariah is, of course, the "young man"[2] to whom the interpreting angel is sent with this elaboration on the symbolic imagery and its meaning. Moreover, the ultimate speaker, the measurer, is identified as divine, for he speaks in the first person as Yahweh (v. 5 [9]).[3] This "man" with the measuring line is then one with the "man" riding on a red horse in vision one, identified there as the Angel of the Lord.

The foregoing analysis is corroborated by the data in the kerygma section (vv. 6-13 [10-17]). The first-person-speaking of v. 5 (9) continues there and, as noted above, so do the themes of v. 5 (9). Nothing would suggest there is a change of speaker. On the contrary, the one speaking in the first person identifies himself as the messianic Angel—the (ultimate) first person speaker in v. 5 (9). For he says that he has been sent by God (vv. 8,9,11 [12,13,15]), and his mission is one of visiting divine judgment on the world powers (vv. 8,9 [12,13]).[4] In short, the kerygma of vv. 6-13 (10-17) is a continuation of the speech of v. 5 (9) and provides confirmation of the identity of the (ultimate) speaker in v. 5 (9)—and thus of the measurer—as the Angel of the Lord.[5]

Supportive of our conclusion that the measurer is the divine Angel are other biblical instances of measuring as a divine activity. Possession and use of the measuring line here signifies that the "man" is not merely some subordinate surveyor gathering information but the Lord himself engaged in sovereign construction.

By the stretching out of measuring lines, perimeters were set. Zech 2:1,2 (5,6) picks up the promise of Zech 1:16 that a line would be stretched forth over Jerusalem as part of the process of rebuilding the city and temple.[6] Like this third vision of Zechariah, Jeremiah 31 prophesies of the new covenant restoration (vv. 31-34) under the imagery of a rebuilding of Jerusalem (vv. 38-40), and the going forth of the measuring line there (v. 39) is explicitly a matter of establishing the boundaries.

As expressed in Zech 2:2 (6), the purpose of the measurer was "to see" (r'h) its breadth and length. This might suggest that he was to ascertain the dimensions of a city already in existence (in the visionary world). If so, the situation would be analogous to that in the creation narrative. There, a sevenfold refrain states that God "saw (r'h) that it was good," signifying that the Maker of heaven and earth subjected the work of the day to judicial scrutiny to ensure that it accorded perfectly with the master plan, and finding, of course, that it did, he pronounced it "good." Similarly, in Zech 2:2 (6), the Angel of the Lord would be seen as going to inspect the future completed Jerusalem, already beheld in his omniscient ken, and as subsequently announcing that it exhibited the vast dimensions he had specified in his architectural plans (v. 4 [8]).

However, the Hebrew r'h occasionally has the sense of choose or provide.[7] Thus, in 1 Sam 16:1, the Lord selects (r'h) a king from among Jesse's sons. In Gen 22:8, God provides (r'h) a lamb for the altar. And in Deut 12:13,14, Israel is commanded not to offer burnt offerings at any place they pleased (r'h) but at the place the Lord chose (bḥr). Alternatively then, Zech 2:2 (6) could mean that the measurer was proceeding to the site of future Jerusalem to mark out what he had determined its dimensions should be. Similarly, in Rev 11:1,2, John's temple measuring is not to discover its size but to register a divine verdict. What he measures is thereby set apart unto God and under his protection; what he leaves unmeasured is thereby rejected and abandoned to profanation and desolation.

Accordingly, the role of the measurer in Zechariah's third vision is, equally with that of the rider of the red horse in the first vision, compatible with the divine dignity of the Angel of the Lord. Ezekiel 40-48 provides another extended example of a visionary appearance of the messianic Angel as a man with a measuring line (cf. esp. 40:3; 43:6; 44:2,5). In that case, the purpose of his measuring is to reveal to the prophet his sovereign design for his temple-kingdom. In the Book of Revelation, possession of the measuring rod is attributed to Christ, and again it is an insigne of his authority over God's house.[8] Thus, in Revelation 11, the one who charges John with the judicial use of the rod (vv. 1,2) is identified as Christ when he goes on to speak of his commissioning of "my" two witnesses (v. 3). Agreeably, in Rev 21:15, it is the angel sent to John by Christ who has the golden reed, with which he measures the new Jerusalem (the purpose here being similar to the measuring in Ezekiel 40-48).[9] Measuring activity is also attributed to God in his creation of the world, his cosmic temple. We read that he stretched out the measuring line at the laying of the foundations of the earth (Job 38:5) and measured out the heavens with the span (Isa 40:12). And according to Job 28:25 (cf. Isa 40:12)[10] God meted out the waters and the land by measure.[11]

This background of divine acts of measuring performed in execution of sovereign decree and in determination of the boundaries of God's house and city corroborates the identification of the man with the measuring line in Zech 2:1,2 (5,6) as the Angel of the Lord. He is the Word of God who was in the beginning with God, who was God, the Maker of all things, visible and invisible (John 1:1-3; Col 1:16). The measurer is the Creator-Lord, seen by Zechariah as now engaged in redemptive re-creation as the architect and almighty constructer of the new cosmos, the heavenly city, New Jerusalem.

B. *City of Glory*. Descending from heaven at the climax of the history of re-creation, the new Jerusalem will be the realization of the goal set for the city of God at the original creation. The garden-city in Eden already enjoyed the presence of the divine Glory on the mount of God as its heavenly cultic focus. And the kingdom mandate to fill and subdue the earth contemplated an expansion of the holy city to world-wide proportions, to the fullness of Megapolis. Then this global city was to be transformed by the Creator-Spirit into Metapolis, the Beyond-City of eternity. There the Glory, no longer a local focus, would fill the cosmos, permeating the fullness of Metapolis. New Jerusalem is that Metapolis arrived at by way of redemptive re-creation. In the symbolic portrayal of it in Zechariah 2, its fullness is the theme in v. 4 (8) and its Glory-focus in v. 5 (9).

As represented in this third vision, eschatological Jerusalem would resemble an open country patchwork of settlements of men and cattle; by reason of its abounding population it would not have the bounding walls characteristic of ancient cities (v. 4 [8]).[12] The outworking of this prophetic symbolism in new covenant history is expounded in the kerygma section (vv. 6,11 [10,15]). The roots of the imagery are ancient. They reach back to the oracle of Noah (Gen 9:25-27).

Noah's pronouncement concerning his descendants began with his curse on Canaan (v. 25) then proceeded to his blessings on Shem (v. 26) and Japheth (v. 27). From Shem would come the covenant line, set apart to bear God's name (Hebrew, šēm), the blessing bestowed in due time in God's covenant with Abraham, particularly in the first stage of the fulfillment of its promise in the old covenant kingdom of Israel. But in the conjoined blessing on Japheth (v. 27), Noah's oracle moved beyond the ethnic particularism of the old covenant: "May God open (yapht)[13] for Japheth (yephet)." What was to be opened is indicated in the following clause: "and may he [Japheth] dwell in the tents of Shem." Tent imagery was prompted by the occasion of the oracle, the event in Noah's tent (Gen 9:21ff.). Shem and Japheth had shared in their godly act within a tent (v. 23) and they were to share the blessing of occupying the (covenant) tents.[14] Until Christ came the covenant tents were for the most part closed to all except the Abrahamic descendants of Shem. Envisioned in Noah's oracle, however, was the day when the entrance flaps of these tents would be flung wide open to welcome the descendants of Japheth—and, indeed, all the Gentiles.

Isaiah, foreseeing this same development, when Zion's children would "inherit the Gentiles" (54:3), employed anew the tent metaphor of Japheth's blessing as he called on mother Jerusalem to make room for all these children from afar. "Enlarge the place of your tent and let them extend the curtains of your dwellings; spare not, lengthen your cords and strengthen your stakes" (54:2; cf. 49:18-23; 60:3-16). In prophesying of this prospect, Isaiah also resumed Noah's image of the opening of an entrance. He describes Zion's gates of praise as wide open continually to welcome the Gentiles coming with their worshipful tribute to the Holy One of Israel (Isa 60:11-14; cf. 26:2). And when Noah's oracle concerning Japheth was being fulfilled in the mission of the apostle Paul to the Gentiles in the regions settled by the Japhethites, the figure of the opened entry surfaced again. The missionaries reported that God "had opened the door of faith unto the Gentiles" (Acts 14:27; 1 Cor 16:9). The feature of the gates perpetually opened to afford access for the nations of the earth is present once more in the typological symbolism of John's vision of the eternal city in Rev 21:24,25.

On this thematic trajectory that leads from Noah's oracle to the Apocalyptic vision of the Beyond-City, the vision of Zechariah 2 finds a place. The Noahic tent imagery is replaced by that of the city, as in the visions of Isaiah and John, but central here again is the theme of the extraordinary expansion to be undergone by the covenant community due to a great influx of Gentiles (v. 11 [15]). It is this unprecedented development to occur in the coming age that Zechariah portrays under the symbolism of a Jerusalem where the customary walls are no more.

The attainment of the destined fullness of Metapolis fulfills Noah's blessing on Shem as well as that on Japheth. For one of the covenant promises to Abraham, son of Shem, was that his seed would be multiplied past numbering (Gen 22:17); through his messianic descendant all the nations of the earth would be blessed (Gen 22:18) and so he would become the father of many nations (Gen 17:14-16).

In another way too the Jerusalem of Zechariah's third vision embodies the blessing that Japheth would find in the tents of Shem. For according to Noah's oracle, the Lord would vouchsafe to Shem his covenantal Name-Presence, and such a divine Presence is promised in Zech 2:5b (9b) for the future Jerusalem: Yahweh will be "the Glory in the midst of her," the cultic focus of her cultural fullness. The new Jerusalem will be paradise restored but it will be more than a simple restoration of the holy garden-city of Eden, for in it the manifestation of the Glory is not confined to a focal center. God's fiery Presence fills the eternal city to its unwalled limits (v. 5a [9a]; cf. Isa 4:5). It is in its entirety a temple, hence has no temple within it.[15] Nor does it require light of sun or moon, for the God of Glory is its everlasting light (Isa 60:19,20; Rev 21:22,23; 22:5).

Paradoxically, the unwalled eschatological Jerusalem of Zechariah 2 has a wall around it (v. 5a [9a]). By filling the city right to its distant horizon, the divine Glory constitutes a wall of fire around it there at its perimeter. However, the idea is not that the city has no ordinary walls because the fiery divine wall replaces such (as though this were analogous to statements about the absence of a temple or luminaries in the heavenly Jerusalem). As we have seen, the absence of the customary walls (v. 4 [8]) is clearly accounted for by the city's overflowing population.

Help in determining the function of the divine wall of fire around the city comes from the Revelation 21 version of this scene. The great, high walls spoken of there (vv. 12-21) serve not as defence against attack but as a sanctifying boundary, setting apart all who dwell within as holy unto the Lord, separating them from those outside, those not written in the Lamb's book of life (cf. Rev 21:27; 22:14,15). Such is the function, apparently, of the divine wall in Zechariah's third vision. This fiery wall, a manifestation of God's holiness, acts primarily as guardian not of the security of the city but of its sanctity. It harks back to the Eden sanctuary and the wall of fire produced by the flaming sword that turned every way to guard the access to the tree of life and maintain the sanctity of the site of God's Glory (Gen 3:24).

While Zechariah's image of the divine wall of fire speaks of the consuming holiness of God that prevents the entry of defiled sinners, remarkably the city is thronged by former outcasts, as the Angel presently declares (Zech 2:11 [15]). We are reminded that the Angel of the Lord who reveals this vision was himself to be pierced by the flaming sword (cf. Zech 13:7) to open a way through the wall of fire and gain entrance for an innumerable multitude out of all nations (cf. Rev 7:9,14-17). The wonder of the burning bush, not consumed, meets us again here, in anticipation of Zechariah's next vision with its gospel of sovereign grace, of the brand plucked out of the fire, removal of defilement, and investment in robes of priestly glory (cf. Zechariah 3).

II. KERYGMA: EVANGEL OF THE MESSIANIC ANGEL

It is still the Angel-Measurer speaking in Zech 2:6-13 (10-17). His words, however, are no longer being relayed to the "young man," Zechariah, but are now directed to the people of Zion (vv. 6-11 [10-15]) and to all the world (vv. 12,13 [16,17]). God's people are addressed as "daughter of Zion" (v. 10 [14])[16] and viewed as in captivity with the "daughter of Babylon" (v. 7 [11]).

To this audience the messianic Angel presents an interpretation and application of the message of the foregoing imagery. In vv. 6-11 (10-15) application in imperative form (call to action) precedes interpretation, the latter functioning not just as explanation of the symbolism but as motivation for obeying the command. By the repeating of this hortatory pattern these verses are structured into two subsections, vv. 6-9 (10-13) and vv. 10,11 (14,15), with imperatives in vv. 6,7 (10,11) and v. 10a (14a) and explanation-motivation in vv. 8,9 (12,13) and vv. 10b,11 (14b,15).[17] An important third element in this pattern is the concluding statement of (messianic) validation (see vv. 9c,11c [13c,15c]). In the final section of the kerygma (vv. 12,13 [16,17]), the imperative (v. 13a [17a]) is again followed by a kî-clause of motivation, but is preceded by a summation (v. 12 [16]).

From the kerygmatic exposition of the imagery it appears that the perfecting of the cosmic temple-city by the messianic Measurer would follow upon a redemptive warfare involving both the dispossession of the world powers for the enrichment of God's kingdom (vv. 6-9 [10-13]) and, paradoxically, a gracious work of conversion, a gathering of multitudes of Gentiles into the community of salvation (vv. 10,11 [14,15]). Christ, the *kerux*, heralds here his coming world-wide victory over the enemy and issues beforehand his efficacious altar call to his own, afar off, to come home. It will be the completion of this universal mission that authenticates his claim to be the Servant-Lord sent by the Lord God of hosts.

A. *Conquest of the Nations.* Continuing the typological idiom of the imagery section, the kerygma pictures the covenant people of the messianic age as Israelites still in the land of Babylon, anticipating deliverance. Old Testament prophets portray Israel's return from captivity as a second exodus and agreeably these two typological events, exodus and restoration, are blended in the Angel's prophetic representations of new covenant history.

The opening directive of the first subsection (vv. 6-9 [10-13]) is expressed in a double imperative: "flee from the land of the north" (v. 6a [10a]) ... "to Zion escape" (v. 7a [11a]).[18] Leave Babylon, head home to Jerusalem. Get out of the oppressive world center and get back to the center of God's kingdom. This had also been the prophetic command of Isaiah: "Go forth from Babylon, flee from the Chaldeans" (48:20) ..."Depart, depart, go out from there" (52:11).[19] Jeremiah picked up the refrain in his oracle against Babylon: "Flee out of the midst of Babylon" (50:8; 51:6a) ..."be not cut off in her iniquity, for it is the time of Yahweh's vengeance" (51:6b).

Between the two imperatives a motivation clause is inserted: "For I am spreading you abroad[20] as the four winds of the heavens, says Yahweh" (v. 6b [10b]). Expounding the promise inherent in the image of an unbounded Jerusalem, the Lord assures those he commands to return that their future back at Zion is one of blessing, of expansion in every direction. This enticing prospect of Jerusalem's coming fullness is amplified in the following motivation clauses, all of which hark back to the basic symbol of vv. 4,5 (8,9).

While return to Zion is encouraged by appeal to its promised prosperity, flight from Babylon, as from Sodom (Gen 19:12ff.), is urged on the grounds of its impending doom (vv. 8,9 [12,13]). The two are closely related: Jerusalem's prosperity would be achieved through the plundering of Babylon.[21] The first and third motivation clauses in vv. 8,9 (12,13) announce Messiah's mission of judgment against the offending world powers. The middle clause affirms afresh the Lord's intense love for his oppressed people. Vision three thus restates the theme of messianic vengeance introduced in vision one and developed as the main point of vision two.

The motivation clause in v. 8a (12a) presents the Angel's announcement of his mission to the nations that plundered the covenant people. It begins with ʾaḥar kābôd, a problematic phrase, especially for those who regard this mission as Zechariah's, not Messiah's. There are two particularly cogent options. One is to translate "after glory" in the sense "in quest of glory."[22] The glory to be won could be the wealth of the nations (cf. Hag 2:6-9) or the honor of God's name, secured through the display of his sovereignty in the avenging of his people. In favor of this interpretation, the nature of the mission as an avenging judgment is the main emphasis in the adjoining clauses, especially in v. 9 (13).

The second attractive possibility is to translate "with (the) Glory,"[23] signifying that the Angel would be accompanied in his mission by the theophanic Presence, the Glory-Spirit. Favoring this view is the fact that kābôd had just been used in the imagery of v. 5b (9b) for the Glory-Presence in the midst of God's people.[24] This would be another allusion to exodus history, for in the mediatorial intercession of Moses after the golden calf episode (Exod 32:34-33:23) the precise issue was whether Israel was to be led to Canaan by the messianic Angel alone or by the Angel attended by the Glory-cloud.[25] Theophany in the form of the Angel alone had been characteristic of the patriarchal age, but the coming of the typological age of judgment at the exodus was marked by

Parousia-Presence. God heeded Moses' plea and his Glory accompanied his Angel on his mission to plunder the nations of Canaan. In Zech 2:8 (12) the Angel would then be giving assurance that his announced eschatological mission against the nations would be a Parousia event, a coming in the glory of the Father and all his holy angels.[26] And when, as the incarnate Messiah, he was about to move beyond his earthly state of humiliation, he, like Moses, prayed for an investment with the Glory-Spirit appropriate to the new stage of exaltation he was entering in the heavenly day of the Lord. "Father, the hour is come ... glorify thou me with thine own self, with the Glory which I had with thee before the world was" (John 17:1,5).[27]

The kî-clause in Zech 2:8b (12b) might be taken as directly supporting the command to return from Babylon (v. 7a [11a]) by assuring God's people that they were precious to him ("the apple of his eye") so that they might confidently anticipate his blessings back at Zion. The point would then be the same as in the motivation clause in v. 6b (10b). Suggesting this direct relation to v. 7a (11a) is the resonance of bĕbābat (v. 8b [12b]) with bat-bābel (v. 7a [11a]) and the irony thus highlighted: "the daughter of" his (God's) eye (v. 8b [12b])—the daughter of Zion (v. 10 [14])—is dwelling with "the daughter of Babylon" (v. 7a [11a]).[28] Alternatively, v. 8b (12b) could relate immediately to v. 8a (12a), explaining God's determination to visit retribution on the nations: the people against whom they had shown malice were precious to him. Indeed, since Israel belonged to God as his personal possession, the nations that dominated her were challenging God's claims on her service.[29] By reinforcing the motivation of v. 8a (12a), v. 8b (12b) would still be supporting, but indirectly, the imperatives of vv. 6a and 7a (10a and 11a).

Again in the motivation clause of v. 9a (13a) the disaster threatening Babylon is the consideration urged for obeying the double command of vv. 6a,7a (10a,11a) to flee from there. Messiah's mission against the world powers would resemble the ancient judgment on Egypt. It would result in a complete reversal, the plunderers becoming a spoil to their former servants, just as the Egyptians were despoiled by their Hebrew slaves (Exod 3:22; 12:36). Messiah would effect this defeat by brandishing his hand over these nations, an action reminiscent of the stretching forth of God's hand and the lifting up of Moses' hand over Egypt. Like Zech 2:9 (13), Exodus 3 combines these two features: commissioning Moses, God declares that he will send forth his hand and smite Egypt with wonders (v. 20) and that Israel in leaving will despoil the Egyptians (vv. 21, 22).

Isaiah, in oracles against Egypt and Babylon, describes God's destroying judgment as a shaking of his hand over them (Isa 11:15; 13:2; 19:16; cf. Job 31:21). He clearly alludes to the lifting of the hand of God and of Moses over the sea at the exodus (Isa 11:15) and under the figure of the typological history of the exodus from Egypt and the return from captivity, Isaiah, like Zechariah, was prophesying of a messianic, eschatological judgment.[30]

What we have found in the first subsection of the kerygma is that the Measurer himself is central in the exposition of the imagery. That the Messiah and his mission is the main theme of the vision becomes even more evident when we notice how each kerygmatic subsection (vv. 6-9 [10-13] and vv. 11,12 [15,16]) concludes by pointing to the prophesied events in Zion and the world as validation of the divine sponsorship of that mission. But before dealing with the validation motif in vv. 9c and 11c (13c and 15c), we will examine the second subsection, its imperative (v. 10a [14a]) and its motivation (vv. 10b,11a [14b,15a]). We will find that it discloses a new aspect of Messiah's mission, a surprising development not suggested by the first subsection (at least, not at first glance),[31] yet essential to explain the image of Jerusalem expanded to unprecedented dimensions, beyond containment.

B. _Conversion of the Gentiles._ "Sing and rejoice, O daughter of Zion" (Zech 2:10a [14a]). The directive that introduces the second division of the kerygma (vv. 10,11 [14,15]) is the perfect prelude for the glad tidings that follow in the motivation section.[32] "Lo, I come, and I will dwell in the midst of you" (v. 10b [14b]; cf. 11b [15b]). With this promise the messianic Angel puts into words what was expressed symbolically in the first vision by the imagery of the rider on the red horse in the midst of the myrtles (1:8; cf. 1:16a). He heralds the Christmas evangel, good news for all people (cf. Luke 2:10). "Joy to the world! The Lord is come ... Let men their songs employ."

Centered between the two assurances that the coming Lord "will dwell in the midst of you" is the disclosure of a distinctive new aspect of Jerusalem's restoration prospects. "Many nations will join themselves to Yahweh in that day and will be my people" (2:11a [15a]). The last clause is the covenantal formula used by Jeremiah when prophesying of the new covenant (31:33; 32:38). Also, the verb _lwh_ ("join") is used elsewhere for covenantal alliance.[33] Reminiscent of Psalm 2, Psalm 83 pictures the nations taking counsel and entering into covenant together against God and his people (vv. 2-5 [3-6]), and Assyria's participation in this covenantal coalition is denoted by _lwh_ (v. 8 [9]). In Jer 50:5, _lwh_ refers to the union of God's people with him "in an everlasting covenant." Of most interest for Zech 2:11a [15a]) is Isaiah's use of *lwh* for foreigners attaching themselves to Israel (14:1) and to the Lord (56:3,6). Alternative terminology is taking hold of God's covenant (56:4,6); keeping the Sabbath, the covenant sign (56:2,4,6); and receiving the everlasting name (56:5) that belongs to those in the new and everlasting covenant (55:3,13).

Incorporation of the Gentiles into God's covenantal people is a recurring theme in Zechariah. He indicates, moreover, that their status is to be one of full participation, including cultic privilege. As noted above, the picture of many nations joined to the covenant community (2:11a [15a]) is surrounded by the doubled promise: "And I will dwell in the midst of you."[34] At the close of the passage which forms the central spine of the overall diptych structure of the book (6:9-15), after its account of a symbolic enactment of Messiah's royal-priestly coronation, the prospect emerges of those far off coming and sharing in the building of the temple (v. 15). Likewise, the introduction to the second half of the diptych (7:1-8:23) concludes with a prophecy that the Gentiles will take hold of the skirts[35] of the covenant people, saying, "We will go with you, for we have heard that God is with you" (8:23). Taking hold of the hem of the garment was a sign of submission to authority. For Gentiles to grasp the tasseled skirts of Jews was to join in the acknowledgement of Yahweh's sovereignty signified by that sartorial symbol. It was to take hold of God's covenant, like those whom Isaiah described as being joined to the Lord and his people (Isa 56:4,6). This symbolic convention is reflected in the Gospel episodes of individuals touching the border of the garment of Jesus, the true Jew and the Lord, combined in one (cf. Matt 9:20,21; 14:36). Though not involving Gentiles, these instances embodied religious confession of the Lord such as Zechariah had envisioned.

Elsewhere Zechariah foretells the conversion of Philistines, who will become as chieftains in Judah (9:7). On a broader scale, he foresees a remnant out of all nations coming to Jerusalem to worship the King, Yahweh of hosts, and to observe the Feast of Tabernacles (14:16). This was in the tradition of Isaiah's assurance to foreigners who were joined to the Lord that they were to be welcomed into the heart of the service of sacrifice and prayer on God's holy mountain (Isa 56:6-8). They would see God's Glory and be admitted into the priesthood of his house (Isa 66:21). God's purpose to make known the gospel unto the nations for the obedience of faith had indeed been revealed by the scriptures of the prophets (Rom 16:26).

Another aspect of Isaiah's large contribution to Zechariah 2 is the connection he makes between the themes of the conquest of the Gentiles and their conversion. In his treatment of Gentiles joining Israel, the first stage finds these former strangers from the covenant assisting in the restoration of God's people, being joined unto them, but as servants. They, the captors and oppressors, are taken captive and are now ruled over (Isa 14:1-3; cf. 60:4-14). Then in Isaiah's later resumption of the theme, this joining of foreigners to the house of Jacob becomes a religious joining unto Israel's God, a gathering into the full fellowship of covenant life and divine service (Isa 56:3-8).

Gentile conversion is also related to Gentile conquest in the passages where Isaiah provides background for the Zech 2:9 (13) imagery of God's brandishing his hand over the nations. In Isaiah 11 the new exodus symbolism of the spoiling of the former oppressor and the drying of the waters by God's shaking his hand (vv. 11-16) is connected to the prophecy of the nations seeking unto the messianic "root of Jesse" (v. 10). And in Isaiah 19 the shaking of Yahweh's hand over the Egyptians in judgment (v. 16) leads to their knowing him and erecting an altar to worship him with sacrifice and oblation (vv. 19-21). Egypt, smitten by the Lord, returns unto him and is healed (v. 22). Indeed, in that day the Assyrians join the Egyptians in the worship of Yahweh (v. 23). "In that day Israel will be the third with Egypt and Assyria" (v. 24), the Gentiles sharing with the Jews in their identification with the Lord and reception of his triune blessing: "Blessed be Egypt my people, and Assyria the work of my hands [cf. Isa 43:7], and Israel mine inheritance" (v. 25). A remarkable disclosure given beforehand in prophetic Scripture of the church in which the Gentiles in the flesh, once far off from God, are brought near in the blood of Christ, who creates of Jews and Gentiles one new man (Eph 2:11ff.).

Zechariah's third vision contains the same association of ideas as these Isaianic passages. Thus in Zech 2:11 (15) the conversion of the Gentiles emerges unexpectedly as a consequence of the conquest of the enemy powers. Likewise in Zechariah 9 the conversion of Philistines (v. 7) occurs in the context of a holy war campaign that dispossesses the ungodly nations occupying God's land. And in Zechariah 14 the overcoming of the universal gathering against Jerusalem is the background of the prophecy of a new gathering at Jerusalem, this one consisting of converts out of all the vanquished nations, come to worship the Lord (v. 16).

It is particularly the act of the spoiling of the aggressor nations by their former servants (Zech 2:8,9 [12,13]) that provides the basis for the idea of converts being won from the ranks of the enemy. In Zech 2:9 (13) the spoiling of the nations is a dispossessing of them in terms of their worldly wealth and glory. It is not the same as the wresting of converts from them referred to in Zech 2:11 (15). The latter is a second kind of spoiling, an act of salvation. Those who move from the world's side to the Lord's side as a consequence of the messianic Angel's mission of judgment on the nations (v. 8 [12]) are to be viewed as having been captives of the enemy power, a prey that had been seized and is now set free. This spoiling of the nations is a redeeming of the nations.

If we follow the thematic trail of Messiah's redemptive spoiling of the nations on into the New Testament, we come in a straight course to the Lord's binding of the dragon, deceiver of the nations, in Revelation 20. The place to pick up this trail is Isa 49:24,25.

Isaiah 49 abounds in parallels to Zechariah's third vision. The voice of Messiah, the Servant of the Lord, breaks through as the speaker (vv. 1ff.). God's people experience an exodus-like homecoming (vv. 9-12), which calls for song and rejoicing (v. 13). Zion's citizenry will so increase as to burst through the old bounds (vv. 19,20). These new children of Jerusalem will come from the Gentile nations (vv. 21,22; cf. v. 12), for the Servant will be a light to the Gentiles and God's salvation to the ends of the earth (v. 6). Hence, the influx of the Gentiles will validate the claims of the servant-Lord to be the God of Jacob and his Savior (vv. 23,26). But of most immediate interest is the coupling of the conquest and conversion of the nations, and particularly the promise that in Zion's warfare, God, the warrior-champion of his people,[36] will take away the captive prey of the terrible adversary (vv. 24,25).

Isa 49:24,25 is translated by Jesus into a saying about himself and Satan (Matt 12:29; Mark 3:27; Luke 11:21,22). Rephrased, the question, "Shall the prey be taken from the strong?" (Isa 49:24) becomes, "How can one enter the house of the strong man and spoil his goods?" (Matt 12:29). And God's answer, asserting that he would himself contend with the strong man and take away his prey (Isa 49:25), becomes in Jesus' saying a declaration that a stronger warrior will overcome the strong man, take away his armor (Luke 11:21,22), bind him, then enter his house, seize his goods and divide the spoil. According to the context, Satan is the strong man and Jesus is the stronger warrior who spoils the prince of demons by rescuing the demon-possessed from his domination.[37]

These messianic acts of deliverance, wrought by the Spirit-finger of

God, heralded the arrival of the kingdom (Matt 12:28; Luke 11:20). They were a harbinger of the penetration of Christ's saving power into all the dark domain of the deceiver of the heathen world. By the gospel the stronger One would take the prey from the terrible foe, bringing former victims of his deception out of all the Gentile nations as converts to serve the triune God of truth. As the stronger One declared at the critical hour of his confrontation with the strong enemy: "Now is the judgment of this world; now shall the prince of this world be cast out. And I, if I be lifted up from the earth, will draw all men unto myself," (John 12:31,32).

Rev 20:1-3 restates the saying of Jesus in apocalyptic style. Here, the messianic Angel from heaven (v. 1), the stronger One, binds the dragon, the strong man, for a thousand years (v. 2). Imprisoned in the abyss, Satan can no longer confine the light of the community of faith within the bounds of Israel, deluding all the other nations with his lie (v. 3). The thousand years are Great-Commission-fulfilling times. All through the millennium the stronger One is rescuing as a prey from the dragon multitudes of converts out of every nation, tribe, people, and tongue (cf. Rev 7:9). Delivered from the devil's darkness and deception, drawn as disciples unto the Light of the world, they become lampstand churches, martyr-witnesses faithful unto death. Beheaded for the testimony of Jesus they are received into the heavenly ministry of the martyrs as priest-kings with Christ before the throne of God (Rev 20:4-6). So complete is the triumph of the stronger One over the draconic foe, he who has the power of death, that dying, for the Christian martyr-witnesses, is transformed into a "first resurrection," an entrance into a sabbatical resting (cf. Rev 14:13) and reigning with their Savior-Victor. In that blessed state they continue during the millennial time of the "the great tribulation" for the church on earth (cf. Rev 7:14), waiting until the full complement of their company is attained (cf. Rev 6:11), eager for the day when that *pleroma* of the seed of Abraham from all the nations, Christ's battle spoils, will be displayed to the glory of God as the fullness of the New Jerusalem (Rev 21:24-26).

Jesus' saying, particularly in its Lucan form, connects Isa 49:24,25 (and Zechariah 2) with Rev 20:1ff. Light is thus thrown forward from Isaiah and Luke on Revelation 20 showing that the binding of the dragon is to be understood in terms of Christ's delivering souls as a prey from Satan's power. The millennium is revealed as the present church age of world-wide gospel testimony and ingathering, an age for exercising all patience through the tribulation of the times (cf. Rev 1:9; 2:2,3,19; 3:10; 13:10; 14:12). Light is also thrown back from Luke 11:21,22 and Revelation 20 on Isaiah 49 and Zechariah 2. Aware that Satan is the ultimate enemy of God and man standing behind the world powers, we can more readily understand the paradoxical prophetic portrayal of the nations both as enemies to be conquered by the divine warrior (for they often act as agents of the Enemy) and as captives held by Satan but set free and united as converts to Zion by the stronger One, sent with the Glory-Spirit.[38]

From our later vantage point in redemptive history we perceive that the soteric spoiling of the nations transpires first. The elect remnant who constitute the *pleroma* of the Gentiles are gathered in during the present church age. Afterward, the nations, spoiled of the elect and now identified with antichrist, the son of perdition, are spoiled of their earthly heritage in the judgment of the last day. It is through this process of the twofold spoiling of the nations, first of their people and then of their property, that Jerusalem becomes enlarged to cosmic horizons (Zech 2:4 [8]).

C. *Validation of the Messianic Commission.* Each of the first two subsections of the kerygma closes with the assertion: "You will know that Yahweh of hosts has sent me" (vv. 9,11 [13,15]). As shown above, the speaker making this claim is the one speaking in the first person throughout the kerygma, the messianic Angel, the Measurer. What he is going to accomplish among the nations in the power of the divine Glory (cf. vv. 5,8 [9,12]) will demonstrate that he is in truth the Messiah sent by God. It will validate his self-identification as the Servant-Branch whom the Lord of hosts brings forth (cf. 3:8).

When the Lord was charging Moses with his role as mediator of the old covenant, Moses raised the question of credentials. God responded that the authentication of his call would be the manifestation of the divine Presence with him and the consequent successful performance of his assignment to deliver the Israelites and establish them in covenant with the Lord. "Surely I will be with you and this shall be the sign unto you that I have sent you: when you have brought forth the people out of Egypt, you shall serve God upon this mountain" (Exod 3:12). The great I Am, God of Glory, would accompany Moses (Exod 3:14-17) and brandish his hand over Egypt (Exod 3:20) so that Israel would despoil their oppressors (Exod 3:21,22) and return from the house of bondage to the house of the Lord in the land of promise (Exod 3:17). It was this presence of the Glory, executor of redemptive judgment, that Moses subsequently insisted on as the quintessential attestation to his divine commissioning (Exod 33:14-16).

In Zechariah the theme of the validating of the messianic mission appears in two other passages besides 2:9,11 (13,15). The first is in vision five (4:1-14), which exhibits extensive correspondence to vision three, its matching member in the chiastic structure of the series. Among the parallels are building imagery, with a messianic figure holding a construction line (2:1 [5] and 4:10); promise of the subjugation of the world power (2:8,9 [12,13] and 4:7); and the consummating of the restoration program (2:4,5,12 [8,9,16] and 4:7,8). Like the third vision the fifth appends to the final universal triumph of God's kingdom the messianic claim: "You will know that Yahweh of hosts has sent me" (4:9).

The validation formula appears again in the crowning episode in Zech 6:9-15, following directly on the announcement that Gentiles from afar will take part in the rebuilding of God's dwelling place (v. 15). Since Messiah, the Branch, is the primary agent in this temple construction (vv. 12,13), the statement that its completion will attest to a divine commissioning clearly refers to Messiah, not Zechariah.

As we have seen, the situation in Zechariah 2 is much the same. Thus in all three passages the evidence that validates messianic identity is the fulfilling of the mission of the Measurer (Zech 2:1,2 [5,6]), namely, completion of the temple/city with the divine Glory within and the inclusion of the Gentiles in the fullness of eschatological Jerusalem. Elsewhere in Scripture the universality of God's work of salvation, particularly the contribution of Gentiles to the glorification of Jerusalem, is cited as the ground for similar validation claims, like: "You will know that I am Yahweh" (Isa 49:23); "My people will know my name" (Isa 52:6—a context abounding in parallels to Zechariah 2); and "You will know that I, Yahweh, am your Savior and your Redeemer, the Mighty One of Jacob" (Isa 60:16). The fact that such analogous phenomena concern claims to deity, not just to prophetic inspiration, corroborates our interpretation of the validation formula in Zech 2:9,11 (13,15) as an assertion not of the prophet Zechariah but of the messianic Angel.

When Jesus arrived, sent of the Father, he renewed the evangel-apologetics he had engaged in as the divine Angel of Zechariah's visions. "The works which the Father has given me to accomplish, the very works that I do, bear witness of me, that the Father has sent me" (John 5:36). The world would know that Jesus was the Christ of God when not only his disciples but all who would believe on him through their word were joined together in one in him, partaking of the glory which the Father gave him (John 17:20-23). When the ascended Jesus breathed out the Spirit, the earnest of that glory, on the Pentecost community, firstfruits of the universal harvest, Peter pointed to this eschatological development as a confirmation of Jesus' claims. Thereby the house of Israel was to know assuredly that God had made this Jesus whom they crucified both Lord and Christ (Acts 2:36; cf. Rom 1:4). In the mission of Moses, mediator of the old covenant, the accompaniment of the Angel by the Glory-Spirit attested to the mediator's divine call (cf. Exod 33:12-17). In the new covenant (the Angel himself now being mediator of the covenant), the validation of the divine commissioning of the covenant mediator is again the presence of the Glory-Spirit—and the resultant extension of the soteric blessings of the kingdom to the Gentile nations.

What John began to do in his Gospel, demonstrating that Jesus was the Christ, the Son of God, by rehearsing his sign-works (John 20:30,31), the apostle continued to do in the Book of Revelation. The Apocalypse is a covenant witness document of Jesus, the faithful witness, presenting his claims as the covenant Lord, testifying that he is the mighty messianic Angel, who was sent, who came and conquered, and is now invested with the Glory-Spirit, all authority in heaven and earth his. In demonstration thereof the Apocalypse confronts us with an overwhelming assemblage of images of his mighty acts as victor over the dragon and the beasts, judge of the nations, possessor of the keys of death and Hades, divine priest-king who redeems a countless multitude out of all people to enjoy and serve God in the heavenly Zion forever.

The final validation of Jesus as the Christ of God will be the consummating of his mission as the Measurer-Builder (Zech 2:1,2 [5,6]) in the eschatological descent of the New Jerusalem from heaven, of cosmic dimensions and having the glory of God (Rev 21:10ff.). In this present age God allows the ungodly to suppress in unrighteousness the knowledge imprinted on their hearts by the self-authenticating witness of the divine revelation in creation and redemptive re-creation. But in that day every knee must bow in acknowledgement that the Lord is God, the Judge of all (Rom 14:10-12), and every tongue must confess that Jesus Christ is Lord to the glory of God the Father (Phil 2:11; cf. Rev 5:13).[39] The validating insignia, always absolutely cogent, will then command cosmic confession.

D. *Summation and Summons.* God's promised presence as the Glory in the midst of Jerusalem is climactic in the imagery section (2:5b [9]), and in the kerygma it is this dwelling of the Lord in the midst of his people that is presented as the ultimate purpose of the messianic advent (2:10,11 [14,15]). Agreeably, God's choice of Jerusalem for his sanctuary dwelling is the theme of the summation in v. 12 (16). Paired with the election (*bḥr*) of Jerusalem (v. 12c [16c]) is the Lord's taking of the entire community of Judah as his own inheritance portion (v. 12a [16a]; *nḥl* the verb, and *ḥēleq* the noun).[40]

Zechariah's thought and terminology go back to the Deuteronomic treaty of the Great King. The divine choice of Jerusalem reflects the frequent Deuteronomic references to the place Yahweh would eventually choose (*bḥr*) as the permanent location of his Glory-Name and central altar (12:5,11, *passim*). In Deut 32:9, recalling the Lord's allotment of national territories, Moses declared that Yahweh's portion (*ḥēleq*) was his people, Jacob was the lot of his inheritance (*naḥălâ*). Similarly, Ps 33:12 and Ps 47:4 [5] (which shares the Zechariah 2 theme of Yahweh's universal kingship) combine *bḥr* and *naḥălâ* in expressing the same idea. And in Exod 15:17 (cf. 33:3,15; 34:9) God's inheritance (*naḥălâ*) is paralleled by his dwelling place in the midst of his people, the sanctuary his hands establish as the site of his everlasting reign

The design of the election of Jerusalem is explicitly stated in the phrase, *ʿal ʾadmat haqqōdeš* (v. 12b [16b]). Giving the preposition *ʿal* its final sense (cf. e.g., Exod 29:36; Deut 27:13), I would translate, "for the sanctuary ground."[41] The use of *ʾadāmâ* (rather than *ʾereṣ*) speaks against translations like "in the holy land." It suggests a particular spot of ground that has been sanctified by a divine epiphany. Illustrative are the episodes in Exod 3:5 and Josh 5:15, in which the immediate presence of the Angel of the Lord made the place where Moses or Joshua stood holy ground (*ʾadmat qōdeš* in Exod 3:5). In choosing Jerusalem, God was vouchsafing to it the divine presence (Messiah and Glory-Spirit) that would make it a sacred place; his purpose was to secure it as the site of his temple.[42]

Deut 32:43, the closing verse of Moses' witness song, has been brought into the discussion of Zech 2:12 (16) because it contains the term *ʾadmātô*, "his [Yahweh's] land/ground," seen by some as comparable to Zechariah's *ʾadmat haqqōdeš* (understood as the entire promised land). Though the specific parallel seems illusory, the broader contexts of Deuteronomy 32 and Zechariah 2 have much in common and comparison proves illuminating. Shared features include: the use of *naḥălâ* and *ḥēleq* for God's heritage (as noted above); the figure of the pupil of the eye for the preciousness of Israel to God (Deut 32:10, Zech 2:8 [12]); the formal combination of summons to all the world plus rationale (Deut 32:43; Zech 2:12,13 [16,17]); paradoxical prospects for the Gentiles, including both vengeance and redemptive action as occasion to praise God (Deut 32:26-43; Zech 2:8,9,11 [12,13,15]).[43]

Interpretation of the notoriously difficult Deut 32:43 best begins with recognition that retribution against the enemy nations is the sustained theme in the immediate context (from v. 26 on) and the main point in v. 43 itself. This emphasis is augmented in the longer textual tradition of the verse, variously represented by the LXX and Qumran, which includes "he will requite those who hate him" after "he will render vengeance to his adversaries."[44] Together they form the middle pair of a four-cola chiasm (ABBA), of which the A-members are "he will avenge the blood of his servants" and "he will make atonement for his land (ʾadmātô) and people" (NIV). It becomes evident that this making of an atonement payment for the land must be understood in terms of the law in Num 35:33, which requires the making of atonement for land[45] stained by innocent blood, crying out for vengeance. Only the shedding of the murderer's blood would accomplish this atonement. Significantly, Deut 32:43 is immediately preceded by God's sworn commitment to exact such gory vengeance against the oppressors of his people (vv. 40-42). The final clause of Deut 32:43 does not, therefore, speak of making expiation for the sins of God's people but of avenging their righteous blood. Thereby, God cleanses "the lot of his inheritance" (Deut 32:9) to serve as his holy dwelling in the midst of Israel—the purpose stated for making atonement for the land in Num 35:34 (cf. Deut 19:10; 21:8).

Given the textual uncertainties in Deut 32:43 and the awkwardness of "his land, his people" at the close, there is a serious possibility that the ʾadmātô reflects an original reference to "the blood" (dam)[46] of his people. A perfect parallel would then obtain with "he will avenge the blood of his servants." Num 35:33 would still be the legal background but the reference to the blood-stained land would be only implicit.[47]

It seems then that ʾădāmâ is not used in either Deut 32:43 or Zech 2:12 (16) to denote the promised land. But examination of the Deut 32:43 context does disclose fundamental correspondences to Zechariah 2 and alerts us to the fact that the promise given in the summation (Zech 2:12 [16]) assuring the choice of Jerusalem/Judah as sanctuary ground entails the messianic mission of retribution described earlier in the kerygma section (vv. 8,9 [12,13]). If this terrain is to serve as a temple site of the holy One of Israel, expiation must be made for its blood-defilement by avenging its sons against the nations that have attacked and slain them.

Isaiah locates the avenging of the martyr-saints at their resurrection triumph over death and the final defeat of Satan. He describes the earth as defiled since the Fall by innocent blood and groaning under death's corruption (Isa 24:4,5; cf. Rom 8:19ff.). But at last Yahweh will come forth to punish the inhabitants of the earth (Isa 26:21a) and to destroy Leviathan, possessor of the power of death, persecutor of the saints, accuser of the brethren (Isa 27:1). Then the earth/netherworld will no more cover over her slain, but disclose their blood, long crying for vindication (Isa 26:21b; cf. Gen 4:10; Rev 6:10; 16:16; 19:2). All this is prophesied anew in the Book of Revelation: the judgment of the bestial world-city and the devil, the resurrection, and the clearing of the cosmos of death and Hades (Rev 19:11-20:15). And here, as in Zechariah's third vision, this work of divine avenging is the immediate prelude to the establishment of the holy temple-city, New Jerusalem, sanctified by the triune Presence, the tabernacle where God dwells with men (Rev 21:1ff.).

To his summation (Zech 2:12 [16]) the divine Angel adds a concluding summons to all mankind (v. 13 [17]). The kerygma had begun with Messiah issuing his evangel-command to those far off (v. 6 [10]; cf. Isa 49:1ff.). It was a call to escape back to the altar/temple of God at Zion (v. 7 [11]). Gospel invitation is an altar call; it creates an altar-centripetal movement. In the new covenant age evangelistic advance finds the witnessing church expanding in a centrifugal mission out from the site of the old earthly altar, out to the nations of the Gentiles. But this centrifugal propulsion of the testimony of Jesus to the ends of the earth still triggers an altar-centripetal gathering, not however back to earthly Jerusalem and its obsolete altar but to the true altar in heavenly Jerusalem. In the universal summons of Zech 2:13 (17) Christ the *kerux* provides a model for his church in fulfilling its great commission as he centers the rapt reverence of the Gentiles on the Parousia-Presence, the Glory of the Zion above.

The messianic Angel announces imminent divine action (v. 13b [17b]), a decisive intervention ending the delay that had prompted his earlier plea of "How long?" (cf. Zech 1:12). He heralds the advent of the Lord, appearing from his heavenly throne (cf. Deut 26:15; Hab 2:20a; Ps 11:4), his zeal stirred up like a man of war to do battle against his enemies (cf. Isa 42:13; 51:9; Judg 5:12).

So, hush! Silence, all flesh (Zech 2:13a [17a]). The summons sounds and the kings of the earth shut their mouths, speechless, awe-struck before the exalted Servant (Isa 52:15b). His mission is authenticated as divine, for they, Gentiles deceived by the devil, now hear and understand what had been unheard of, what the prince of darkness had kept from them, the gospel tidings of peace with God through the sacrifice and intercession of this amazing Servant. He has come and overcome Beelzebub. He has rescued the prey from many nations. He has been exalted and his claim to be Christ, sent forth by the Lord of hosts, has been validated (Isa 52:13-53:12).

Hush! Silence, all flesh before Yahweh. The day of the Lord is at hand (cf. Hab 2:20b; Zeph 1:7; Rev 8:1). "This is the day in which the Lord is up and doing; let us be glad and rejoice in him" (Ps 118:24; cf. Mal 3:17; 4:3 [3:21]).

---

1 Cf. further the Appendix.

2 Though the Hebrew na^car can serve as a technical term for officials of various sorts, it probably alludes here simply to the prophet's youthfulness (cf. Jer 1:6).

3 If the other angel is the measurer, not just his personal spokesman, he is the Angel of the Lord. On the indefiniteness of his designation as "another angel," compare the appearance of Christ as "another strong angel" in Rev 10:1 (cf. 14:17; 18:1,21; 20:1).

4 Unable to accept the high mystery of the Angel who describes himself as sent by Yahweh of Hosts (v. 11 [15]) and yet speaks as Yahweh of hosts (v. 8 [12]) or the reality of the presence and participation of the pre-incarnate Christ in these visionary proceedings, many commentators treat the claims to be sent by God (vv. 8,9,11 [12,13,15]) as parenthetical interjections by Zechariah. It is alleged that the prophet repeatedly interrupts the divine oracle he is supposedly voicing in order to boast of the future authentication of his prophetic call (cf. Deut 18:21,22). But the claims to be sent are thus severed from the attached statements of the purposes of this sending (viz., judgment of the nations and dwelling in Zion) which do not fit Zechariah's role.

5 The first-person-speaking in v. 5 (9) cannot be explained then as simply the voice of God breaking through in the words of a spokesman, for this divine one who speaks in the first person is a sent one, the messianic Angel, and is, therefore, to be sought among those who appear in the vision.

6 Cf. our comments on Zech 1:16 in the first vision. In vision five (counterpart to vision three in the chiastic arrangement of the visions) another line appears, a plummet, it too employed in the reconstruction process.

7 In postbiblical Hebrew, forms of r^ph are used to express notions of approval, selection, designation.

8 In Mesopotamian iconography the measuring reed and line are found as a symbol of the authority of the god. Thus, on the stele of Ur-nammu at Ur, the moon-god Nannar is seen holding these measuring insignia when approached by the king for instructions concerning the building of a ziggurat. Cf. A. Parrot, *Babylon and the Old Testament* (New York 1958), 145-47.

9 Cf. also Amos' picture of Yahweh with the plumb-line of judgment in his hand (7:7,8).

10 God's measuring is associated in Job 28:25 with an act of divine seeing (r^ph) in his ordering of the world (v. 24).

11 Of Marduk it is related that as he began to construct the world out of the carcass of vanquished Ti'amat he "measured the dimensions of the Apsu," the subterranean abode of Ea, preparatory to establishing the earth structure on it (*Enuma Elish*, IV, 143).

12 Cf. vision one where the stretching of the line over Jerusalem is followed by the Lord's declaration that his cities would be spread abroad by reason of great prosperity (Zech 1:17). Again in Zech 10:8-10 the motif appears of the available space not able to contain God's people, divinely sown, increased, and brought back from captivity (cf. Isa 49:20).

13 "Open wide" is the meaning suggested by the sparse evidence for the root *pth*; cf. Prov 20:19, where the object is "lips". *Pth* is perhaps used instead of *ptḥ*, the common verb for "open," to obtain the pun on Japheth.

14 That Japheth's occupying of the tents of Shem signifies a participation in Shem's covenant relationship to God is intimated by the wordplay between *ʾĕlōhê šēm*, "the God of Shem," (Gen 9:26) and *ʾohŏlê šēm*, "the tents of Shem," (Gen 9:27).

15 Similarly, Zech 14:20,21 envisions the elevation of the entire Jerusalem and indeed all Judah to sanctuary status. Cf. in Dan 2:35 the new mount Zion, which fills the whole earth, and in Rev 21:10ff. the new Jerusalem, a cosmic holy of holies.

16 Even if the genitive is regarded as appositional (i.e., "maiden Zion") the city represents its occupants.

17 The latter are all introduced by *kî*, "for," or "for lo I" (v. 9a [13a] and v. 10b [14b]).

18 Accusative defining place whither may be placed first for emphasis, especially with imperatives. This adverbial rather than vocative rendering of Zion achieves the syntactic pairing suggested by the phonic correspondence of *ṣāpôn* (north) and *ṣiyyôn* (Zion).

19 He too pictured the departure in exodus terms as an act of redemption, with God's Presence before and behind as protector and provider, guiding through the wilderness, bringing forth water from the rock (cf. 48:21; 52:12).

20 If the verb *prś* is given its less frequent sense of scatter, the clause becomes an insipid parenthesis referring to God's past dispersing of the Israelites to account for the fact they are now in Babylon. It would then differ from the other *kî*-clauses, all of which point to present circumstances or future prospects as reasons for compliance with the imperatives.

21 In Noah's oracle in Genesis 9 there is a correlation between the curse on Canaan (v. 25) and the blessings on Shem and Japheth (vv. 26,27). This is indicated by the repetition of the curse after each blessing. Dispossession of Canaan is the other side of Israel's taking possession. Cf. Isa 54:3.

22 Cf. the use of *ʾaḥar* in Gen 37:17; Ezek 33:31; Hos 2:5 [6]; Job 39:8.

23 The meaning "with, in the company of" for *ʾaḥar* is attested in Hebrew and Ugaritic.

24 The motivation clause of v. 8 (12) would thus fit the pattern of the others in developing the implications of the introductory imagery.

25 See the discussion in my *Images of the Spirit* (Grand Rapids: Baker, 1980), 71-75.

26 In Isa 48:16, in the context of judgment on Babylon (v. 14), is the statement (evidently to be attributed to the Son of God): "the Lord Yahweh has sent me and his Spirit." In Ps 73:24 *ʾaḥar kābôd* modifies "you will take me (into heaven)." Some translate "with glory." Other options are "with (the) Glory" or "afterwards (by your) Glory."

27 Note also the associated theme of validation of mission in John 17:22,23, as in Zech 2:9 (13).

28 On "daughter (*bat*) of the eye," see Ps 17:8; Lam 2:18; cf. Deut 32:10. This reading of *bĕbābat* assumes either a doubling of the preposition or a diminutive doubling of the noun. It may also be read "gate" of his eye. In that case, *bat-bābel* would be understood as "the daughter of Gate-of-god" (Babel, according to the common etymology). Perhaps a double pun is intended.

29 This would be the same emphasis found in the oracle in vision one. See the comments above on Zech 1:14,15.

30 Hand (*yād*) is a designation for the Glory-cloud and it is paralleled in these passages by other such designations—"Spirit" (Isa 11:15) and "banner" (Isa 13:2). In Zech 2:8,9a (12,13a) the fact that the "hand" of v. 9a (13a) stands in a corresponding position to the *kābôd* of v. 8a (12a) in the chiastic arrangement of the three clauses argues for the translation of *ʾaḥar kābôd* as "with the Glory."

31 Actually, the deliverance of God's people from exile, which is involved in the judgment on the nations, is to be understood of all who are in a far off, Lo-Ammi condition, Gentiles as well as Jews. The new element in vv. 10,11 (14,15), the conversion of the Gentiles, is thus discernible in vv. 6-9 (10-13).

32 Announcing the same hope of the coming of the Savior-King to speak peace to the nations, Zech 9:9ff. similarly begins: "Rejoice greatly, O daughter of Zion."

33 Leah puns on *lwh* in naming Levi, expressing the hope that her husband will now be joined to her (Gen 29:34). Does this reflect on the marriage relationship as a covenant? A similar word play is found in the Lord's promise to Aaron that the Levites will be joined to him to keep the charge of the sanctuary (Num 18:2,4).

34 Some arbitrarily apply this promise to Israelites only. They see it as a restrictive qualification on Gentile participation that betrays the author's failure to attain fully to the new covenant concept of universalism. The root prophecy, Noah's oracle, is similarly misinterpreted by those who identify the subject of "he will dwell in the tents of Shem" (Gen 9:27) as God rather than Japheth, thus making the passage say that while Japheth would have worldly blessings, God's covenantal presence would belong to Shem exclusively.

35 In Num 15:38,39 and Deut 22:12 the term *kānāp*, "skirt," is used for the border of the garment to which tassels with a blue strand were to be affixed as a reminder of the covenant stipulations of the Lord.

36 Cf. also the imagery of God's lifting up his hand and military banner unto the nations (v. 22).

37 In Isa 53:12, dividing the spoil is a feature of the exaltation of the Servant of the Lord as a reward for the redemptive suffering whereby he sprinkles many nations (Isa 52:15).

38 Significantly, Satan, latent in the world powers in Zechariah's third vision, appears in the immediately following vision as the Adversary, whom the Angel of the Lord overcomes, so saving the elect from his power.

39 Isa 45:23, cited by Paul in Rom 14:11 and Phil 2:11, is set at the conclusion of an on-the-offensive apologetics challenging the folly of the idolaters. The Lord simply points to his self-revelation in his work of creation and his words of prophetic predisclosure as the incontrovertible manifestation of himself as God, sole sovereign of space and time. As in Zechariah 2, this validation of divine claim comes in connection with a universal summons to salvation (Isa 45:22). Biblical apologetics has an evangelistic thrust; it is a function of the church's witness to the name of the Creator-Savior-Consummator.

40 Zechariah's first three visions form a unit. Visions two and three develop the two main themes introduced in vision one, with vision two emphasizing retribution against the nations and vision three the restoration of Jerusalem and return of the Glory. In rounding out the triad, vision three echoes several features of the opening vision, including the coupling of the choice of Jerusalem and the favoring of the cities of Judah (cf. 1:12,17 and 2:12 [16]).

41 V. 12b (16b) might be taken with v. 12a (16a), but a better balance is gained if it is construed with v. 12c (16c), the opening *waw* of which is then emphatic with postposition of the verb. Possibly v. 12b (16b) pertains to both the a and c parts of the verse.

42 If v. 12b (16b) goes with the selection of Judah in v. 12a (16a), the sanctuary concept is extended beyond the temple in Jerusalem. Similarly, Zech 14:20,21.

43 The same combination appears in Ps 47:1ff. See the quotation of Deut 32:43a in Rom 15:10.

44 Another addition found after the first clause in LXX and Qumran, and providing a parallel to it, is adopted in the quotation in Heb 1:6.

45 Used here is *ʾereṣ* which at times refers to soil (cf., e.g., Deut 11:6; 12:16; 29:22).

46 Cf. Accadian *adamatu*, "dark blood."

47 In Num 35:33 the making of atonement is "for the blood" (*laddām*) as well as for the land (*lāʾāreṣ*).

Vision Four (3:1-10)

GUARDIAN OF GOD'S COURTS

Introduction.

1. *Compositional Center:* A key position is occupied by the fourth vision (Zechariah 3) within the series of seven night visions and within the macrostructure of the book.[1]

Zechariah's work as a whole is built on a three-hinge framework with Zech 6:1-15 as the middle hinge between the two main panels of the overall diptych. Each of these panels in turn is a diptych with its own central hinge, Zechariah 3 for the first panel and Zechariah 11 for the second. A formal feature shared by the three hinge passages, and exclusive to them in the book, is the personal participation of Zechariah himself in the symbolic action. Another is the involvement of specific historical individuals in the episode. Further, coronation is their common theme, all three portraying the commissioning of Messiah to his royal-priestly task. By presenting this theme at each of these key structural points in the book, the formal framework brilliantly highlights "the figure of the coming Christ, ordained to priestly sacrifice and subsequent highest royal glory, the one who is the central hinge and focus of prophetic revelation."[2]

Within the structure of the seven visions, Zechariah 3 occupies the center position. It is set apart from the three visions before and after it by the fact that it does not fit into the pattern of introductory formulae that characterizes these two triads (cf. 1:7,8; 2:1; 2:5; 3:1; 4:1-2; 5:1; 6:1). It is also distinguished from the other six visions by the peculiar features it shares as one of the trio of hinges in the macrostructure of the book. Thus, while the other visions symbolize earthly realities by imaginary forms, actual persons (Joshua and his fellow priests) appear in Zechariah 3. And the prophet intervenes in the fourth vision to forward the action, whereas his role elsewhere in the visions is limited to witnessing the scenes and seeking explanations from the hierophant angel.

The centerpiece position of the fourth vision is accentuated by the chiastic form of the balancing triads on either side, producing an ABCDC′B′A′ schema. One aspect of this concentric arrangement has to do with the locus of the divine action in the several visions. The scene of the symbolic drama proceeds from the nations of the world in the outside (A and A′) visions, to the land of Judah-Israel in the B and B′ visions, to Zion, the theocratic capitol, in the C and C′ visions. Then in Zechariah 3, the central D vision of the chiasm, we find ourselves at the holy of holies, the ultimate center of the cosmos where the Lord is enthroned in the midst of his angelic council.

2. *Christological Climax*: Here at the center of the visions stands the Christ-figure, present as the Angel of the Lord and typified by Joshua in his reinvestment as royal highpriest. And here Messiah's mission of salvation is set forth in the radical terms of its hidden, underlying dimension as a decisive encounter with Satan. The contention revolves about the Lord's claim to the sinful but chosen people represented by Joshua (the Joshua still in his defiled garb at the outset of the vision). And the outcome of the ordeal between the messianic Servant and the diabolical serpent turns on the question of Joshua's fate in the divine judgment: will this representative sinner be condemned and abandoned to the dominion of the devil or will he be justified and consigned as a holy minister to the service of the God of glory?

Implicit in the third vision were intimations that ultimately Satan was the enemy power threatening the people and kingdom of God and that the coming of the kingdom involved not just an overwhelming exercise of might to destroy the enemy but a working of Spirit-power in the conversion of enemies, transforming them into builders of the city of God. It required a coming of Christ to bind Satan and spoil his house, rescuing the prey from his grasp. All this becomes graphically explicit in the fourth vision. Moreover, the process of spiritual reclamation and transformation is now more precisely depicted as one of justification in the face of Satan's accusations and as one of renewal in the image of the divine Glory. Present also are indications that the victory over the accuser will require the atoning sacrifice of the messianic Servant. In vision four we see ourselves—for we are Joshua—as in ourselves sinners in the hands of an angry God but, as God's chosen in Christ, sinners in the pierced hands of the suffering Servant-Savior.

Biblical-theological climax, with focus on Christ, thus coincides with the compositional center of the visions. Remarkably similar to this fourth vision of Zechariah is the middle section of the Book of Revelation. Like Zechariah 3, Rev 12:1 (or 11:19)-14:20 occupies the central point of an overall seven-member chiasm, and here again it is at the structural center that the depths of the redemptive-historical process are explored and exposed. The preceding apocalyptic visions of the seven letters, seven-sealed book, and seven trumpets display further parallelism to Zechariah. They lead up to the climactic centerpiece of the chiasm with themes and imagery that recall Zechariah's first three visions. The Messiah figure in association with the Glory council dominates scene and action. He stands in the midst of his persecuted saints and sends forth agents of judgment on the world. These heavenly agents are symbolized as horsemen. Intimations are given that lurking in the shadows of the world's hostility to the church is the primeval leviathan. But, as in Zechariah, it is in the center-section of the Apocalypse that the conflict of the ages is directly and dramatically revealed as the contention of Christ with Satan over the church. And once more, as in Zechariah 3, it is the role of Satan as the accuser of the redeemed before God's throne that is prominent (Rev 12:10). And again, the messianic man prevails in judgment against the dragon (Rev 12:5,9), a victory for the accused saints attributable to the blood of atonement shed by the suffering Servant (Rev 12:11).

Comparison of Zechariah 3 and Revelation 12 constrains recognition of their common rootage in Genesis 3. Further connections between Zechariah 3 and the Genesis 3 context will be noted in the exposition of the fourth vision below, but here we simply cite some major features of Genesis 3 that reappear in both Zechariah 3 and Revelation 12: the emergence of the gospel of salvation in the rebuke-damnation of the devil; the three principals of the redemptive drama—Messiah, his people, and Satan; Messiah's identity as the royal offspring, born of the woman; Messiah's contention with the devil; the two stages in Messiah's mission of vanquishing Satan—his sufferings and the consequent glory. These central visions of the books of Zechariah and Revelation bring us back to the radical roots and fundamental realities of the holy war first announced in Genesis 3:14,15 and destined to rage on through history from the loss of Eden's holy paradise until its consummatory restoration in the new Jerusalem.

I. THE REBUKE OF SATAN

A. *Before Messiah's Judgment-Seat:* Common to all seven visions, as at least their background, is the divine council setting, represented directly by the divine presence (as in visions one, three, four, five and seven) or at least indirectly by agents of the council sent forth on missions (as in visions two and six). But the heavenly scene is most immediately and realistically displayed in this central fourth vision. Here the heavenly court coalesces with the holy throne room on earth, celestial beings whose proper sphere is the invisible, supernal realm appearing alongside the earthly high priest Joshua. Such an interlinking of heavenly archetype and earthly ectype is what was involved in the non-visionary, external reality of the presence of the Glory-Spirit, the epiphany of the heavenly court, manifested in the Israelite tabernacle or temple.

Towering over the judgment scene, sovereignly directing the proceedings, stands the messianic figure of the Angel of Yahweh.[3] He appeared in the first vision both as Judge of all the earth engaged in surveillance of the world powers through his angelic agents (Zech 1:8-11) and as the Intercessor, effectively pleading the cause of God's oppressed people (Zech 1:12-17). Here in the fourth vision he is seen in this same dual role; he is the Judge who renders the verdict on the basis of reports from various sources and he also acts as Advocate for the covenant people. His double office of Judge and Advocate is the more remarkable here in that the party he is to judge, accused Joshua, is the same one he proceeds to defend.

As in vision one, it turns out to be the enemy power against whom condemnation and doom are actually pronounced. Here it is the enemy himself. He appears in the vision as a second principal, seen by Zechariah as taking his stand in court[4] to oppose (*śṭn*) the defendant (hence his name, Satan) with slandering charges (for which he is known as *diabolos*/devil). The verb *śṭn* and the derived noun are used for others besides Satan himself, but the terms clearly refer to the prince of the evil principalities and powers in the prologue of Job, 1 Chr 21:1, and Zech 3:1,2.[5] Development of the usage of the noun as applied to the devil from an appellative to a proper name should not be misconstrued as evidence that the notion of a personal devil gradually emerged out of some more general concept. We are not dealing with the evolution of a metaphysical notion in the Israelite mind but with the progressive divine revelation of a specific historical entity. The fact of the existence of the personal devil confronted mankind at the outset of earthly history in Eden and it is presented to us in the revelation of that primeval encounter in Genesis 3, with occasional further disclosures concerning him in the subsequent biblical record.

Satan's confrontation with the Angel of Yahweh in Zechariah 3 will be better understood if seen within the pattern of satanic enmity exhibited in the episodes narrated in Genesis 3 and the prologue of Job. But before tracing that dark labyrinth, notice must be taken of the third principal figure in the visionary trial scene—Joshua, the accused.

As the high priest, Joshua represented the covenant congregation. This representative relationship was signified by working into the design of the high priest's vestments a double set of the names of the twelve tribes of Israel. They were engraved on the precious stones located on the shoulder straps of the ephod and again in the gems in the breastpiece (cf. Exod 28:9-12,21-29). While representing his contemporary Israelites, the highpriest also foreshadowed the future in that he was a type of the coming true priest-king over the house of God, the mediatorial priest who would bring the people he represented to God through the blood of the everlasting covenant.[6]

The typological dimension of Joshua's priestly identity becomes explicit later in this vision. But when the scene opens Joshua appears in his capacity as the representative equivalent of Jerusalem-Israel,[7] more specifically, covenant-breaking Israel defiled by sin, for he appears in filthy garments, a shocking deviation from the ceremonial requirement that the high priest enter the heavenly court of the holy of holies in his vestments of holy glory. Though the people of God are thus depicted in old covenant idiom, Joshua is not a symbol for the old covenant faithful only. The messianic significance of Joshua later in the vision indicates that this vision as a whole, like the others for which it is the centerpiece, concerns all the elect of God in Christ, the holy company which attains perfection under the new covenant.

B. *Har Magedon Crisis:* One thing that was obviously at stake in this judicial encounter was the destiny of Joshua. Although the specific charges made against him by the accuser are not quoted, they can be surmised from the context. Satan will have pointed to the transgression of the covenant symbolized by Joshua's soiled garments. Apparently he will also have cited the fact that the Lord of the covenant had himself judged the Joshua community guilty and had condemned them to undergo the extreme curse of exile, a judgment whereby he repudiated the nation as Lo-Ammi, "Not-My-People." Such an argument by the accuser-prosecutor would account for the subsequent rejoinder of the Angel-Advocate reminding Satan that Joshua was a brand plucked from the consuming fire of God's vengeance (v. 3c), restored to the covenantal status of Ammi, "My-People."

Would Satan's charges prevail or would they be overcome by the considerations adduced in Joshua's defense?

But something beyond Joshua's fate was at issue in this court. With subtle indirection Satan was affronting the majesty of the divine Judge, challenging him as to his divine claims and prerogatives. Satan's tactics here are similar to those he resorted to in his opposition to God's servant Job.

As in Zechariah 3 the setting of the Book of Job is the heavenly council on a day when the court was in session (Job 1:6; 2:1). Again Satan is present and assumes the role of accuser of man. That his chief purpose is, however, to offer blasphemous challenge to the enthroned Lord is more readily discernible here. Confronted by God's claim that Job was his loyal servant, a faithful family priest (Job 1:5,8), a trophy of his redeeming grace, Satan contradicts: No—Job is no true servant. The prophetic gospel-decree of Gen 3:15 is not being realized in Job or anyone else. God cannot snatch from Satan the prey he seized at the Fall. Job's religious profession is false. He is a hypocrite, using a pretense of piety as the price of prosperity and God is guilty of complicity in this pious fraudulence (Job 1:9-11). God's boast of Job's devotion to him is an empty lie.

The trial by ordeal that follows is designed to test the validity of Satan's accusations against Job and in that sense Job is on trial.[8] But clearly the larger issue concerns the truth of the gospel, the validity of God's claim to be the Savior of his elect from Satan, sin, and death. Under contention ultimately is the identity of Yahweh as true God, the God of truth, and so the rightful One to be Judge of heaven and earth.

Job serves then as the champion of God's name. Through Job's trial by ordeal God triumphs in the trial by ordeal between himself and Satan. The vindication of Job is the vindication of the Lord, Job's sovereign Savior. The silencing of Job's accuser is the victory of the divine Judge and his rebuke of Satan.[9]

The differences between the situations in the Book of Job and Zechariah's fourth vision are only on the surface. To be sure, it is the genuineness of the piety of the family priest Job that is stressed while it is the sinfulness of the high priest Joshua that is conspicuous. But both these priests figure in the accounts as sinners saved by the grace of God. Both are examples of the efficacy of God's redemptive wisdom and program. In

Zechariah 3, no less than in the prologue to Job, Satan is then attacking the Lord for accepting the ministry of an allegedly unfit priest at his altar-throne. Posing as a cherub-guardian of the sanctity of God's sanctuary, Satan challenges the presence of Job and Joshua; filthy and false, they defile the holy temple. To challenge them was in effect to call into question the holiness of the God who consorts with such sinners, welcomes their presence and delights in the worship they offer (cf. Matt 11:19; Mark 2:16; Luke 5:30,7:34).

The temptation event in Eden sheds further light on Satan's secret objective in his incrimination of Joshua and Job. That episode differs from the other two in that Satan there maligns God to man rather than accusing man before God. Once man has fallen into sin, the attack on God gets camouflaged behind surface accusations against the sinners with whom God identifies in redemptive covenantal union. But before the Fall, Satan vilifies the Lord God more openly (Gen 3:1-5), insinuating that his imposition of the unique prohibitory stipulation was dictated by jealous self-interest and a lack of benevolence (v. 1b) and blatantly alleging that the death sanction was a deceptive, empty threat (v. 4).

Exhibited in this behavior of Satan in Eden is what may be called the Har Magedon-revolt syndrome. Eden was the site of Har Magedon, "the mountain of meeting," i.e., the judicial assembly of God and his angels (cf. Ps 82:1; Isa 14:13). The proceedings in that heavenly council are the background of Satan's appearance in the garden. A disclosure made to the council that God purposed to create man, like the angels a creature in the divine likeness, crowned with glory and given dominion over the creation (Gen 1:26; Ps 8:5-8), evoked in the cherub-prince evil emotions— threatened pride, envy, malicious hate. He must thwart the announced development. He must redirect the man-creature's covenantal allegiance from the Lord God to himself. He must challenge the Sovereign enthroned on Har Magedon. His must be the glory, the power, and the kingdom forever, his throne exalted above all that is called Elohim.

So Satan schemed and his subtle strategy was successful—seemingly, for a second. Then suddenly, heralded by thunder, the King of Glory appeared (Gen 3:8). A new decree was proclaimed: doom for the devil, reconciliation for God's elect through a second Adam, the destined slayer of the dragon (Gen 3:14,15). Henceforth, until the final realization of all God decreed, Satan's Har Magedon revolt would be a conspiring against this messianic champion set as God's anointed king in the midst of heaven's hosts on the holy mountain. But the Almighty laughs at Satan's raging against the Son (Ps 2:4). He makes the hostility Satan instigates contribute to the fulfillment of his decree and the redemptive triumph of his messianic Servant (cf. Col 2:14,15). Satan's continuance as a factor in human history is permitted according to God's unfathomable counsel so that he can play his guilty part in the crucifixion (Acts 2:23-36), the bruising of the Servant's heel, which by the alchemy of divine grace turns out to be the crushing of the serpent's skull. Well named, the place called Golgotha.

Satan's undertakings in the episodes depicted in the prologue of Job and Zechariah 3 are instances of his ongoing Har Magedon rebellion, the desperate, irrational, but relentless enmity that finally produces the man of sin, son of perdition. When his role in Zechariah's vision is perceived as part of this continuing undercurrent of antichrist evil, his ultimate point of attack is seen to be not the defendant but the Judge, not Joshua but the Christ-Angel.

By establishing the fact that Joshua was unclean, unacceptable on the holy hill of Zion (cf. Psalm 15), Satan would demonstrate that God's announced program of redemption had proven a failure. Further, he would make the case that the Angel of the Lord was not worthy to sit as judge in the Har Magedon council, for in countenancing the priestly service of defiled Joshua he was responsible for the contamination of God's holy courts. The messianic Angel would thus be guilty of the very failing that had resulted in the expulsion of the first Adam from Eden's holy garden and would thereby be disqualified for any future mission as the righteous Servant, a second Adam, a savior of sinners.

Satan repeats here a tactic employed in Eden. In each case it was his own evil presence that confronted a guardian of God's house with the duty of repulsing such an unholy intrusion, and each time Satan's strategy was to divert attention to something else and so maintain his own position at Har Magedon. Would the strategy succeed with the Angel of the Lord as it had with Adam? The answer was not long in coming.

C. *Trampling the Serpent:* "Yahweh rebuke you, O Satan" (Zech 3:2a). The Angel of the Lord dealt directly and decisively with the accuser and his blasphemous challenge. Yahweh's thunderous[10] rebuke does more than parry the thrust of the opponent; its effects are devastating.

Similar to the divine rebuke of Zech 3:2 is that in Psalm 9. The scene there too is judicial with the Lord seated on his throne judging righteously. He maintains the cause of his people against the enemy by rebuking the wicked nations (v. 5a [6a]), and by this action (whether understood as past or precative) he destroys them, blotting out their name forever, reducing them to perpetual ruin (vv. 5b,6 [6b,7]). God's roaring rebuke forces the waters of the sea to retreat (Isa 50:2; Nah 1:4; Ps 18:15 [16]) and turns to flight the tumultuous onrush of the nations (Isa 17:13). In Ps 18:15 (16) God's "rebuke" against the deep as he delivers his people from the strong enemy (vv. 16ff. [17ff.]) is paired with "the blast of thy nostrils," the phrase used in Exod 15:8 for God's vanquishing of the leviathan of the deep at the redemption of Israel from Egypt. Since the sea is the realm of Satan from which he brings forth the draconic enemies of the saints (Dan 7:2ff.; Rev 13:1ff.), Ps 18:15 (16) is thematically of a piece with Zech 3:2. At times divine rebuke seems tantamount to a destructive curse (cf. Ps 119:21; Mal 2:2,3). Indeed, the rebuke formula found in Zech 3:2 came to be used in execratory incantation.[11] In the "Yahweh rebuke you, O Satan," of Zech 3:2 we can hear reverberating the primal "Cursed are you" of Gen 3:14.

The Angel of the Lord's rebuke silenced the accusations, but further it constituted a condemnation of the accuser himself, repulsing him from the station he presumed to occupy in the divine council. It was a scornful repudiation of the devil's pretensions to the throne on Har Magedon.

Here portrayed in advance is the history of our Lord as the stronger One, who by his rebuking of Satan, the deceiver-captor of the nations, sets his captives free. In the accounts of Jesus' rebuking action in the Gospels[12] we find the same objects as in the Old Testament references to divine rebuke. Jesus rebuked the roaring wind and waters of the sea, brought them to silence (Matt 8:26; Mark 4:39; Luke 8:24), and so rescued his perishing disciples. "Who then is this?" The very Creator Lord who commanded the waters to respect his bounds and made the dry land appear. The very Redeemer Lord who divided the sea and made the waters a way of salvation for the Israelites. And Jesus rebuked Satan. He did so when he saw him behind Peter's counsel (Mark 8:33), and again when, repeatedly, he encountered him in his demonic agents, defeating them and delivering their victims from satanic tyranny (Matt 17:18; Mark 1:25; 9:25; Luke 4:35,41; 9:42; Acts 5:16; 8:7; 19:12). Jesus is the divine warrior who at last repels Satan's final antichrist attack by the Spirit-breath of his mouth, the rebuking blast of his nostrils (2 Thess 2:8).

The judicial confrontation of Messiah and Satan depicted anticipatively in Zechariah 3 is presented as actualized in Revelation 12. The dragon's attempt to do away with Jesus fails (vv. 3,4); the anointed Son ascends and occupies the throne on heavenly Zion (v. 5; cf. Ps 2:6-9). Assumption of the throne meant warfare in heaven, Messiah-Michael with his angel-agents of the divine court suppressing the revolt of the dragon and his demons (v. 7) and casting Satan, accuser of the brethren, out of heaven, down from Har Magedon (vv. 8, 9). So began the execution of the messianic Angel's word of judgment: "Yahweh rebuke you, O Satan."

Comparing what is disclosed in the Old and New Testaments, it appears that prior to Christ's exaltation Satan was permitted some kind of access to the heavenly council and was suffered to pose in some way as prosecuting attorney against the saints before God's throne. But with the enthronement there of Christ as priest-king, prevailing in his advocacy of the cause of his own on the basis of his accomplished atonement, Satan's anomalous, attenuated tenure in the divine council was terminated—and his time until final doom was short (Rev 12:12).

D. *Law and Gospel:* Like the primeval curse pronounced on the serpent, which was at the same time the primal promise of salvation in Christ (Gen 3:15), so Messiah's rebuke of Satan in Zechariah 3 was tantamount to a verdict rendered in favor of the Joshua-community (vv. 4,5). For Satan's assault on God's throne came disguised as a feigned concern for the sanctity of heaven's holy court, a concern expressed in the form of accusations against the sinners God would welcome there. Similarly in Revelation 12, it is as a victory of the redeemed over their accuser (vv. 10,11) that the Lord's ejection of Satan from the heavenly court is celebrated.

In Revelation 12, the explanation of the triumph of the saints who overcome Satan and his demons is the blood of the lamb. Such is also the explanation for the rebuking of Satan and the dismissal of his charges in Zechariah 3. The principle governing the judicial decision and action of the Angel-Judge is revealed in his amplified repetition of the verdict-curse: "Yahweh who has chosen Jerusalem rebuke you; is not this a brand plucked out of the fire?" (v. 2b,c). Those whom Satan would have condemned were God's elect, and who shall lay anything to their charge (Rom 8:33a)? The principle that operates in their case is grace, sovereign grace, not works. They were chosen in Christ before the foundation of the world, foreordained unto adoption according to the good pleasure of God's will, to the praise of the glory of his grace bestowed on us in the beloved, in whom we have our redemption through his blood, the forgiveness of our trespasses (Eph 1:4-7). It is God that justifies; who is he that condemns (Rom 8:33b,34)?

In accusing the brethren Satan directs attention to their status in the first Adam, in whom they have transgressed the original covenant of works and become liable to its curse of death. In relation to that breakable covenant all are deserving of a verdict of condemnation and a sentence of expulsion from the holy garden of life and abandonment in the abyss of Hell. Satan would pretend that history was frozen in the situation produced by his success as tempter of the first Adam. He would ignore and would have the court ignore the divine decree announced immediately after the Fall of the first Adam, declaring God's eternal purpose of grace for a countless throng of elect and revealing the opening up of a new redemptive way to justification and life through a second Adam, a serpent-trampling Savior (Gen 3:15).

The story of the typological kingdom of Israel was an historical parable in which mankind under the covenant of works in Adam was represented by Israel under the law. For according to Jeremiah the Torah-covenant viewed as a grant of the land of Canaan to Israel for a temporal typical inheritance was another breakable works-arrangement, unlike the new covenant of grace to be made in the days to come (Jer 31:31). The apostle of that new covenant, the apostle of justification by faith, proclaimed justification through Christ from all things "from which you could not be justified by the law of Moses" (Acts 13:39). "That no man is justified by the law before God is evident," said Paul, "for, 'The righteous shall live by faith,' and the law is not of faith, but 'He that doeth them shall live in them'" (Gal 3:11,12). And again, "For if the inheritance is of the law, it is no more of promise" (Gal 3:18). It is the typological story of Israel's history under its covenant of works that provides the symbolism of the prophet's gospel for mankind in Zechariah 3.

The half-truth lie urged by Satan is expressed in that figurative idiom: Behold Joshua/Israel standing before the tribunal in filthy clothes, shamefully defiled transgressors of the Torah-covenant of works. Consider the exile—God himself repudiated Israel, drove them out of their inheritance, handed them over as captives to serve the enemy.

The Angel-Judge's rebuke of the accuser is also cast in that typological idiom: "Yahweh who has chosen Jerusalem rebuke you." He refers to the elect in Christ, the second Adam, as Jerusalem. To express their predestination to be a holy temple, builded together into a habitation of God in the Spirit (Eph 1:4; 2:21,22; cf. 1 Pet 2:5), he uses the Mosaic formula for God's selection of the location of the temple-city where his name would dwell under the old covenant (cf. e.g. Deut 12:5,11). Employing this typological metaphor, the Angel brings to light the decisive factor the accuser had concealed—God's eternal purpose of grace.

Before the foundations of the world a covenant was sealed in heaven. The Father covenanted to grant the Son a kingdom of glory as the just reward for the accomplishment of an earthly mission. Through incarnation the Son was to undertake the office of a second Adam and fulfill all righteousness in behalf of an elect people, securing for them justification and earning for them title to heaven's glory. By the obedience of this One, the many were to be made righteous (Rom 5:19) and Satan vanquished.

The Angel-Judge rejects the charge of Satan and proceeds to justify Joshua on the basis of what he, the messianic Angel, was one day to do. He would become flesh and perfectly discharge the office of second Adam in faithfulness to his covenant of works with the Father, thereby becoming the mediator of a covenant of grace to his redeemed. The salvation-kingdom covenanted unto him by the Father he would in turn covenant unto his people as his co-heirs (cf. Luke 22:29,30), conferring it on them as a gift of grace, received by faith. Satan is rebuked because he reduced the judicial picture to the dimension of the first Adam and ignored the second Adam. He pointed the finger at Joshua and discounted the Angel-Judge, the Redeemer-Advocate of Joshua-Jerusalem.

The fallacy of Satan's case against Joshua may also be analyzed from the perspective of the relationship of the law to the prior covenant with Abraham. When Paul identified the Torah-covenant as a works arrangement, "not of faith," he had to face the question whether it negated God's promissory commitments to Abraham. The apostle was eager to insist that the covenant of grace confirmed long before was not disannulled by the law so as to make the promise void (Gal 3:17). Satan, on the contrary, by identifying Joshua exclusively in terms of his filthy garments (i.e., his transgression of the law) insinuated an interpretation of the Mosaic covenant of works as overriding and abrogating the Abrahamic covenant.

In doing so, Satan was suppressing counter-evidence of the continuing validity of the program of grace. Though God had indeed cast off Israel for breaking the Mosaic covenant of works, when the appointed seventy years were completed (cf. Zech 1:12), he had regathered a remnant from exile in remembrance of his covenant with Abraham (Lev 26:42; cf. 2 Kgs 13:23) and with a view to the true fulfillment of that covenant in the eventual coming of Christ from Israel as the promised seed of Abraham. This act of restoration from the Babylonian captivity was in fact a prophetic portrayal at the typological level of the promised antitypical restoration of the elect to covenant fellowship with God as a heavenly kingdom of priests and holy nation, the fruit of the redemptive accomplishment of the second Adam.

What Satan would conceal, the Angel-Judge cited as telling evidence: "Is not this a brand plucked from the fire?" (Zech 3:2). From the consuming curse of the exile-judgment God had saved a remnant, like the survivors of the fiery overthrow of Sodom and Gomorrah (cf. Amos 4:11). That divine act of redemption attested to the truth that a principle of sovereign grace was operating in the trial of Joshua as the decisive factor that must result in a verdict of justification.

The accusing serpent, he with the power of death (Heb 2:14), was overcome by divine rebuke because the messianic Servant would give his life as a ransom, the One for the many (Matt 20:28; Mark 10:45), to redeem them from the lake of fire, the second death (Rev 2:10,11; 12:11; 20:6). Joshua overcame in judgment because of the atoning blood of the Lamb, the priestly self-sacrifice to be offered unto God by the Christ of whom the high priest was a type (Zech 3:4-10), the Judge before whom he stood (Zech 3:1,3; 2 Cor 5:10).

II. THE RE-INVESTITURE OF JOSHUA

A. *Reckoning of Righteousness.*

1. *Removal of Sins:* Zech 3:3 goes with the preceding verses. It repeats the opening statement that Joshua was standing before the Angel of the Lord (v. 1a), adding the alarming detail that he appeared at that awesome tribunal in filthy garments. By thus indicating what the basis was for Satan's accusations (v. 1b), verse 3 underscores the wonder of God's elective grace revealed in his rejection of those charges (v. 2). But verse 3 also belongs with what follows, for the clothing imagery it introduces is continued in vv. 4ff. in the symbolic portrayal of the happy consequences of the Angel's rebuke of the adversary: the removal of Joshua's offending garb (v. 4) and

his reclothing in priestly vestments (v. 5).

The process of Joshua's justification and reinstatement is patterned after the ceremony prescribed in the Law for the installation of Aaron and his sons as priestly guardians of the tabernacle. (Exodus 28-29 contains the relevant legislation; Exodus 39-40 and Leviticus 8 narrate the event.) Included in the ritual in both cases are the elements of divine choice, cleansing, clothing-crowning, and charism. Moreover, the setting of the two transactions is the same, for Aaron's consecration took place at the tent of meeting, the earthly projection of the heavenly court. It is then from this distinctly priestly perspective that Zechariah 3 presents the drama of man's salvation in Christ and interprets humanity's historical role and eschatological goal.

Concerning the high priesthood it is written: "No man taketh this honor unto himself, but he that is called of God, as was Aaron" (Heb 5:4). The Pentateuchal directives for the order of Levitical priests begin with a declaration of God's choice of Aaron and his sons to be peculiarly his own and to draw near and minister unto him (Exod 28:1; 29:44). Similarly in the trial scene in Zechariah 3, the Angel's favorable verdict, which results in Joshua's reinstatement as high priest, is traced to God's choice of Joshua/Jerusalem (v. 2).

In the performance of his office the priest finds himself standing at the place of judgment. For the temple is God's royal court where he is enthroned between the cherubim. Ministering there the priest comes under the direct scrutiny of the holy Judge of heaven and earth. Freedom from sin is therefore a prime prerequisite of the priestly calling. Such a state of righteousness characterized Adam at his creation, qualifying him for his priestly role at the holy mount in Eden. In his unfallen condition, without sin, he could stand unthreatened before the Glory-Presence and behold the beatific vision in rapturous delight and adoration. In the post-Fall world, priestly vocation requires first of all a restoration of righteousness to the sinner by the removing of the guilty stains which would otherwise prove his fiery undoing when he stood before God's face.

Accordingly, the regulations for the installation of the chosen Aaron and his sons as priests stipulated that Moses, having brought them to the entrance of the council tent, must first of all wash them with water (Exod 29:4; 40:12; cf. Lev 8:6). This ablution was a juridical rite symbolizing pardon of transgressions rather than subjective purification. Psalm 51 illustrates this kind of washing. There the plea to be washed (v. 2 [4]) is preceded by the petition that transgressions be blotted out, erased from the criminal record (v. 1 [3]), and it is followed by a confession of transgressions (vv. 3,4a [5,6a]), all anticipating the divine tribunal (v. 4b [6b]). Similarly in the lawsuit of Isa 1:15-18, the washing to which the covenant breakers are summoned is a forensic cleansing from the crimson stains of their blood-filled hands and from their scarlet sins, a cleansing that will lead to the verdict of the Lord, their Judge, that they are whiter than snow (cf. Ps 51:7 [9]).

The regulations for the Levitical priesthood also provided for a continuing ritual of cleansing from sins. In the instructions concerning the brass laver located between the altar and the tent of meeting, it was commanded that whenever Aaron and his sons were to minister at the altar or enter the holy tent they were to resort to the laver to wash their hands and feet, lest they die (Exod 30:17-21; 40:30-32). Within the schema of the tabernacle's cosmological symbolism the laver represented the waters of the heavenly sea, which, flowing from the throne of God, are the instrument of divine judgment ordeal (cf. Rev 15:1).[13] They function as a curse, becoming a flood to wipe out life from the earth or a river of fire to consume the beast and the little horn. They also function as a blessing, taking the form of a river of life that makes glad the city of God, watering the trees of life whose leaves are for the healing of the nations in the eternal Eden. At the exodus these judgment waters performed both functions, destroying the Egyptian army but delivering the chosen, priestly nation of Israel. Paul identified these judicial waters of the exodus as a baptism (1 Cor 10:2), reflecting the fact that baptism symbolizes the undergoing of a judgment ordeal. The waters of baptism are a death passage with forensic significance. Thus, for those who by faith undergo baptismal death in Christ's baptism-crucifixion, baptism is unto the remission of sins (Acts 2:38; cf. Mark 1:4; Luke 3:3).[14] Such was the meaning of the washing of the Levitical priests at the brazen laver. It was a forensic baptism, signifying the judicial clearing of the record, the pardoning of the evil deeds of the hands which must minister at the altar, the forgiving of the evil paths trodden by the feet which must enter the house of God. And the legal ground of the judicial pardon was Christ's atoning sacrifice in the baptism of his death (Luke 12:50), typified in the sacrifices offered on the altar next to the laver.

There was an alternative ritual of purification in which uncleanness was symbolized by dirty clothing (cf. Isa 64:6; Rev 3:4), with laundering as the usual means of purification. When the Israelites were being constituted a holy kingdom of priests at Sinai, they were sanctified for the epiphany on the third day by the washing of their garments (Exod 19:10,14). Also, the cleansing of the Levites for their sacred service included the laundering of their clothes (Num 8:7,21), as did the ritual of restoration for various specific instances of defilement (cf., e.g., Lev 11:25; 14:8,9; 16:26,28; Num 19:7ff.). The plea for cleansing in Ps 51:2 (4) uses a verb (*kbs*) that normally denotes the washing of clothes rather than the bathing of the body. It is this sartorial alternative that is found in Zechariah 3. The soiled clothing of Joshua serves as the symbolic equivalent of the defiled flesh of Aaron and his sons in the priestly installation ceremony on which the Zechariah 3 transaction is patterned. By the same token, the removal of Joshua's soiled clothes—a variant of the laundering treatment—is the equivalent of the washing of the body which was the first step in the ceremony prescribed for the consecration of the priests.

The cleansing of Joshua clearly has forensic significance. Removal of his offending clothes answers to the rejection of Satan's accusations and therefore symbolizes the clearing of all recorded offenses from his judicial transcript. Explaining the act of divestiture, the Angel of Yahweh tells Joshua: "See, I have caused your iniquity to pass from you" (v. 4b). The verb *h‘br* is used here in the sense attested in passages dealing with the forgiveness of the sins of king David (2 Sam 12:13; 24:10; 1 Chr 21:8) and of Job (Job 7:21).[15]

Similar to the installation procedures of both Leviticus 8 and Zechariah 3 is Isaiah's inauguration to prophetic office (Isaiah 6). The setting is the heavenly court (vv. 1,2) and again the dilemma is that of the unclean human who finds himself in the presence of the holy Lord of glory (vv. 3-5). As in Zech 3:4,5 the cleansing, effected by applying a purificatory stone to the prophet's unclean mouth, is carried out by an angelic agent (vv. 6,7a). Once again the cleansing is judicial, explained by the assurance: "Your iniquity is taken away and your sin is atoned for" (v. 7b). And as the priests' laver-cleansing was based on atoning altar-sacrifice, so here the expiatory stone is obtained from the altar, which means that this cleansing too is grounded on sacrificial atonement. In the course of Isaiah's prophetic ministry he would eventually identify the suffering Servant of the Lord as the one who would accomplish this cleansing sacrifice. Likewise in Zechariah 3 attention is directed to this future messianic priest-sacrifice, the Servant-Branch of whom

Joshua was a type (v. 8).

The key features we have noted in the episodes involving Aaron and Joshua are met again in the vision of Rev 7:11-17. Induction into priestly ministry, the heavenly court setting, the symbolism of priestly clothing, and judicial washing accomplished through atoning sacrifice—all these elements come together in the imagery of the redeemed myriads, white-robed, standing before the throne and the Lamb, appointed to serve God in his temple day and night, and identified as those who "washed their robes and made them white in the blood of the Lamb" (v. 14).

Strange detergent, staining blood. But such is the forensic chemistry of the justification of God's chosen priesthood. Jesus, lamb of God, must pour out his blood in the baptism-judgment of his crucifixion that there might be a baptismal laver filled with blood, a fountain opened where sinners lose all their guilty stains (cf. Zech 13:1). By this blood the accuser of the brethren is overcome in the court of heaven (Rev 12:10,11). "Unto him who loves us and has freed us from our sins by his blood and has made us to be a kingdom, priests to his God and Father, to him be glory and dominion for ever and ever. Amen" (Rev 1:5b,6; cf. 5:9,10). This is the doxological climax of the biblical testimony concerning God's Servant, the bruised and bleeding but serpent-crushing seed of the woman promised in Eden (Gen 3:15); the coming Shiloh of Jacob's blessing on Judah, with whom the prophecy associates a donkey slain to ratify covenants and a mysterious washing of garments in the blood of grapes (Gen 49:10,11).

The trajectory of judicial ablutions along which the vision of Zechariah 3 finds a niche thus extends from Genesis to Revelation.

2. *Robes of Righteousness:* In the cleansing rituals that involve the washing of garments the very act that purges away the dirt produces the clean robes (cf. Rev 7:14). But in Zechariah 3, where the dirty clothing is removed rather than laundered, a second, separate step is needed to complete the process—an act of reclothing. It is the Angel of the Lord who continues to exercise the sovereign initiative in this further action. Explaining to Joshua the meaning of the removal of his offending garments (v. 4b), he appends the promise that he will reclothe him in new apparel (v. 4c).[16] As Zechariah watches the visionary drama unfold and recognizes that the new garments are high priestly vestments, he interjects the prayer that the high priest's mitre in particular be placed on Joshua's head (v. 5a).[17] A statement that

this specific act of crowning took place (v. 5b) is followed by a general summary of the re-investiture (v. 5c) and a concluding observation that the Angel of the Lord stood there (v. 5d).

Since the divestiture and investiture of Joshua are complementary acts, *maḥălāṣôt*, the rare term used for the new clothes, must denote something opposite to the soiled garb it replaces. We know that it is the regalia of the high priest in which Joshua is being robed. This plus the fact that in its only other appearance *maḥălāṣôt* refers to elegant finery (Isa 3:22) suggest that this term denotes garments of a special, ornate character that would be kept in mint condition. As such the *maḥălāṣôt* serve here as an apt antonym to dirty clothing. Significantly, the one specific item singled out for special attention, the head-dress, is described as a "clean" mitre.

The complementary relationship of the divestiture and investiture also provides an index to the precise theological significance of the reclothing. Removal of the unclean clothing symbolized the legal blotting out of sins, the rebuttal of Satan's accusations, forgiveness, the imputation of the sins of God's elect to Christ. As the complementary act to that, the reclothing will signify the judicial declaration of their righteousness, justification through the imputation to them of the righteousness of the messianic Servant, the righteousness of his active obedience in fulfillment of the probationary task of vanquishing the serpent. Chosen Joshua's reclothing was his vindication as the one who was in the right in the sight of the heavenly Judge in the case of Satan against God's elect. "I will greatly rejoice in Yahweh, my soul shall be joyful in my God; for he has clothed me with the garments of salvation, he has put on me a robe of righteousness, as a bridegroom adorns himself like a priest" (Isa 61:10; cf. Ps 45:13,14 [14,15]; Isa 52:1; Matt 22:11,12).

B. *Re-creation in the Glory Image.* From the entire context it is evident that the reclothing of Joshua is a ritual of reinstatement as high priest;[18] his new clean clothes are high priestly vestments. While the reclothing viewed as the complement of the symbolic removal of sins signifies the reckoning of righteousness, a further soteric grace is discovered in the symbolism of reinvestiture when we focus on the nature of the new clothes as the official regalia of high priesthood.

The production of these vestments (as recounted in Exodus 28 and 39) is the second of a remarkable pair of replications of a divine archetype. The archetype is the Glory-Spirit, the heavenly Glory-temple whose earthly manifestation is the Shekinah. Replication of this Spirit-Archetype is a major motif in the biblical record of the original creation process. It was the likeness of the Spirit-temple that was reproduced in the structuring of the heaven and earth as a cosmic temple (cf. Gen 1; 2; Isa 66:1) and again in the fashioning of mankind in the image of God's Glory.[19] This phenomenon recurs in redemptive history. The forming of Israel as a priestly nation at the exodus is a re-creation event. The Glory-Spirit of Genesis 1:2 appears again, hovering over Israel in the *tōhû*-like wilderness (cf. Deut 32:10,11), and presently, by the fiat-command of God, the tabernacle is brought into existence, a cosmic temple in symbolic miniature, a replica of the Glory-Spirit constructed according to the archetypal design revealed to Moses on the mountain of the Glory-theophany.[20]

Next in the biblical account, following immediately upon the directions for the construction of the tabernacle (Exodus 25-27), are the prescriptions for Aaron's sacred garments and his investiture (Exodus 28-29; cf. 39:1-13). And when examined these high priestly vestments turn out to be a scaled down, sartorial version of the tabernacle—and thus another replication of the Glory-Archetype.[21] Their likeness to the tabernacle can be traced in the aspects of their materials, form, function, and general purpose. Their identity as a replication of the Glory-theophany is most strikingly displayed in the impression of radiance they conveyed, the effect of their flame-colored materials with the gleam of the precious gem-stones and gold. It was indeed the explicit design, stated at the beginning and close of the prescriptions concerning them (Exod 28:2 and 40), that they were "for glory and beauty" and both of these terms are elsewhere applied to the Glory-theophany (cf. Isa 4:2; 28:5). By commanding into being the figure of the high priest so adorned, the Lord was, in symbolic idiom, re-creating man in the divine image. The exodus history repeated the creation history in its reproduction of the Glory-Spirit likeness in both the cosmos and humanity.

In the ordination of Aaron the putting on of the holy garments followed as the second step after the washing at the laver (Exod 40:12,13; Lev 8:6-9). Correspondingly in Zechariah 3 the removal of the filthy garb (the equivalent of the laver lustration) is followed by Joshua's investiture, which must then be understood, like that of Aaron, as a putting on of the image of God.

To be created in the divine image includes, ultimately, three glory components present in the Glory-Spirit-Archetype. One is the ethical glory of purity and truth. That is the component Paul focuses on when he adopts this metaphor of putting on God's likeness like clothing (Eph 4:24; Col 3:10). Interestingly, in the apostle's adaptation of the theme, the putting on of the clothing of holiness follows, as in Zechariah 3, a putting off of unfit clothing (Eph 4:22; Col 3:9).

A second component of the image of God is dominion comparable to that exercised by God and the Elohim-like angels of the divine council (cf. Ps 82:1,6). Agreeably, Joshua's re-investiture was an appointment to the office of the high priest, which afforded admission into the holy of holies, with a place in God's court. This is mentioned in the commission given to Joshua: he was to govern God's courts and to be given access among the angel-attendants of the heavenly King (Zech 3:7). Of the high priest's vestments it was the mitre in particular that expressed the royal, governmental aspect of his office. The terms used for this turban are also used for a royal diadem (cf. Isa 28:5; 62:3; Ezek 21:26 [31]). Special attention is called to the mitre by Zechariah's request for its inclusion in the reclothing of Joshua (v. 5). And this singling out of the mitre prepares for the climactic role to be played later in the vision by this majestic head-dress, or more specifically by the golden consecration "stone" affixed to its forefront and most distinctly imparting to the mitre the nature of a royal crown (v. 9; cf. Zech 6:11). Joshua's re-investiture proclaims that all who are created anew in God's image are crowned with the dignity of dominion; they live and reign with Christ.

The third component of the Glory likeness is the visible glory of transfiguration, an outward luminosity befitting and bespeaking the lucid purity and integrity within, a physical radiance that manifests the majesty of regal station. This visual glory, not included with the other two elements in the original creation endowment of man, is an eschatological honor. It is the Spirit-wrought glorification the redeemed will experience when they behold Jesus, arrayed with the Glory-Spirit, coming in the clouds of heaven. It was portrayed by the dazzling beauty of Aaron's holy garments. In the vision of Zechariah 3, Joshua, by being re-invested with the radiant high priestly regalia, is transfigured into the brilliant Glory-likeness of the messianic Angel of the Glory-Presence before whom he stands.

Our introductory comments on Zechariah's fourth vision noted its rootage in Genesis 3. Another link is the investiture motif. There too we read of human defilement, registered in a sense of shameful nakedness, and of a divine covering of the guilty pair with skin clothing (Gen 3:21), symbolizing the restoration of the image of God.[22] The term for "skin" is part of a three-cornered pun, also involving the term "naked" used for Adam and Eve (Gen 2:25) and the term "subtle" used for the serpent (Gen 3:1). By the paronomasia it is suggested that as a result of the Fall the culprits had lost their original likeness to the Glory-Spirit (cf. Gen 1:26,27) and had taken on the image of the devil, but by God's grace were to be renewed in likeness to their Creator. The holiness component of the *imago Dei* is prominent (cf. Rev 3:18; 16:15), but the glory of royal-priestly dominion is also present. Priestly office and function had been given to man; he was to be the guardian of God's sanctuary-garden (Gen 2:15). This office he had forfeited by the loss of original righteousness so that he had to be expelled from the sanctuary, his priestly task now taken over by the cherubim (Gen 3:24; cf. Exod 20:26; 28:42). In this context the act of clothing in the divinely provided garments of skin takes on the nature of a re-investiture with priestly status and dominion.

Clothing made of animal skin had to be procured through sacrificial death; an act of atonement was the judicial basis for the priestly reinstatement and restoration of divine image and righteousness. From the nearby context we also learn that it was the messianic seed of the woman who would undergo the necessary substitutionary, sacrificial suffering (Gen 3:15). Only at the cost of the bruising of his heel would he trample the head of the serpent. Only by his atoning death for the sins of the rest of the woman's seed, the Joshua-people of Zechariah 3, does the Servant silence the serpent. Only through this rebuking of Satan by the Messiah is the way opened for Joshua to be re-invested as high priest and to enter once more into the holy courts of the Lord.

Several features of the sartorial symbolism under survey are curiously combined in Ezekiel's marriage allegory of God's covenanting with Israel at the exodus (Ezekiel 16). The Lord finds Israel in a helpless state, cast out and naked (vv. 6,7). He washes and anoints her and covers her nakedness (vv. 8,9). He clothes her in bridal adornments, which are designed to resemble in a variety of details both Aaron's vestments and the tabernacle. And so the bride is fashioned into an ectypal image of the archetypal Glory of the Groom. Her beauty, the Lord declares, was perfect, by virtue of his placing his splendor on her (v. 14).[23]

Similarly, in the allegory of the messianic king and his bride-people in Psalm 45 special attention is given to the bride's finery (vv. 13,14 [14,15]), the terms for which are elsewhere in the Old Testament mostly confined to descriptions of the priests' regalia and the tabernacle. A corresponding emphasis on the apparel of the king (vv. 3,8 [4,9]) suggests that the royal splendor is a paradigmatic glory that is replicated in the bride's raiment. Reinforcing this is a further parallel: praise of the king's surpassing beauty (the verb yph, v. 2 [3]; cf. Isa 33:17) is echoed by a reference to the beauty of the bride (cognate noun, yŏpî, v. 11 [12]; cf. Ezek 16:13,14). Since the king is divine (cf. v. 6 [7]), this bridal investiture is a metaphor for re-creation in the image of God.

Originating in Gen 3:21 and surfacing in various genres in Pentateuchal law, the psalms, Zechariah 3 and elsewhere in the prophets, the theme of priestly re-investiture in the image of God continues into the New Testament, culminating in the Apocalypse, where it is a fundamental motif. Towards the close of that book it appears combined with nuptial imagery, as in Psalm 45 and Ezekiel 16. The church-bride, ready for the marriage of the Lamb, is arrayed in fine priestly linen (Rev 19:7,8). Other details of priestly dress are interwoven in the description of the bridal adornments in Revelation 21 and 22. As seen in this final portrait, the bride-church appears clothed in priestly glory, a replica of the likeness of Christ as he is delineated in the opening epiphany, with transfigured high priestly robes, invested with the Glory-Spirit (Rev 1:13-16).[24]

The account of Joshua's reclothing concludes: "and the Angel of Yahweh was standing" (Zech 3:5d). This verb (ᶜmd), a common technical term for participation in various roles in judicial procedures, had already been used for Joshua (vv. 1,3), Satan (v. 1), and the angel attendants (v. 4, cf v. 7). The first vision, which corresponds to the fourth in many ways including the theme of renewal in the divine image, speaks of the messianic figure as "standing"—in the midst of the myrtles (God's people) over against the deep (the hostile powers).[25] Commander of the angelic hosts (cf. Josh 5:13), he was present with his people as their Immanuel-Advocate and that meant vindication and victory for them while it spelled the devil's doom (cf. Exod 14:19; Zech 14:4). Similarly the reference to the Angel's "standing" at the close of Joshua's re-investiture in Zechariah 3 accents the dominance of his presence and the decisiveness of his advocacy for Joshua's justification and reinstatement. With respect to Satan, the messianic Angel's "standing" there at the end of the judicial encounter proclaims that the Servant tramples the serpent and is the victor in final judgment.[26]

III. REVELATION OF THE MESSIAH

A. *Proposal of a Celestial Priesthood.* According to the Pentateuchal accounts, after the installation ceremonies of washing, putting on the holy vestments, and anointing, Aaron was given instructions concerning his cultic duties (cf. Exod 29:38ff.). So it is in Zechariah 3. After the re-investiture of Joshua the divine Angel addressed to him a solemn charge, recommissioning him to his high priestly functions (vv. 6,7).

Joshua's duties are expressed as conditions whose fulfillment would bring high privilege and honor. The transaction was tantamount to a covenant of grant proposal, offering special reward in recognition of faithful services to be rendered. Joshua's recommissioning took this form because the high priestly order epitomized the Torah-covenant with Israel and therefore, like it, was informed by the works principle. As previously observed,[27] the Mosaic Covenant was indeed a covenant of works at the level of Israel's typological kingdom. In that respect it recapitulated the original covenant of works with Adam. Hence the proposal made to Joshua was also after the pattern of that covenant of creation with its proposal of a grant of heightened blessings to be merited by Adam's obedient discharge of the stipulated services, particularly the priestly guardianship of God's sanctuary.

There is disagreement as to how many of the five clauses in Zech 3:7 after the messenger formula, "Thus says Yahweh of hosts," describe the conditional duties. Clearly the first two do so, but the question is whether the next two belong with them in the protasis or with the fifth clause in the apodosis. In other covenantal formulations with similar stipulations a change of person in the subject of the actions marks the transition from obligations imposed or undertaken to benefits promised, or vice versa (cf., e.g., Gen 17:1-21; Deut 26:16-19). In Zech 3:7 the second person subject continues through the first four clauses (underscored by an emphatic "you" at the beginning of the third clause), changing to the first person only in the fifth clause (cf. Gen 17:9). On the other hand, evidence for starting the apodosis with the third clause is found in a similar syntactic construction in Psalm 132. This psalm abounds in parallels to Zechariah 3 in theme, terminology, and imagery; in fact the passage in question (v. 12) is, like Zechariah 3:7, part of a divine commitment involving a charge to a theocratic appointee (protasis) and a promise of perpetual tenure (apodosis). And the introductory particle used to introduce the apodosis in Ps 132:12 also introduces the third and fourth clauses in Zech 3:7.

To walk in God's ways and keep his charge (the duties mentioned in clauses one and two) are at times equivalent to the general requirement of keeping the covenant (cf. Deut 8:6; 10:12; 26:17; 28:9; 30:16; Mal 3:14), but they could refer here specifically to the guardian function of the priesthood (cf. Num 3:7). Judicial governance and guardianship of the temple complex are clearly described in the third and fourth clauses, and even if regarded here as promised honors (i.e., as part of the apodosis) they are still indicative of the functions of the office with which Joshua was being charged. Like Adam's probation mission in Eden (Gen 2:15), Joshua's commissioning set him on guard against the hostile incursion of the evil one into God's holy house. He must stand against Satan's challenge at Har Magedon.

As the reward for fighting the good priestly warfare against the devil, God promised: "I will grant you access among these who stand by" (Zech 3:7f.). This is the acme of honor even if the royal privileges of the third and fourth clauses are also construed as part of the promised grant. The word translated "access" (derived from *hlk*, "walk") seems more literally to mean a passageway or entryway (cf. Ezek 42:4). To be accorded entrée among the angelic attendants standing by the Lord is to be admitted into the heavenly court, into the very presence of God and a close, confidential relationship with him. That prerogative was the supreme privilege vouchsafed to prophets. Zechariah was experiencing this exalted privilege as he received the night visions. But on the occasion of his entering the holy of holies the high priest also enjoyed this entrée into the presence of the Lord enthroned between the cherubim standing by the ark-throne. Malachi speaks of faithful priests walking (*hlk*) with God (Mal 2:6; cf. Mic 6:8; Gen 5:22; 6:9).

The final fulfillment of the Angel's promise to Joshua is found in the New Jerusalem, the celestial city constituted a temple by the presence of the Lord God enthroned in the midst of the heavenly hosts (Revelation 21-22). There God tabernacles with his people, who (as we have seen) are portrayed as a bride-priest, the wife of the Lamb, her bridal garments priestly vestments, the ultimate realization of redemptive renewal in the image of the Lord of Glory.[28] In a word, the Joshua-priesthood was promised heaven. There God's holy servants dwell eternally in the secret place of the Most High, under the shadow of the Almighty. There the longing spirit finds rest and says "Amen and amen" to the psalmist's word of faith, hope and love: "Afterwards you will conduct me into your Council; yea afterwards you will take me up into your Glory. Having you, what else need I in heaven; having you, what more do I desire on earth?" (Ps 73:24,25).

Heaven, however, was not to be attained through the Mosaic covenant of works. Israel, like Adam, failed to fulfill the stipulated probationary conditions; the Aaronic priesthood, embodied in Joshua in the days of Zechariah, did not faithfully discharge its commissioned duties. The proposed grant was forfeited and the curse of the covenant was incurred instead. Adam was driven out of Eden's garden-sanctuary; Israel, with its priesthood, was expelled from its symbolic paradise. Heaven must be won by another, a promised one yet to come, mediator of a new covenant of grace.

B. Prophecy of the Coming Day.

1. *Joshua: Sign of the Servant:* The covenant of works proposal to Joshua lifts our thoughts above to the Father's covenantal proposal to send his Son to replace the Aaronic priesthood and to be a second Adam. This Son-Servant would be an obedient Adam, keeping his covenant of works, faithfully performing his priestly charge, and thereby he would merit for himself and those the Father gave him the promised place of acceptance, audience, and access in heaven. And in God's typological arrangements under the old covenant, Joshua, high priest of Israel, was a sign of that coming Servant of the Lord.

"Hear now, Joshua the high priest—truly you and your colleagues who sit before you are a prophetic sign [literally, men of a sign]—behold, I will bring forth my Servant the Branch" (Zech 3:8). The announcement proper, marked by "behold," is that God will send the Servant (v. 8c), while the statement about the symbolic nature of Joshua (v. 8b) is parenthetical. Yet their logical relationship is that the prophetic announcement identifies what Joshua symbolizes: he is a prototypal portent, a type, of the coming messianic Servant.

More specifically, the sign consists of Joshua—the high priest consecrated and commissioned to his office (vv. 4-7)—presiding in a judicial council.[29] Whether or not the colleagues are priests, their sitting before him indicates they are under his authority. A passage in the Qumran document,

The Manual of Discipline, dealing with protocol in various communal situations, insists on the presence and prerogatives of a priest in these gatherings and describes the others as sitting in his presence (IQS vi,4-6; cf. 2 Kgs 4:38; 6:1; Ezek 8:1). The term "sit" in Zech 3:8 is probably used in the sense of sit in judgment (cf. Exod 18:13,14; Isa 28:6; Dan 7:9,10; Ps 122:5; Ruth 4:4). It is the royal-judicial aspect of the high priesthood that is prominent here as it was in the charge to Joshua (v. 7). It is Joshua the priest-king, invested with authority over God's courts, who is a prophetic type of the coming One.

Corresponding to the dual priest-king office of Joshua is the compound designation of his antitype, "my Servant the Branch" (v. 8), a dual title that identifies him as both priest and king. The mission of the antitypical, messianic priest-king would be set in motion by God: "Behold, I will bring forth" (literally, "cause to come;" cf. Jer 32:42). This note of God's sovereign initiation was already sounded in the earliest disclosure concerning the Messiah and his salvation: "The Lord God said unto the serpent ... I will put enmity" (Gen 3:14,15)

The designation "my Servant" summarizes the sublime Isaianic message of the suffering Servant of the Lord. The Zech 3:8 announcement, "behold, I bring forth my Servant" recalls the introductory "Behold, my Servant" in Isa 42:1 and 52:13. As delineated in Isaiah's climactic passage (52:13-53:12), the Servant's ministry is priestly: he presents an offering for sin, he sprinkles many nations, he makes intercession for transgressors. Central to the portrait is his passive obedience unto death during his state of humiliation as he fills the role of priest and sacrifice. But there is a second stage in his history. The reward for his priestly service is highest exaltation; the Servant-priest is crowned with royal glory (52:13; 53:12; cf. 49:7). He is a priest-king.

The name-title, "the Branch" (*ṣemaḥ*) brings out more distinctly the royal dimension of the Servant title to which it is joined in Zech 3:8. For this title encapsulates the teaching of previous prophets concerning Messiah as scion of the stock of king David, son of Jesse. Isaiah used such plant imagery: "A shoot shall come forth from the stump of Jesse and a branch (*nēṣer*) from his roots will bear fruit" (Isa 11:1). Again, "the branch (*ṣemaḥ*) of Yahweh will become beauty [a term applied to a royal crown in Isa 28:5] and glory for the remnant" (Isa 4:2). Two similar passages in Jeremiah, each beginning "Behold the days come" and prophesying of the advent of the messianic king of David's dynasty, call him the Branch (Jer 23:5,6; 33:14-17). In Jer 33:15 the metaphor is verbal: "I [Yahweh] will cause a shoot of righteousness [i.e., a legitimate royal heir] to shoot forth (ṣmḥ) unto David" (cf. Zech 6:12).[30] Similarly, Ps 132:17 (as customarily rendered) presents God's promise that in fulfillment of his covenant oath to David he will make a horn sprout forth (ṣmḥ) to him.

Combining the priestly Servant and royal Branch titles was natural enough since they overlap conceptually in various ways. We have observed that Isaiah's suffering Servant is at last elevated to highest royal honor. Like the Davidic Branch his origins are as a tender plant and root out of dry ground (Isa 53:2). Messianic "David" is also called "my servant" (Ezek 34:23; cf. Pss 78:70; 89:3,20). Attributed to both Servant and Branch are endowment with the Spirit, wisdom and success, deliverance of those bound in prison and darkness, and the bringing of salvation to Israel and all nations and of judgment and righteousness to the earth (Isa 42:1-4, 6,7; 49:6-12; 52:13; 53:11; 61:1-4 and Isa 11:2-4,11; Jer 23:5,6; 33:15,16). The fact is that the two titles refer to one and the same individual.

The New Testament bears witness that this combination of suffering priest and righteous king seen in Zechariah 3 (and 6:9-15; 9:9-11; 11; and 13:7) and elsewhere in the Old Testament (notably Psalm 110 and Dan 9:24-27) finds its realization in Jesus the Christ. At his baptism the Father's voice identified him in a blend of phraseology drawn from God's inaugural decree to his King-Son in Ps 2:7 and his word of approbation to his Servant in Is 42:1 (Matt 3:17; Mark 1:11; Luke 3:22). Jesus himself summarized all that was spoken of him in the law, the prophets, and the psalms in terms of this dual identity and function—the sufferings and the glory that would follow (Luke 24:25-27,44-47). And Jesus, identifying himself as the majestic Son of Man of Daniel 7 declared repeatedly that the Son of Man must undergo sufferings to ransom the many, as was foretold of the Servant in Isaiah 53. As seen by John in apocalyptic vision (Rev 5:5,6), Jesus was both the slain lamb (cf. Isa 53:7) and the lion of the tribe of Judah, the root of David (cf. Gen 49:8-10).

2. *The Stone: Seal of the Spirit:* A second "behold" (*kî hinnēh*) at the beginning of Zech 3:9 marks part two of the Angel's prophetic announcement. As in part one, a typological sign of what is predicted in the announcement proper is first introduced, viz., the stone.[31] A series of declarations follows concerning the antitype, the true once-for-all event.

Insertion of an additional "behold, I" in the midst of this series emphasizes the point that the Lord God is the author of the antitypical fulfillment of the stone's symbolism.

The relation of the sign-types in the two parts of the Angel's announcement (v. 8 and vv. 9,10) reflects the structure of the previous re-investiture ritual with its general symbol of the vestments as a whole but also its particular focus on the head-dress. Thus, in v. 8 the figure of the presiding Joshua harks back to the overall reclothing in v. 4 while the stone in v. 9 resumes (as we shall see) the special attention directed to the turban in v. 5. This relationship between the earlier and later portions of the vision and, in particular, the fact that the stone belongs to the symbolism of the reclothing is demonstrated by the last clause in v. 9. There the significance of the stone is expounded in terms of a divine removing of iniquity, a clear reference to v. 4 where the symbolism of Joshua's reclothing is explained in the same way. Once this relationship is recognized, along with the thoroughgoing dependence of the Zechariah 3 investiture procedure on the regulations for the installation of the high priest in Exodus 28 and 29, there should be no difficulty (the great variety of interpretations notwithstanding) in perceiving the identity of the stone.

Pursuing the suggested connection between the stone and the high priestly mitre placed on Joshua, we turn back then to the Exodus account of Aaron's investiture and discover that the unusual combination of images and ideas that expound the meaning of the stone in Zech 3:9 appears there in the legislation concerning the high priestly head-dress (Exod 28:4,36-38; 29:6; cf. 29:30,31; Lev 8:9).

On the forefront (mûl pĕnê) of the mitre was affixed (ntn, "give," Exod 29:6) a plaque of pure (tāhôr)[32] gold, called a "blossom" (ṣîṣ) as an ornamental flowering of the mitre. In the ancient Near East kings and gods, and they alone, are depicted wearing tiaras decorated on the front with blossom-shaped phylacteries. In Isa 28:1-5 ṣîṣ is used as a parallel to crown. Isaiah prophesies that the crown of Ephraim will be overthrown but in that day Yahweh of hosts will be a diadem of beauty for the remnant. This same prospect is presented in Ps 132:18, which foretells the blossoming (verb ṣîṣ) of the crown of the Messiah whom God makes to branch (verb ṣmḥ) from David's line. Such blossoms were carved on the walls and doors of God's royal house (1 Kgs 6:18,29,32,35). With its gem-like ṣîṣ, the mitre was a crown exhibiting the royal character of the high priestly office.

The golden plaque was also called a *nēṣer*, "consecration" and "crown" (as a sign of consecration). Its significance as an emblem of sanctification to God's service was spelled out in the inscription "Holy to Yahweh" which was engraved on it like the engravings of a signet-stone (Exod 28:36; 39:30). The mitre being placed on Aaron's head, its frontal diadem would be positioned on his forehead (Exod 28:38). There it must be whenever he came before God bearing the iniquity (*ʿāwōn*) of Israel's holy gifts, so that the Lord's eyes might fall at once on his holy seal of consecration, prerequisite for the acceptance of his priestly ministry.

Unmistakably it is this Exodus legislation concerning the golden plaque on the high priest's mitre that is the source on which Zech 3:9 draws and that provides the identification of the stone. The stone appertains to the high priest; it is something which "I [the Lord] have given before *ntn* with *lipnê*] Joshua." This may simply mean it was committed to Joshua's possession.[33] But the choice of words seems to reflect their use in the passages concerning the mitre-diadem, in which case the idea is that the stone was positioned over Joshua's forehead. There is then a natural connection to the next statement, "upon one stone will be seven eyes": the eyes of the Lord would look directly upon the stone on the forehead of the high priest standing before him. The identification of the seven eyes (not as seven facets of the stone or seven letters of its inscription or seven springs of water but) as the sevenfold Spirit of God is clear from Zech 4:10 and Rev 5:6. The one chosen stone was the focus of the full sevenfold divine concentration.

"Eyes of the king" was a title for certain officials in Persia and elsewhere whose duty was to be informants. Often they would be accusers, an imperial analogue of Satan. But in their general function of surveillance these royal officials provided a model to depict God's reconnaissance of the earth conducted through his angelic agents with a view to ordering all things for the good of his people (2 Chr 16:9; Ezra 5:5; cf. Zech 4:10; 1 Kgs 8:29; Ps 11:4; Jer 24:6; 1 Pet 3:12).[34] In Zechariah 3 the seven eyes of the Lord submit to the Angel-Judge a counter-report to that of Satan.[35] Satan's eyes fastened on Joshua's soiled garments but the seven eyes of Yahweh look on the stone on Joshua's forehead, the stone that wins acceptance before the throne in heaven.

In Zech 3:9 God's fastening his gaze on the stone on Joshua's forehead leads to the promise that he will remove the iniquity of the land in one day. This is the counterpart to the assurance given the similarly crowned Aaron of acceptance in his role of bearing iniquity in behalf of Israel. Further, God's declaration that he would engrave the stone's engraving corresponds to the engraving of Aaron's diadem-stone and was a promise that he would effect in Joshua the sanctification signified by the plaque's inscription, "Holy to Yahweh."

The use of *'eben*, "stone," for metal objects, gems and weights (cf., e.g., Zech 4:10; 5:8; Exod 25:7; 35:9) helps explain its use for the mitre plaque, an object of gold, in Zech 3:9. Noteworthy in view of the diadem nature of the plaque is the phrase "stones of a crown" in Zech 9:16. Also, the plaque was engraved and in the Exodus background of Zechariah 3 precious "stones" of the high priest's vestments are engraved too (cf. Exod 28:11,21; 39:6,14). Of special interest is the signet seal design of the plaque, for signet seals were usually precious stones. Evidence that the plaque was patterned after signet seals is the specification that its engraving be that of a signet seal (Exod 28:36; 39:30). Also, the plaque was suspended on a cord (Exod 28:37; 39:31), as was, for example, Judah's engraved signet seal (Gen 38:18,25). Further, the plaque's inscription, "Holy to Yahweh," expressed ownership, a function of signet-stones.[36]

Other data support our seeing signet-seal imagery in Zech 3:9 and at the same time suggest further reasons why the plaque was called a stone. Signet imagery was in vogue; just two months before Zechariah's night visions God's word through Haggai likened Zerubbabel to a signet (Hag 2:23). In Zechariah's own next vision he pictures Zerubbabel with a plumb stone in his hand (Zech 4:10), an object whose form (i.e., a stone hanging on a line) matched that of a signet-stone on its cord. (Was the symbolism of the golden plaque polyvalent, portraying the plumb line standard of holiness that prevailed in God's house[37] as well as the signet seal of sanctification and ownership?) In fact, in Zech 4:10 the seven eyes of the Lord look upon Zerubbabel's plumb stone as they do upon Joshua's stone in Zech 3:9, suggesting that the choice of "stone" in Zech 3:9 was with a view to calling attention to this parallelism between these two similar objects and thereby highlighting a paired set of priestly and royal typological symbols of the Messiah.

The identity of the stone as the signet-seal on the high priest's mitre explains Zechariah's zealous concern that this head-dress be bestowed on Joshua (Zech 3:5). For it was the Lord's seal of acceptance (Exod 28:38). It was a stamping of God's name (signet impressions being signatures) upon the forehead of his priestly servant, acknowledging him as his own personal possession, sanctified unto him.

In Pauline theology sealing is synonymous with the anointing of the Spirit (2 Cor 1:21,22; Eph 1:13; 4:30; 2 Tim 2:19). This sealing is a stamp of ownership which reserves believers unto the eschatological redemption (Eph 1:13,14).[38] Reflecting on this in 2 Tim 2:19, Paul quotes from Num 16:5, where the Aaronic priesthood is identified as belonging to the Lord, accepted as holy into his presence. Read in the light of this sealing with the Spirit, the placing of the signet-seal on Joshua in Zech 3:9 fills out the ritual pattern of high priestly installation with the act of anointing, climactic in the ritual of Exodus 28 and 29.[39] With this symbol of Spirit-anointing on Joshua's head, the messianic typology of high priestly investiture is completed. Joshua stands before us as a prismatic sign of the Anointed One, Messiah the Servant-Branch, Christ our priest-king.

The imagery of the sealing of God's people for priestly service by the stamping of God's name upon their foreheads reappears in the Book of Revelation (7:3; 14:1; 22:4). The connection between the sealing and the name is established by the fact that the same ones who receive a seal on their foreheads in 7:3 are said to have the name of the Lamb and his Father on their foreheads in 14:1 (cf. 22:4).[40] Those so marked by God are his "servants" (7:3; 22:3), "purchased for God" (14:4). The priestly nature of their service is plain—they stand before his throne and see his face (14:3; 22:4).

A further point of contact between the sealing with God's name in the Apocalypse and the stone in Zech 3:9 is that such sealing is equivalent to re-creation in the image of the Glory-Spirit.[41] "The equivalence of the bearing of God's name and the bearing of God's image appears strikingly in Rev 22:4. Here, in the midst of the description of the glorified covenant community, renewed after the image of the Lord, it is said: 'They will see his face and his name will be on their foreheads.' This marks the fulfillment of Christ's promise to incorporate the overcomer in his temple as a pillar and to 'write on him the name of my God, and the name of the city of my God, the New Jerusalem which comes down out of heaven from my God, and my new name' (Rev 3:12). The church's bearing of Christ's new name is exponential of its new nature as the new city-temple, the priest-bride arrayed in tabernacle-glory, the image of the Glory-Spirit-Lord, the glory of the bridegroom-Son. Behind the imagery of Rev 22:4 are the figures of Moses and Aaron. Aaron bore on his forehead the name of the Lord inscribed on the crown on the front of the priestly mitre. The very countenance of Moses was transfigured into a reflective likeness of the Glory-Face, the Presence-Name of God, when God talked with him 'mouth to mouth' (Num 12:8) out of the Glory-cloud. As the Name and the Glory are alike designations of the Presence of God in the theophanic cloud, so both name and glory describe the reflected likeness of God. To say that the overcomers in the New Jerusalem bear the name of Christ on their forehead is to say that they reflect the glory of Christ, which is to say that they bear the image of the glorified Christ."[42]

Within the high priestly investiture symbolism the stone, the name of God sealed on Joshua's forehead, is the supreme sign of renewal in the glory-image of the Spirit. It is the type par excellence of restoration to royal priesthood with dominion over creation and governance of God's cosmic courts. By crowning Joshua with this diadem stone the divine Angel was symbolically fashioning Joshua in his own archetypal image—and at the same time was constituting this regal priest a portent-sign of himself in his future manifestation as the Lord's Anointed, crowned with glory and honor, all things in subjection under his feet, set over the house of God as a Son (cf. Heb 2:6-9; 3:5,6).

The diadem nature of the stone-plaque centers attention on the royal dominion aspect of the image of God and thus on God's inheritance grant to his people of a kingdom of glory, productivity, and peace. "In that day, says Yahweh of hosts, you shall invite each one his neighbor under the vine and under the fig-tree" (Zech 3:10). Blessing sanctions in the old covenant regularly include the outward realm as well as the spiritual sphere.[43] So did prophetic promises concerning the consummation phase of the new covenant (cf., e.g., Deut 30:9; Jer 32:40,41).

Zechariah's picture of the coming day is drawn from the prosperity of Solomon's days, when "Judah and Israel dwelt safely, every man under his vine and under his fig tree" (1 Kgs 4:25 [5:5]). Micah had already used the same typical imagery (Mic 4:4) when prophesying of the kingdom "at the end of the days" (4:1)—the eschatological formula behind Zechariah's "in that day." Later in Zechariah's prophecy we hear repeatedly a reprise on the theme of paradise restored (cf. 8:3-5,12; 9:17; 10:10; 14:8-11).

Antitypical fulfillment and eschatological finality are keynotes in the announcements of Zech 3:8-10. Through the coming One, the messianic Son sent from heaven in the power of the sevenfold Spirit, God would bring to pass all that was symbolized by the typical priesthood of the order of Aaron. A divine engraving would replace the work of the Israelite craftsman of old: "I will engrave its engraving" (v. 9c). By his Spirit-anointed Servant God would accomplish in truth the sanctification of his elect which was expressed by the inscription on the golden plaque, "Holy to Yahweh." "In one day"[44] by the priestly offering of Jesus, God would effect once and for all the removal of the iniquity of that land (v. 9d),[45] perfecting forever them that are sanctified (cf. Heb 7-10; esp. 7:27; 9:12; 10:10). What the "land flowing with milk and honey" prefigured, God would bestow as an antitypical cosmic inheritance on the joint-heirs of Christ (v. 10). In that day, Messiah the Branch, the righteous king, would bring forth justice and security, prosperity and peace, in all the earth.

The mission of the messianic priest-king has a double portrayal in Zechariah 3. It is typified by the figure of Joshua and his diadem-stone, but it is also set forth by the acts of the Angel of the Lord described in verses 1-5. All that the divine Angel is seen doing for Joshua in the vision he would later do as the incarnate Servant-Son. In that day he would in historical fact vanquish the serpent, accuser of the brethren; remove the guilty stains of his people and clothe them in righteousness; seal them with his Spirit, renewing them in the image of God; and restore them as a royal priesthood, heirs of heaven's glory, blessed with access into the throne-presence of the Lord their God. Behold the Angel of the Lord, the coming One. Behold my Servant, the Branch.

"Arise, O Lord, from your Sabbath-throne; arise from the ark of your sovereignty.[46] Let your priests be clothed with righteousness, let your consecrated ones shout for joy" (Ps 132:8,9).

---

1 For discussion of the structure of the Book of Zechariah see the Appendix.
2 Cf. the Appendix, 256.
3 His designation can be abbreviated to "Yahweh" (v. 2) or "the angel" (v. 3).
4 Cf. Acts 25:18.
5 Cf. Ps 109:6, where, as in Zechariah 3, the reference is to a prosecuting attorney.
6 Messianic typology is present in all priestly functioning after the Fall that involves the symbolism of atonement, the effecting of reconciliation between God and sinners. In Israel

that messianic aspect of the cult was accentuated by the separation of the chosen Aaronic line to an exclusive priestly office that served as a mediatorial bridge between the rest of the covenant people and God. This special arrangement did not, however, negate the universal office of priesthood that is always the privilege of God's people.

7 Accordingly the decision reached on Joshua is based on the divine election of Jerusalem (v. 2).

8 For an analysis of the juridical framework of the Book of Job see my "Trial by Ordeal" in *Through Christ's Word: A Festschrift for Dr. Philip E. Hughes,* ed. W. R. Godfrey and Jesse L. Boyd III (Phillipsburg, 1985) 81-93.

9 Implicit in the presenting of Satan's appeal for a trial by ordeal before God's judgment seat was an acknowledgment that the Lord was the God of truth, the One who determines the outcome of judicial ordeals. Satan thus contradicted his charge that God was not true God in the very process of making it.

10 Cf. Ps 104:7; Isa 17:12,13.

11 A pronouncing of this rebuke-curse on the devil is cited in Jude v. 9, whether in allusion to Zech 3:2 or its appearance in the Assumption (or Testament) of Moses. If the latter, we would have to assume that this work preserved a true tradition not recorded in the canonical literature about an historical encounter between Michael and Satan on the occasion of Moses' burial. In the former case, the "body of Moses" concept must be understood after the analogy of the body of Christ as a designation of the community under the covenant mediated by Moses (cf. 1 Cor 10:2), the people of Jerusalem represented by Joshua the high priest. If Jude v. 9 refers to Zech 3:2, it clearly identifies the Angel of the Lord by the name Michael. On the other alternative, this identification would still not be contradicted. On either view, what Jude recommends is the recognition that final judicial authority resides in God. The episodes in both Zechariah 3 and the Assumption of Moses involve the idea that whatever claim Satan makes on sinful believers, it is countermanded by the Lord God's redemptive claim on them.

12 The verb employed, *epitimaō*, is used in LXX for *g^cr*, "rebuke," in Zech 3:2.

13 Cf. my *Images of the Spirit* (Grand Rapids, 1980), 41.

14 Cf. my *By Oath Consigned* (Grand Rapids, 1968) 65ff.

15 The choice of this verb in Zech 3:4b was probably prompted by the fact that it is also used for the removing of clothing. An example that provides an interesting comparison to the case of Joshua the high priest is Jonah 3:6, which narrates the removal of the royal robe by the king of Nineveh, to be replaced by sackcloth and ashes. Cf. Ezek 26:16.

16 The verb (*halbeš*) is understood with imperative force (and the object is changed to "him") on the view (supported by LXX) that v. 4c does not continue the Angel's explanation to Joshua (v. 4b) but resumes the directives to the angelic attendants (v. 4a).

17 In our introduction to vision four it was noted that this intervention by the prophet in the visionary action is one of the features peculiar to the three hinge sections in this book. There is considerable support in the ancient versions for a different textual reading which would make v. 5a a continuation of the Angel's words in v. 4.

18 Cf. Num 20:26, where the transfer of the high priestly office is effected by stripping Aaron of his holy garments and placing them on Eleazar.

19 For an elaboration of this subject see my *Images of the Spirit.*

20 Cf. ibid., 35-42. For a discussion of the tabernacle as a replica of the Glory-temple and the theme of re-creation in the image of God, see also the earlier comments on Zechariah's first vision.

21 Cf. *Images of the Spirit*, 42-50.

22 See further my *Kingdom Prologue*, 93-95.

23 For detailed discussion see *Images of the Spirit*, 50-53.

24 See further ibid., 48,49.

25 Cf. comments on Zech 1:8 in our discussion of the first vision.

26 The verb ʿmd has at times the meaning of "endure," "hold firm." Like the statement about Joshua's standing before the angel in v. 3, v. 5d is a transition, concluding what precedes but introductory to what follows.

27 See above under the heading "Law and Gospel".

28 Cf. *Images of the Spirit*, 48-56.

29 Only Joshua is addressed in the summons to attention (v. 8a) and he is the main subject ("you") of the parenthetical statement. The subject (including the colleagues) is placed before the introductory kî, which in such cases has emphatic force ("truly"). The third plural pronoun at the end does not single out the colleagues, for a third person pronoun can be used to strengthen a previous pronoun of first or second person (cf., e.g., Isa 43:25; Jer 49:12; Zeph 2:12).

30 Jer 33:17 links royal and priestly roles in an affirmation of the perpetuity of the Davidic Covenant.

31 In v. 9a the stone is the immediate object referred to by hinnēh, "behold," which then also seems to do double duty (reinforced by another hinnēh at v. 9c), introducing the announcement proper.

32 Cf. the use of ṭahôr (Exod 28:36) in Zech 3:5 for the mitre itself.

33 Note the use of ntn in Exod 29:6 for placing the crown on the mitre.

34 Cf. the comments on the horsemen in our discussion of the first vision.

35 According to Rev 5:6 it is Christ, the Lamb, who has the seven Spirit-eyes and according to Zech 1:10,11 it is the messianic Angel who sends the surveillance agents on mission and to whom they report.

36 Bearer of God's signet-seal, the high priest was God's steward-representative with authority to stamp God's mark of ownership (consecration) on persons and things.

37 If the binding of the covenant stipulations as a symbol to the forehead (Deut 6:8; 11:18; cf. Exod 13:9,16) is a cognate practice, it supports understanding the mitre plaque as a holy standard.

38 For divine protection as a correlate of divine ownership, authenticated by sealing, cf. Rev 7:3; 9:4; Ezek 9:4-6.

39 This is another parallel between Zechariah's fourth and fifth visions, for Spirit-anointing is the dominant motif in Zechariah 4.

40 The Satanic pseudo-equivalent is the mark-name of the beast on the forehead or right hand of his followers (Rev 13:16,17). Inclusion of the right hand in this counterfeit supports the cognateness of the Deut 6:8 practice to the mitre plaque (mentioned above, note 37).

41 Renewal in God's image is implicit in Paul's explanation of sealing as anointing with the Spirit. On the correlation of the biblical concepts of the image of God and Spirit-anointing or messiahship, see *Images of the Spirit*, 70.

42 Ibid., 54,55.

43 Of interest for the connection of verses 9 and 10 in Zechariah 3 is the way Deuteronomy 11 attributes the productivity of the land (a blessing associated with covenantal fidelity, vv. 8,13) to "the eyes of Yahweh your God" being upon it all year long (v. 12).

44 Decisive victory accomplished in a single day was a distinguishing mark of the great king in the ancient Near East. Cf. Douglas Stuart, "The Sovereign's Day of Conquest," *Bulletin of the American Schools of Oriental Research* 221 (Feb 1976), 159-164.

45 Instead of its inhabitants, the land, as a type of heaven, is mentioned in Zech 3:9, preparing for the paradise-land theme in v. 10.

46 Cf. Num 10:35,36. Solomon's quotation of the psalm (2 Chr 6:41) is prefaced by a request that the Lord's eyes be upon his suppliant people (v. 40; cf. Zech 3:9).

Vision Five (4:1-14)

ANOINTER OF GOD'S TEMPLE

Introduction. Vision four took us into the holy of holies to witness the critical encounter between the messianic Servant and Satan at the throne of God. Christ was typified there by the priestly figure of Joshua, invested with his holy robes, crowned with the golden diadem—seal of the Spirit, granted access among the angels in heaven, and entrusted with the rule over God's courts. Vision five reveals the sequel to Christ's victory over the dragon. We behold him, typified by the royal figure of Zerubbabel, building the house of God in the power of the Spirit, here symbolized by the golden oil flowing into the golden lampstand.

Christ and the Spirit is the theme of both these visions, with Christ the focus in Zechariah 3 and the Spirit central in Zechariah 4. The fifth vision also sustains a close relationship to vision three, its counterpart in the chiastic structure of the seven visions, and to vision one, with which it is paired when the opening and closing triads of visions are construed as in linear parallelism.

Zechariah 4 presents the symbolism of the lampstand and the two olive trees in verses 1-3, with their interpretation in verses 4-10, and then the symbolism of the two olive-shibboleth's [to use a popular transliteration] in verses 11 and 12, with the interpretation in verse 13. Our comments will diverge somewhat from the verse sequence as we develop the themes: I. The Spirit and the Menorah, and II. The Spirit and the Messiah.

I. THE SPIRIT AND THE MENORAH

A. *The Spirit as Pattern for the Menorah.*
1. *Mosaic and Zecharian Menorahs:* Menorah is the Hebrew word for the lampstand in the tabernacle.[1] The menorah was a stylized tree with central trunk and three branches on either side, all with floral detailing.[2] Its material was gold, described as pure, whether in the sense of technical quality or cultic cleanness. Apparently it was constructed by molding a sheet of gold foil over a wooden form (which was necessarily retained and provided stability). The menorah held seven lamps, either one on each of the seven arms or all seven made from the receptacle atop the central shaft by pinching its rim into wick-holders at seven places (a well attested ancient

lamp design). The people brought the oil for the lamps, which were trimmed each morning and lit each evening by the priests.

Like the tabernacle menorah, the one in Zechariah's fifth vision has seven lamps (Zech 4:2). However, nothing is said of side branches.[3] If this menorah consisted of only a single pedestal, the seven lamps would be arranged around the bowl on top of it. Each of the seven lamps is itself of the seven-wick design mentioned above, giving a total of forty-nine lamp-lights. But the most remarkable new feature in Zechariah 4 is the two flanking olive trees and the connecting apparatus by which a continuous supply of oil flows from these trees to the menorah lamps, fueling their perpetual flames.

2. *Arboreal Theophany and Menorah-Church:* In Zechariah 4 it is not the lamps aflame but the two olive trees that represent the divine Presence. Specifically, the trees are a symbolic depiction of the theophanic Glory, associated with the menorah in the tabernacle. The way the olive trees overarch the lampstand from both sides reflects the scene in the holy of holies where the two cherubim of the Glory-Presence spread their wings over the ark of the covenant. The duality of the cherubim and of the olive trees corresponds to the two-pillar formation of the Glory-cloud, itself a representation of the two legs of God as he would take his stand, particularly in judicial actions.[4]

The presence of the divine Glory among the covenant people was portrayed in Zechariah's opening vision (1:7-17) by the figure of the Lord of Glory with angelic retinue stationed in the midst of the myrtles. As seen in the fifth vision under the symbolism of the golden oil of the olive trees flowing into the menorah, the Glory-Spirit is again a divine presence in the midst of, indeed within, God's people. And as in the first vision with its myrtle trees, so here it is a tree, the menorah-tree into which the divine oil flows, that represents the covenant people.

Though fueled by the Spirit-oil, the flames of the menorah lamps are the shining of the covenant community. This is corroborated by the hierophant angel's interpretation of the menorah in terms of the temple, which housed the menorah and performed on a larger scale and more publicly the menorah's function as an illuminating witness to the world (vv. 4-10). Now the temple, though the residence of the divine Glory within, is to be identified with God's people. At the New Testament level the church is the temple, the holy structure of living stones built on the foundation of Christ Jesus to be the habitation of God in the Spirit (Eph 2:20-22; Heb 3:6). The menorah is quite directly interpreted as the church when the seven lampstands of John's vision in Revelation 1 are identified as seven churches (Rev 1:20), and when, conversely, the two prophets representing the witnessing church in the symbolism of Revelation 11 are explained as equivalents of the lampstand of Zechariah 4 (Rev 11:4). Enhancing the menorah's prefiguration of the new covenant church is its assemblage of forty-nine lights, suggestive of the Jubilee and so pointing to the new covenant (cf. Luke 4:18-21).

3. *Menorah, Replica of the Theophanic Glory:* Israel's tabernacle-temple (the conceptual equivalent of the menorah in Zechariah 4) and the church temple are distinguishable from their divine Resident. But antecedent to them is the archetypal heavenly temple, which is not distinguishable from God but is God manifested, the effulgence of his Glory. Filling the cosmos, the epiphanic Glory constitutes the architectural space and structure of this divine temple.

Invisible to earthlings now, this Glory-Spirit temple will be unveiled to us in the revelation of the new heavens and earth at the Consummation. At that time the cosmos as a place where the present distinction between dimensions visible and invisible to us will cease to exist as a result of the heightening of our perceptive capabilities through glorification. Then will be realized the beatitude, "they shall see God," the archetypal Glory-temple (cf. Rev 22:4).

According to Rev 21:22 there will be no further need of temples in the world of New Jerusalem since God himself is the temple there, his own Glory his holy house (cf. Isa 66:1; Acts 7:48ff.; 17:24). But while there will no longer be local, symbolic, man-made sanctuaries like Solomon's temple in the consummated cosmos (and such are in fact already obsolete in the present church age), Rev 21:22 does not mean to deny the perpetuity of the church-temple. Not a temple made by human hands, the church is God-built, a temple created by the Spirit, and God, even though he is his own temple-dwelling, will yet condescend to tabernacle forever in the church-temple. Wondrous this union: we dwell in him, the divine temple, and he dwells in us, the temple he has made (cf. Isa 57:15; 66:2). It is in Christ that we are that temple; indeed, Christ is that temple (cf. Mark 14:58; John 2:19ff.). And Christ, "the Lamb," is mentioned along with the Lord God as the temple in the New Jerusalem. Church-temple and Glory-temple coalesce there.

Like the old tabernacle and temple, which were constructed after the heavenly archetypal pattern revealed to their human builders, so the church-temple is made according to the paradigm of the Glory-temple. This is brought out in Zechariah 4 by the way various features of the olive trees and oil, symbol of the Glory-Spirit, are replicated in the menorah, symbol of the church-temple. The menorah turns out to be another of the Bible's numerous parables of the (re-)creation of man in the image of God. Just within Zechariah's visions we have already found this motif in the imagery of the tabernacle-like myrtles of the first vision and in the symbolism of the tabernacle-like high priestly vestments in the fourth vision.

Most closely related are the treatments of this image-renewal theme in Zechariah 3 and 4. The Spirit and the symbol of oil play a part in both visions. In Zechariah 3, Joshua's holy vestments, themselves replicas of the Glory-Spirit, are crowned by the diadem-stone on the mitre, a seal of the Spirit, a sign of Spirit anointing. Also, by virtue of the anointing during the investiture ritual the high priest was saturated with oil, symbol of the Spirit. Together the anointing and the enrobing in the glory garments were a double portrayal of creation in the image of the Glory-Spirit. Zechariah 4 similarly symbolizes the same concept. Here, the Spirit, by filling the lampstand-community, creates his likeness in it.[5]

By reason of the gold and gems worked into the high priest's vestments they shone like the theophanic Glory in whose likeness they were fashioned. Of similar but even more radiant appearance is the menorah of Zechariah 4. Again gold is the material but now it is aglow with reflections of the jubilee of flames, themselves an even brighter and more literal copy of the theophanic fire. The likeness of the golden menorah to the Glory-Spirit is highlighted by denoting the oil, symbol of the Spirit, as "the gold" (v. 12). Flowing into the lampstand, the golden oil reproduced its shining golden lustre there.

Replication of the Spirit-likeness in the menorah is also expressed in a sharing of arboreal imagery. Though the tree features of the tabernacle menorah are not explicitly mentioned in the description of the lampstand in Zechariah 4, it is possible that the seven-branched structure and other floral detailing of the familiar Mosaic menorah are simply taken for granted. If not, the arboreal form of Zechariah's lampstand may still be maintained, for the sevenfold cluster of seven-lamp receptacles on top of it may then be seen as modified equivalents of the seven branches of the tabernacle menorah.

As a stylized tree the Zecharian menorah, symbol of the community, matches the two olive trees, symbol of the Glory-theophany. This correspondence is enhanced by the linkage of each of these arboreal symbols with the two golden cherubim. When observing above that it is particularly the manifestation of the Glory in the two-cherubim formation above the ark that is reflected in the two olive trees, we cited their common feature of duality. A further point of connection is that the cherubim in Solomon's temple were carved out of olive wood (1 Kgs 6:23). The menorah is linked to the same cherubim structure not only by the gold material used in both cases but by a shared mode of fabrication. Within the Exodus legislation the *miqshah* technique (the molding of metal foil) is mentioned only in the making of the cherubim (25:18; 37:7) and the menorah (25:31,36; 37:17,22).[6] Revelation 11, appropriating the symbolism of Zechariah 4, carries the correspondence of the menorah to the olive trees a step further. The single menorah there becomes two lampstands (v. 4) and thus a numerical likeness to the two olive trees is added to the other points of correspondence between them.

The Book of Revelation provides another intimation that the menorah-church bears the divine Glory-image when it depicts the Glory-Spirit by symbolism similar to menorah flames. Thus, the seven torches of fire burning before the throne are identified as the seven Spirits (Rev 4:5).[7] The biblical roots of this symbolism can be traced to God's covenant-ratifying appearance to Abraham in the menorah-like form of fire-pan and torch with their ascending columns of flame and smoke (Gen 15:17). This anticipated the two fiery columns of the Glory-cloud theophany at the exodus, of which the dual cherubim structure, insignia of the Glory-Spirit, was an adaptation, and of which, in turn, the two olive trees of Zechariah 4 were a further adaptation.

Re-creation in the divine likeness is treated in Zechariah's fourth vision from the perspective of its significance for personal deliverance from sin and judgment. What is in view in the fifth vision is the meaning of the church's acquisition of the image of the Glory-Archetype for the performance of its historical menorah-mission of prophetic witness. As we shall see, displaying the divine likeness is a major element in that witness of the church; its form serves its function. This was illustrated in the experience of the Israelite prophets, for whom acquisition of the Glory-Spirit image was an essential part of their formation for office, a concomitant of the Spirit-anointing prerequisite to their witness function.[8]

B. *The Spirit as Power for the Menorah Mission.*

1. *Menorah: Witness Light:* God is light (1 John 1:5) and God is truth (I John 1:6; 2:21-23; 5:7,20),[9] the true and living God of Glory, the One (Zech 14:9). And it pleased him to glorify himself by calling into being a creation to serve as a medium of his luminous self-manifestation, a vehicle of theophanic revelation to creatures, themselves displaying ectypally the likeness of his Glory. The seven eyes of the sevenfold Spirit would take delight in seeing his own archetypal Glory-likeness shining back from the temple of his human images on earth (as well as from his angel-sons in heaven). For mankind this reflective radiating of the light of God would be an exhibiting on a creaturely level of the glory of divine dominion and divine holiness, righteousness and truth. Further, at the promised consummation of this created order the human temple-community was to assume an outward luminosity that reflected the light of the heavenly Spirit-temple. With mankind's eschatological glorification the natural darkness they had experienced in the original cycle of night and day would become a thing of the past. For then the hitherto invisible Glory-light of heaven would become visible, illuminating all the cosmos in perpetual day (cf. Isa 60:19,20; Zech 14:7; Rev 21:25; 22:5)—the perfected revelation-replication of the God who is light.

Glorifying God by reflecting the light of his Glory back to him remains after the Fall the chief purpose of man's light-bearing. Moreover, the full realization of that highest goal through the ultimate glorification of the saints is still the predestined omega-point of human history. But in the interim between the Fall and the Consummation the diffusing of light by God's people serves some partly or totally new purposes as this function is carried out in the spiritual darkness of a fallen world.

One of these partly new objectives was the confrontation of evil. Before the Fall of man on earth a fall had transpired in heaven, so that even in Eden man's displaying of the light of God's image would have been an exercising of God-like dominion and righteousness and a confessing of the

Truth over against the dark presence of the devil. Donning the divine image was already a putting on of the armor of light to do battle with the prince of darkness and to overcome him. Radiating light was even then the bearing of a legal witness to the true God in dispute against the tempter, the liar from the beginning. However, though this confrontational aspect of covenant witness is not something altogether new after the Fall, there is this difference, that now the darkness is entrenched and pervasive within mankind. The witness-light must be presented not just in defiance of a would-be usurper and his minions but in the face of conflict with satanic powers that are currently "the rulers of the darkness of this world."

There is also a totally new purpose involved in the luminary function of the righteous in the post-Fall world—it henceforth serves the redemptive objectives of the Covenant of Grace.

The Mosaic-Zecharian menorah symbolizes the diffusing of the light and truth of God by his people, not in the daylight of the original pristine order of creation but in the postlapsarian night. Lit each evening to burn through the night, the menorah in the holy place of the tabernacle was a light shining in the darkness. The Israel of God performs its menorah mission in the darkness of a world blinded by Satan's anti-theology, worshiping in the cult of no-gods. The shining of the menorah-church is a witnessing to the true God of heavenly Glory that has the effect of condemning the counter-claims of the satanic idol, which is a lie and pitch darkness.

This confrontational, anathematizing aspect of the church's witness is brought out in Zechariah 4 when it interprets the menorah mission in terms of the role of the temple, standing on Zion and magnifying the name of Yahweh, the God of heaven and earth, in the face of the great mountain (v. 7). For the great mountain is the hostile imperial power and its idol-cult, lifting itself up as a rival to the mountain of God's temple, as a pseudo-Zion, an antichrist Har Magedon.

The condemnatory aspect of the menorah mission is again prominent in Rev 11:1-13. In this adaptation of the Zechariah 4 lampstand imagery, the symbolism of the menorah light is clearly interpreted as the light of truth. For the menorah is identified with God's two prophetic witnesses (vv. 3, 4).[10] And the purpose of the menorah mission as seen here in the career of these witnesses is emphatically the bringing of judgment on their enemies. The picture is one of radical opposition. So intense, so demonic is the world's hatred of the exposing, condemning light of the truth (cf. John 3:19,20), that when the two witnesses have finished their testimony the beast from the abyss kills them and peoples from all the nations celebrate this pseudo-triumph with hellish glee (vv. 7-11).

Maintaining a judicial-apologetic witness against the deceived, unbelieving world is then one dimension of the menorah program. The field of history is a courtroom in which God's people give testimony to his name over against the blasphemies of the idol-worshipers.[11] This piercing of the darkness with light, exposing falsehood, anticipates the day of the Lord, when by the brightness of his coming he shall bring to light for judgment all the hidden things of darkness (1 Cor 4:5; cf. Gen 3:8; John 3:19,20).

But the menorah mission is also a summoning of the lost to salvation in Jesus Christ. Indeed, it is the primary and proper function of the menorah to serve God's purpose of redemptive grace, that totally new aspect of light-radiating not present before the entrance of sin and death at the Fall. The menorah community is commissioned to proclaim the gospel of him who says: "I am the way and the truth and the life" (John 14:6). "I am the light of the world; he that follows me shall not walk in darkness but shall have the light of life" (John 8:12; cf. 12:46). The true heavenly Light declares to his disciples, renewed after his image, "You are the light of the world" (Matt 5:14), and he bids them, "Go, therefore, and make disciples of all the nations" (Matt 28:19).

This gospel-witnessing function of the menorah-people is readily discernible in the situation of the menorah in the tabernacle. It was located between the altar of sacrifice and the mercy seat, a place redolent of atonement and gospel pardon.

The menorah flames illuminated the way to the throne of grace in the holy of holies. In the setting of the Solomonic temple, where there were ten lampstands arranged in two rows on the north and south sides of the holy place (1 Kgs 7:49), the menorah lights themselves actually formed a passageway—from the site of judgment in the court to the Glory-throne beyond the second veil (cf. Heb 9:2-5), the way from Golgotha to God's holy heaven.

As we have observed, Zech 4:4-10 interprets the menorah mission in terms of Zerubbabel's temple building project. The counterpart to that enterprise in the new covenant is the program of building the church, the assignment to disciple those God calls to be living stones in the temple founded on Christ. The menorah mission is mandated by the Lord in the Great Commission.

Both old and new covenant temples are lights of the world set on hills (the old temple quite literally so); they are both lamps put on a stand to shine before men that they might glorify the Father in heaven (Matt 5:14-16). The mission of the old menorah-temple and that of the new menorah-church alike is to summon men out of all nations to the holy city on Har Magedon (whether the old earthly, typological Jerusalem or the new heavenly, true Jerusalem), to call them on a faith pilgrimage to the altar of atonement and the throne of grace. The mission of the menorah community, old and new, is to light the way to the Father's house.

2. *The Spirit and the Menorah Light:* Some have speculated that the middle section of Zechariah 4 (vv. 6b-10a) is misplaced because, allegedly, it is not connected with what precedes. Actually, this word of the Lord addresses itself to the very heart of the preceding symbolism. It interprets the oil, which is obviously, if implicitly, included in the imagery of the menorah and olive trees as described in vv. 1-3, and is explicitly mentioned in the supplementary details of vv. 11,12 (all already seen by the prophet Zechariah at the outset). It was this golden oil that would have rivetted Zechariah's attention, this supernatural provision pouring endlessly from the olive trees in a miraculous mechanism that dispensed with the ordinary human participation, whether by way of contributing the oil for the menorah or tending its flames. This wonder oil, the secret of the perpetual flame, was the spectacular feature of the vision that demanded an immediate explanation (cf. vv. 4,5). And the Lord's reply to the prophet's query was right to the point: "Not by might nor by power but by my Spirit" (v. 6b). God's Spirit, the Light of life, is the oil, the inexhaustible fuel of the true menorah, the limitless energy source of the ever burning church-lamp (cf. 1 Kgs 17:14-16). As source of that Spirit-oil, the olive trees on either side were trees of everlasting life for the people of the menorah (cf. Rev 22:1, 2).

The Lord's reply went on to apply this truth to the program of building the temple. Here was a current instance demonstrating that Spirit-power is the secret of success in the menorah mission. Despite every adverse circumstance, the project would surely be finished. The day of outwardly unpromising beginnings would be succeeded by a time that witnessed the leveling of the hostile world mountain and the celebration of the elevating of the temple. And it would not in the last analysis be due to the efforts of Zerubbabel and the covenant people that the temple would be completed; the ultimate accomplishing of the mission must rather be attributed to the Spirit. For we are told that "these seven, namely, the eyes of the Lord that run to and fro through the whole earth" (which, according to Rev 5:6, represent the Spirit) are fixed with joy upon Zerubbabel (v. 10). This signifies that the Lord has authorized the enterprise, that he takes special interest and pleasure in it, and by his Spirit is sovereignly supervising it— the guarantee of sabbatical success.

Those who allege that this section of Zechariah 4 is discontinuous with the opening description of the menorah assert that not until the phrase "these seven" in v. 10b is the subject of the menorah resumed. "These seven" refers then not to the Spirit-oil but to the seven lamps, identifying them as the eyes of the Lord. One objection to this is that something other than the seven eyes must be construed as the subject of the seeing spoken of in v. 10a. But the natural connection between eyes and seeing is obvious. Furthermore, the lamps represent the covenant community, the recipients of the Spirit-oil, and therefore cannot be identified as the seven eyes of the Lord, which represent the Spirit. "These seven" does not refer to the seven lamps in Zech 4:2 but to the "seven eyes" in Zech 3:9, as Zech 4:10c indicates.

Closing (v. 10) on the note it began (v. 6), this section of the vision points again to the Spirit and his universal sovereignty (the seven eyes engaged in judicial surveillance of "the whole earth") as the explanation and guarantee of the final accomplishment of the menorah mission. What must be done to fulfill that mission in the future had been done by the Spirit in the past. Was the creation of a people in the luminous image of God central to that mission? Then remember how the Glory-Spirit in the beginning was the power of the Most High overshadowing the lifeless dust of the earth to quicken the man-creature, so bringing forth a son of God, a replica of the Creator's glory (cf. Gen 1:2, 26, 27; Luke 3:38). Did the menorah mission entail the bringing low of the high world mountain? Did it require victorious battle against the armies of the satanic beast-power? Then recall how, in the hour when the dragon-power of Egypt threatened to overwhelm the Israelites, the Glory-Spirit vanquished lofty pharaoh and all his military might (Exod 14:4; Ps 136:15). It was "from the pillar of cloud and fire" (i.e., the Glory-Spirit theophany) that God looked down upon the Egyptians (Exod 14:24) and cast chariots, horses, and riders into the depths of the sea, triumphing gloriously (Exod 14:28; 15:1,4). That was the "power" by which he brought forth his people out of Egypt (Exod 32:11). Singing, "Yahweh is my strength and my song" (Exod 15:2), the Israelites confessed the truth of Zech 4:6—salvation is not by human might or power but by God's Spirit. Psalm 33 makes the same confession: "No king secures victory by his massive army, no warrior is delivered by his great strength" (v. 16) ... "The eye of Yahweh is on those who fear him" (v. 18a) ... "Our soul waits for Yahweh, our help [or warrior] and our shield is he" (v. 20).

"By my Spirit," the power of God in creation and redemption hitherto—that is the word of exhortation and promise to Zerubbabel and all henceforth who are called to the menorah mission.

II. THE SPIRIT AND THE MESSIAH

God's presence in the midst of his people is a key theme throughout Zechariah's visions. He is present in the person of the Messiah. This Immanuel presence takes the form of the messianic rider of the red horse, stationed in the midst of the myrtles (vision one); and of the Angel-measurer, who proclaims the evangel, "Behold I come and will dwell in the midst of you" (2:10,11 [14,15]), and who testifies that his messianic appointment will be validated by his finishing his building mission (vision three). Again in vision four the messianic Angel is present with the covenant community, represented by Joshua the high priest, who is also identified as a type of the messianic Servant. And once more here in vision five, now under the typological figure of Zerubbabel, Messiah is seen participating with his people in the work of restoration. Also, the voice of the Messiah is heard here in the word of the Lord, declaring (as in vision three) that the triumphant completion of his rebuilding commission will confirm his identity as one whom the Lord has sent into the midst of the menorah-community.

Constantly bound up with Messiah's presence is a presence of the Spirit. The mounted rider is attended by agents of the Glory-Spirit, emissaries of the court of heaven symbolized by the horsemen in vision one and by the expert destroyers in vision two. The divine measurer in vision three states (according to the preferable rendering) that he had been sent "with the Glory-Spirit" (2:8 [12]). In vision four the combination of the sign of the Messiah-Servant and the seal of the Spirit suggests the intimate association of the two. It is this theme of the interrelationship of the Son and the Spirit as it is developed in the vision of the menorah and its mission that we shall now explore.

Here in summary outline is what we shall find. The Son is anointed with the Spirit and he is the anointer with the Spirit. As the Spirit-anointed one, Messiah is himself the model (i.e., perfect) menorah. He is therefore also a model (in the sense of paradigm) for the menorah mission of shedding light in the dark world, the mission-imperative entailed in the menorah identity. Now curiously the menorah mission involves making the menorah. Hence, the Messiah as ultimate executor of the menorah mission is the maker of the menorah, the builder of the church. Expressed in the typological idiom of the fifth vision, Zerubbabel is the builder of the temple (Zech 4:7-10). Further, in the course of making the menorah, Messiah commands the menorah to fulfill its mission as a light to the Gentiles, the mission which he models,[12] and thus to participate in making itself. That is, Christ promulgates the Great Commission. And in order to empower the menorah-church for that mission, which is accomplished not by human might but by God's Spirit, Messiah, the anointed with the Spirit, becomes the anointer with the Spirit. In the symbolism of vision five, he becomes the channel of the oil from the olive trees to the menorah (Zech 4:11-14). To be the menorah-maker means Messiah is mediator of the Spirit. Christ pours out the Spirit upon the church. He complements the charge of the Great Commission with the charism of Pentecost. So he creates the menorah-church a likeness of the Spirit.

A. *Messiah—Anointed with the Spirit: Model for the Menorah.* As shown by his designating the Messiah "my Servant the Branch" (Zech 3:8), Zechariah draws upon Isaiah for his messianic portraiture. And in Isaiah's prophecy, anointing with the Spirit is a hallmark both of the coming branch from David's line (Isa 11:2) and of the Servant of the Lord (Isa 42:1; 61:1; cf. Luke 4:18). Now, Spirit-anointing imparts Spirit-likeness and, agreeably, in Isaiah 11 the anointing presence of the Spirit of Yahweh on the messianic shoot out of the stock of Jesse endues him with the wisdom and power characteristic of the Spirit (vv. 1,2). Translated into Apocalypse idiom − the messianic lion of the tribe of Judah, the root of David (Rev 5:5), is the Lamb with seven horns (power) and seven eyes (wisdom), which are the seven Spirits of God (Rev 5:6, an allusion to Zech 4:10).

Also, according to Isaiah, the Anointed of the Lord bears the likeness of the Spirit's radiant splendor, the Glory-light aspect of the Spirit which is replicated in the menorah. To his chosen Servant, on whom he puts his Spirit (Isa 42:1), the Lord says: "I give you ... for a light to the Gentiles," to illuminate those in darkness (Isa 42:6,7; 49:6; cf. Luke 2:32; Acts 26:22,23). The advent of this divine prince to occupy David's throne forever is the shining of a great light on the people who walked in darkness (Isa 9:1,2 [8:23-9:1]; cf. 60:1-3).

Christ, the true anointed Servant, the true Israel, is the true menorah-light, the perfect likeness of the Glory-Spirit. And as the true menorah, Christ carries out the menorah mission of witnessing to the living God, who has "given him for a witness to the peoples" (Isa 55:4).

Perfect image of the archetypal Glory-Spirit by virtue of his anointing, Christ serves along with the Glory-Spirit as a model which is replicated in the menorah community. Fashioned anew in the likeness of the Anointed one, the members of that community too are God's servants (Isa 41:8,9; 44:1,2), God's witnesses (Isa 43:10,12; 44:8), and as such a light to the Gentiles (cf. Acts 13:47; 26:22,23).

Like Zechariah, Daniel exhibits this same Isaianic complex of themes. After the pattern of Isaiah's suffering Servant, the *māšîaḥ nāgîd*, "Anointed Prince," of Dan 9:24-27 is cut off to make an atonement for the many, so ratifying the covenant of grace and becoming a covenant of the people. In Dan 7:13,14 the Messiah appears as the heavenly son of man, whose Parousia with the clouds of heaven is a revelation of him as the perfect image of the Glory-Spirit. All the glory-components that constitute the *imago Dei* are present here: the glory of dominion over a universal and everlasting kingdom, the glory of holiness prerequisite to his reception and exaltation before the ancient of days at the white throne, and the glory of luminous majesty as one invested with the clouds of Glory.

Also, as in Isaiah and Zechariah there are indications in Daniel that the Messiah is a model that is reproduced in God's people. For the interpretation given of the vision of the son of man identifies the saints of the Most High as participating with him in the glory of his kingdom's dominion (7:18,22,27). And in Dan 12:3 the faithful are likened to the archetypal Anointed one in his specifically menorah character as light and witness. They have been witness-lights who turned many to righteousness, and at their resurrection-glorification they will be radiant lights, replicas of the son of man adorned with the Glory-clouds, shining as the brightness of the firmament, as the stars for ever and ever.

The menorah vision of Zechariah 4 receives explicit canonical exposition in the lampstand symbolism of John's Apocalypse. Our examination of this begins with a brief notice of John's broader use of the metaphor of light for Christ and his mission. In John's Gospel, Christ's identification as light (John 1:4b,5,9) is related to his identity as the Logos-declaration of God, the one who shows us the Father (John 1:1,14a,18; 3:34; 8:19,28; 12:49,50; 14:6-11, esp. v. 9; 17:8; cf. 1 John 1:2), who is light (1 John 1:5). It is particularly through his advent that the Logos is light. He is light in relation to men (John 1:4).[13] He shines as a light among us (John 1:14), in this world and its darkness (John 1:5,9,10a). He identifies himself as the light of the world, designed to give opening of eyes to the blind and the light of life to those in darkness (John 8:12; 9:5).

In the terms of Zechariah's fifth vision, Christ as Logos-light performs the menorah mission. He, the Word of God, speaks the words of God whose word is truth (John 17:17; cf. 14:6). These words are the words of eternal life (John 6:68; cf. 63) which he gives to his disciples (John 3:34; 14:10; 17:8) to evoke faith in God, who delivers from the judgment and transports believers from death to life (John 5:24; cf. 4:14,41; 6:63,68; 8:51). The light of the Logos is a witness-light shining to bring those without the knowledge of God to the light of the knowledge of God radiating from him, the image of God (John 1:10b,14b; 12:35,36,46; cf. 2 Cor 4:4-6), the glory of Israel and a light to the Gentiles. The Logos-Lamb is the lamp (Rev 21 :23).

Further, the Logos-light is an archetypal model for the menorah, a light that is replicated in believers. He is the true, the heavenly light (John 1:9; cf. 1 John 2:8); they become "sons of light" (John 12:36; cf. Matt 5:14-16). Illustrative of this reproduction of the Logos as the menorah or witness-lamp is John the Forerunner-herald, the witness to the true light (John 1:6-8,15,19ff.), the lamp that lit the way to the Lamb (John 5:35).

There are two passages in the Book of Revelation where Zechariah's lampstand imagery is taken up by John, and in both the idea is clearly conveyed that the model of the glorified Christ is being replicated in the menorah-church. In the opening vision, the heavenly son of man, his countenance like the sun, his eyes like flames of fire, appears in the midst of the radiant lampstand churches. Lights in the world, they are fashioned in the likeness of their glorious Lord, the archetype light of the world (Rev 1:12-20; cf. 21:11).

In Revelation 11 (esp. v. 4), the most explicit reference to Zechariah's fifth vision, the menorah symbolism is applied to the two prophet figures representing the church. An extensive parallel between the nature and historical course of the missions of Christ and the prophet-menorah community directs attention to the way the church is being formed in the Lord's menorah image. "As their [the two prophets'] career unfolds in verses 3-12, the reader cannot miss the similarity of its pattern to that of Jesus' ministry. A time of proclamation and signs, issuing in satanic opposition and the violent death of the witnesses in the great city, 'where also our Lord was crucified' (so verse 8 adds, making the parallelism explicit), is followed by the resurrection of the martyrs and their ascension in a cloud."[14]

As the canonical connections of Zechariah 4 reveal, the Spirit-anointed one of whom the prophet speaks is the model for the menorah-community and its world mission. Christ is the *kerux* who issues his evangel-command to all afar off and so sets the pattern for the church in fulfilling the Great Commission.[15] The identification of Messiah's people by the symbol of the menorah indicates that the *kerux*-likeness of the Light of the world is being reproduced in them. In the midst of a crooked and perverse generation they "are seen as lights in the world, holding forth the word of life" (Phil 2: 15, 16). So is fulfilled the eternal purpose of him who works all things after the counsel of his will: "For whom he foreknew he also foreordained to be conformed to the image of his Son, that he might be the firstborn among many brethren" (Rom 8:29).

B. *Messiah—Agent of the Spirit: Masterbuilder of the Menorah.* The menorah epitomizes the temple and accordingly in Zechariah 4 the menorah's mission is expounded in terms of a building of the temple. To build the temple—to make the menorah—is the historical task of the menorah. Since Messiah provides the model for the menorah-church and its mission, he is the maker of the menorah, the masterbuilder of God's temple-church. A typological picture of this is given in Zechariah's fifth vision under the figure of Zerubbabel engaged in the rebuilding of the Jerusalem temple (Zech 4:7-10).

Zech 4:6-10 is a double oracle of Yahweh, with introductory formulae in verses 6a and 8. Each oracle contains three sections, the two sets paralleling each other to produce an ABCA'B'C' pattern. The B-sections pose challenging questions to the antagonists and gainsayers (vv. 7a and 10a), and the C-sections refer to the temple building activity of Zerubbabel, each reference involving the symbolism of a stone (vv. 7b and 10b). The A-sections present the primary affirmation, an assurance that the house of God will be built. Verse 6b attributes success in this enterprise directly to God's Spirit. Verse 9 focuses on the royal messianic agent of the Spirit. It declares that the hands of Zerubbabel have laid the foundation of this house and his hands shall finish it" (v. 9a). The messianic Angel speaking here also states that this successful completion of his mission—"his" because he is "Zerubbabel"—will attest that he is indeed the Anointed agent of the Spirit, the Christ of God: "You will know that Yahweh of hosts has sent me unto you" (v. 9b).

1. *Temple-building: Crown and Covenant*

(a) *Crown Construction:* Building a temple is a royal task. We shall presently trace the biblical history of this royal enterprise back to the first Adam, but it will suffce here to cite the temple Zerubbabel was rebuilding. Planned by king David, executed by king Solomon (cf. Ezra 5:11), the Jerusalem temple was clearly crown construction. The incorporation of the commission to build the temple in a covenant that was predominantly a confirmation of the perpetuity of David's royal dynasty emphasizes the peculiarly royal nature of temple building (2 Sam 7:13a; 1 Chr 17:12; cf. Psalm 132). Such a commission indeed validated the appointed builder's right to the crown (cf. 1 Chr 28:5-7).

In the extrabiblical accounts of temple building in the ancient world the same situation obtains: it is the king who plays the main role. He was not merely titular director of the project but took an active part, especially in key symbolic rites. How important such projects were for the king's reputation is indicated by the inclusion of this function among the royal titles, as well as by the celebration of temple building in royal documents. The peculiarly royal responsibility for various other major construction projects, particularly cities, is also evidenced by references to such achievements in summaries of royal reigns.[16]

In keeping with the royal status of temple builders, Zerubbabel, the one selected as the type of Christ the masterbuilder in Zech 4:6-10, was a scion of David's dynasty. He and the high priest Joshua are a complementary typological pair in visions four and five. Together they prefigure Messiah's dual office and function as priest-king. Since there is a royal dimension to the high priest's office, which is reflected in the crowning of Joshua and the association of the Branch title with him in vision four and again in the episode of Zech 6:9-15 (which, moreover, speaks of the Branch as building the temple), the choice of the Davidic Zerubbabel instead of Joshua as the messianic type in vision five is significant. It points up the fact that however the high priest might be associated with the monarch in the project (cf. Hag 1:12,14; 2:2,4), temple building is properly and distinctly the function of the king (cf. Hag 2:21,23).

(b) *Divine Commission and Covenant:* Divine commissioning is a conspicuous feature of accounts of royal temple construction in the Bible and elsewhere in the ancient world. In the extrabiblical accounts the decision of the gods was expressed in a command to build revealed to the chosen royal builder through dreams or omens, or possibly through a prophet. At times a king might take the initiative but he must secure divine approval through mantic means before proceeding. Divine commission provided necessary legitimation and carried assurance of success. According to the biblical narratives, the erection of holy dwellings for God is likewise a matter of divine mandate, and if, as in the case of David, the human king conceives the purpose to build, the Lord's approval must first be sought (2 Sam 7:1ff.; 1 Kgs 5:5; 8:17ff.; cf. Ps 132:2ff.).

Throughout the biblical history of temple building the divine commission is more specifically a covenantal commission; the building mandate is incorporated in the terms of a particular covenant. The following sketch of this history to Zechariah's day will seek to indicate primarily how the project is in each case a covenantal commission and a royal enterprise. Subsequently we will supplement this by observing how the several accounts consistently include the features of conquest as prelude to construction and of temple building as an imitation of creation.

The relevant biblical accounts are found to belong to a standardized Near Eastern literary pattern used in narrating temple building events from at least the second millennium on. It will be useful to present in summary at this point the several main topics in this thematic structure. This may be done by identifying them within the record of the construction of Solomon's temple.[17]

Standard elements included: the decision and commission to build (1 Kgs 5:15-19); the acquisition of building materials (1 Kgs 5:15-26) and drafting of craftsmen (1 Kgs 5:13ff.; 7:13); description of the temple and its furnishings (1 Kings 6 and 7) with statement of completion as specified (Kgs 6:9,14,38); dedication and deity's entry of his residence (1 Kgs 8:1-11,62-66); dedicatory prayer (1 Kgs 8:12-61); blessings and curses (1 Kgs 9:19). There are further significant details in the biblical accounts, like the divine provision of an exemplar, that also belong to the common pattern.

(i) *Adam and the Covenant of Creation:* God is the original temple builder, the builder of the heavenly Glory-temple. His epiphanic Glory constitutes the ultimate temple; God is his own temple. The Glory-filled cosmos is a royal house of the divine King, with heaven his throne and earth his footstool. On earth, the Creator made a microcosmic copy of the Glory-temple in the form of the garden of Eden, with its mountain of God, the throne site of a visible, localized projection of the heavenly Glory-Spirit.

The creation "week" saw the beginning of another kind of divine dwelling as God brought forth creatures made in the likeness of the Glory-Spirit temple. By the provisions of the Covenant of Creation man was commissioned to enter into the process of constructing this people-temple. As the Creator fathered Adam as a son in his image (cf. Luke 3:38), Adam was to father sons in his likeness (cf. Gen 5:1-3). Through the ongoing procreative multiplying of humanity the human temple would be produced, each new person another "living stone" in the growing holy edifice.

Envisaged as the consummation of the covenant order was a human temple transfigured into a radiant replica of the archetypal Glory-temple. Glorification, that final step in the construction of the temple, would be an act of the Creator. But meanwhile the cultural mandate of the covenant called on man to participate in this temple building by multiplying his kind, so producing the global community of mankind, God's people-temple. Embodied as it was in a royal mandate to subdue and occupy the earthly domain, this assignment to build the people-temple was also a royal commission. The covenantal service of temple building was a function of kingship. At the same time, since the temple is a house of prayer and worship, it is evident that performing the cultural task of the king served the purposes of the priest's cultic functioning. The telos of the kingdom is that God may be all in all.

Because the history of man in Eden terminated abruptly in the Fall, the narrative of the Covenant of Creation contains only the commissioning of the human king to his part in building the people-temple, not the other elements that round out the accounts of redemptive temple construction. However, the Genesis prologue does record the Creator's work of constructing the cosmic temple, a project that was brought to completion. Though this temple building was unique in being the work of God alone and the account of it does not, therefore, exhibit precisely all the usual features of the standard temple building accounts, the essential components are nevertheless present, mutatis mutandis.

Though there is no commissioning of a human king, there is the divine decision to build, registered in the succession of divine fiats.[18] Though there is no conscription of laborers or acquisition of materials, there is the creative word of God which by itself effects all, producing all the materials, doing all the work. And the other major components of the standard pattern are quite plainly present. Within the six-day schema the process of construction is delineated and the form and furnishings of the temple are described. The record of the seventh day contains the statement of the completion of the project and the approval of the work as in accord with the divine plan and exemplar; the celebration of the enthronement of the deity within the temple and its dedication to him; and, in the instituting of the Sabbath ordinance, a declaration of sanctions. The creation prologue of Genesis is then actually the archetypal temple building account.[19] To portray the building of later temples after this pattern was to identify these redemptive projects as acts of (re-)creation (a theme we shall return to below).

(ii) *Noah and the Ark Covenant:* The story of Noah's building of the ark fits into the present survey, for the ark was a temple structure. It was designed to be a copy of the cosmic temple made by the Creator. Its three stories correspond to the cosmos conceptualized as divided into the three levels of the heavens, earth, and the sphere under the earth. Its window corresponded to the window of heaven and its door to the door of the deep (cf. Gen 7:11).[20] The ark's temple identity is corroborated by the reflection of its architecture in the Mosaic tabernacle and the Solomonic temple. Their structure too reproduced the three story pattern of the cosmos both in their horizontal floor plan and in their vertical sectioning.[21] Note also the three-storied side chambers of the temple. In addition, the temple had the features of the door and upper window, and it shared the ark's vertical dimension of thirty cubits.

Further, the narrative of the building of the ark exhibits in a comprehensive way that complex literary form conventionally employed in biblical and extrabiblical accounts of temple building. It begins with the divine decision that the chosen human agent should build the ark. This purpose is disclosed as a covenantal commission with a divine commitment to prosper the undertaking (Gen 6:13ff.). Other standard elements are the description of the ark and its occupants, the design being given by divine revelation (Gen 6:14ff.); the acquisition of materials (Gen 6:14) and the assembling of the furnishings, here in the form of the representatives of the plant, animal, and human spheres that occupied this holy cosmic kingdom structure (Gen 6:18ff. and 7:1ff.); the statement that the ark was built according to specifications and completed (Gen 6:22); date formulae (Gen 7:6,11,13); and the dedication of the ark-kingdom (Gen 8:20), followed by a declaration of future sanctions.[22]

Constructing the ark-temple was a covenantal project. The commission to build the ark is given within the divine revelation in which the actual term *bĕrît*, "covenant," first appears in the Bible (Gen 6: 18). In fact, the verses containing the commission and the covenant declaration (vv. 14 and 18 respectively) occupy parallel positions in the literary structure of the flood account.[23] Implicit but unmistakable in the commission thus equated with the covenant is a commitment on the part of the Lord, the divinely sanctioned commitment that qualifies this arrangement to be called "covenant". In commanding Noah to make the ark (v. 14) the Lord was covenanting to prosper the enterprise. This becomes more explicit in verse 18 where there is an immediate association of the two; God's promise to fulfill this covenant is at once followed by further details of the commission, instructing Noah to enter the ark to be kept alive when God brings his judgment on the rest of the world (v. 17).[24] The commission to build the ark-temple was then clearly a covenantal commissioning.

The ark was crown construction, for Noah had royal status within the kingdom-typology of this covenantal event.[25] Within the holy bounds of the theocratic ark-world Noah's role was a redemptive resumption of Adam's royal position and prospects under the Covenant of Creation. He was king of that temple-kingdom, with all the creatures placed under his rule, with the creation and all its tempestuous forces made subservient to his honor and blessing. Royal dominion as experienced by Noah in the ark-theocracy exceeded what Adam enjoyed as an original endowment of the creation covenant; it was a symbolic equivalent of the lordship Adam was to secure as a reward for success in his probationary mission. Noah's kingship was thus prophetic of the kingship of Jesus, the second Adam, who accomplishes the act of probation-righteousness and thereby attains the position of glory and honor where all things have been effectively put in subjection under his feet (Heb 2:6-9). It was the ark-covenant that invested Noah with this royal dignity and it was as type of the messianic King, the masterbuilder of the church-temple, that Noah was commissioned to build the ark-temple.

(iii) *Moses and the Old Covenant:* The interrelation of the tabernacle and the covenant mediated through Moses at Sinai is patent. Construction of this divine dwelling was the immediate, major assignment stipulated for the vassal community of Israel in this covenant. A house of God is already mentioned (Exod 23:19) within the account of the ratification of the covenant (Exodus 19-24), which is at once followed by the detailed prescriptions for the tabernacle (Exodus 25-31) and by the narrative of its actual construction (Exodus 35-40). This amounted to a record of the confirmation and inauguration of the covenant order, for the tabernacle was the supreme expression of God's covenant relationship to Israel. Even the interruptive episode of the golden calf (Exodus 32-34) attests in its negative way to the correlation of the tabernacle and covenant by showing how the loss of covenant status (through Israel's covenant-breaking) meant the loss of God's Presence and the forfeiture of his tabernacle-residence in their midst.[26]

Like the narrative about Noah's ark-temple, Exodus 25-40 exhibits the pattern of the common Near Eastern temple building accounts, including the following elements: the divine decision to build revealed as a covenantal commission to Moses (Exod 25:1,8) and mediated by him to the people (Exod 34:29-35:19); the prescriptive description of the tabernacle and its furnishings (Exod 25:10ff.), along with its priesthood and their accoutrements (Exod 28:1ff.)—a human replication of the tabernacle, affording an intimation of the living people-temple to be built by the messianic masterbuilder; the heavenly exemplar (Exod 25:9,40); the acquisition of materials

(Exod 25:3-7; 35:4-29; 36:3-7) and the securing of expert craftsmen (Exod 35:30-36:9); the actual building process (Exod 36:8-40:33) with notice that all was completed according to specifications (Exod 39:32,42,43; 40:16,19,21,23, 25,27,29,32,33); the blessing on the people (Exod 39:43; cf. Lev 9:22,23); the dedication by symbolic anointing (Exod 40:9-16; cf. 30:22-23; cf. Lev 8:10; Numbers 7) and by the entry of God's Glory into his holy house (Exod 40:34; cf. 29:44; Lev 9:23, 24).[27]

Though the covenant stipulation to build the tabernacle was given to the covenant community as a whole and the entire nation, especially its gifted artisans, was engaged in the work, it was more particularly a divine commission to Moses as mediator of the covenant program. Completion of it all is attributed to him (Exod 40:33). Building the house of God was, therefore, in the case of the tabernacle once again crown construction. For Moses was the shepherd-king of God's flock, the one set as royal ruler over the entire theocratic community (cf. Num 12:7; Heb 3:2).

(iv) *Solomon and the Davidic Covenant:* We have already seen that the biblical narrative of the building of the Solomonic temple is an outstanding example of the conventional Near Eastern literary form used for such affairs. This episode is also a classic instance of temple building as a task for kings, the project having been proposed by king David and carried out by king Solomon. And here again there is a close correlation of temple building and covenant. The Lord's approval of David's proposal, revealed through the prophet Nathan, was incorporated in and was a central feature of a divine covenant of grant (2 Sam 7:4ff.; 23:5; Ps 89:3 [4]).

The covenantal context of Solomon's temple building is underscored by repeated rehearsal of the terms of the Davidic Covenant in the narrative of the process of construction: in David's preparatory charge to Solomon (2 Chr 22:6ff.) and his related address to Israel's leaders (1 Chr 28:2ff.); in Solomon's communication to king Hiram of Tyre when launching the actual project (1 Kgs 5:3-5 [17-19]; 2 Chr 2:4ff.); in a revelation of God to Solomon recorded in the midst of a description of the temple structure and its furnishings (1 Kgs 6:11-13); in Solomon's pronouncing of blessing at the completion of the project (1 Kgs 8:15ff.; 2 Chr 6:4ff.) and his prayer of dedication (1 Kgs 8:23ff.; 2 Chr 6:14ff.; cf. Psalm 132); and in a further revelation of God to Solomon when the temple was finished (1 Kgs 9:4ff.; 2 Chr 7:12ff.).

When defining the function of temple building in the Davidic Covenant we must distinguish between the two levels of the kingdom covenanted to Abraham. In relation to the typological level administered through the old (Mosaic) covenant,[28] the Davidic Covenant was a covenant of grant, rewarding David for faithfully waging the war of the Lord. This works principle, operating at the typological level of the kingdom, was further evidenced in the fact that the continuance of the typological kingdom under the Davidic dynasty was made dependent on the continuing allegiance of the Davidic kings to their heavenly Suzerain, as expressed in their compliance with the probationary stipulations of his covenant. Within this covenant of grant, the temple building commission was a covenant stipulation to be obeyed, and the obedient performance of this service would function as the meritorious ground for dynastic confirmation and continuance (cf. 1 Chr 28:5-7).[29] At the same time, this commission was a high honor and privilege, a sign of God's favor, for the temple represented the dwelling of Immanuel with his people, the ultimate blessing of the covenant.

In relation to the messianic level of the kingdom inaugurated and defined by the new covenant, the Davidic Covenant was one of sovereign grace. It guaranteed the everlasting dynasty and kingdom as a gift of redemptive love. As in the case of the typological kingdom, bestowal of this antitypical kingdom-temple grant involved the accomplishing of a probationary act of righteousness—not, however, by David and his successors in the old Jerusalem. This grant was rather a reward given to the messianic son of David for his meritorious service in fulfillment of the intratrinitarian covenant made in heaven before the world began. At this antitypical level too, temple building functions as validation of royal claim. The bringing of the church-temple to consummation, the work of the ascended Christ through the Spirit, demonstrates the validity of his claim to the crown of heaven and earth. It attests to the Father's establishment of the Son as King of kings on the throne of David at the right hand of the Majesty on high.

In Zechariah 4 this validating messianic achievement is proclaimed in the announcement that the Christ-figure, Zerubbabel, begins and finishes the temple (v. 9a) and the conjoined declaration by the messianic Angel of the Lord (cf. v. 8): "You will know that Yahweh of hosts has sent me unto you" (v. 9b).

(v) *Postexilic Temple and the Davidic Covenant:* In the resumption of the Mosaic-Davidic covenantal order after the exile (cf. Hag 2:5), the Davidic Covenant still provided the primary authorization for the erecting of God's house in Jerusalem (cf. Ezra 5:11). Divine confirmation of the temple (re)building commission came through the prophetic ministry of Haggai and Zechariah, prompting the community to proceed with the task forthwith (Ezra 5:1,2; 6:14).

This commissioning of temple construction was, as usual, a royal mandate, even though no Israelite king occupied the throne in Jerusalem. For at this juncture in the history of the theocratic nation, when Israel was being restored to their typological heritage after the exilic lapse in the Mosaic Covenant relationship, it pleased God to draw king Cyrus, the Persian ruler of the Israelites, into the typological drama of redemption in the role of restorer. By special divine appointment, king Cyrus was constituted a prefiguration of Messiah, who would one day restore the true Israel of God from their exile east of Eden and who would build the true temple of God. "Yahweh stirred up the spirit of Cyrus king of Persia" so that he issued a decree for the restoration of God's house in Jerusalem, asserting therein that he had been charged to do so by the God of heaven (2 Chr 36:22,23; Ezra 1:1-4; 5:13; 6:14). This happened in fulfillment of God's remarkable word through Isaiah, beforehand identifying king Cyrus as his anointed shepherd-king, whom he would commission to build his city and temple (Isa 44:28; 45:1 ff., esp. v. 13).

The narrative of the building of the postexilic temple in Ezra 1-6 contains most of the standard features of such accounts. In addition to the divine commissioning of king Cyrus, these include: the acquisition of materials and enlisting of workmen (Ezra 1:5ff.; 3:7ff.); description of the structure (Ezra 6:3,4) and the progress of the building to completion, in accordance with God's command (Ezra 3:2,11; 5:2; 6:14), with dates (Ezra 3:8; 6:15; cf. Hag 1:1,15; 2:10); and dedication festivities (Ezra 6:16-18).

This history of the restoration of the temple was, of course, the immediate context in view in Zechariah's fifth vision, providing the typological imagery for the prophecy of Messiah, the royal masterbuilder of the menorah-temple. As previously indicated, the choice of Zerubbabel as the type of Christ related to the principle that temple building is a task for kings, Zerubbabel being a prince of David's dynasty.

Christ, the true theocratic king, would lay the foundation of the true temple, typified by Noah's ark, Moses' tabernacle, and the Solomon/Zerubbabel temple, and he would complete it. His temple would be a Spirit-people-temple, such as was envisaged in the royal mandate given to Adam under the Covenant of Creation. Christ received his royal commission in the eternal intratrinitarian covenant with the Father and as agent of the Spirit he carries out the holy building task in his administration of the new covenant, by the Great Commission enlisting his followers as his fellow-workers in the menorah mission.

(vi) *Excursus:* God's covenanting with man is a controlling element in biblical religion, but elsewhere covenant is not so evident a feature of the relation of deity to men. However, the divine commissioning of kings to build temples, as narrated in the standard accounts, involved the essential ingredients of a suzerain-vassal covenant. By charging the king with the task of erecting the temple, the deity exercised his sovereignty over him and facilitated the ongoing administration of the tributary relationship inasmuch as it was in the temple that the vassal king's tribute offerings were brought before the divine suzerain. Also, inherent in the commission to build the temple, and specified in the king's dedication prayer, was the deity's commitment to grant various boons: the entrance of the deity into the temple; the exaltation of the king and extension of his scepter to distant days; and the fertility of his land.[30] Such divinely sanctioned commitment is definitive of covenant. And since, according to the dedication prayer, the promised blessings were to be bestowed on the king for his good services (i.e., for his obedient performance of the commission), divine commission to build a temple was tantamount, more particularly, to a proposal-of-grant covenant.

This covenantal arrangement was established by divine declaration,[31] no treaty text functioned as an instrument of ratification. But the affair was documented by the inscription containing the temple building account, and the possibility suggests itself that the conventional treaty form has influenced the shaping of these accounts. For the basic sections of suzerainty treaties find their counterparts in the building inscriptions: the preamble and historical prologue sections presenting the suzerain's claims on the vassal's service; the stipulations section stating the suzerain's commandments; and the sanctions section enunciating the constraints on the vassal's loyal obedience. In the building accounts, the suzerain's claims are presented in the very identity of the divine author of the decision to build and in his authoritative communication of the assignment. The contents of the commission are, of course, the covenant stipulations, and the benefits promised to the royal builder are the sanctions. Of special interest is another variety of the sanctions found in many building accounts, one that is reminiscent of the treaty form (though also present in other kinds of texts). It consists of a closing section pronouncing curses and blessings on future rulers, according to their treatment of the temple and its building inscription. At times this was modified into a more general appeal to future kings to show piety towards the gods, with promise of divine blessings.[32] This obviously reflects the concluding section of curses and blessings in the classic treaty form,[33] but in addition the sanction relating to the treatment of the building inscription is akin to the curse against tampering with the treaty text found in the distinctive document clause of the treaties.

2. Temple-building: Conquest and Creation:

(a) *Conquest, A Corollary of Construction:* In the ABCA'B'C' arrangement of the double oracle in Zech 4:6-10, the two A-sections (vv. 6b and 9) declare that the temple will be completed by the power of the Spirit, exercised through his messianic agent, "Zerubbabel." This declaration is made in the face of difficulties whose presence is reflected in the challenging questions issued in the two B-sections (vv. 7a and 10a). It is evident that construction of the temple, promised again in the C-sections (vv. 7b and 10b), is going to involve conquest of the enemy.

"Who[34] are you, O great mountain before Zerubbabel? (Before Zerubbabel you will become) a plain" (Zech 4:7a). This is the kind of interrogative challenge the apostle Paul used to defy all that threatened God's elect. "If God is for us, who can be against us?" (Rom 8:31). "Who shall separate us from the love of Christ?" (Rom 8:35). No hardship, nothing in all creation; we are more than conquerors through our God who is with us (Rom 8:31-39). The apostle was echoing Psalm 118. " Yahweh is for me; what can man do to me?" (v. 6). Zech 4:6-10 and Psalm 118 share the primary theme of God as the strength of his people (cf. Ps 118:14 and Zech 4:6) and the distinctive motif of the stone in the messianic temple that signifies the overcoming of opposition (cf. Ps 118:22 and Zech 4:7b, 10b). Note also that in Psalm 118: 13 the enemy whom the Lord cuts off is addressed in the second person singular (cf. Zech 4:7a). These correspondences suggest that Ps 118:6 is the inspiration for Zech 4:7a as well as for Rom 8:31.

The hostility (not merely rivalry) of the great mountain becomes more explicit if "before (*lipnê*) Zerubbabel" is taken with what precedes. The mountain power is then pictured as putting the battle in array against Zerubbabel (cf.the use of *lipnê* 1 Chr 14:8; 2 Chr 14:9 [10]). If "before Zerubbabel" is taken with what follows, the mountain is depicted as being humbled in the presence of a superior Zerubbabel (cf. the use of *lipnê* in Exod 9:11; Deut 1:42; Judg 2:14; 20:32; 1 Sam 4:2). Our translation of verse 7a above reflects the possibility that this is a case of the poetic device in which a word written once applies in both directions, sometimes with different meanings.[35]

Interpretations of the great mountain include: the pile of ruins on Zion that had to be cleared away in the preparing of a foundation platform for the temple; the difficulties in general that beset the building enterprise; and the particular local adversaries of the project. But the context of the night visions favors the view that the great mountain symbolizes the hostile imperial power seen as a satanic counterfeit of Zion, the temple mountain of God and seat of his sovereignty (cf. Zech 6:1).[36] Especially relevant is the treatment of the horn-nations in Zechariah's second vision: the titanic world power lifts up its head-horn on high against the living God of Zion but its idolatrous challenge is brought low by God's expert agents of vengeance.[37] In the fifth vision the leveling of the self-exalted imperial power is conveyed by the word "a plain." Isa 40:4 speaks of mountains leveled into plains and Isa 41:15 assures lowly Israel, warred against by enemies (vv. 11-14), that the Lord their Redeemer will make them his instrument to reduce these "mountains" to dust. In Zech 4:7, however the phrase "before Zerubbabel" is connected to the rest of the sentence, the picture is one of conflict between Zerubbabel and the great mountain, so that the leveling of the mountain to a plain marks an overcoming of the world-power before Zerubbabel, a casting down of Satan's kingdom by the messianic king.

God's challenge to the hostile world, "Who are you?" (v.7), is issued at a time when the covenant community is outwardly weak. The world mountain towers over them. The restoration of the temple on Zion is just beginning (cf. Hag 2:3). This is reflected in the parallel challenging question of verse 10a: "Who is despising the day of small things?" God's challenge sets the stage for the announcement of a total reversal on both sides; not only will the high world mountain be brought low but lowly Zion will be exalted—Zerubbabel will complete the temple of heavenly glory (cf. Hag.

2:9). God will shake heaven and earth, overthrowing royal thrones and world kingdoms, while making Zerubbabel as his own signet ring (cf. Hag 2:21-23).

Conquest of the world is the corollary of temple building. Holy war must clear the way for the holy work of building God's house.

(b) *Construction, A Copying of Creation:* The theme of the construction of God's kingdom-temple that follows on the victory against the world mountain is found in both the A-sections (Zech 4:6b and 9) and C-sections (Zech 4:7b and 10b). Together they declare that Zerubbabel begins and finishes the temple. Verse 9a provides a clear, comprehensive statement to this effect, and verses 7b and 10b supply graphic details of either the founding or completing of the building, depending on how one understands the two stones.

Some understand "the head (*hārōšâ*) stone" brought forth by Zerubbabel as the cornerstone (cf. "head of the corner" in Ps 118:22). On the basis of customs elsewhere in the biblical world, others take it as a former stone, i.e., a stone derived from the previous temple on this site and deposited in the foundation of the new temple to assert the continuity of the two. Van der Woude interprets it as "the stone Beginning ... the primeval stone from which the creation of the world commenced," an allusion to the mythological idea of a primal hill that emerged from the chaos waters as the starting point and center of creation.[38] On this view too verse 7b would refer to the foundation stage. But the laying of the foundations of the postexilic temple (which is the immediate, typological perspective here) had already taken place. Also, what we expect in verse 7b as the corollary of the leveling of the lofty world mountain (v. 7a) is the exaltation on high of the lowly house of God. The reference would then be to the completing of the temple and the stone would be the final topstone. An expectation that *hārōšâ* will have the meaning "top" here is prompted by the *rōšāh*, "its top,"[39] in verse 2, referring to the menorah. Further, the concluding words of verse 7b have been understood as a public acclamation such as might attend the completion of a project (cf. 2 Sam 6:15), in the present case, the closing ceremonies dedicating the temple (cf. 2 Chr 7:4-6). The exclamation, "*ḥēn, ḥēn,*" would be appropriate to such an occasion whether interpreted as praise of the beauty of the edifice or petition for God's continuing blessing on the temple (cf. 1 Kgs. 8:29, 43).[40]

On the other hand, Ezra 3:10,11 records joyful shouting at the laying of the foundations of the postexilic temple.[41]

The occasion of the challenging question in verse 10a is a time of "small things," characterized by disparaging comments of the gainsayers, a relatively early phase in the temple restoration project. The stone mentioned in verse 10b, the stone in the hands of Zerubbabel described as *habbĕdîl*, will also belong to that earlier stage. *Bĕdîl* means tin and the major ancient versions interpreted this stone as a plummet.[42] A plumb stone could refer to any stage in the building process. Other identifications include: one of the sacred objects, including precious stones or metallic tablets, deposited in foundations; and a set aside or chosen stone (cf. the verb *bdl*, "separate, divide"), whether the stone of verse 7b, understood as a stone taken from the ruins of the former temple, or as a special stone selected to be a keystone.[43] With emendation to *bĕdōlaḥ*, "bdellium," the stone could be a symbolic signet.

Zerubbabel's temple building, like all temple construction, had as its archetype God's original creation of the cosmic temple. As we have seen, the Genesis prologue exhibits in prototypal form the standard literary pattern of temple building texts.[44] The Zech 4:6-10 account parallels the Genesis prologue in such fundamental features as the dual role of paradigm and power assigned to the Spirit in temple construction and the emphasis on the commencement and completion of the project. Of incidental interest here is the similarity of the record of Zerubbabel's temple building in Zech 4:6-10 and the creation event as reflected in the Lord's interrogation of Job (cf. Job 38 and 39). Each account contains these elements: challenging questions put to human wisdom and power (Job 38:2,4,5, passim); laying the foundation (Job 38:4) with mention of a particular stone (in Job 38:6, the cornerstone); reference to a line, measuring or plumb (Job 38:5); acclamation over the architectural achievement (Job 38:7).

Throughout its history temple construction is depicted as creation activity. A short survey of the matter will be presented in the following chronicle, which will also note the recurring correlation of conquest to temple building.

(c) *Chronicle of Conquest and Construction:*

(i) *Covenant of Creation:* Although the creation of the cosmos as a house of God was the archetypal temple building, it differed from all postlapsarian temple building in that it was a purely constructive process with no prelude of conflict and conquest. The mythological versions of the creation tradition posit evil as present in precreation reality and characteristically make the creator-god's vanquishing of rival forces of chaos a preliminary step in the creational ordering of the cosmos and the associated building of the hero-god's palace. But Genesis 1, allowing no place for evil before creation, reveals the creation to have been an exercise of simple sovereignty, with no pre-existing rival powers to be overcome by the eternal God.[45]

However, there was also the temple building commission given to Adam, and under the terms of the Covenant of Creation there was a probationary conflict to be endured and an enemy to be overcome before the temple program could proceed. By this time satanic evil had arisen in the world and Adam's immediate task was to confront and judge the challenge of that evil and so maintain the sanctity of Eden. Only then would the program of filling the earth with the family of Adam and Eve, the living people-temple, go forward. Royal temple building was a covenantal grant proposed on the basis of a probationary obedience in warfare against the devil. Faithful service issuing in triumph in this holy war was prerequisite to construction of God's holy house.

(ii) *Ark Covenant:* The ark was a symbolic replica of the cosmos-temple; Noah's building of the ark-temple was a re-enactment of creation. This creation aspect of the event is brought out by the literary form of the flood narrative, whose structure and style parallel the creation narrative in the Genesis prologue. Also, the physical phenomena of the episode recall in a remarkable, if limited, way the original creation history. There is a return to the situation of unbounded waters dealt with in "day two," a re-emergence of the dry land, and a reappearance on the earth of the representatives of the vegetable and animal kingdoms, and of man. Of special interest in view of the role of the Spirit (*rûaḥ*) in temple building in Zechariah 4 is the role Gen 8:1 assigns to *rûaḥ* (echoing the *rûaḥ* of Gen 1:2) in the restructuring of the earth out of the deluge waters. These cosmological correspondences were recognized by Peter who boldly expounded the flood event as the creation of the heavens and earth that now are (2 Pet 3:5-7).[46]

Antecedent to this creation of the present heavens and earth was the conquest of the opponents of God's rule, the persecutors of his people who had dominated the old world.[47] Noah had opposed the antichrist world in his prophetic witness, declaring its condemnation, and God, the ultimate temple builder, triumphed over the enemies in judgment, destroying them by drowning their world in watery chaos. The vanquishing of the satanic powers was thus a precursor of the arrival of the ark-temple, the holy kingdom-city, at its sabbath rest on the high mountain in the re-created heavens and earth.

(iii) *Old Covenant:* With Moses as his messianic agent, Yahweh triumphed over Egypt and its gods in acts of judgment, which Scripture figures as a divine slaying of the satanic dragon (Ps 74:12ff.; Isa 51:9f.; cf. Ezek 29:3ff.; 32:2ff.). The Egyptian sea is also identified with the draconic powers whom the Lord defeats in redemptive judgment for the salvation of his people.[48] At the same time, the mastery of the sea by the Glory-Spirit, consisting as it does in the dividing and bounding of the waters so that the dry land appears, is a reproduction of the creation process. A re-creation setting is thus evoked for the temple building that takes place under Moses, whether we are thinking of the forming of the nation as the holy house of Israel, God's people-temple, or of the erection of the tabernacle. Agreeably, the tabernacle is designed to be a replica of the cosmic temple created in the beginning.[49] Tabernacle construction is a copying of creation; however, being a redemptive (re-)creation event, building of the tabernacle was preceded by the conquest of pharaoh and his forces, the manifestation of Yahweh's supreme sovereignty in anticipation of his enthronement in the exalted sanctuary to be prepared for him.

(iv) *Davidic Covenant:* At its typological level the Davidic Covenant proferred temple building prerogative and continuance of dynasty on the condition of the continuing faithfulness of God's royal representatives. Indeed, God's making of this covenant of grant was itself a benefit bestowed on David for faithful service he had already rendered, particularly in fighting the wars of the Lord (cf. 1 Kgs 3:6). Significantly, the account of the revelation of the Davidic Covenant (2 Samuel 7) follows upon the record of his conquest of the enemies of the theocratic kingdom, his capturing of Zion, and his locating the ark of the covenant there (2 Samuel 5 and 6). David's military service was the ground for God's granting to his dynasty the privilege of building the temple. Thus, conquest was the prelude to temple construction.

The same pattern emerges when the matter is viewed from the perspective of the Lord as the divine warrior. The battle was the Lord's; David was merely his agent. And in the building of the temple too the human king was only the agent of the Lord, whose house it was and who was its ultimate architect and builder. It was as the victorious divine warrior that God proceeded with the building of his temple as the seat of his enthronement as King of kings. Pointing to the pattern of divine conquest as prelude to divine temple construction is the statement in 2 Sam 7:1 that it was Yahweh who had given David rest, making him victorious over all enemies round about. The Lord had initiated the conquest of his theocratic domain under Moses and Joshua (cf. 2 Sam 7:5-7) and had now finished it through his servant David (cf. 2 Sam 7:9-11), and it was this completing of the conquest that opened the way for his ordering the erection of his more permanent house of enthronement (cf. 2 Sam 7:7,13). Appropriately, the covenant oracle providing for the building of the Lord's holy palace was cast in the genre of the victory hymn.[50]

(d) *Conclusion:* Under the typological figure of Zerubbabel's temple building, Zech 4:6-10 prophesies of Christ's temple building. Zerubbabel's carrying forward the temple project from foundational commencement to dedicatory consummation is a redemptive repetition of God's original creation of his cosmic temple. And the leveling of the imperial mountain before Zerubbabel as he engages in raising up the head of God's house on Zion exemplifies the pattern, constant from the first to the second Adam, that finds the slaying of the dragon to be the precursor of the erection of God's royal residence.

The New Testament depicts the work of Christ as a fulfillment of this typological paradigm, particularly so in the drama of the Apocalypse. It is Christ, the Son of Man who has decisively overcome the satanic dragon and has been established in supreme heavenly authority with cosmic dominion (cf. Rev 1:12ff., 2:1,8,12,18; 3:1,7,14; 12:1ff.; 20:1-3), who then proceeds to fashion the seven menorah-churches, the true temple-city, by his authoritative, creative word through the power of the Spirit (cf. Revelation 2 and 3). At the climax of the Apocalypse, the consummating of this holy architectural enterprise in the manifestation of the new Jerusalem, the glorified temple-city, follows as the sequel to Christ's "final judgment-conquest of the dragon and his hosts (Rev 20:10; cf. v. 2), by which the son of David secured rest forever from all the enemies round about."[51]

C. *Messiah—Anointer with the Spirit: Mediator to the Menorah.*

1. *Mediator Symbolism:* Zechariah had received the interpretation he requested for the two olive trees and, in particular, their product, the olive oil (Zech 4:4). This symbolism represented the theophanic Spirit, the archetypal pattern for the menorah-church and the power for fulfilling the menorah mission (Zech 4:1-10). The prophet's interest then focused on the coupling of the trees with the menorah (vv. 11-14). Commentators who have mistakenly identified the menorah as a symbol for the Lord are understandably uncomfortable with the consequences of that for verse 12. For on their view verse 12 would depict deity (the menorah) as dependent on a flow of energy (the oil) from his servants (the trees). Some would resolve the problem by dismissing verse 12 as a later editorial addition. Of course, even without the explicit account in verse 12 of the flow of oil through the connecting apparatus, the thought would naturally present itself that the two flanking olive trees served as the source of oil for the menorah. Moreover, as we shall see, that thought is also conveyed by the identifying phrase "sons of oil" in verse 14.

"What are these two olive trees?" asks Zechariah (v. 11). Then, repeating his question, he adds the term *šibbōlet* to the description of the trees (v. 12). In this passage *šibbōlet* is usually translated "branches," but elsewhere it regularly refers to an ear of grain, though it is apparently applicable to the harvestable inflorescence of other plants. A grammatical question also requires attention. In the phrase "the two *šibbōlet*'s of the olive trees," the genitive (the olive trees) is usually regarded as subjective. Thus construed, the *šibbōlet*'s are a part of the trees; hence the customary translation "(end) branches" or "tufts." The genitive should, however, be taken as explicative, the olive trees specifying the particular genus of *šibbōlet*, i.e., an olive tree kind of *šibbōlet*. In effect, the *šibbōlet*'s are then a metaphor for the olive trees, likening them in their flowering of fruit, about to be harvested and processed, to a spike or inflorescence of grain.

A second noun *šibbōlet* means "flowing (or deep) stream" (cf. Ps 69:2, 15 [3,16]) and the rest of the symbolic picture in Zech 4:12b suggests that the prophet's question plays on this double meaning. In relation to the conduits that connect the trees to the menorah, *šibbōlet* would signify the flowing stream of olive oil that issues from each tree. As they pour out their golden oil through the channels the olive trees become olive oil rivers. In the combination of the two meanings of *šibbōlet* the images of the tree of life and the river of life merge (cf. Ezek 47:1-12; Zech 14:8; Rev 22:1,2; John 7:37-39).

A curious parallel to Zechariah's treatment of *šibbōlet is* found in Isa 27:12 (which may well have been his inspiration). There again *šibbōlet* seems to refer to olive trees rather than grain.[52] The Lord is pictured gathering his people like fruit "from the *šibbōlet,*" that is, from the olive tree inflorescence. But the second meaning, from the flowing stream, is required by the following words describing the extent of the harvest: "(from the flowing stream) of the River (Euphrates) to the Wadi of Egypt."

In Zechariah's vision the process of pressing the fruit of the *šibbōlet*-trees to extract their oil for the menorah is not delineated; it is contained, hidden as it were, in the compression of the olive trees ripe for harvest and the streams of olive oil within the pun on *šibbōlet*. More evident is the copious quantity of oil that results from the wondrous transformation of the trees into streams. The large volume of oil flow indicated by the term *šibbōlet* (cf. Ps 69:15 [16]) is also intimated by the term *ṣantārôt*, which denotes the two golden shafts through which the oil is channeled to the menorah.[53] Definitely, the picture is not that of two end tufts adjoining narrow pipes into which they trickle oil. The indications of a supply of oil in abundance support the interpretation of the two *šibbōlet*'s (in their arboreal meaning) as the two olive trees in their harvestable fullness.

Responding to Zechariah's inquiry about the two *šibbōlet*-trees, the angel identifies them as "the two sons of oil who stand by the Lord of all the earth" (v. 14). Fittingly, "sons of oil" signifies a plentiful source of oil. "Sons of " expresses here the idea of a source, as it does in Isa 5:1, where a fertile hill is called "a son of fatness (or oil)."[54] *Yiṣhār,* the term for oil, denotes fresh olive oil, and it consistently connotes abundant harvest. The angel's answer thus confirms the understanding of the symbolism of the *šibbōlet*-trees as the (mediatorial) source—an inexhaustibly rich source—of the oil.

But what historical persons are meant? Who are the two sons of oil?[55] Since the *šibbōlet*-trees are the source of the oil, not the recipient, their identification as "sons of oil" does not signify that they were anointed ones. In fact, not *yiṣhār* but *šemen* would be used for anointing oil. The misunderstanding of the sons of oil as anointed ones has led to the common interpretation of the two as the royal and priestly offices, represented in Zechariah's day by Zerubbabel and Joshua. But if the trees are the (mediatorial) source of the oil that streams to the menorah, if the sons of oil are not the anointed but the anointers, we must think of prophets, not kings or priests. "The prophets, outstandingly the paradigm prophet Moses, were God's chief agents for anointing."[56] Moreover, in Rev 11:4 it is the two prophetic witnesses that are explicitly said to be the two olive trees. Further, the description of the sons of oil as "standing by the Lord of all the earth," that is, as his servants, comports with the familiar designation of the prophets as God's servants (cf. Amos 3:7; Jer 7:25; 25:4; Rev 10:7; 11:18). This description also points to prophetic identification in that it denotes the status of those admitted into the divine council (cf. its use for angelic members of the council in Zech 3:7), a special privilege of prophets.

Why there are two prophet-trees is a matter of the total design of the vision, which mirrors the symbolic setting of the Glory-Presence in the holy of holies with its dual-cherubim pattern (of which, more presently). We need not seek particular candidates, therefore, like Haggai and Zechariah, or Moses and Elijah (although their careers do supply the details of the picture of the career of the two prophet-witnesses in Rev 11:3ff.).

Though the symbolic representation of the divine Presence is to be found not in the menorah but in the olive trees, Zech 4:12 shows that these two trees as such represent the prophet-mediators of the Spirit and, therefore, it is more precisely the oil of these olive trees which is mediated through them to the menorah that symbolizes the Spirit-Presence. The Mosaic prophets were part of the menorah community[57] and yet in their office were distanced from the covenant people and became the representatives of God, the mediators of his word and the mediators of his Spirit-Presence to the community. Hence they appear in Zechariah's vision, in the form of the two *šibbōlet*-trees, as the insignia of deity, in a manner analogous to the two cherubim figures that stand by the enthroned Glory in the holy of holies. Cherubim and prophets, members alike of the retinue of the King of Glory, bespeak his Presence. It is in keeping with this that the dual, overarching pattern of the theophanic cherubim is reproduced in the Zechariah 4 vision of the two prophets of the Spirit-Presence. Here is the justification for speaking of the two olive trees as a symbolic depiction of the theophanic Glory.

It is evident that the Old Testament prophets could only in a typological manner be the source or mediators of the Spirit. "'The two sons of oil' in Zechariah 4 may be identified with the Old Testament prophets only in the limited sense that they were prototypal of the Lord Christ, the archetypal-antitypical prophet, who in the fullest measure possessed the Spirit, who was one with the Spirit, who was in truth the mediatorial source of the Spirit for his lampstand-church."[58] And once it is recognized that ultimately the two *šibbōlet*-trees are Christ, they may be identified without qualification as representing the divine Presence. The trees and their oil—Christ and the Spirit.

2. *Messianic Mediator:* Christ's mediating of the Spirit-oil to the menorah-church, typified at the close of the fifth vision, sets in motion the working of the Spirit symbolized in the first part of the vision—the Spirit's functioning as creator-paradigm who fashions the menorah-church in his Glory-likeness and as the divine power by which the church performs its menorah mission. With these prophetic themes, Zechariah's vision directs us to the Great Commission and Pentecost. The church's world witness is undertaken in obedience to the charge of Christ, who summons it to imitate him, the model light of the world. In the Great Commission he calls his disciples to be colaborers with him in building the menorah, in fathering the church in his image, the perfect image of the Spirit. Then by pouring out the charism of Pentecost, the messianic mediator implements his covenantal commissioning of his church.

(a) *Christ and the Covenantal Commission:* What we commonly refer to as the Great Commission (Matt 28:18-20) is of larger significance than "commission" would suggest. It is more broadly a covenantal pronouncement. It performs a critical role in the inauguration of the new covenant, a role similar to that of the revelation on the two tables of the covenant in the establishing of the old covenant.[59] In both cases the setting is that of covenant ratification.

At Sinai there was a declaration of the terms of the treaty (eventually written on the two tables) before the ratificatory act (Exodus 20-23; 24:3). This provided the Israelites with the knowledge necessary for them to take the oath of acceptance, which, with the accompanying altar ritual, ratified the old covenant (Exod 24:3-8). A communion meal celebrated by Israel's representatives in the presence of the Lord on the mount of Glory sealed the establishment of the covenant relation (Exod 24:9-11). And the divinely inscribed treaty tablets, deposited at the footstool of God's throne in the tent of Glory (Exod 34:27-29; 40:20) constituted a permanent documentary witness to the covenant as in effect.

Jesus' covenantal declaration on the occasion of his ascension was also in the context of covenant ratification, not however as preparatory to but consequent to the ratificatory act. Ratification occurred at the Lord's shedding the blood of the new covenant on the cross. Jesus' pronouncement recorded in Matt 28:18-20 served to confirm the already accomplished fact of ratification. It was the promulgation of the new covenant, a summary formulation of its terms and a declaration that this new constitutional order was now in operation. In addition, the new covenant like the old is sacramentally sealed in a communion meal and its status as ratified and in force is attested in divinely inspired documentation, the four Gospels deposited in the canon of new covenant Scripture.[60]

Analysis of Matt 28:18-20 indicates that it exhibits the essential structure of the old covenant documents deposited in the holy of holies—the two tables of the covenant and the "book" of Deuteronomy. Like them it contains: (1) the claims of the covenant Suzerain, establishing his sovereign status in the arrangement by assertions of who he is and what he has done for his people in the past; (2) his commands, stipulating the duty of his servants; and (3) threats and/or promises, which can function as constraints on the loyalty of the covenant servants or as commitments on the Lord's part.[61] We will trace in more detail these basic treaty elements in Matt 28:18-20, and in the process will also observe points of contact with the contents of Zechariah 4.

Jesus began with his coronation claims, declaring himself invested with cosmic authority (Matt 28:18b). It had come to pass according to the Scriptures. In the Psalms God disclosed the eternal covenantal grant to the Son: coronation as theocratic king on holy Zion and entitlement as inheritor and judge of the nations to the uttermost part of the earth (Ps 2:6-9). He would be enthroned at God's right hand, ruling in might in the midst of his enemies, judging among the nations, adoringly served by his priestly people (cf. Psalm 110). In prophetic vision the Son of Man was revealed as annihilator of the satanic beast, granted by the Ancient of Days universal glory and power, everlasting dominion, an imperishable kingdom, the worshipful submission of all peoples, nations, and tongues (Dan 7:9-14). Similarly, Zechariah highlighted the universal sovereignty of the coming messianic mediator of the Spirit and author of the menorah mandate. The prophet portrayed him stationed by "the Lord of the whole earth," whose seven eyes "run to and fro through the whole earth" (Zech 4:10,14).

At the promulgation of the new covenant, close upon his covenant-ratifying death, Jesus announced to his disciples that these Scriptures were that day fulfilled in their ears; the Father had given him all authority in heaven and earth.

The New Testament resounds with praise of the Son who has received universal dominion as the reward of his faithfulness in the covenant made with the Father in eternity. Fulfilling the messianic obligations stipulated in that covenant of works, he had been made in human likeness and had been obedient unto death on a cross. Therefore the Father had now bestowed on him the promised and merited reward, enthronement at the Father's right hand, the dignity of lordship in administering the new covenant, the name above every name at which every knee in all the universe must bow (Phil 2:6-11). In similar vein Jesus is extolled in Hebrews 2 as the one who, made a little lower than the angels, had suffered death and because of that was now crowned with glory and honor, all things put in subjection under his feet. To him, the covenant fulfilling second Adam, thus belongs the eschatological glory originally proferred the first Adam in his covenant of works in Eden (vv. 6-10).

The risen Savior stood before his disciples as the victor, the slayer of the dragon, the conqueror of Satan and his power of death (cf. Rev 12:5-11). He was the living one. He was dead—behold his hands and side—but was now alive forevermore, possessor of the keys of death and Hades (cf. Rev 1:17,18). He was the Son of Man exalted to the pinnacle of heaven with authority over all creation (Matt 28:18b). This self-identification of Christ the Lord in the hour of his ascension, confronting his disciples with who he was and what he had done for them, constituted his claim on their covenantal confidence and commitment.

Proceeding from his holy claims to his sovereign charge, Jesus issued the new covenant commission (Matt 28:19,20a). Formally, this corresponds to the commandments section of the Mosaic covenants, but functionally it differs as the gospel of grace and truth that came by Jesus differs from the law given through Moses (John 1:17). Israel's obedience to the stipulations of the works arrangement mediated by Moses would be accepted as the legal ground of their continued possession of the typological kingdom. But Jesus does not summon the church to earn the eternal kingdom by obedience to the demands of the new covenant. Rather, it is as the one who, by the active and passive obedience of his life and death, has already merited salvation and the glory of the kingdom for his church that Jesus addresses to his disciples the great commission.

Nor is it only in this functional respect that the stipulations of the old and new covenants differ from each other. The central corporate commissions of these two covenants belong to two vastly different eschatological times. The mission of Moses introduced an age of (typological) final judgment and agreeably his covenant commission to Israel was: Go ye and destroy the Canaanites. With the inauguration of the antitypical kingdom at our Lord's first advent an age of salvation was introduced, and with a view to that Jesus' great commission to the church was: Go ye and disciple the nations.[62]

Jesus' great commission is a menorah mandate, a charge to the church to shed abroad the light of its gospel witness. Followers of the Light of the world are to be lighting individual menorah flames and multiplying lampstand churches all over the earth. In so doing these replicas of "the (model) faithful witness" are fathering a growing family of witness-children in the Lord's image—the redemptive fulfillment in the Spirit of the original assignment to mankind to multiply and fill the earth with God's people-temple.

Jesus spells out the discipling task in terms of baptizing into the triune name and teaching his lordly commands. The aim is to extend throughout the globe the sceptre-claims of the King of grace and so elicit everywhere a confession of Jesus as Lord, the confession that is made unto salvation (cf. Rom 10:9,10)

The great commission calls the church to a construction project, a building of the holy temple of God. Risen from the dead, slayer of the dragon and so validated as true King of kings, Jesus fulfills the ancient typological pattern by advancing from victory in the battle ordeal against the enemy of God to the erection of the house which (in his case) is at once the throne site of his sovereignty and God's holy dwelling place. He is himself the Masterbuilder, but he commissions his people to enter into this work of redemptive re-creation with him, promising them that afterwards they shall also sit down with him on his throne (Rev 3:21). As in previous temple-building episodes in Scripture, this divine commission to construct God's temple is covenantal. The menorah-temple mandate of Jesus is issued in the context of his promulgating the new covenant and occupies within it the place of covenantal stipulation.

Our Lord's closing promise to be with his people to the conclusion of this world-age (Matt 28:20) corresponds to the section of sanctions, the third major component in the formulary for old covenant documents. Threats of curse and promises of blessing addressed by Moses to the Israelites were calculated to constrain the obedience by which continuation of God's favor would be secured and his dire judgments averted. While from Israel's perspective the sanctions were constraints to covenant loyalty, viewed from the Lord's perspective these sanctions were his commitments to enforce the terms of the covenant. They were divine guarantees that he would punish rebellion to the third and fourth generation and that he would infallibly confer his promised blessings on covenant-keepers to the thousandth generation. Akin to that kind of guarantee of blessing was Jesus' climactic promise to be with his church always. It envisaged the church, however, not as under probation and having to earn the perpetuation of God's blessings but as the persevering people for whose salvation Jesus was the surety and whom he was sending forth into the world as the Father had sent him into the world (John 17:18). Matt 28:20 is Jesus' commitment to that apostolic community of witnesses, the commitment of a constant presence, which assures the success of their menorah mission.

By the promise, "Lo, I am with you," our Lord identified himself as one with the I Am who so identified himself to Moses (Exod 3:14), promising, "surely I will be with you" (Exod 3:12) and "with your mouth" (Exod 4:15b). The settings of the two promises are similar: the commissioning of Moses to witness to the name of Yahweh before the hostile world power and the sending forth of the church to witness to the name of the Father, Son, and Holy Spirit before a world that hated them because Christ, whom the world hated, had chosen them out of the world (John 15:18-21). In each case the commissioned party is assured of all-sufficient enablement for an otherwise impossible task, the assurance of the divine Presence with them and with the witness of their mouths.

Jesus' promised presence would be in and through the Paraclete-Spirit whom he promised to send, the Spirit of truth sent forth from the Father to witness to the Son (John 15:26), teaching the witnessing church all things and guiding it into all truth (John 14:26; 16:7-14; cf. Exod 4:15c). Our Lord's covenantal commitment thus identifies him as the realization of Zechariah's vision: as the source of the oil channeled to the menorah in a perpetual supply "unto the end of the age" (Matt 28:20b); as the Prophet-Mediator of the Spirit, the seven eyes of the Lord whose sovereign superintendence encompasses "all the earth" (Zech 4:10b,c), matching the scope of the menorah mission to "all the nations" (Matt 28:19a); the Spirit-might by which the hostile world mountain is leveled and the exaltation of the house of God accomplished (Zech 4:6ff.).

(b) *Christ and the Covenanted Charism:* At Pentecost, Jesus the true son of oil poured out the fire-fuel of the Spirit from his heavenly throne and flaming tongues lighted upon the heads of the assembly of commissioned witnesses (Acts 2:2). The Zechariah 4 vision of the menorah with a jubilee of flames had come to life. Here was a reproduction of the symbolic picture in historical reality. The actual menorah lamp was lit. Jesus had inaugurated the church's menorah-mission of world-wide witness, testifying to the new covenant in his blood, showing forth his death until he come.

The fiery Spirit with which Jesus baptized the church at Pentecost (cf. Acts 1:5) represented the enabling presence of Jesus promised in his covenantal commissioning of the disciples (Matt 28:20b; John 14:16-20). In epiphanic form this divine presence was similar to that seen by Moses at his commissioning. But while the flaming Glory burning in the unconsumed bush was a token of the redemptive grace of I Am, the tongues of flame on the apostolic assembly spoke of the Spirit's might available for menorah mission.

By virtue of this presence of the Lord in the Spirit, the church would be empowered to carry out its world-witness commission. For this promise of the Father the disciples must wait. Before they were to go, before they proceeded from Jerusalem to the ends of the earth, the Spirit must come (Acts 1:4). For the Spirit was the Witness who would convict the world of sin and righteousness and judgment (John 16:8). By the presence of the Spirit with their tongues the witnesses of Jesus would be able to stand before rulers and authorities and confess the Son of Man (cf. Luke 12:11, 12). The inauguration day of the menorah mission already demonstrated the effectiveness of the apostolic witness through the power of the Spirit in convicting an international array of sinners of their desperate plight (Acts 2:37ff.; cf. 1 Cor 2:4; 2 Cor 3:1-6; 4:7). And the fruits of this Pentecost day were an earnest of the world-wide harvest that would follow.

For the Pentecost charism the disciples must wait because the menorah mission was one of reproducing the glory of the Light of the world, of fathering children of light. And only the Spirit can accomplish this regeneration, this birth from above, this re-creation in the Glory likeness.

Moses' shining face, while a typical foretaste of this transformation, was the flower on a stem that was to be cut off. It was the glory of a covenant that was to be invalidated (2 Cor 3:7,11,13)[63] because it was not of faith but works (cf. Gal 3:12), a covenant of the letter, written on tables of stone, that could not fulfill the promise of righteousness but was rather a ministration of condemnation and death (2 Cor 3:6,7).

The new covenant, however, is not of works but of grace, a ministration of the Spirit writing on the heart, a ministration of righteousness and life (2 Cor 3:6,8,9). Unlike the old covenant, the new is not terminated in abrogation but endures unto consummation (2 Cor 3:11). Its glory is seen in the face of Jesus Christ (2 Cor 4:6), the model menorah, and that glory shines in our hearts, transfiguring us into the same glory-image (2 Cor 3:18). By the Spirit he sends on Pentecost, Christ replicates his likeness in us, so lighting the menorah of myriad lamps unto the glory of God.

Typologically, the episode in the Sinai history (Exodus 19ff.) that affords the best parallel to the Pentecost event is the twofold anointing of the tabernacle: the symbolic anointing with oil by Moses (Exod 40:9-16) and the anointing with the Spirit-cloud as the Glory filled the tabernacle (Exod 40:34). Linking this old covenant "Pentecost" and the new is the description in Daniel 9 of the mission of Messiah-Prince (vv. 25-27) in the prophecy of the seventy weeks. There, the final purpose of the appointed period of ten jubilees is the anointing of the holy of holies (v. 24).

For Moses to be mediator in the Glory-Spirit's covering and filling the tabernacle was the seal of his mediatorial vocation. Similarly the Pentecost event in fulfillment of Jesus' covenantal commitment to send the Spirit was the confirmation of his claim to be Lord of all, with cosmic authority (Matt

28:18). For to be mediator of the promise of the Father demonstrated that he was enthroned with the Father in the heavens, head over all. Pentecost proclaimed that God had made him both Lord and Christ. It attested that, as prophesied in the psalm, the Father had declared to Jesus, "Sit thou on my right hand till I make thine enemies the footstool of thy feet" (Acts 2:34-36; cf. Zech 4:9).

The two lampstand-witnesses carry out their menorah mission in the confidence that Jesus their Lord is Lord of lords and that he is present with them by his almighty Spirit (Rev 11:4-6). It is he who ordains that they shall maintain their Gospel testimony to all peoples, tribes, tongues, and nations throughout the present Great Commission age (Rev 11:3). Though the beast that comes up out of the abyss at the behest of the dragon will then silence them (Rev 11:7b-11), it will not be until they have completed their global historical task (Rev 11:7a). And the Lord who has loosed Satan with his beast agent from the abyss will quickly quell this Har Magedon challenge and exalt his own witnesses to glory (Rev 11:11,12). Age of testimony—hour of trial—eternal triumph: that is the eschatological course of the menorah-church, patterned after the mission of the Light of the world.

At Pentecost the hands of Zerubbabel-Messiah laid the foundation of the menorah-house of God—and his hands shall finish it (Zech 4:9). Let the heavens ring: Glory in the highest.

---

1 Cf. Exod 25:6,31-40; 27:20,21; 30:7,8; 35:8; 37:17-24; 40:4,24,25; Lev 24:2-4; Num 8:2-4. On the construction of the menorah see Carol L. Myers, *The Tabernacle Menorah* (Missoula, 1976).

2 The chiastically arranged night visions of Zechariah, a triad of visions on either side of the central hinge, might be seen as a literary translation of the menorah structure.

3 In this respect Zechariah's menorah would be more like the ten separate lampstands in Solomon's temple (cf. 1 Kgs 7:49) or the seven individual lampstands of the vision in Rev 1:12.

4 See further *Images of the Spirit*, 86.

5 Ibid., 86. A difference in the two treatments of the theme is that Zechariah 3 presents a priestly model of the *imago Dei*, while the model in Zechariah 4 is prophetic.

6 Cf. also Num 10:2.

7 In relation to the identification of the seven Spirits as seven eyes (Rev 5:6; cf. Zech 3:9; 4:10) note Jesus' comparison of eyes and lamps (Matt 6:22; Luke 11:34).

8 Cf. *Images of the Spirit*, 57-64.

9 Ps 43:3 (cf. 119:105) brings out the conceptual bond of light and truth: "Send forth your light and your truth, let them lead me; let them bring me to your temple mount, unto your dwelling place."

10 Cf. *Images of the Spirit,* 91.

11 Cf.Isa 43:10,12; 44:8,9.

12 The Isaianic Servant figure introduced in Zechariah 3 is thus interpreted in Zechariah 4 as both an individual and corporate servant.

13 This is not to deny that the Logos-designation may refer in the first instance to the ontological pre-incarnational relation of the Son to the Father. But John 1:4, like 1:10, should be understood in terms of the incarnation, not of the general divine providential government of creation. Identification of the light of the Logos with life in John 1:4 and 8:12 is compatible with its revelatory, witness function, for this life is knowledge: "This is life eternal that they should know thee, the only true God, and him whom thou didst send, Jesus Christ" (John 17:3). Cf. E. L. Miller, "The Johannine Origins of the Johannine Logos," JBL 112 (1993), 446, n. 7.

14 *Images of the Spirit,* 90,91 . See the context of this quotation for a detailed account, which leads to the conclusion: "In sum then, the scenario of the whole Revelation 10 and 11 complex is taken over from the Old Testament model of the Angel-prophet directing the prophets, fashioning them in their covenantal office in his own prophet-likeness. Under this figure of the Angel, the Apocalypse portrays Christ structuring the apostle-church in his prophetic image"(93).

15 Cf. the development of this theme in our comments on vision three.

16 For biblical examples, cf., e.g., 1 Kgs 9:15-19; 15:23; 22:39; 2 Kgs 20:20. The messianic temple building of Zechariah's fifth vision amounts to a resumption of the theme of messianic city building in vision three, the counterpart to the fifth vision in the chiastic pattern of the seven visions.

17 Our treatment of this subject is much indebted to V. Hurowitz, I *Have Built You an Exalted House: Temple Building in the Bible in Light of Mesopotamian and Northwest Semitic Writings* (Sheffield, 1992). Hereafter cited as *Hurowitz.*

18 For a related decretive word of God to the heavenly council, cf. Gen 1:26.

19 The mythologized mutations of the true creation tradition also preserve the temple building perspective of the event. So, for example, the gods construct the Esagila sanctuary in honor of Marduk at the conclusion of the "creation" in the *Enuma Elish* (VI, 45ff.). The conventional pattern for building accounts attested in the extrabiblical literature and in the Bible alike stands in continuity with the literary traditions of creation accounts.

20 For details see my *Kingdom Prologue,* 139, 140.

21 See the discussion in my *Images of the Spirit,* 39-42.

22 The account of the making of the vessel in the Gilgamesh epic, as narrated there by Utnapishtim (the Noah figure) exhibits this same pattern. The form-critical evidence of the integrity of the temple-building pattern in Genesis itself and the comparative evidence of the acknowledged unity of the Gilgamesh text contradict the customary source-critical partitioning of the biblical text.

23 For details see my *Kingdom Prologue,* 142.

24 This administration of the salvation and kingdom blessings of the Covenant of Grace reported in Gen 6:13ff. is to be sharply distinguished from the common grace covenant with all the earth recorded in Gen 8:21-9:17.

25 Whether or not Noah was king of his earthly city (as the flood hero is in the Mesopotamian tradition) is not relevant to the theme of temple building as a task for a king, for the common grace world is not the holy sphere to which God's temple and his royal messianic temple builder belong.

26 Parallels have been noted in Mesopotamian texts where the account of the building of the temple is interrupted by a rebellion against the divinely designated builder. See *Hurowitz,* 111.

27 With reference to Pentateuchal origins, it is significant that the structural pattern of the Exodus account of the tabernacle is particularly close to building accounts of the mid-second millennium B.C. (cf. *Hurowitz,* 64,110).

28 The connection of the Davidic Covenant, with its temple building commission, to the Mosaic Law-Covenant is reflected in the attention given by the building narrative to the presence of the two tables of the Torah-covenant in the ark in the temple (cf. I Kgs 6:19; 8:3,9; 2 Chr 5:2ff., esp. v. 10). This interrelationship is also attested in the echoes of the concepts and expressions of the Mosaic Covenant (as forrnulated in its Deuteronomic renewal) which are found, especially, in Solomon's dedication prayer and God's response. Cf. *Hurowitz,* 301.

29 The correlation of temple building and the establishment of dynasty is indicated by the incorporation of the account of the construction of Solomon's palace in the story of the building of the temple (I Kings 7). Construction of the palace waited on the completion of the temple, which confirmed Solomon's right to the theocratic throne.

30 Cf. *Hurowitz,* 298,303,322.

31 Cf. P. Kalluveettil,*Declaration and Covenant* (Rome: Biblical Institute Press, 1982), 93ff.

32 Cf. *Hurowitz,* 304, 306.

33 In the account of Solomon's temple building, God's closing reply to the king is a statement of blessing and curse on the Davidic dynasty and the nation Israel, conditioned on their fidelity or failure in meeting the demands of the Torah-covenant (1 Kgs 9:4-9), and the wording of the sanctions is taken from the Deuteronomic treaty (cf. Deut 28:1,37,45,63; 9:23-26).

34 The *mî* here might be rendered as the indefinite, "whatever (you are)." So Adam van der Woude, "Zion as Primeval Stone in Zechariah 3 and 4" in *Text ant Context: Old Testament and Semitic Studies for F. C Fensham*; ed. W. Claassen (Sheffield, 1988) 240. (Hereafter, *Primeval Stone.*) Favoring the interrogative meaning is the parallel *mî* in Zechariah 4:l0a.

35 See below the discussion of *šibbōlet* in verse 12.

36 Cf. Jer 51:25. The religious dimension of the political reality in view is suggested by the use of the Akkadian equivalent of "great mountain" as a title for various gods, including Enlil and his temple. See B. Halpern, "The Ritual Background of Zechariah's Temple Song," *CBQ* 40 (1978) 187.

37 In our discussion of vision two we noted the Babel-Daniel background of the motif of God's judgment on the pseudocosmic mountain.

38 *Primeval Stone,* 241.

39 The Hebrew has a mappiq in the final *He.*

40 *Ḥēn* can mean either grace or beauty (cf. Prov 17:8).

41 Appealing to ancient versions van der Woude translates *tĕšu'ōt* as "splendor" rather than "shoutings" (*Primeval Stone,* 240,241).

42 Cf. our discussion of the stone in Zech 3:9.

43 Van der Woude (*Primeval Stone,* 243) renders it as the stone "Separation," another name for the stone "Beginning" (v. 7b). Appealing to the use of *bdl* in Genesis I for the separation of the waters, he sees in the stone "Separation" a reference to the rising of the cosmic mountain from the primal sea.

44 Cf. my *The Structure of Biblical Authority,* 86 for the view that Prov 8:22ff. portrays the creation process as a building of the divine wisdom's house.

45 For further discussion of this, see my *Kingdom Prologue,* I 7-20.

46 On these literary and cosmological parallels, see further my *Kingdom Prologue,* 136-139.

47 Cf. *Kingdom Prologue,* 132,133.

48 See the discussion of the deep in our comments on Zech 1:8 and cf. *The Structure of Biblical Authority,* 79-82.

49 Cf. *Images of the Spirit,* 35-42.

50 On this and the similarities of 2 Samuel 7 to Egyptian hymns of victory see *The Structure of Biblical Authority*, 82-84. (Re-)creation aspects of the Solomonic temple building are noted in connection with the discussion of the tabernacle in *Images of the Spirit*, 39-41.

51 *The Structure of Biblical Authority*, 86.

52 Note that the harvesting is "one by one."

53 Ṣantārôt is taken as related to ṣinnôr, "water channel" (cf. 2 Sam 5:18; Ps 42:7 [8]), on which see T. Kleven, "Up the Waterspout," *BAR* 20,4 (1994) 34,35.

54 Šemen is used here for "oil".

55 On the following see further *Images of the Spirit*, 86ff.

56 Ibid., 87.

57 Accordingly, in Rev 11:4 the two prophets are also identified with the two lampstands.

58 *Images of the Spirit*, 88. In their servant status too as those "standing by the Lord," the prophetic sons of oil typified the Messiah as Servant of the Lord (cf. Zech 3:8). In Rev 11:4 the two witnesses identified as the two olive trees symbolize the witnessing church of the new covenant not as typological of Christ, like the Old Testament prophets, but as the body of Christ, which represents him, the head of the body, in his world witness and is thus identifiable with him.

59 "The ten commandments," the common designation of the contents of the stone tablets, likewise does not bring out the full nature of these documents as entire treaties.

60 Cf. *The Structure of Biblical Authority*, 172-203.

61 Cf. my *Treaty of the Great King*, 13-22.

62 Blind to this simple, fundamental difference, practitioners of consistent theonomist theory would apply the policy expressed in Israel's commission to the present new covenant age, and thus, in effect, they advocate that the church, as soon as it is possible, should obliterate the mission field rather than harvest it.

63 In all these verses the verb *katargeō* refers to the old covenant. The passage does not, therefore, say anything about the glow on Moses' face as such fading away or becoming somehow inoperative.

Vision Six (5:1-11)

DESOLATOR OF THE APOSTATES

Introduction. According to the pattern of the introductory formulae (cf. 1:7-8; 1:18 [2:1]; 2:1 [2:5]; 3:1; 4:1-2; 5:1; 6:1) there are seven visions in Zech 1:7-6:8, not eight, for Zechariah 5 is not to be divided into two visions but regarded as a unit, the sixth vision. The introductions to the two triads of visions bracketing the central hinge vision (Zechariah 3) all include the phrase, "I saw and behold," but that is absent from Zech 5:5, where many commentators would begin a separate vision. The phrase we find instead at v. 5 is like one which marks the middle, not beginning, of a vision at Zech 2:3 (2:7).[1]

The unity of the two parts of Zechariah 5 is also indicated by certain interdependencies of grammar and terminology. Thus, the suffix in "their appearance" (v. 6) has as its antecedent the thieves and perjurers of v. 3. And the phrase "in all the land" (v. 6) resumes "all the land" in v. 3. Most compelling, however, are the clear thematic interrelationships of the two parts of the chapter and the remarkable intermeshing of their symbolism. The sixth vision portrays the judgment curse of exile, distinguishing its two distinct stages: destruction of the victims' holdings in their homeland (vv. 1-4) and deportation with relocation in a foreign land (vv. 5-11). Details of the interlocking imagery of the two parts will emerge in the exegesis below.

Within the chiastic arrangement of the two triads of visions the second (1:18-21 [2:1-4]) and sixth (5:1-11) correspond. Each is composed of two parts. Also, as the range of the night visions moves from the world in the first and seventh visions towards Zion and the holy of holies in the central three (the third through the fifth), the focus comes to the theocratic land in the second and sixth. Moreover, each of these deals with the removal of unholy elements from the holy land through instruments of divine judgment.

When the parallelism is traced between the visions and the likewise concentrically structured burdens of Zech 9:1-14:21, the sixth vision and Zech 13:2-9 correspond. Their common message is "judgment within the covenant realm, referred to in both as 'all the land' (5:3,6; 13:8). Apostates are cut off from their place in the holy land (5:4,9-11; 13:8). Associated with this removal is the motif of uncleanness, the unclean stork (5:9) and the unclean spirit (13:2). Prominent in the indictment is swearing or speaking lies in the name of the Lord (5:4; 13:3)."[2]

I. DISPOSSESSION OF THE APOSTATES (5:1-4)

A. *The Flying Scroll.*

1. *Covenant Curse:* By identifying the scroll Zechariah saw as a "curse" (Zech 5:3), the angel tells us it is a covenant document, the Lord's treaty given through Moses. Ratified by the vassal's oath of submission, such suzerainty covenants threatened dire curses in case of perfidy. Hence the terms "oath" and "curse" became synonyms for "covenant."[3] A standard section of the treaties was the sanctions, which (in their classic form) included blessings but were heavily weighted on the curse side (see Deut 28:1-68; 29:16-28; cf. 27:11-26; Lev 26:3-39).[4] It is the execution of this curse sanction of the old covenant that is portrayed in Zechariah 5.

The expression in Zech 5:3, "on this side ... on the other side," is possibly a specific allusion to the covenant tablets of Sinai, since it is used in Exod 32:15 to describe those stone tablets as inscribed on both sides.[5] But the idea might also be that the curse strikes here and there, that is, everywhere throughout "the whole land" (cf. Deut 28:16-19).

When calling upon Israel to swear their covenant loyalty Moses forewarned: "It shall come to pass, if you do not obey Yahweh your God, ... that all these curses will come upon you ... They will pursue you and overtake you until you are destroyed" (Deut 28:15,45). Ultimate among the threatened curses would be the siege and destruction of their dwellings in the holy land and banishment to an alien land. "Yahweh will bring a nation against you from afar... swooping down like an eagle" (Deut 28:49). "They will besiege you in all your cities until your high and fortified walls come down throughout all your land" (Deut 28:52). "You will be plucked off the land ... and Yahweh will scatter you among all peoples" (Deut 28:63-4). By Zechariah's day such an exile judgment had befallen Israel and Judah alike, and now those recently restored from that Babylonian captivity are warned by Zechariah that again in the future such a curse would descend on the covenant community. The houses of the covenant breakers in the promised land would be consumed (Zech 5:1-4) and they would themselves be removed to the land of Shinar (Zech 5:5-11).

"'I will cause it [the curse scroll] to go forth,' declares Yahweh of hosts" (Zech 5:4). In international vassal-treaty relationships the gods invoked as witnesses had the role of visiting the curse sanctions on the offending vassal. But Yahweh, covenant Lord of Israel, is also the God of Israel's oath. He would, therefore, himself be the one who would bring the fierce foreign nation against his disobedient people, as Moses warned (Deut 28:49). When his anger was kindled against them for forsaking his covenant, it was he who would bring on them all the curses written in his treaty (Deut 29:25-28 [24-27]).

2. *Twenty by Ten Cubits:* The dimensions of the curse-scroll were those of the forecourt of the temple (1 Kgs 6:3), a precinct associated with judicial process (1 Kgs 8:31-2). They were also the dimensions of a kindred holy space, the area spanned by the cherubim figures in the holy of holies, the golden setting of the brilliant gem of theophanic Glory. For each cherub was ten cubits high and each outstretched wing of the two cherubim was five cubits (their inside wings touching in the middle above the ark and their two outside wings extending to the walls on either side) for a total width of twenty cubits (1 Kgs 6:23-7).[6]

The flying scroll's dimensions thus direct us to the site from which it issued forth, to the ark in the holy of holies, where the Mosaic treaty texts were kept under the feet of their Author and Administrator, the Lord of the covenant. This documentary witness to the oath-ratified covenant, deposited in the ark, was the reality behind the visionary flying scroll. Judgment would be administered according to the standards stipulated in these covenant documents for life in holy fellowship with the Lord God in his kingdom of love and glory. The King of Glory, enthroned above the ark of the covenant scroll, would maintain the sanctity of his holy house and land according to the covenant's stipulations, cleansing them of all that failed to satisfy its demands, punishing all such according to its sanctions. "According to it ... according to it" (Zech 5:3), they must be cut off.

To carry out this anathema mission of the flying scroll, the Lord sends forth the heavenly agents of judgment, the angels symbolized by the winged cherubim figures flanking the ark of the scroll in the holy of holies. These celestial beings, the guardians of God's holy Presence and the tree of life from the beginning, wielders of the flaming sword at the entrance of Eden, would bring the curse-scroll winging over the land, cutting off with their fiery sword all that profaned God's holy land and temple.

Adoption of the dimensions of the area occupied by the cherubim as the measurements of the flying scroll indicates that it represents the angelic executors of judgment as well as the covenant document, the standard of judgment. The fact that the scroll was flying recalls the exile curse of Deut 28:49, which foretells the coming of the agents of Yahweh's judgment "as the eagle flies." And, of course, the agents of the deportation of the woman in the ephah in the second part of Zechariah's sixth vision also fly. Moreover, as seen by Zechariah, the flying scroll was perhaps actually winged, like the women carrying the ephah (Zech 5:9). Such wing appendages would suggest the figures of the cherubim more immediately and graphically than the scroll's dimensions. Further, the impressionistic image conveyed by the scroll, a large sheet of parchment or leather sailing through the sky, would be that of a cloud.[7] Here was a judgment cloud moving over the land, the winged cloud identified with the cherubim, the cloud-chariot on which the divine warrior-judge advances over the earth (Pss 18:9-15 [10-16]; 104:3).

Now this cherub-winged chariot cloud is one and the same as the theophanic cloud of Glory, the divine Presence revealed in the holy of holies above the ark. In the configuration of symbols there in the holy of holies all the elements of the Zecharian scroll image come together: the ark of the covenant was the provenance of the flying scroll and the ark was the footstool of the enthroned King of Glory, guarded by the overshadowing wings of the cherubim. Scroll and cherubim betoken the presence of the Lord of hosts. Hence the flying scroll not merely symbolizes the standard of the covenant judgment and its angelic agents, it also represents a Parousia of the covenant God and Judge himself. It images an anathema advent of the Lord of hosts riding through the heavens in the midst of his vehicular angel agents.

B. *Thieves and Perjurers.* From the nature of the flying scroll as an administrative instrument of Yahweh's treaty with Israel it is evident that its sphere of judgment is the covenant nation rather than the kingdoms of the world. Other details confirm this. The term *hāʾāreṣ*, though it can mean "earth," in Zech 5:3 must mean "land" (i.e., Canaan), for in the sequel the guilty who are detected in all this "land" (v. 6) are removed to another land, "the land of Shinar" (v. 11). Also, one of the offenses mentioned, namely, swearing falsely by the name of Yahweh (vv. 3,4), implies that the offenders have been avowed subjects of Yahweh within the sphere of his covenant domain.

The particular sins specified as the ground of the curse judgment, perjury and theft, comprise transgression of the first and great commandment and the second, like unto it. Dishonoring God's name by perjury violates the requirement to love him supremely and stealing from one's neighbor is failure to love him as oneself. The selection of theft to individualize sins against neighbors may be due to the connection of sins of embezzlement with swearing oaths of clearance in theocratic judicial process (cf. Lev 6:1-7 [5:20-26]). When the false swearing of an oath of innocence is added to robbery, trespass of the eighth commandment becomes a direct offense against Yahweh too (Lev 6:2 [5:21]).[8] Haters of God and man, godless and lawless, breakers of the covenant, apostates—against such was the scroll curse aimed.

A distinctive feature of the Zechariah 5 portrayal of the offenses that come under judgment is their association with the market place. All the details of the vision, the standards of measurement and weight (cubits, ephah, talent), the theft perpetrated through false balances and aggravated by lying oaths, all this symbolism conducts us into the world of commerce, its business and its sins. What characterizes the apostates targeted by the covenant curse is a mercantile idolatry. They repudiate Yahweh, King of Glory, prostituting themselves to the love of the glory of the world, to the worship of Mammon. Tolerated within the covenant ranks they would change the holy community into something indistinguishable from the world. They would turn Jerusalem into Babylon. Therefore, the King of Zion sends the curse scroll over the whole face of the land to excise them.

C. *Demolition of the Houses of Mammon.* Zech 5:3-4 describes the first stage of exile: siege and destruction. The verb *nqh* in v. 3 is rendered by some "acquit" rather than "cut off." "Acquit" is the usual meaning of the Piel and if the Niphal form in v. 3 reflects that, the guilty are viewed as having resorted to the oath of clearance procedure (cf. 1 Kgs 8:31), swearing falsely in God's name to get themselves acquitted. The point would be that in the eyes of the heavenly Judge, who does not hold those guiltless who swear covenant oaths falsely (Exod 20:7; 34:7), their false oaths have compounded not cleared their sins, and they will not escape his vengeance. However, the Niphal of *nqh* may mean "be made desolate, empty" (cf. Isa 3:26). Also attested is a corresponding meaning of the Piel, "to clear away, purge" (cf. Joel 3:19-21 [4:19-21]; Deut 19:10,13; 21:9; 32:43; Isa 26:21). And it is more natural to understand v. 3b as referring to the desolation effected by the curse God sends forth—specifically mentioned just before (v. 3a) and after (v. 4)—than to the clearance resulting from an oath of innocence that had only supposedly been sworn.[9]

This cutting off takes the form of the demolition of the apostates' houses (Zech 5:4). When threatening Israel with the exile curse, Moses mentioned the leveling of walls associated with siege (Deut 28:52). Concerning the disobedient he also said they would build houses but not live in them (Deut 28:30). The extra-biblical treaty-curse repertoire also included overturning of the victim's house (cf. the eighth century Aramaic Sefire treaty I, C. 21-23). In Zechariah's nearer background are the threats of Nebuchadnezzar (Dan 2:5; 3:29) and Darius (Ezra 6:11) that the houses of any defying their edicts would be laid in ruins.

Entering the houses of the thieves and perjurers, the curse consumes (klh; cf. Deut 28:21) them. Destruction by fire is probably meant. In a similar context in Ezekiel, God declares: "I have poured out my indignation upon them; I have consumed them with the fire of my wrath" (Ezek 22:31). The covenant breakers will discover that the fiery doom of the curse cannot be averted. The arrogant Jehoiakim tried. He took the scroll on which God's prophet had transcribed the covenantal curses, cut it in pieces, and cast them into the fire until all the scroll was incinerated (Jer 36:1-26). But he was not done with it. The curse-scroll rose from the ashes, rewritten, with many like curses added to it (Jer 36:27-32). And, applying the lex talionis, it flew over the land, incinerating the houses of all who despised its warning, people and king alike (cf. Jer 39:8).

This fire-curse has a supernatural intensity for it has been sent forth (Zech 5:4a) by the One of whom Isaiah wrote: "And the Light of Israel will be for a fire and his Holy One for a flame; and it will burn and devour his [i.e., the Assyrian foe's] thorns and his briers in one day" (Isa 10:17). In the ordeal at Carmel this Holy Light demonstrated that he was God indeed by sending a fire that devoured not only the burnt offering and the wood but the stones of the altar as well—a miraculous melt-down (1 Kgs 18:38). The miracle of judgment is repeated in Zech 5:4; the fiery curse consumes the houses "with their timbers and stones." The demolition is total. The apostates are completely despoiled of the heritage they forfeited as false sons of the covenant. "Surely you make them fall into ruin ... they become a desolation in a moment" (Ps 73:18-19).

While the combination of wood and stones in Zech 5:4 underscores the completeness of the destruction, another nuance is suggested by its use in the treaty sanctions that inform the curse-scroll image. Twice Moses describes idols as wood and stone, the idols of the nations encountered by Israel at their national beginnings (Deut 29:17) and the gods of the nation that would eventually take Israel into captivity, the gods of wood and stone that the accursed covenant breakers would themselves worship there in exile (Deut 28:36). In Zechariah 5, where the idolizing of material wealth is the peculiar evil of the offenders, their houses sum up their idolized acquisitions, and the wood and stone represent those houses. Already in Yahweh's land they were worshipping gods of wood and stone. Their houses were temples of Mammon. Continuing this theme, the second part of the sixth vision repeats the curse-threat of Deut 28:36 as it pictures the apostates removed to Shinar and established as an idol-cultus there.

D. *Reversal of the Tenth Plague.* The scroll judgment of Zechariah 5 bears a striking resemblance to the tenth plague on Egypt.[10] In each episode God launches the attack (Exod 11:1; Zech 5:4a), an aerial assault in both cases. The curse-scroll flies over the whole land and enters houses to inflict destruction; the angel destroyer passed over all the land of Egypt (Exod 11:6; 12:12) and entered the houses of the Egyptians to smite the households with death (cf. Exod 12:23). The tenth plague took place during the night, and the description of the scroll-curse as "passing the night" (literally) in the doomed houses possibly echoes that. The Glory-Presence is the reality represented by the winged scroll, and God was present in that same theophanic form in the paschal event (cf. Exod 13:21).

There was, however, one great difference between the two episodes and that difference constitutes the tragedy of Israel symbolized by the flying scroll. Whereas in the night of the tenth plague the Lord had protectively hovered over[11] the Israelite houses, guarding their blood-marked doorways against the entrance of the destroyer, it is precisely Israelite houses that he targets for the devastating penetration of the scroll-curse. He no longer affords them covert under the shadow of his wings. He treats the apostate Israelites as he did the hardened pharaoh and Egyptians of old.[12]

Zechariah 5 warns those restored from the Babylonian exile of a future recurrence of national cutting off. Israel would again forfeit, this time beyond recovery, their national election to the heritage of the typological kingdom offered in the blessing sanctions of the old covenant. In that respect, they would be disowned and suffer dispossession and dispersion as the vengeance of the covenant Lord, a coming of the wrath of God upon them to the uttermost (cf. 1 Thess 2:16). This fate foretold in Zechariah 5 overtook the old order in 70 A.D., the doom Jesus announced in language recalling Zechariah 5: "Your house is left unto you desolate" (Matt 23:38).

Clearly pointing to the fall of old covenant Israel as the (at least) initial furfillment of the flying scroll judgment is the interpretive recasting of the sixth vision in Zech 13:2-9, the parallel to Zechariah 5 in the matching chiastic structures of the two parts of the book. There again we read of a judgment affecting "all the land" (v. 8), and again of a cutting off: "two parts therein shall be cut off and perish" (v. 8). And connected with this judgment is the prophecy of the messianic shepherd's rejection and the scattering of his followers (v. 7; cf. Matt 26:31-2; Mark 14:27). The cutting off befalls the generation that knew not the hour of its messianic visitation. In its leadership and as a whole it was a generation of thieves and perjurers. They turned the house of God into a den of thieves (Jer 7:11; Matt 21:13) and bore false witness against the Son of God. Refused and cast out by them, the vindicated, exalted Messiah-Prince sent the Roman legions as his army to destroy their temple-city, pouring out on their abominable apostasy the desolations foretold in covenant sanctions and prophetic visions (Deut 9:26-7).

II. DEPORTATION OF THE APOSTATES (5:5-11)

Siege and its devastation are followed by the deportation of the conquered to the land of their captors. The Deuteronomic treaty sanctions foretold a day when it would be said of Israel that "because they forsook the covenant ... the anger of Yahweh was kindled against this land to bring upon it all the curse that is written in this book; and Yahweh rooted them out of their land ... and cast them into another land" (Deut 29:25-28 [24-27]; cf. 28:63). Zech 5:5-11 portrays a final carrying away of Israel into exile as the transporting of a woman, Wickedness, in an ephah-container borne by two stork-winged women to the land of Shinar. The first part of the sixth vision had pictured the destruction of the apostates' idolized houses in Canaan; this second part concludes with the construction of an idol-house for them in Babylon. Like the curse-scroll in the first part, the ephah in the second is seen in flight and here too the passage through the air indicates that the judgment issues from heaven, from the throne of the Lord of heaven and earth. The wind was in the wings of the two women (v.

9), the propulsive power for their aerial journey, and the winds are ministers of God sent forth to do his bidding (cf. Ps 104:4; Zech 6:5).

A. *The Flying Ephah.*

1. *Ephah and Talent:* Continuing the motif of standard measures (cf. the cubits, v. 2), measures of volume and weight are now introduced into the vision. Zechariah sees a container, described only as to its capacity as an ephah (v. 6)—estimated at about two-thirds of a bushel. It probably looked like a vessel customarily used for holding grain. Covering its round opening was a lid, which is denoted as a circular talent (v. 7)—estimated at some 75 pounds. It is also referred to as a "stone" (v. 8), Hebrew *ʾeben*, which can mean "weight." The material of this talent-weight was lead.

These standardized weights and measures represent God's holy standards of covenant life, also symbolized by the twenty-by-ten-cubit flying scroll. A point of interest here, significant for the unity of Zechariah 5, is that the emblem of the flying scroll (or the related winged solar disk) has been found on the handles of jars (like the ephah container) stamped with the royal seal (apparently identifying the containers as royal standards). The two standards of Zech 5:6-8, the ephah and the talent-weight, are mentioned together in laws concerning just weights and measures (Lev 19:36; Deut 25:15) and in passages where false ephahs and balances are condemned as "an abomination to Yahweh" (Prov 20:10; Mic 6:10-11). Such abuse of ephah and talent, sins of market place traffic, is thievery and perjury (falsification of the standards and vain exploitation of the name of God). Evidenced again is the interrelation of the two parts of the sixth vision.

It was because of the sins associated with the ephah and talent that the apostates were under the curse of the covenant. That idea is conveyed in the symbolism of Zech 5:5ff. by having the talent-covered ephah function as God's instrument of judgment, carrying off the guilty into exile (cf. Prov 13:6). The woman "Wickedness," symbol of the accursed deportees, is confined within the ephah (visionary symbolism is not concerned with such incongruity of scale). The lead-talent is brought into the picture as part of a dramatic introduction of the woman. After identifying the ephah (Zech 5:5,6a), the angel prepares Zechariah for the emerging of the woman with the announcement: "This is their appearance in all the land" (v. 6b).[13] To reveal the woman sitting within, the lead cover of the ephah had to be momentarily lifted, and afterwards it was slammed down again. The role of the lead-talent was to ensure that the captive within could not escape; it made the ephah a prison. The heaviness of lead would suit it to that function, but there may be more to it than that. A parallel to this imagery is found in Hittite incantations, in which demons and various evils are dealt with by putting them in bronze cauldrons with lead lids so that they cannot come out and by setting the cauldrons in the depths of the sea or netherworld.[14] Such a background would add dark overtones to Zechariah's symbolism, suggestive of the satanic character of the wickedness placed under the divine anathema.

2. *The Winged Women:* In the apparition of the two stork-winged women who lift the ephah into the air[15] and fly it away to Shinar we have an unholy counterpart to the theophany of the Glory between the cherubim above the ark. This variation on the motif of the winged scroll (and solar disk) is another item in the remarkable symbolic linkage of the two parts of Zechariah 5.[16] Specification of the wings as those of a stork might be due simply to the suitability of the strong wings of the stork for this assignment, but in this unholy configuration the stork's unclean status must be relevant (cf. Lev 11:19; Deut 14:18). Unclean agents are used by the Judge of Israel to remove the defilement from his holy land to unclean Babylon, habitation of demons and a hold of every unclean spirit and unclean bird (Rev 18:2). His use of these evil beings as instruments of his wrath against the apostates here is like his employing of the ungodly Assyrians and Babylonians to take rebellious Israel into exile.

The choice of female figures to depict the unclean agents might be by attraction to the symbolism of the woman "Wickedness." Or, as with the lead weight, there is possibly an adaptation of a legendary concept. Quite similar are the harpies of Homeric epic, winged female beings, spirits of wind and storm who snatch people and carry them away.[17] Here again the symbolic details would be conjuring up the demonic dimension of the drama.

B. *The Woman Wickedness.* "This is their appearance in all the land" (v. 6b). "This" in v. 6b does not refer back to the ephah (v. 6a) but forward to the woman (v. 7b). "Behold" (*hinnēh*) in v. 7a begins the fulfillment of the expectation created by the special call to attention in v. 6b,[18] and "this is a woman" (v. 7b) identifies what v. 6b was pointing to. Then the final "this" in v. 8a introduces the interpretation of the figure of the woman referred to in vv. 6b, 7.

"Appearance" in v. 6b is Hebrew *ʿayin,* "eye,"[19] in the sense of what the eye sees, as when it is said God does not look on the outward appearance (*ʿayin*) but on the heart (1 Sam 16:7; cf. Exod 10:5; Lev 13:55; Num 22:5). The antecedent of the plural suffix in "their appearance"— extremely puzzling to those who suppose a separate vision begins at v. 5— is the thieves and perjurers of vv. 3,4.[20] In the first part of the vision they are referred to as individuals and identified by their particular infractions of the covenant stipulations. Here the guilty are gathered into a collective symbol: "this is their appearance." This woman Wickedness pictures what they are in the eyes of God as he judicially scans "all the land" (cf. Zech 4:10).

The idolatrous, spiritually adulterous nature of the objects of God's anathema is intimated by the symbolic figure of the woman. Israel, unfaithful to her marriage covenant with Yahweh, is often portrayed as a harlot, an unfaithful woman who forsakes the Lord God and commits whoredom with her idol-lovers (e.g. Hosea 1-3; Jeremiah 2; 3; Ezekiel 16; 23). As taken up into the symbolic fabric of the Book of Revelation, the woman of Zechariah 5 is the great harlot, unfaithful to the Lamb and prostituting herself to the Beast and the world.

The woman's name, "Wickedness" (Heb. *rišʿâ*),[21] also connotes harlotry, the harlotry of apostasy from the covenant Lord. In tracing the evidence for this we include the use of related terms like *rešaʿ:* "wickedness;" the adjective *rāšāʿ,* "wicked;" and the denominative verb *ršʿ* "be wicked, act wickedly." The dominant use of the verb (especially in exilic and postexilic texts) is with reference to Israel's breaking of the covenant in spite of God's faithfulness in keeping it (1 Kgs 8:47; 2 Chr 6:37; Dan 9:5,15; 11:32; 12:10; Neh 9:33), the wickedness of departing from God (2 Sam 22:22; Ps 18:22). The adjective is used as the antonym of "righteous" in statements about the contrasting conduct and the diametrically opposite final destinies of the covenant faithful and unfaithful: "him that serves God and him that serves him not" (Mal 3:18; Ps 1:5,6; Prov 3:33; 14:11). At times the imagery of harlotry is explicitly applied to the way of the wicked. Psalm 106, referring to the Israelite covenant breakers as "the wicked" (v. 18), charges them with playing the harlot (v. 39). Similarly Psalm 73, wrestling with the perplexing prosperity of "the wicked" (vv. 3,12), identifies their conduct as playing the harlot from God (v. 27b).

Noteworthy in the usage of these terms are points of contact with distinctive features in Zechariah 5. As in the case of the sins of the thieves and perjurers in Zech 5:1-4, the reprobated behavior of "the wicked" is an idolatry of Mammon (Pss 37:21; 73:12; Prov 10:2), involving the use of lying ephah and false weights (Mic 6:10,11). The scroll's curse on the houses is paralleled in Prov 3:33, "The curse of Yahweh is on the house of the wicked, but he blesses the abode of the righteous," and in Prov 14:11, "The house of the wicked shall be overthrown, but the tent of the upright shall flourish" (cf. Prov 10:2). In the same vein are Ps 73:19, which says of the ultimate fate of the wealthy wicked, "How are they become desolate in a moment, utterly swept away by terrors," and Mal 4:1 (3:19), which warns that "all who work wickedness (*rišᶜâ*) shall be stubble, and the day that is coming shall burn them up, so that it will leave them neither root nor branch." And then there is the extraordinary parallel in 2 Chr 24:7. Reporting how the sons of the notorious Athaliah, daughter of Ahab and (likely) of Jezebel, had (at her instigation, cf. 2 Chr 22:3) taken what was dedicated to the Lord's house and used it for the Baalim, the account refers to the queen herself as "the wickedness" (*hammiršaᶜat*). Surely this embodiment of wickedness in the apostate Athaliah is the historical model behind Zechariah's image of wickedness personified as the woman in the ephah.[22]

C. *Construction of the Shinar Shrine.* Shinar, the exile destination of the captive woman, Wickedness (Zech 5:11), was the site of postdiluvian humanity's ancient challenge against the Lord of Har Magedon (Gen 11:2; cf. 10:10; 14:1,9).[23] The Babel project stands in Scripture as the representative attempt of an idolatrous world in revolt to exalt itself to heaven by its own strength for its own glory. It was a repudiation of the redemptive grace of God that had been manifested in his ark-covenant with Noah (Gen 6:18) and it serves in the Genesis record as a foil for the immediately following narrative of the covenant of promise given to Abraham (Genesis 12ff.). Babel in the land of Shinar is the great apostasy. In the final days of Judah and its monarchy Nebuchadnezzar revived the ancient apostate ideology there in Babylon, the world city. It was to the land of Shinar that he carried the captives of Judah, along with the vessels of the house of the Lord in Jerusalem, which he placed in the house of his god there (Dan 1:2). That is the pattern reproduced in the visionary deportation of the woman in the ephah to the land of Shinar. For the harlot Wickedness to be reestablished in this Shinar location is to be absorbed back into the apostate, idol-worshipping world (cf. Deut 28:36) from which Israel had been separated by national election and redemption.

Construction of a house for the apostates in Shinar at the close of the vision (v. 11) balances the destruction of their houses in Canaan in the first part of the vision. The houses destroyed by the curse-scroll had been virtual temples of Mammon, and in the account of the house prepared for the ephah in Shinar the Hebrew *bayit* is evidently used in the sense of "house of a god, temple." The god to be enshrined here is the same— Mammon, the idolized treasures of this world represented by the ephah with the talent cover. Indicative of the cultic character of this house is the setting of the ephah on its "base" (*mĕkônâ*). Such bases were features of temples in the historical background of Zechariah's visions. There were the bases from Solomon's temple that Nebuchadnezzar carried off (2 Kgs 25:13-16; Jer 52:17-20; 27:19-22; cf. 1 Kgs 7:27ff.) and the base on which the altar was set in the restored temple (Ezra 3:1-3). Possibly the word ephah contains a hint that the house where it gets installed on its base is a temple, for a pun may be intended on the names of ziggurats in which the first element was *E* (Sumerian, "house"), and one of which (at Lagash) was *E.pa,* "summit house."[24]

Curiously, no mention is made of the woman apart from the ephah at the destination in Shinar. Zech 5:11 answers a question about the ephah (v. 10) and, therefore, the ephah is to be taken as the direct antecedent of the feminine pronouns in v. 11. Yet the woman held captive in the ephah would be implicitly included in the question (v. 10) and the answer (v. 11). Since nothing is said about the woman being released from the ephah she must share in the disposition made of it. Now the enshrinement of the ephah-god is an act of enthronement.[25] Agreeably, the verb used for depositing the ephah in Zech 5:11 is *nûaḥ,* from which derives *mĕnûḥâ,* "resting place, rest," a term that denotes Yahweh's royal sabbatical session (1 Chr 28:2; Ps 132:7,8,13,14; Isa 66:1; cf. Exod 20:11, where the verb *nûaḥ* itself is used for God's Sabbath enthronement).[26] If then the woman shares in the treatment received by the ephah, she too would be enthroned at the prepared place. She would "sit a queen" (cf. Rev 18:7) over the great city Babylon.

D. Reversal of the Exodus. Comparison with Israel's experience under Moses once again proves instructive. What we found in comparing the flying scroll with the tenth plague episode, namely, formal similarity in the phenomena but with totally opposite effect on the Israelites, we find again in comparing the flying ephah with the exodus deliverance. The image of the soaring stork-winged women carrying the ephah recalls the eagles' wings on which the Lord bore the Israelites on their way out of Egypt, through the sea and wilderness. Like the flying scroll, the flying women with the ephah bring to mind the cherubim-winged chariot-cloud of the Lord.[27] But whereas the flying scroll represented the divine Presence, the flying escort of the apostate Israelites in Zechariah 5, though used by God as his agent of judgment, is a demonic impostor. It is an anti-Glory Spirit. It does not shepherd a flock to the promised inheritance in Canaan (cf. Ps 78:52-55) but marches a captive band far off to unholy Babylon, away from the true sanctuary on Zion's mount of assembly to a shrine belonging to the pseudo-Har Magedon ziggurat tradition of Shinar.

Envisaged as the final objective of the exodus redemption was the preparing of a dwelling for the Glory-Presence enthroned between the cherubim above the ark containing the covenant revelation, the ark with golden "mercy-seat" cover bespeaking atonement. A satanic antithesis of this looms at the end of the Zechariah 5 deportation: the preparation of a house for the enshrinement of the idol-ephah, the ephah with lead cover bespeaking alienation and with the personified revolt against the covenant confined within.

Exile-repudiation, a complete reversal of the exodus-redemption—that is the fate of the accursed apostates. How this plays out in history is not disclosed in Zechariah's sixth vision. Zech 5:11 hints at a future for the woman Wickedness enthroned in the Shinar shrine. Another chapter in the story of the harlot Babylon is adumbrated here, something beyond the end of the old era in the 70 A.D. destruction of the temple, a mystery that unfolds in the apocalyptic visions of the new covenant.

III. BEYOND THE FALL OF ISRAEL

A. *Mystery: The True Israel.* Though sweeping through all the land, the curse of the flying scroll is a surgical strike that selectively targets the apostate thieves and perjurers for dispossession and deportation. A spared, surviving remnant is implied. This remnant becomes more explicit in the parallel prophecy of the judgment of Israel in Zech 13:8,9. In that passage, alongside two-thirds who are cut off and die there is one-third that is left alive, a remnant whom God acknowledges as his genuine people.

Other Old Testament prophecies of the fall of Israel also join to it the hope of the promised fullness of Israel. An outstanding instance is the second of Isaiah's two vineyard songs. The first, Isa 5:1-7, foretells only that God will lay waste his vineyard, Israel. In this respect it matches what is explicit in the message of Zechariah 5. But the second song, Isa 27:2-13, while it speaks of a smiting, a breaking off and fiery consumption of branches, and a turning of the city into a forsaken wilderness, adds the idea of a purgative effect and the prospect of great fruitfulness, of an ingathering one by one from Egypt to Assyria. It promises an ultimate fullness in spite of the fall.

In the light of such passages we may detect in the implicit presence of a remnant in Zechariah 5 an intimation that purgation as well as punishment was at least an indirect purpose of the mission of the volant scroll. However, this purifying effect of the judgment that culminated in the destruction of Jerusalem in 70 A.D. was not intended as a reformation of the Mosaic covenant order, with a view to its continuation. On the contrary, this judicial purge was a removing of this old order off the stage of history to make room for the true fulfillment of the kingdom covenanted unto Abraham, fulfillment at the new covenant level. The national election of Israel as the people of the provisional Mosaic kingdom was cancelled in curse and the typological order terminated in desolation and diaspora. But for the individual election of sovereign grace there was no failure of the guaranteed blessings; the Torah Covenant of works with its typological kingdom had not annulled the earlier promise-faith covenant. That covenant of grace continued and underlay the typological-works level of the Law, finding expression in the ever present elect remnant (Rom 11:1-6) and at last in that "one third" not cut off, who continued through the collapse of Israel to become the nucleus of the community of faith under the new covenant of grace.

Within the total compass of Zechariah's night visions the message of the covenant curse in the sixth vision is more than balanced by assurances of the covenant's eschatological blessings. Indeed, the curse was to contribute to the realization of the blessings for all the seed of promise, the true Israel. Vision six and vision two, which form a pair in the concentric structure of the seven visions, describe a centrifugal movement of unclean elements out of the holy kingdom. Vision two deals with the removal of oppressive aliens from the holy land; vision six, with the expunging of the apostates. This is complemented by a counter-movement in visions three and five, a centripetal, conversion dynamic by which those afar off come to Zion to help build God's house; more than that, to become part of God's Spirit-temple (cf. Zech 10:8ff.). Towards this glorious development, the termination of the old typological order and the destruction of its temple made a negative contribution by clearing the way.

The anathema mission of the flying scroll was thus a prelude to the completing of the true temple through Messiah's menorah mission of blessing to the nations (cf. Zechariah 4). This is an aspect of the mystery of the hardening in part that befalls Israel until the fullness of the Gentiles comes in (Rom 11:25). That the fall of Israel should lead to the salvation of the Gentiles (Rom 11:11) and the realization of the fullness of both the Jews (Rom 11:12) and Gentiles (Rom 11:25) excites praise for God's unsearchable wisdom in the apostle who, in dependence on Isaiah's second vineyard song, provides us with a profound biblical-theological exposition of this wonderful counsel of salvation (Rom 11:33-36).

Zechariah's night visions point beyond the passing away of the old Israel under Moses to the mystery of the true new Israel in Christ. What Zechariah and other Old Testament prophets foresaw dimly, new covenant revelation brilliantly illuminates: a realization in the fullness of time of the mystery of God's will, whereby he sums up all things in Christ (Eph 1:9,10), gathering Gentiles as fellow-members of the body and fellow-partakers of the promise in Christ Jesus through the gospel (Eph 3:2-4). The remnant that was not cut off in the collapse of the typological Israelite kingdom was an earnest of the glory of Christ's church, "which is his body, the fullness of him that fills all in all" (Eph 1:23).

In the New Testament Apocalypse, the true Israel, the election, is represented by the figure of a woman, who is first seen (Rev 12:1ff.) adorned with heavenly glory and giving birth to the messianic male child, and at the close of the book (Rev 21:9ff.) appears as a bride, the wife of the Lamb, shining with the glory of God. The Book of Revelation is concerned primarily with the woman as the mystery church of the messianic age, but her role in bringing forth Christ as to the flesh also implies her previous presence in the premessianic era. Spanning the old and new covenants, she evidences the underlying unity and continuity of the ongoing covenant of grace.

We shall be considering the relation of this woman to the harlot Babylon figure in the Book of Revelation, and as we do so we will be commenting on the influence of Zechariah 5 on the Apocalyptic treatment of the career of the harlot. At the moment, we want to note allusions to Zechariah 5 in the Revelation 12 account of the woman who represents the true Israel.[28] Her deliverance from the dragon is pictured in exodus imagery. She is threatened by a river poured out of the dragon's mouth, but the waters are swallowed by the earth, an event akin to Israel's crossing of the sea (Rev 12:15,16). Her flight from the dragon takes her into the wilderness, as did Israel's from pharaoh (Rev 12:6,13,14), and as God carried Israel on eagles' wings (Exod 19:4), so the woman is given the two wings of a great eagle to fly to safety (Rev 12:6,13,14). It is at this point that the influence of Zechariah 5, specifically its depiction of the deportation of the woman Wickedness, is evident, not just in the motif of flying but in the description of the destination as "the place prepared for her" (Zech 5:11; Rev 12:6,14). These allusions to Zechariah 5, by calling attention to the exodus-like event in the career of each of the two women, actually brings into focus the difference between the two. For the exodus in the case of the woman Wickedness of Zechariah 5 is in fact a reversal of the exodus, an abandonment to the world, while the exodus experienced by the Revelation 12 woman is the true, antitypical exodus, a deliverance from the satanic world power accomplished by the man-child this woman brings forth, the mighty mediator of the new covenant.

B. *Mystery: The Harlot Babylon.* A second mystery is revealed in the symbolism of the New Testament Apocalypse, the mystery of another woman over against the woman who represents the mystery of Christ's church. Carried away in the Spirit into a wilderness, John the Seer was shown a woman on whose forehead was written a name: "Mystery, Babylon the Great, the Mother of Harlots and of the Abominations of the Earth" (Rev 17:5). In this harlot Babylon we see again the Zecharian figure of the woman Wickedness, who, exiled from Canaan, becomes identified with Babylon in Shinar, set there as its enshrined queen (Zech 5:7-11). The equation of the Zecharian and Johannine images, highlighted by their sharing of the striking symbolic combination of a wicked woman and the city Babylon, is supported by many other links to the Zechariah 5 context found in the Apocalyptic treatment of the great harlot city. The connection proves mutually interpretive. The identity of the woman Wickedness in Zechariah 5 as the apostate covenant community confirms the indications within the Book of Revelation itself that her equivalent there, the harlot

Babylon, is an image of the false church. And the elaboration of the career of that harlot church in the visions of the Apocalypse opens up for us the history of the woman in the ephah that is latent in Zech 5:11.

We shall present first the data within the Apocalypse pointing to the identity of the harlot Babylon as the apostate church, then the evidence for her identification with the woman Wickedness of Zechariah 5.

1. *The False Church:* Babylon is called "the great city" in the Book of Revelation (16:19; 18:10,16,18,19,21), or simply "Babylon the Great" (14:8; 16:19; 18:2). This city-name identifies the mystery woman, the harlot. She is called "Babylon the Great" (17:5), "the great city that rules over the kings of the earth" (17:18). References to harlot Babylon in these terms in Rev 14:8 and 16:19 before her formal introduction and the full account of her career in Revelation 17 are not altogether abrupt; highly important preparation is provided in Rev 11:8. Indeed, the proper interpretation of the harlot Babylon, the great city, is established by the identification of the great city in Revelation 11 with the erstwhile "holy city" of Jerusalem (11:2), where the two witnesses are slain and "where also their Lord was crucified" (11:8). The great city is then the covenant institution in a state of apostasy.

The apostate, anathematized character of the great city is expressed in Rev 11:1,2 in the act of separating between the true people of God (symbolized by the temple and altar) and the false members of the covenant (symbolized by the outer court and the city of Jerusalem). The former are owned by the Lord as his peculiar possession for his acceptance and ministry (symbolized by measuring them). The latter are repudiated as not genuinely consecrated to the Lord (symbolized by excluding them [cf. Matt 8:12] from the measured area); they are cut off from the true temple community and abandoned to be trampled by the world (cf. Luke 21:24), whose vain idols they have preferred. The old Jerusalem thus becomes a symbol for the apostate deformation of the "the holy city" it originally and properly was.[29] It becomes "the great city which spiritually is called Sodom and Egypt" (Rev 11:8) and (elsewhere in Revelation) "Babylon the Great."

Clearly identifying the harlot city Babylon as an apostate form of the covenant community is the elaborate contrastive parallelism observable between the two central female figures, between the harlot Babylon and the bride, the wife of the Lamb. The latter, like the harlot, is identified as a city, not, however, the old, unfaithful Jerusalem but the holy city, New

Jerusalem (Rev 21:2,9,10), city of the great King (cf. Ps 48:2; Matt 5:35). Each woman has a spectacular portraiture: the true and pure one adorned with the radiance of heavenly glory (Rev 12:1; 21:11ff.) and bright linen, the righteousness of saints (Rev 19:8), an image of Christ (cf. Rev 1:13ff.);[30] the other draped with the glittering trappings of a whore, a likeness of the beast (Rev 17:3,4), itself a likeness of draconic Satan (Rev 12:3). Each woman is a mother: the one is delivered of the messianic son (Rev 12:5), with reference also being made to the rest of her offspring, those who hold to the testimony of Jesus (Rev 12:17), a virgin company not defiled with women (Rev 14:4); the other is "the mother of the harlots and the abominations of the earth" (Rev 17:5). The holy woman and her offspring are persecuted unto martyrdom (Rev 12:11,17), The harlot is their persecutor, drunk with their blood (Rev 17:6); in Babylon is found the blood of prophets and saints (Rev 18:24; cf. 18:20; 19:2), a mark of its continuity with the old Jerusalem (cf. Matt 21:35-39; 23:31-35; Acts 7:52; Rev 11:8). Of other such antithetical pairings that might be cited we note just one more, the association of the two women with the wilderness. The mother of the son who is caught up to God's throne flees into the wilderness for refuge from the dragon and his beast-agent (Rev 12:13,14; 13:1-7). Then—strange sequel—there in the wilderness John sees a woman, the harlot Babylon, sitting on the satanic beast (Rev 17:3). The impression given is that the harlot is a corrupted derivative from the holy woman who had fled into the wilderness, a devolution out of the true covenant community, a false church.

2. *The Harlot Babylon and the Woman Wickedness:* The conclusion that the harlot Babylon is the covenant institution in an apostate condition (not just some political-economic dimension of pagan society) is corroborated by the data demonstrating that this Apocalyptic figure is a continuation of the woman Wickedness in Zechariah 5.

Zecharian influence is strong in Revelation 11; indeed, the Zechariah 4 symbolism of the menorah is central in the delineation of the two witnesses (Rev 11:3,4). In the opening verses of that chapter the influence of Zechariah 5 is clear. The sixth vision's scenario of the cutting off and separation of the apostates from the holy sphere provides the model for the anathematizing of the great city (Rev 11:2). In each case the false is distinguished from the true, and this judicial discrimination is again in Revelation 11 a matter of applying the holy standards of God's temple, expressed here in the measuring rod that recalls the (twenty-by-ten cubits)

196

measurements of the flying scroll. References to various temple courts also link the two passages. One referent of the twenty-by-ten cubit dimensions of the scroll was the inner court of judgment, and that court falls within the measured area holy to God in Rev 11:1. Left outside the measured area is the outer court (Rev 11:2), which, along with the great city, symbolizes the rejected apostates. Both outer court and city are given over to trampling by the nations, that is, there is a merging of the excluded group with the invasive Gentile world, and this corresponds to the coalescence of the woman in the ephah with the Babylonian world in Zech 5:11.

According to the announcement at the outset (Rev 17:1), the harlot Babylon, especially her judgment, is the main theme of Rev 17:1-19:10. For present purposes a sampling of the connections of this section with Zechariah 5 must suffice. Elaborated in considerable detail is the mercantile activity of the great city, described in imagery reflecting Ezekiel's prophecy of the doom of the great commercial city of Tyre (Ezekiel 27). This is not inconsistent with the ecclesiastical nature of the harlot city for it is precisely the nature of the false church that it despises its calling to be distinct from the world and proceeds to make itself indistinguishable from the world. Moreover, it is sin in this very sphere of merchandizing, the sphere of the ephah and talent, that characterizes the apostates from God's covenant who are portrayed as the Babylon-bound harlot of Zechariah 5.

Other points of connection: Babylon the Great is decried as a hold of every unclean bird and a habitation of demons (Rev 18:2), recalling the stork-winged demonic vehicle that transports the ephah to Shinar in Zechariah 5. The harlot of Rev 18:7 boasts that she "sits as a queen" in the world city, making the kings of the earth drunk with the wine of her fornication (Rev 17:1,2), a status that is anticipated in Zechariah's vision of the woman Wickedness enthroned like the fertility goddess in the temple in Babylon (Zech 5:11). "The punishment of the great harlot who sits on many waters" (Rev 17:1) reminds us of the curse inflicted by the flying scroll of Zechariah 5 on the thieves and perjurers and their houses. She is left desolate (Rev 17:16; 18:19). All her luxuries are consumed by fire (Rev 18:8,14). Dramatizing Babylon's fall, a strong angel takes up a stone like a great millstone and casts it into the sea (Rev 18:21), a symbolic variation on the scene in Zechariah 5 where the angel lifts up the stone talent (circular in shape like the millstone) and casts it on the ephah, which was to be deposited in the depths of the sea of the nations (vv. 7,11; cf. Rev 17:15).[31]

One further point of linkage: The letters to the seven churches in Revelation 2 and 3 introduce in more recognizable form the various parties that appear in less apparent symbolic guise elsewhere in Revelation. Particularly relevant is the woman Jezebel. There is no mistaking the relationship of this woman and her adulterous idolatry within the church in Thyatira (Rev 2:20-23) to the harlot Babylon. Infamous queen of Israel, inciter of Ahab to idolatry (1 Kgs 21:25,26), worshipper of Tyrian Baal, a woman of whoredoms and sorceries (2 Kgs 9:22), Jezebel was (it would seem) the mother of Ahab's daughter Athaliah—quite literally, a mother of harlots and abominations (Rev 17:5). And Athaliah in turn was (as we have seen) the historical model behind the woman Wickedness of Zechariah 5 (cf. 2 Chr 24:7). The symbolic individualizing of the two harlot-Babylon figures of Zechariah and Revelation by these two intimately related evil queens, Athaliah and Jezebel respectively, attests to their equivalency.

As evidenced by this set of correspondences, the great city of Revelation is to be identified with the woman Wickedness of Zechariah 5 and, therefore, is to be understood, like its Zecharian equivalent, as a perversion, a deformation, of the covenant institution.

3. *Fallen is Babylon the Great:* Just as the Revelation 12 woman symbolizes the true people of God before and after Christ, so the harlot Babylon represents apostasy in the old Israel as well as the false church of the present age. The remnant of Israel became the nucleus of the ongoing community of faith of the new covenant and similarly unbelieving Israel, infiltrating the church of Christ with its Judaizing perversion of the gospel of grace, had a continuing existence there as synagogues of Satan, as the apostate harlot church.

The Apocalypse traces the careers of the two women, and in so doing unfolds the chapter on the future of the woman Wickedness that was left tantalizingly incomplete at the close of Zechariah's sixth vision (5:11), a chapter on developments beyond the fall of Israel in 70 A.D. This history of the harlot Babylon is set within the framework of an eschatological pattern consisting of an extended period in which the church carries out the great commission, followed by a short final crisis of satanic opposition, which is countered by the Parousia and its consummating judgment.

In Revelation 11 this pattern emerges as the shape of the historical course of the true church, and also of the false church (the great city) as its career is interwoven with that of the two witnesses. Throughout the relatively long period (symbolized in Revelation as three and a half years, or its equivalents, forty-two months and 1,260 days) the two witnesses are so empowered of God that they overcome all opposition and finish their menorah mission (11:3-7a). During this time the great city is allied with the imperial world power in opposition to that testimony, and it is the site of the martyrdom of the two witnesses in the relatively short (three and a half days) crisis marked by the rising of the beast from the Abyss, the final stage of the beast-power (11:7b-10). God's judicial response to this, while vindicating the two witnesses by resurrection and welcome to heaven, brings earthquake devastation and death to the great city (11:11-13).

The themes introduced in Revelation 11 are developed in the major treatment of the harlot Babylon in Rev 17:1ff. Again there is the sharp antithesis to the true church, the loss of holy identity, and mutation into an institution indistinguishable from the world and its idolized culture. Again there is the persecution of those who proclaim the testimony of Jesus. And fully developed here is the alliance with the bestial imperial power, symbolized by the woman sitting on the beast (17:3). The course of this relationship is traced within a survey of the history of the beast in the form of an explanation of its seven heads (17:7-11). The pattern noted in Revelation 11 reappears here, prefaced by an earlier age. The first five heads belong to an age in which the beast "was" (the premessianic age). The sixth head, the beast that "now is not," stands for the era of three and a half years (cf. Rev 13:5); he "is not" during this period in that he cannot prevent the church from carrying out its mission of universal witness. The seventh head that continues only a little while, coming up out of the Abyss but quickly going into perdition, represents the final crisis. This crisis issues in the last battle, which finds the beast (itself an eighth head) with his ten horns (cf. Rev 16:14; 20:8) arrayed against the Lamb-Lord. In this Har Magedon conflict (cf. Rev 16:16) the beast is vanquished and descends into perdition (17:11-14; cf. 19:19-21; 20:7-10).[32]

It is during the time of the sixth head, when there are restraints on the beast so that he "is not" (cf. 2 Thess 2:3-7; Rev 20:2,3), that the alliance obtains between the harlot and the beast, a relationship in which the harlot "rules over the kings of the earth" (17:18)—or, in terms of Zechariah 5, the woman Wickedness sits on her shrine-throne in Babylon. In church history to date the papal system is the most obvious instance of this political ideology. It is also an outstanding example of both the coalescence of the institutional church with the paganized culture of the world (cf. Revelation 18) and the ecclesiastical persecution of the true followers of the Lamb (Rev 18:24; 19:2).[33]

A surprising development occurs in connection with the rising of the beast from the Abyss at the end of the age and his gathering of worldwide forces to make war against the Lamb. He not only besieges the true community of the saints (Rev 20:9), silencing the true witnesses (Rev 11:7), but in the process of exalting himself above all other religious claimants he shatters his alliance with Babylon, the false church. Turning on the harlot with hatred, the beast and the ten horns make her desolate and burn her with fire (Rev 17:16).[34] Babylon's fall is described at great length (Rev 18:1-24; cf. 14:8) and celebrated with doxology in heaven (Rev 19:1ff.).[35]

Such then is the destiny awaiting the woman Wickedness of Zechariah 5 at the end of this age, a desolating judgment like the one that terminated her old covenant career. The harlot's ruin, loss of earthly treasure, and fiery consumption as recounted in Rev 17:16-18:24 recall the effects of the flying curse in Zech 5:1-4. Another point of correspondence is that the accounts of both these occasions of destruction at the hands of the world power stress that they are an infliction of God's own verdict against the apostates (Zech 5:4; Rev 17:17).

But though the two judgments of the woman Wickedness are similar, their significance for their respective covenant orders, old and new, are quite different. The fall of Israel in 70 A. D. put an end to the typological kingdom blessings of the old covenant; it terminated the old covenant order itself. The fall of Babylon in the still future final crisis does not terminate the new covenant order but is one of the more immediate precursors of the consummation of the blessings of the new covenant in the coming of the kingdom of glory. Accordingly, cries of "Woe" at the catastrophic end of the harlot church (Revelation 18) are followed by shouts of "Hallelujah" in heaven, shouts of praise to God because he has avenged the blood of the true church on the great whore and shouts of joy because now the wedding of the Lamb and his holy bride has come (Rev 19:1-9).

Beyond the fall of Israel in 70 A. D. (Zech 5:1-4) lies the era of the woman Wickedness in the land of Shinar (Zech 5:5-11), moving towards another, final fall of this harlot-corrupter of the earth. Execution of this final anathema on the mother of harlots signals the hour of fulfillment for the *"Marana tha"* prayer of mother Zion.[36]

---

1 For further details see the Appendix.

2 Op. cit.

3 Cf., e.g., Deut 29:12 (11); 2 Chr 34:24,30; Ezek 16:8; 17:13; Dan 9:4,11.

4 In connection with the covenant of Suppiluliuma and Kurtiwaza there is a separate tablet devoted to sanctions, with a listing of the gods who are to enforce them.

5 For writing on both sides of a scroll, see Ezek 2:10.

6 It has been observed that the two-to-one proportion of the scroll's dimensions matches the ratio between the width of a column and the height of biblical scrolls at Qumran. Even if this was regular practice centuries earlier, it would probably be due to practical considerations and would have only coincidental relevance for Zechariah's scroll.

7 In Isa 60:8 clouds are spoken of as flying.

8 The oath of innocence procedure took place in the temple forecourt area (cf. 1 Kgs 8:31), which, as noted above, had the twenty-by-ten cubits dimensions of the flying scroll— a further interlocking of the details of the sixth vision.

9 Conceivably the choice of *nqh* involves a play on its two meanings, which we might paraphrase in English: "Though they cleared themselves, God cleared them out."

10 Evils threatened in the Deuteronomic sanctions are identified as the afflictions of Egypt (Deut 28:27,60).

11 For the translation of *psh* in Exodus 12 as "hover over," not "pass over," see my "The Feast of Cover-Over." *JETS* 37:4 (1994) 497-510.

12 We shall find that the exodus history continues to provide a counterpoint to the sixth vision in Zech 5:5-11.

13 For further analysis of this, see below.

14 See Harry A. Hoffner, Jr., "Hittite Tarpis and Hebrew Teraphim," *Journal of Near Eastern Studies* 27:1 (1968) 61-68.

15 The phrase "between the earth and the heaven" possibly contains an allusion to the role of heaven and earth as witnesses to the covenant oath-curse (Deut 30:19; 31:28; Isa 1:2).

16 The circular shape of the lead cover adds to the similarity to the round solar disk symbol.

17 Also from classic mythological sources, Pandora's box has been compared with the ephah. Cf. note 14 above.

18 For a similar "this is (*zōt*) ... behold (*hinnēh*)" sequence, cf. Amos 4:12-13.

19 Following LXX and Syriac, many read *ʿāwōn*, "iniquity."

20 The extent of their appearance, "in all the land" (v. 6b), corresponds to the range of the flying curse against the thieves and perjurers, "over all the land" (v. 3).

21 Note the assonance of *ʾiššâ* (woman) and *rišʿâ* (wickedness).

22 In Zech 5:11 the ephah containing the woman is treated like an idol (see below). This might suggest that Zechariah's woman symbol was influenced by the fertility goddess Astarte, the Babylonian Ishtar, Queen of Heaven, whose worship in Judah and Jerusalem prompted God's fiery wrath (Jer 7:16-20).

23 On this, see our comments on the four horns in vision two.

24 The ziggurat motif is found in the parallel second vision, on which see note 23.

25 In the Babylonian setting, the preparation of a house for deity recalls the account in *Enuma Elish* of the construction at that site of Esagila for royal Marduk.

26 Isa 66:1 is an especially close parallel to Zech 5:11, for it too combines with the

resting-place terminology the idea of building a house as a place of enthronement.

27 One thinks too of the similar yet dissimilar experience of Elijah. The ephah's aerial escort with the wind in their wings mimics the prophet's rapture by whirlwind in the chariot of fire (2 Kgs 2:1, 11). But the destinations are polar opposites: Elijah translated to heaven and the ephah transported to a station on the way to hell.

28 See the comments on the relation of Revelation 12 to Zechariah 3 in our introductory remarks on the fourth vision.

29 For the use of Jerusalem in its Judaistic apostasy as an antithesis to the true covenant community, cf. Gal 4:25,26.

30 On the bride in priestly array as a likeness of Christ's appearance in Revelation 1, cf. our comments on the priestly vestments in the fifth vision.

31 The influence of passages besides Zechariah 5 is, of course, also seen in the delineation of the great city Babylon and its judgment. The prophecy of Babylon's fall in Jeremiah 51 is a notable example. Thus, on Rev 18:4, see Jer 51:45 (cf. Zech 2:6 [2:10]); on Rev 18:21, see Jer 51:63; and on Rev 19:1-5, see Jer 51:48,49.

32 Preterist views of the harlot Babylon and her judgment are contradicted by the synchronizing of her career with the eschatological pattern covering the entire church age to the final judgment.

33 Other significant affinities of ecclesiastical Rome with the prostitute Babylon are its Mariolatry and its neo-Judaizing distortion of the gospel of grace.

34 Jer 4:30 and context contain a close parallel, which, significantly, concerns the apostate covenant community. The prophet indicts Judah as a whore, dressed in crimson and gold, courting the nations and their gods (cf. Jer 2:17,18). In the day of God's judgment her lovers despise her and seek her life.

35 The "man of sin," whose *parousia* with satanic deception provokes the *parousia* of Christ in final judgment, the "Antichrist" in popular usage, represents the imperial reality symbolized by the beast and horn imagery in Daniel and Revelation (compare Dan 11:36 and 2 Thess 2:4). Antichrist is thus the destroyer of the false church (the harlot Babylon) and therefore is not to be identified with the papacy, an embodiment of the false church (cf. *Westminster Confession of Faith* 25, 6).

36 Cf. 1 Cor 16:22. On Zion as mother, cf., e.g., Isa 66:7,8, and see the extended context of this passage for Isaiah's recurring depiction of the city Jerusalem as a woman.

JUDGE OF THE WORLD

In the concentric series of seven visions, the final vision (Zech 6:1-8) parallels the first (Zech 1:7-17), resuming its theme and imagery. Vision seven answers to the eschatological longings voiced in the "How Long?" cry of the opening vision. The *marana tha* prayer raised heavenward there was prompted by the state of the world report brought to the messianic rider of the red horse. As discovered by the celestial horsemen in their world reconnaissance, the nations were displaying defiant indifference to the Lord God, particularly by their oppressive domination of God's people, and they were doing so with apparent impunity. Their hostile arrogance had, however, provoked the Lord to jealous anger, which he makes known in an oracular response to the intercession of the messianic Angel (Zech 1:14-17). God assures his suffering servants of his presence with them and his determination to deal in his wrath with the nations at ease. Vision seven announces the fulfillment of that divine commitment. Equine imagery is again employed for the heavenly agents and the scope of their judicial mission is again global. Visions one and seven thus form an inclusion, framing the series of visions.

Immediate preparation for vision seven and its prophecy of final judgment is provided in vision six (Zech 5:1-11). One way it does so is by completing a two-directional sorting out process that transpires on a world-wide scale. The third vision had prophesied of a messianic evangel that would summon the dispersed people of God out of Babylon back to Zion, an efficacious call that would result in many nations being joined to Yahweh in that day (Zech 2:6-11 [10-15]; cf. Zech 6:9-15). Then the sixth vision foretells a movement in the opposite direction, an anathema-expulsion from Zion of those false to the covenant, carrying them away from Jerusalem to Shinar-Babylon. By means of this twofold movement God effects a clear-cut separation between his seed of promise, the children of heaven, and the denizens of the world, children of the devil. The stage is thus set for Zechariah's closing vision of the chariots of judgment.[1]

I. PAROUSIA

A. *God's Presence in Glory.* A site marked by two bronze mountains is the starting point of the mission of four chariots (Zech 6:1). The identification of this site is given in the hierophant angel's statement that the chariots came forth "from standing before the Lord of all the earth" (v. 5).[2] The setting alluded to is the heavenly court where the cosmic Sovereign sits enthroned in Glory. It is there that his angel-ministers stand in attendance upon him, harkening unto the voice of his word (cf. Job 1:6; 2:1; Ps 103:19,20; Zech 4:14). This closing vision thus fits the consistent pattern according to which the celestial council is the background or even immediate setting of each of the seven visions. We may speak of this divine self-manifestation as a *parousia* in the sense of "presence."

1. *Two Mountains:* The imagery of two mountains with the God of Glory between (and above) them is a variation on symbolism we have observed previously, the symbolism of the divine Presence enthroned between matching objects on either side. In vision one, the messianic rider of the red horse is stationed between what may well be two myrtles, representing the holy community of God's servant-people. In vision five, the two olive trees overarching the menorah reflect the Shekinah theophany complex in the holy of holies, with the Glory-cloud above the ark, footstool of God's throne, and the two cherubim on the right and left.[3] And as we have suggested, behind this imagery is the two-pillar theophany of the Glory-cloud, representing God standing on earth, particularly in oath-taking stance and in other judicial capacities. There is also an architectural dimension to this polyvalent imagery. The Glory above with the flanking cherubim were the lintel and side columns respectively, framing an entryway that leads from the terrestrial world into heaven. This gate of heaven symbolism found in the holy of holies was repeated in the entrance into the temple with its two bronze pillars (1 Kgs 7:13-22).[4]

Similar symbolism of deities associated with a pair of cosmic mountains is found in Near Eastern mythological traditions. The sun-god is represented as appearing between two mountains, and two mountains mark the point of access to the realm of the netherworld deity. It has been suggested that the sunrise motif informs Zechariah's seventh vision. Appeal might be made to Psalm 19 as affording a biblical instance of the imagery of the sun, in a manifestation of God's glory, coming forth from a heavenly tent and entering on a world-traversing mission. But the concept conveyed in Zech 6:1-8 is rather that of chariots of war passing through the boundary gate of heaven and earth, dispatched by the heavenly Suzerain-Judge on an earthly mission of world judgment.

One likely tributary of this two-mountain imagery is the scene of the covenant ratification ceremony conducted by Joshua at the adjacent mountains of Ebal and Gerizim (Josh 8:30-35; cf. Deuteronomy 27). There too the enthroned divine presence, symbolized by the ark, stood in the center between the two mountains. That ceremonial scene at Shechem in the center of the promised land proclaimed Yahweh's sovereignty over the whole land. The altar erected on Ebal was a virtual victory stele celebrating the Lord's defeat of the gods and nations of Canaan and the vindication of his claims to this domain, the prototype of his cosmic kingdom.[5] It is this sovereign status of the God of Israel, Potentate of all the earth, that is also signified by the two-mountain scene in Zech 6:1-8.

Within the Book of Zechariah, and indeed in the section of the second half of the prophecy that parallels the seventh vision in the first half,[6] another pair of mountains appears, identified as the Lord's (Zech 14:5). These two mountains are produced in the course of a Parousia event, an advent of Yahweh with his holy ones.[7] As the Lord stands on the Mount of Olives before Jerusalem, it is divided into two mountains (v. 4; cf. Exod 19:18; Judg 5:5; Ps 68:8 [9]), the feet of the towering figure of the Lord now standing astride the two (cf. Rev 10:1,2,5). The valley created between the parted halves of Olivet provides a passage to safety for God's people, a mountain guarding both their flanks, the overarching Presence of the Lord a shield above them. This eschatological deliverance prophesied in Zech 14:4-5 is antitypical to the exodus passage through the Egyptian sea.[8] Zechariah 14 thus includes more explicitly than Zech 6:1-8 the soteric aspect of the two-mountain Parousia episode, but the association of the two-mountain imagery with the Parousia in Zechariah 14 supports the interpretation of the two mountains in Zech 6:1 as symbolic of the Lord's Parousia-Presence.

2. *Bronze Mountains:* The two mountains were mountains of bronze and prominent in the use of bronze elsewhere in biblical symbolism is its association with Glory-theophany, more particularly with the legs of the theophanic figure, and with related celestial beings. Ezekiel's chariot-throne theophany is a conspicuous source of the imagery in Zech 6:1-8 and the fiery cherubim creatures who bear this vehicular throne of the Glory-Spirit are pictured with legs of gleaming bronze (Ezek 1:7), harmonious with their total shining appearance, a reflection of the Glory-light of God's Presence (Ezek 1:13). The luminous human form on the throne above the cherubim (Ezek 1:26-28) appears in Daniel 7 as the one like a son of man and again in

Daniel 10 as a man with face of lightning, eyes of flame, and arms and legs of burnished bronze (Dan 10:5,6; cf. Ezek 40:3). This same son of man, with face shining like the sun, appears in the opening vision of John's Apocalypse and once more his legs (as visible below a robe reaching to his feet) are likened to glowing bronze (Rev 1:15; 2:18). We may also recall here the related symbolism of the two bronze pillars (lit. "standing things") at the temple entrance (1 Kgs 7:13-22). In this gate of heaven symbolism, the two bronze pillars represented the side columns, an architectural translation of the anthropomorphic image of the bronze legs of deity standing on the earth.

When dealing with Zechariah's second vision (1:18-21 [2:1-4]) we interpreted the four horns as the horns at the corners of an altar, and, viewing the altar as a stylized ziggurat, a structure also capped by four horns, we observed that in the case of both the altar and ziggurat the horns were bronze. Since ziggurats represented the cosmic mountain of the gods, their bronze horns would have a significance appropriate to the divine realm. In the context of the second vision the bronze horns would signify divine power. Similarly the bronze nature of the two mountains in Zech 6:1-8 might be taken as secondarily connoting the invincible strength of the Lord who resides there and the impregnable permanence of his kingdom. But primarily the bronze here reflects the identity of the two mountains as the site of brilliant divine Presence, the locus of the radiant Parousia of the God of Glory. Indeed, the allusive connections we have noted indicate that the two bronze mountains represent the resplendent Lord as planting his feet on the earth, taking his stand in the midst of his people. They thus symbolize much the same reality as the scene of the rider of the red horse stationed between the myrtles by the deep in Zechariah's first vision.

3. *Mount Magedon/Zaphon/Zion:* As a representation of the Lord's place of enthronement, the two bronze mountains are a bifid by-form of what elsewhere appears as a single holy mountain. One of the designations of that mountain of God is *har mô'ēd*, "mount of assembly," referring to the gathering of the council of angelic beings there in the court of the King of heaven and earth (cf. Isa 14:13). In Greek transcription *har mô'ēd* becomes *har magedōn* (Rev 16:16). An overlooked but decisive clue indicating that *har magedōn* does indeed mean "mount of assembly (or gathering)" is that it is identified in Rev 16:16 as *Hebraisti,* "in Hebrew," a label consistently accompanied in the Johannine usage by a contextual explanation. And Rev 16:16 is no exception. The explanation of the "Hebrew" term there is

found in the main verb: "And they gathered[9] them together unto the place called in Hebrew Har Magedon (Mount of Gathering)."

In apposition with *har môʿēd* in Isa 14:13 is another designation for this mountain: *yarkĕtê ṣāpôn*, "the heights of Zaphon." A secondary meaning which *ṣāpôn* acquired was "north," but in Isa 14:13 *yarkĕtê ṣāpôn* refers to the heights of the mount of assembly, the polar opposite on the cosmic axis from the *yarkĕtê bôr*, "the depths of the Pit" (Isa 14:15). Zaphon was the name of a mountain to the north of Israel that was regarded as the residence of Baal, an earthly localization of the cosmic abode of the gods. Possibly Zaphon appears in Babylonian magical texts as the name of a city (Zabban) mythically interpreted as a cosmic city, guardian of the entry-point into this world for denizens of the netherworld and heaven. In addition to Isa 14:13, other biblical instances of *yarkĕtê ṣāpôn* denoting God's mountain-city of Har Magedon or a pagan equivalent are Ps 48:2 [3] and Ezek 38:6,15; 39:2. Also, *ṣāpôn* by itself may refer to this heavenly realm, as in the introduction to the chariot-throne theophany of Ezekiel 1. Echoing his opening statement that the heavens were opened and he saw visions of God (Ezek 1:1), the prophet in verse 4 says he saw the storm-cloud theophany coming out of *ṣāpôn*. *Ṣāpôn* here is the heavenly Zaphon, site of God's Glory-Presence (not the geographical north, as usually interpreted).[10]

The Zaphon designation of the mountain (more specifically *yarkĕtê ṣāpôn*) provides a connection between Har Magedon (*har môʿēd*), to which it is appositional in Isa 14:13, and Zion, with which it is equated in the opening two verses of Psalm 48:

> Great is Yahweh, and greatly to be praised, in the city of our God;
> the mountain of his sanctuary, paragon of peaks, joy of all the earth;
> Mount Zion, the heights of Zaphon, city of the Great King.

Zion is the earthly ectypal manifestation of the archetypal heavenly reality of God's temple-city, Mount Zaphon/Magedon.

In keeping with the typological idiom of the prophets, it is the earthly temple-city of God's theophanic Presence, Mount Zion, that is represented by the two bronze mountains of Zech 6:1-8. Indicative of this earthly location of the royal Presence in the seventh vision is the geographic perspective of the account of the chariots' mission—they issue from a

Palestinian site and proceed in various directions relative to that Palestinian point of origin. As Mount Zion, the two bronze mountains speak of the Immanuel Presence of the God of heaven—Ichabod reversed (cf. 1 Sam 4:21; Ezekiel 10-11). They promise the return of Glory (cf. Ezek 43:1-7; 40:2), which is fully realized in the antitypical New Jerusalem/Mount Zaphon/Magedon, where the heavenly and earthly become one.

B. God's Advent in Power. *Parousia* means presence and also coming. In Zechariah's seventh vision the static imagery of the two bronze mountains symbolizes God's presence-*parousia* and the emergence of the dynamic chariots to charge throughout the earth portrays his advent-*parousia*. Divine advent-*parousia* is a majestic coming of heaven's King with his myriad of holy angels, mighty agents of his judgments on the earth (cf., e.g., Zech 14:5; Matt 24:30,31; 2 Thess 1:7).

1. *Divine Transport:* It is on the chariot-agents speeding on their several ways that Zechariah's vision focuses. But it is not as though the divine Presence has been left behind at the two bronze mountains. This is a *parousia*-advent, a coming of the Lord himself. We may think of the visionary action in terms of the four-directional chariot-throne of the Glory-Spirit in Ezekiel 1, a living creature and a wheel facing and moving in each direction. What we have in Zechariah's vision is a dividing of that one chariot complex of four faces into four individual chariots, or better, an explosive extension of it to the four winds of heaven, without, however, the loss of the coherence of the one chariot-throne and without separation from the unifying divine Presence. Like the one chariot-throne, the four chariots are bearers of the Glory-Spirit; the Spirit is indeed their Driver (Ezek 1:12,20; 2:2; Ps 104:3).[11] This explains how the arrival of the chariots at their ultimate destination involves a presence and working of the Spirit there (cf. Zech 6:8).

Procession of the Lord from his mountain, advancing on a mission of redemptive judgment, answers to the Sinai prototype. As celebrated in Psalm 68,[12] the God of Sinai went forth from his holy habitation (vv. 7,8 [8,9]) as the Rider of the clouds (vv. 4,24 [5,25]), amid the thousands of his chariots (v. 17 [18]), to show himself the Savior of the righteous from their enemies (vv. 19ff. [20ff.]). Such is the agenda of the advent of the Lord of the two bronze mountains. It is a time for the injunction of Zech 2:13 [17]: "Be still before Yahweh, all people, for he has roused himself from his holy dwelling place."

2. *Universal Mission:* The heirophant angel's response to Zechariah's inquiry concerning the chariots (Zech 6:4) revealed their provenance and their destination (v. 5). In disclosing the source of their mission, that they came forth from standing in the presence of the Lord, he was identifying the chariots as ministers of the Lord of Glory. The chariots would still be so identified, indirectly, even if we translated: "These are the four winds of heaven." On that translation, the servant-agent status of the chariots would be further suggested by the familiar role of the winds as messengers in God's service (Ps 104:4). If the chariots are thus equated with the winds, an indication would also be given of the nature of their mission, for elsewhere the four winds of heaven carry the connotation of destructive power (e.g., Jer 49:36; Rev 7:1,2; cf. Dan 2:35).

However, the preferable translation is: "These to the four winds[13] of heaven are going forth." A four-direction mission is entailed in our understanding of the four chariots as a development out of the four-direction Glory-chariot of Ezekiel 1. Also, on this rendering of v. 5 as a general statement that the chariots as a group went to all the cardinal points of the compass, v. 6 follows naturally as a specifying of the particular direction each of the chariots took. Moreover, the equivalent phrase employed in the summary statement in v. 7 is "over the earth," signifying the universal scope of the judicial mission of the agents of the one who is "Potentate of all the earth" (v. 5).

In the Masoretic Hebrew text, the account of the directions taken by the individual teams of horses (with the chariots) omits reference to the red horses, the first of the teams listed in vv. 2,3. And while the second (black) team goes north and the fourth (piebald) team heads south, it is uncertain whether the third (white) team is said to go along after (or with) the black team to the north, or whether *ʾaḥărêhem* (either alone or with some addition to the text) signifies "to the west." Understandably but not necessarily correctly, many suggest that the original text supplied the apparent omission by including the red team and directing them to the east. The related attempt to demonstrate an association of each color with the assumed direction of its chariot is not persuasive. If we limit ourselves to the data in the extant text, there is a change in perspective when the account proceeds from the general statement in v. 5, which indicates the global scope of the four chariots, to the specifying of the directions of the individual chariots in v. 6. The orientation of the latter is adjusted to the peculiar topography of Palestine and to the visionary circumstance of an (evidently) north-south valley running between the bronze mountains. In that scenario the chariots would emerge from that valley in just those two directions, north and south.[14]

The list of the chariot teams in Zech 6:2,3 concludes with a summarizing epithet, "powerful ones." Again in v. 7 the whole contingent of horses is designated by this term. Whereas the first vision of the horses on world-wide surveillance evinces the divine omniscience, the divine omnipotence is to the fore in vision seven. The strength of the horses and their high-spirited eagerness to be on their way (v. 7) highlight the nature of the four-chariot mission as a *parousia* in power. It is an advent of the Almighty.

II. FINAL JUDGMENT

A. *Chariots of Wrath.* Chariots were mainly employed in warfare and were indeed the pride of the royal military establishment. Accordingly, the chariot symbolism of Zechariah's seventh vision is to be understood as signifying an advent of God as the divine warrior, advancing in wrath against his enemies. Similarly the boast of Psalm 68 that God has at his command thousands of thousands of chariots (v. 17 [18]) is set in the context of his smiting the head of his foes (v. 21 [22]). And in Isaiah 66 the whirlwind-like chariots of the Lord accompany him as he comes to show fury against his adversaries and to execute judgment on all mankind (vv. 14-16). As extensions of God's chariot-throne of Glory, the four chariots of Zech 6:1-8 are insignia of his supreme sovereignty, but the primary military association of chariotry indicates that their particular purpose as they break forth from between the bronze mountains is the judicial enforcement of that divine dominion. They are chariots of wrath. It is the day of the Lord.

In the introductory comments on the seventh vision we noted that the theme of God's wrath against the hostile nations appears in the first vision in the form of the Lord's determination and promise to bring them into judgment, a promise whose fulfillment is depicted in vision seven. Meanwhile, in the intervening visions the theme of the Lord's judgment on the satanic world powers has surfaced repeatedly, leading up to the climactic treatment of it in the final vision, and preparing the reader to recognize it there.

Within the first triad of visions, the second (Zech 1:18-21 [2:1-4]) develops the divine threat of Zech 1:14,15. The bestial powers that have lifted their horns to assault the saints and usurp Zion will be overthrown by God's agents of vengeance, four expert destroyers. In vision three (Zech 2:1-13 [2:5-17]), the messianic Angel declares that he will shake his hand over the nations that have plundered the sons of Zion and the plunderers will become a spoil to their former victims. Vision four (Zech 3:1-10) unveils the underlying conflict of Christ with Satan, the instigator of the enmity of the nations against the Lord and his people, and reveals the redemptive secret of the believers' victory. In vision five (Zech 4:1-14), Messiah, typologically prefigured by Zerubbabel, overcomes the imperial world enemy, symbolized by a great mountain that is leveled into a flat plain before him.[15] And as the culminating contribution to this pervasive theme of judgment, vision seven prophesies of an apocalyptic intervention of God. Through his chariot agents sent forth from heaven the divine warrior directs his final judicial vengeance against the nations guilty of offering their affront against his holy majesty.[16] God's retributive justice is satisfied. The Judge of heaven and earth can declare: It is finished.

B. _Land of the North._ Whatever questions there may be as to which direction each of the several chariot teams went, the conclusion of the vision (Zech 6:8) makes it clear that "the land of the north ($\bar{sapon}$)" was the chief target. Babylon is this "land of the north." Another instance of this identification in Zechariah is in vision three, where the exiles dwelling in Babylon are summoned to flee "from the land of the north" back to Zion (Zech 2:6,7 [10,11]). This usage is frequent in Jeremiah's warnings of the judgment to be brought on Jerusalem and Judah by the Babylonians (cf., e.g., Jer 1:14; 4:6; 6:1,22; 13:20; 25:9), although Jeremiah also identifies the north with other nations whose hostile entry into Palestine would be from that quarter (e.g., Jer 1:15). In fact, Jer 50:9 foretells an alliance of nations from the north which God will bring against Babylon.

Babylon is an appropriate symbol of the world in its opposition to the Lord because it was Babylon that destroyed Jerusalem, took captive the Davidic king, and exercised dominion over God's people. Babylon was the head of gold in the imperial colossus of Nebuchadnezzar's dream and the first of the beast kingdoms in Daniel's vision. Babylon was the revival of Babel in Shinar, center of the world in its antichrist propensity to build a pseudo-Har Magedon and to exalt itself against the God of heaven. As we have seen, Isaiah portrays the king of Babylon as a prototype antichrist, scheming to ascend to a place of preeminence in the divine council, above the heights of $\bar{sapon}$, the celestial Zaphon (Isa 14:13,14). In terms of its ideological connection with this celestial ṣāpôn, Babylon, land of the north (ṣāpôn), was an apt symbol not just for the hostile world in general but for the satanic world in the final antichrist stage that evokes God's final judicial wrath.

Daniel's treatment of the antichrist theme had similarly associated this development with the north, but he used a different historical situation as his typological model. The Seleucid king Antiochus Epiphanes, adversary of God's faithful in the second century B.C., is "the king of the north" whose career in Daniel 11 becomes transmuted into a prophecy of the man of sin who exalts himself above all gods (vv. 36ff., cf. 2 Thess 2:4).[17] In this king of the north/man of sin of Dan 11:36ff., the world power symbolized by the bestial little horn of Daniel 7 comes to a climactic individual expression of satanic working.

Corresponding to Daniel's little horn is the beast from the sea in Revelation 13, more specifically that beast at the stage symbolized by the sixth and seventh heads. And Daniel's antichrist king of the north would be the one who heads up the final eruption of evil represented by the eighth king (Rev 17:11). It is he who leads the deceived kings of the earth to Har Magedon for the battle of the great day of God Almighty (Rev 16:16; 17:12-14) and is overwhelmed by the *parousia* of Christ, the King of kings, coming in the furious wrath of God Almighty (Rev 19:11-16; cf. 2 Thess 1:7-10; 2:8).[18] This judgment of the antichrist king of the north is what is signified in Zechariah's seventh vision by the *parousia*-advent of the four chariots with the land of the north as ground zero of their attack.

Ezekiel 38-39 is also part of the allusive background of "the land of the north" in Zech 6:1-8. There again the world to the north of Israel is drawn upon for the figurative depiction of the ultimate outbreak of evil. As in Daniel 11, an individual leader of the world power comes into view, Gog by name, a king of kings whose more immediate domain is the nations to the north in the Asia Minor area (Ezek 38:2,3,6; 39:1). There too Magog is located, Gog's imperial base, which is called "your [Gog's] place" (38:2,15; cf. 39:6).[19] Of key import is the identification of Gog's place as the yarkĕtê ṣāpôn, "heights of (Mount) Zaphon" (38:6,15; 39:2). We have seen that yarkĕtê ṣāpôn is har môʿēd/magedōn, "the mount of assembly" (Isa 14:13). We have also seen that Mount Zion represents this celestial court; it is the true yarkĕtê ṣāpôn (Ps 48:2 [3]). That means that Gog's establishing of Magog as a yarkĕtê ṣāpôn was the erecting of a pseudo-Zaphon (a kind of Esagila tower of Babel) in the land of the north. Ezekiel thus presents the remarkable picture of a coming of Gog with his hordes from pseudo-Zaphon/Magedon to challenge the Lord on Zion, the true Mount Zaphon/Magedon.

From Gog's claim to lordship over Zaphon and his universal gathering of armies against Zion/Har Magedon, it is evident that he is to be identified with the antichrist of the final Har Magedon crisis of Rev 16:14-16; 19:17-21 (and other passages in Revelation). This is confirmed by other features in Ezekiel 38-39, like the beast symbolism applied to Gog (38:4; 39:2) and numerous parallels to the judgment of the beast of Revelation in the description of God's destruction of Gog, most striking of these the feasting of the birds and beasts on the slain hordes (Ezek 39:4,17-20 and Rev 19:17,18). Likewise, parallels between Gog's career in Ezekiel 38-39 and that of the Pauline "man of sin" in 2 Thessalonians 2 corroborate Gog's antichrist identity. Thus, Gog's advance against Israel in a storm-cloud theophany (Ezek 38:9,16) matches the (pseudo-) *parousia* nature of the man of sin's appearance (2 Thess 2:9). Also, in both cases the Lord responds in the true Parousia-advent with almighty vengeance (Ezek 38:18-23; 39:1-21 and 2 Thess 2:3-10).

The Ezekiel 38-39 Gog crisis, which has been found to be the same as the Har Magedon/antichrist crisis of Rev 16:14-16, the prelude to Christ's parousia, is also to be identified, of course, with the Gog-Magog event of Rev 20:7-10. Since the latter follows the thousand year era, so does the Gog/Har Magedon battle (and the Parousia). This falsifies the idea that the millennium follows the Parousia; the millennium must be the church age which issues in the antichrist/Har Magedon/Gog-Magog crisis. The Parousia which visits final judgment on antichrist-Gog does not introduce a transitional stage in the coming of God's kingdom in glory, but the eternal consummate reign of God.

Comparison of Zechariah's seventh vision with these kindred prophecies leads us to recognize in "the land of the north" in Zech 6:7 an allusion to the world's final satanic insurrection. In the light of Ezekiel 38-39 we perceive that the Parousia movement of the four chariots from the two bronze mountains against the land of the north is a judicial response to a previous titanic challenge of the northern pseudo-Zaphon power under antichrist-Gog against the Lord enthroned on the original, authentic Har Magedon.[20] Agreeably, in the Zechariah 14 development of this theme, the

Parousia-advent of the divine warrior is clearly a counter-attack against the nations that have gathered against Jerusalem.

If the mission of the four chariots symbolically prophesies the Lord's advent in final judgment against the Har Magedon challenge of antichrist, the consequence of that mission will be the inauguration of the eternal order of God's kingdom. And that is what we shall find to be the case as we move on to examine the oracle of Zech 6:8, which concludes the seventh vision.[21]

C. *The Spirit's Sabbath.* A kerygmatic oracle interprets the accompanying imagery in visions one, three, five, and seven. The oracle in vision one (Zech 1:14-17) conveys the Lord's promise of his eschatological return to his people; at that time he would vent his wrath on the enemy nations and his house would be rebuilt in restored Jerusalem. The oracle in vision seven (Zech 6:8) proclaims the fulfillment of that prospect: "Lo, those who go to the land of the north have set my Spirit at rest in the land of the north."

Here is a vista of the world to come. The holy war is over. At the great battle of Har Magedon the Lord has triumphed; he has eliminated the hostile forces. The final trumpet has sounded and there is "delay no longer;" the mystery of God has been finished as he announced to and through his servants the prophets (Rev 10:6,7). Sabbath time has come.

Some have interpreted Zech 6:8 as describing God's punitive judgment on the wicked. It is argued that the main verb in this verse (Hiph. of *nwḥ*) can be used for a visitation of God's anger, whether in the sense of bringing it down on someone or of causing it to rest by giving full expression to it so that it is satiated and satisfied (cf., e.g., Ezek 5:13; 16:42; 21:17 [22]; 24:13; Zech 9:1). Moreover, the term *rûaḥ*, object of this verb in Zech 6:8, at times means "wrath" (cf. Judg 8:3; Eccl 10:4; Prov 16:32). However, that does not appear to be the sense of these terms here. Although the destruction of the wicked is indeed assumed to have transpired, what this oracle itself contemplates is something subsequent to the act of judgment, the designed consequence of it.

In the context of this set of visions, *rûḥî* is to be understood as God's Spirit rather than his anger. That is its meaning in vision four. There, in connection with the assertion that the hostile world mountain would be

215

leveled as God's temple was raised to completion, the secret of this triumph is revealed: "by my Spirit" (*rûhî*, Zech 4:6; cf. Hag 2:5). In vision three the messianic mission of vengeance against the evil nations (the mission executed by the four chariots in Zech 6:1ff.) is carried out in conjunction with the Glory-Spirit. But most conclusive is the imagery in vision seven itself. The four chariots are individualized extensions of the chariot-throne of the Glory-Spirit; they are bearers of the Spirit. It is the Glory-Spirit they have carried to the land of the north and therefore it is the Glory-Spirit that they set down at rest in the land of the north. Also to be noted here is the sixth vision's counterfeit parallel to the imagery of the chariots carrying the Spirit. There it is the woman Wickedness who is carried by the winged women and is then set down at the destination point. This parallel elucidates more than the carrying action of the four chariots in vision seven, for the verb *nwḥ* is used for the act of setting down in both visions. The meaning of the verb in Zech 6:8 will, therefore, parallel that in Zech 5:11, where it signifies the setting of the woman at rest on a prepared site. More precisely, and highly significant for the interpretation of Zech 6:8, the locating of the ephah with the woman in Zech 5:11 is an act of enthronement.

Looking beyond the pouring out of the last bowl of wrath, beyond the final judgment on the antichrist world, the oracle of Zech 6:8 announces the eternal glory of the Spirit. The enthroned Glory-Spirit's sovereign Presence, which was represented by the two bronze mountains, will be established even in the north country, and, if there, then everywhere. In the consummate state Mount Zion, throne of the Spirit, will be universalized.[22]

We have compared the two bronze mountains to the scene at mounts Ebal and Gerizim reported in Josh 8:30-35. The Lord was present there as the victor, taking possession of the land he had claimed for himself in the Abrahamic Covenant, setting up his victory stele in his typological kingdom. Zech 6:8 represents the universal antitype, the Presence of the Glory-Spirit as the victor celebrating the enforcement of his perfect rule over his creation-wide domain.

The basic outline of the seventh vision: the going forth of the Glory-Spirit from the bronze mountains for battle and his victorious coming to rest, follows the Conquest paradigm. On the larger scale this Conquest pattern covered the history from Sinai to Zion, but it was also reproduced repeatedly on a smaller scale in the order of the Lord's procession through the wilderness. "When the ark set out, Moses said, 'Rise up (*qûm*), Yahweh, and let your enemies be scattered and let those who hate you flee before you.' When it came to rest (*nwḥ*), he said, 'Return, Yahweh, to the midst of the ten thousand thousands of Israel'" (Num 10:35,36; cf. Ps 68:1 [2]). This ascending of the Lord refers to the Glory-cloud's rising up from its session on the ark-throne in the Tabernacle to proceed above Israel and the ark on the ground below, directing the tribes to a resting place (*měnûḥâ*, Num 10:33,34). Num 9:17-23 (cf. Exod 40:34-38) indicates this was the procedure followed during all Israel's journeying. Similar to Moses' plea for Yahweh to rise up is that of Solomon at the temple dedication, calling on the Lord to be up and doing in behalf of Israel and their anointed king: "Now rise up (*qûm*), Yahweh God, from your resting place (*měnûḥâ*, cf. Ps 132:8); arise, (from) the ark of your strength" (2 Chr 6:41; cf. Ps 132:8).[23]

Zechariah's seventh vision answers to these prototypes. It prophesies the ultimate granting of Solomon's prayer for God's saving action and the perfecting of the pattern of the wilderness procession from Sinai to establish the Lord's sovereignty over Canaan on Zion. The Lord rises up from his royal resting place on the mountains of bronze, up from the ark of his strength, and, as symbolized by the going forth of the chariots, he sets out on his judicial mission accompanied by the heavenly forces associated with his ark-throne. Then, the mission of judgment concluded, the Lord resumes his sovereign repose on his chariot-throne, which has brought him to rest in what had been enemy occupied terrain but now and forever is his unchallenged royal domain.

Such is the interpretation of the seventh vision endorsed by its counterpart in the burdens half of the prophecy. Presented there in Zechariah 14 as the sequel to the eschatological advent of the divine warrior to destroy the hostile nations (vv. 3-5) is an elaborate picture of the eternal order of the new creation (vv. 6ff.). The saints will possess a holy and blessed world, purged of all God's enemies. The consummation of joy and glory typified by the Feast of Tabernacles will be realized. And echoing Zech 6:8, Zech 14:9 characterizes that day as the time when Yahweh alone will be king over the whole world.

The key verb of Zech 6:8, *nwḥ*, and its derivative noun, *měnûḥâ*, are used in Num 10:36 and 2 Chr 6:41 (cf. Ps 132:8), as we have seen, for God's royal rest, his session on his ark-throne. In Isa 25:10 the enthronement of the Glory ("hand") on Zion in the day of resurrection triumph is denoted as a coming to rest (nwḥ) on the mountain. Isa 66:12 identifies God's resting place (měnûḥâ) with his heavenly throne. And in Isa 11:10 that "Glory" throne-site is said to be the eschatological měnûḥâ of the royal messianic Root of Jesse.

The Sabbath connotation of these terms is clear. Indeed, in the Exod 20:11 reference to Gen 2:2, the verb nwḥ takes the place of the verb šbt used in the original account for God's seventh day rest. The throne-session that is identified with God's měnûḥâ is in fact the essence of the divine Sabbath.[24] Accordingly, when Zech 6:8 speaks of setting God's Spirit at rest, what is signified is the Spirit's Sabbath.

The Spirit enthroned over the world at the beginning (Gen 1:2) was the quintessential Sabbath reality. In the Creator's seventh day rest this Sabbath reality was translated into temporal-eschatological dimensions,[25] and this royal Sabbath rest of God, the archetype Sabbath, was symbolically replicated in the ordinance of the Sabbath. The Sabbath ordinance in turn is the type that points to man's eschatological arrival at the consummation of kingdom history, at the archetype Sabbath become antitype Sabbath. The setting of God's Spirit at rest, as presented in Zech 6:8, is the dawning of that antitypical, eternal Sabbath, the epiphany of the Parousia-Presence of the Glory-Spirit enthroned in the new heavens and earth.

---

1 Similarly, Zech 13:2-9, the parallel to Zech 5:1-11 in the burdens section of the book, prepares for the prophecy of final judgment in Zechariah 14 by its account of the removal of apostates from the covenant community.

2 Even if we so translate Zech 6:5 as to identify the chariots with the four winds, this last statement in the verse will refer to the chariots. On the translation question, see further below.

3 An unholy version of this theophanic formation appears in vision six in the imagery of the two stork-winged women carrying away the ephah.

4 Cf. my *Images of the Spirit*, 40.

5 Cf. my *Kingdom Prologue*, 229,230. By the same token the Joshua 8 transaction represented to the Lord's people a fulfillment of the land grant promised to them in the Abrahamic Covenant. Cf. A.E. Hill, "The Ebal Ceremony as Hebrew Land Grant," *JETS* 31:4 (1988), 399-406.

6 For the striking parallel features, cf. the Appendix.

7 This exegesis follows the Masoretic text. According to another view, suggested by alternative readings in the versions, "my (God's) mountains" would be Zion and Olivet, with the Kidron as the valley between.

8 The final judgment is a time of salvation for God's elect, a safe passage through Jehoshaphat, the valley of judgment (cf. Joel 3:2,12 [4:2,12]), only because the Lord

himself has first undergone the passage through the dark valley of death, suffering the divine judgment in their place (cf. Gen 15:17).

9 This verb, *synagō*, is used in LXX for the Hebrew *y^{c}d*, root of *mô^{c}ēd*. For a full discussion of the term *har magedōn* and of related topics dealt with under the present heading see my "Har Magedon: The End of the Millennium," *JETS* 39:2 (1996) 207-222.

10 Cf. also Job 26:7; 37:22; Ps 89:12 [13].

11 See discussion of the mounted divine warrior in our comments on vision one.

12 Cf. Deut 33:2; Hab 3:3; Ps 18:9ff. [10ff.].

13 This is an accusative of place whither put first for emphasis (*GKC* 118f.). Cf. *ṣiyyôn* in Zech 2:7 [11]. The preposition *ʾel* is avoided after *ʾēlāy ʾēlleh*. For the concept, cf. Zech 2:6 [10].

14 Similarly in the first vision the horses are possibly divided into just two groups. Another shared feature of these visions is that the colors in both are natural colors of horses and not to be taken as symbolic of particular forms of judgment in the absence of explicit indications to that effect, such as are found in the vision of the four horsemen in Revelation 6.

15 On the special preparation for vision seven in vision six (Zech 5:1-11), see the introduction to this chapter.

16 Also confirming the military-punitive nature of the mission of the four chariots in Zech 6:1-8 is the warrior role of Yahweh in Zechariah 14 (the parallel passage in the second half of the book), where he goes forth to fight against the world-wide gathering of nations to attack Jerusalem (v. 3).

17 If the chariots in Zechariah's seventh vision are understood as moving from Zion in just the two directions, north and south, the geo-political outlook of Zech 6:1-8 is comparable to that in Daniel 11 with its concentration on the Ptolemies to the south and the Seleucids to the north, threatening the covenant people in between.

18 In Dan 11:45 the antichrist king of the north challenges "the temple-mount of glory" (Har Magedon/Zion) and there comes to his end at the advent of Messiah-Michael (Dan 12:1).

19 The name Gog apparently arises by interpreting the term Magog as "place (*ma-*) of Gog."

20 Depiction of God's judgment on Gog in Ezekiel 38-39 contains only a suggestion that retaliation against Gog's Magog-base in the north is involved (cf. Ezek 39:6).

21 Similarly, the consummation of the kingdom is presented as the direct consequence of the equivalent crisis episodes of Gog-Magog in Ezekiel 38-39, the king of the north in Daniel 11-12, and the universal gathering against Jerusalem in Zechariah 14.

22 Cf. Isa 2:2; Dan 2:35; and, in Zech 2:6 [10], the Lord's promise to spread his kingdom people to the four winds of heaven.

23 The synonymous parallelism is missed in the usual translations (which also lose the connection with Num 10:33,34). "Your resting place" and "ark of your strength" are obviously equivalent, and the personal pronoun *ʾattâ*, "you", in the second half functions resumptively for the remainder of the first half, i.e., for the verb and vocative. (This stylistic feature can be shown to resolve perplexities in a number of passages, as I hope to show elsewhere.) "From" is, of course, an attested meaning of the preposition *la*.

24 On this see my *Kingdom Prologue*, 22,23.

25 Cf. my *Images of the Spirit*, 111.

Centerpiece (6:9-15)

KING OF GLORY

Introduction. Zech 6:9-15 is the central hinge[1] linking the two halves of the prophet's diptych composition, the axis between the night visions (1:7-6:8) with their introduction (1:1-6) and the burdens (9:1-14:21) with their introduction (7:1-8:23). Each half is itself a diptych having a hinge section, Zech 3:1-10 for the visions and 11:1-17 for the burdens. Common to the three hinge passages is a focus on the figure of the coming Messiah and in particular on his priest-king office.

Messianic symbolism and interpretation alternate in CH as follows: Symbolism of the preparation of a crown with the participation of returnees from far-off exile and the placing of the crown on the head of Joshua, the high priest (vv. 10,11). Interpretation of the coronation of Joshua (vv. 12,13). Symbolism of the depositing of the crown in the temple as a memorial of the contribution of the returned captives (v. 14) and interpretation thereof (v. 15). Our comments will follow this sequence except that the opening verses (vv. 10,11)[2] will be treated in connection with vv. 14,15, which resumes the subject of the returned exiles, so producing an envelope pattern.[3]

CH recapitulates major messianic themes found throughout the seven night visions: Messiah's dual priest-king office; his regathering of the distant exiles and building of the temple; and his intratrinitarian associations. The most conspicuous connections of CH are with the third, fourth, and fifth visions, the closest relationship being with the fourth. In addition to the formal features distinctive of the three hinge sections of the book,[4] other features shared by CH and vision four include: the figure of Joshua as a type of Christ; the crowning of Joshua and his investiture in glory array; his identification as the Branch; the union of the priestly and royal offices; the exalted privilege of presence in God's heaven; and the principle of faithful service as prerequisite to eschatological blessings.[5] One difference between these two closely related passages is that in Zechariah 3 the investiture of Joshua with the priestly regalia transpires within a vision, whereas the crowning of Joshua in Zech 6:9-15 was a real life occurrence. However, this actual historical event, like the visionary episode, had symbolical significance; it too was a typological prefiguration of Messiah's ministry and exaltation.

I. CROWN RIGHTS (6:12,13b)

A. *Royal Scion.* Interpreting the figure of Joshua the high priest with the crown set on his head, the word of the Lord declares: "Behold a man— his name is Branch (*ṣemaḥ*). From his place he shall branch forth (*ṣmḥ*) and he shall build the temple of Yahweh" (Zech 6:12b-d). The significance of the name "Branch" is explained by earlier prophecies concerning Messiah as one who springs up from David's royal stock (cf. Isa 4:2; 11:1; Jer 23:5,6; 33:14-17). In Zechariah 3 the messianic reference of the Branch title is confirmed by the further identification of the Branch with the Isaianic Servant of the Lord (v. 8).

It is Joshua not in himself but as a symbol of Christ who is in view in both Zechariah 3 and Zech 6:9-15. Many modern commentators, however, reluctant because of their naturalistic bias to admit the prophetic-typological character of the CH episode, try to construe it in political terms as the making of a public statement about the roles of the cultic and civil authorities in the governance of the postexilic community. And since in those terms it would seem that Zerubbabel, the governor and a Davidide, was the one who should receive the royal crown, he gets arbitrarily substituted in the text for Joshua the high priest. Or he gets added as a second figure alongside Joshua (with citation of ancient diarchic practices). On the latter approach two crowns would be involved, and in support of that appeal is made to the apparently plural form *ʿăṭārôt* in v. 11. But this form, if it is a plural and not an old Phoenician singular, may be understood as the superlative plural of excellence or as a reflection of the composite structure of the crown as consisting of separate gold and silver circlets (cf. v. 11 and Rev 19:12). Certainly the Masoretes understood only one crown to be involved for in v. 14 they vocalize *ʿṭrt*, the subject of the singular verb *tihyeh*, as *ʿăṭārôt*. Indeed that singular verb demands the conclusion that only one crown is in view in the entire passage. An attempt has been made to maintain the two-crown view while acknowledging that a single crown is referred to in each instance. But this involves an obviously contrived argument to distinguish the crown of v. 14 from that in v. 11. It becomes evident that no satisfactory explanation of the data is possible apart from the adoption of the typological-messianic interpretation.

B. *Messianic Temple Builder.* Conjoined with the Branch's identity as one who comes forth as the royal scion of David's dynasty is his role as temple builder (Zech 6:12c,d). This role belongs to the portrayal of Messiah as king, for temple building was a royal function. Agreeably it was the Davidide governor, Zerubbabel, who was the primary leader in restoring the temple in Zechariah's day and who appears in Zechariah's fifth vision as the prototype of Christ as builder of the eschatological temple (Zech 4:6-10). In CH Joshua is selected as the messianic type, even though the temple-building theme is present, because the basic symbolism in CH is the crowning of the Branch and that is resumed from vision four, where Joshua was the typological figure. The choice of the priest rather than the governor there was dictated by the cultic setting and rituals of that vision. In CH itself there is also a climactic focus on the priestly prerogative of heavenly association with Yahweh (6:13d,e), which makes Joshua a more suitable symbol here. Another possible factor, remembering that the CH episode was not visionary but actually occurred, is that a public coronation of Zerubbabel, a prince of the royal house, might result in suspicion and punitive reaction on the part of the Persian authorities.

Repeating the twofold identification of the Branch given in Zech 6:12c and d, v. 13a and b declares: "And he (wĕhûʾ) shall build the temple of Yahweh and he (wĕhûʾ) shall bear the glory." As the grammatical parallelism indicates, these two clauses constitute a pair, with the repetition of the independent personal pronoun pointing back to the Branch as the one who receives the twofold attestation of his identity as Yahweh's anointed king, namely, endorsement as builder of the temple (v. 13a) and reception of the royal regalia (v. 13b).

Taken together the four clauses in v. 12c,d and v. 13a,b form an ABB'A' chiastic quatrain, with the middle members (B and B') being a virtually identical pair of statements concerning the building of the temple. The A and A' members of the chiasm both deal with the Branch's succession to the throne. The A clause (v. 12c) declares him the legitimate royal heir and the A' clause (v. 13b) celebrates his investiture with the majesty of kingship. Rather than the more abstract rendering, "he shall bear the glory," v. 13b may be translated, "he shall wear the royal robes."[6] Such investiture in royal robes would be a natural accompaniment of the bestowing of the crown. In fact, in the symbolism of Joshua's crowning in vision four, the setting of the royal diadem on his head is integral to his being clothed in the priestly glory garments (Zech 3:5), the diadem being part of the royal mitre.

C. God's Covenant Promise (2 Samuel 7). The two royal distinctions attributed to the Branch in CH, his right to the throne and his prerogative of constructing the temple, remind us at once of God's covenant with David (2 Sam 7:5-16).[7] The same two royal honors are the featured blessings promised in that dynastic grant. At the typological level these royal promises were fulfilled in David's son Solomon and his successors, but Zechariah's prophecy looks beyond that to their ultimate fulfillment in the messianic Branch, that Son of David to whom it would be given to build an enduring house for God's name and the throne of whose kingdom God would establish forever (2 Sam 7:13).

The covenantal origins of the royal grant to Christ go back before the making of the covenant with David to the intratrinitarian counsels before the world was, back to a primal divine pact.[8] Though the covenants made between God and man in the course of human history were determined upon in eternity in the all-embracive divine decrees, the actual covenanting between the parties does not occur until the creature party is on the scene. However, since all parties of the intratrinitarian covenant are present at the determination of the eternal decrees, that decretive predestinating is at the same time an actual eternal covenanting of the persons of the Godhead with each other with respect to their relationships in all that they decree concerning creation and redemption.

It was in that eternal covenant that the cosmic kingdom of glory was guaranteed to the Son as the reward for his faithful execution of the work the Father gave him to do (cf. Luke 22:29; John 17:4,5). This covenantal commitment to the Son was renewed in the course of the historical administration of the Covenant of Grace.[9] It came to earthly expression in the Abrahamic and Davidic covenants: Christ was the promised seed of Abraham to whom pertained the promise of kingship and kingdom (Gal 3:16) and Christ was the son of David to whom the dynastic promises of the Davidic covenant were directed. What Zech 6:9-15 prophesies is the Father's fulfillment of the eternal covenant by bestowing the promised kingdom grant on the Son who came to earth as Jesus, the Christ of God, the son of David, the son of Abraham (Matt 1:1), and obediently carried out the stipulated task.

II. HEAVENLY THRONE (6:13c-e)

A. *Enthronement of the Priest-King.* Following the quatrain on kingship and the temple of Yahweh is a bicolon (Zech 6:13c and d), in which the parallelism of the two cola is established by the shared phrase, "by his throne" (ʿal kisĕʾô).[10] This pair is capped by a climactic third colon (v. 13e), which is the apex of the entire prophetic celebration of the glory of the messianic Branch.

Throughout the interpretation of the symbolism of the crowned high priest in terms of the Branch (vv. 12,13a,b), he, the messianic priest-king, is the subject of all the verbs. Certainly he continues to be the subject in v. 13c: "and he shall sit and rule," which echoes the declarations of his reception of the royal office in vv. 12c and 13b. And there is no good reason to read v. 13d: "there shall be a priest by his throne," as though there were some other priestly figure standing by the side of the enthroned king. The messianic Branch is himself this priest, the antitype of Joshua the high priest, and the intrusion of another priest alongside Christ, the priest-king, would be superfluous at best. It also requires that the phrase ⁽al kisĕʾô be taken in a different sense in v. 13d than in v. 13c. The only warranted translation of wĕhāyâ kōhēn in v. 13d is: "and he shall be a priest."

Having rejected the notion that different individuals are referred to in v. 13c and d, we face the question of the meaning of the phrase "between the two of them" in v. 13e. The traditional view, rightly holding that the Branch is both king and priest, would explain the problematic "two of them" by personifying the two offices of Christ as two individuals. But this view proves unsatisfactory. If, as it assumes, "his throne" in v. 13c and d is the Branch's throne,[11] then, if the royal figure of v. 13c and the priestly figure of v. 13d are treated as two persons, we are left with the odd imagery of two figures sitting on one throne. Jer 33:14-18, which prophesies of the Davidic kingship and Levitical priesthood continuing together forever in Christ, the priest-king, uses the more appropriate imagery of the actual typological situation, with the king sitting on his throne and the priests ministering before the Lord in his temple. Moreover, the traditional view is mistaken in its appeal to vision five as another instance of the representation of Christ's twofold office of priest-king by two separate figures, the "two sons of oil" symbolized by the two trees (Zech 4:11-14). For the two trees there symbolize the prophetic office.

For a more satisfactory solution of the problem raised by "the two of them" (v. 13e), we must return to the phrase ⁽al kisĕʾô in v. 13c and d and reconsider the question of the antecedent of "his"—usually taken to be the king. In the structure of vv. 12 and 13 there are three pairs of clauses, each marked by the repetition of a key term. The repetition focuses attention on "the temple of Yahweh" in the first pair (vv. 12d and 13a) and on "his throne" in the third pair (v. 13c and d), while the middle pair (v. 13a and b), marked by the repeated personal pronoun "he" (hûʾ), overlaps the first and links it to the third by emphasizing that the Branch is the common subject: he (hûʾ) builds the temple and he (hûʾ) is the one invested with the right to the throne. The connection thus made between the throne and the temple of Yahweh argues for the conclusion that the throne, like the temple, is to be identified as Yahweh's. Other evidence of the bond of the throne and temple supports this conclusion. Architecturally, temple and throne belong together. The temple is a sacred palace; it houses God's throne. The Lord identifies the eschatological temple as "the place of my throne" (Ezek 43:7). Indeed, the throne and temple coalesce in the heavenly city, the identity of both of them being absorbed by the New Jerusalem, the city which as a whole is the temple so that there is no separate temple there (Rev 21:22), the city which is called "The Throne of the Lord" (Jer 3:17). That "his throne," the coronation site of Messiah in Zech 6:13c and d, refers to Yahweh's throne is confirmed by the fact that the throne that appears in biblical depiction of the exalted Messiah's reign is regularly the throne of God.[12] It is then Yahweh who is referred to by the suffix pronoun "his"; he is the second person in view in this context along with the messianic priest-king. And it is to these two, the Lord and his Anointed, that the phrase "the two of them" in v. 13e refers.[13]

Just how we are to picture the relation of the Branch's enthronement to the throne of Yahweh is the question of the meaning of the preposition ʿal in v. 13c and d. Should we translate "on" or "by" the throne? In the heavenly throne scenes in the Bible the customary imagery is that of Messiah stationed at the right hand of God's throne. That is the case, for example, in Psalm 110, the most significant source behind CH. There the Lord invites the Messiah: "Sit at my right hand until I make your enemies a footstool for your feet" (v. 1). The proper translation of ʿal in v. 13c and d is then "by" his throne. By the right side of the throne of Yahweh a throne is set up for the Branch, an arrangement illustrated in 1 Kgs. 2:19, which describes how Solomon sat on his throne and set up a throne for his mother, Bathsheba, and she sat at his right hand. The Apocalypse softens the distinction of the two thrones. It describes the Lamb as in the midst of the throne (Rev 5:6; 7:17; cf. 3:21), which it even calls "the throne of God and the Lamb" (Rev 22:1,3). This reflects the closeness of the union of God and his Christ in their co-enthronement over creation. Another factor here is the way elements of the Glory-Spirit and the Ancient of Days theophanies are blended into representations of the priest-king figure of the Son of Man, producing a single triune figure, at times in the context of a revelation of the divine Presence on the heavenly throne (cf. Rev 1:13ff.; Dan 7:13; Ezk 1:26-28).

What an astounding advance is marked by Christ's priesthood. It was the greatest privilege afforded by the old covenant cult that the high priest might enter the earthly holy of holies, he alone, once a year (Heb 9:7), to stand and minister before the throne of God. But to Christ, the royal priest, it is given to enter the true temple above, to be continually in the heavenly holy of holies, and—the utterly astonishing thing—to ascend the throne and share in the Glory of God between the cherubim (cf. Heb 10:11,12). In contemplation of this priest-king, fairer than the children of men, arrayed in divine glory and majesty, the psalmist exults: "Thy throne, O God, is for ever and ever" (Ps 45:6 [7])

B. *Christ and the Glory-Spirit Temple.* In his ascension and heavenly enthronement Christ received from the Father the Glory he rightfully claimed in anticipation of his obedience unto the death of the Cross, the Glory identifiable as the Father's own self, the Glory the Son had with the Father before the world was (John 17:5). That eternal divine Glory is knowable by us only as it is manifested within the creation. It was for the manifestation of that transcendent Glory that the world was created. Heaven and earth thus have the character of a temple, a place where God's Glory-Presence is revealed, a place where priestly creatures—angels and men made in Elohim likeness (cf. Psalm 82)—behold and reflect back God's Glory, where they worship and adore him.

According to Scriptural representations, the cosmic temple is not simply a place where God manifests his Glory; it is actually identified with God himself (Rev 21:22), that is, with the self-manifestation of God within creation. (Needless to say, the intention is not that God is identical with creation in a pantheistic sense.) More precisely, this Glory-temple is identified with the realm of heaven, the Glory-dimensioned realm presently invisible to mortals but to be opened to the redeemed at the Consummation. Created in the beginning and continuing forever, the cosmic Glory-temple, as God's own self-manifestation, constitutes a perpetual epiphany, a permanent entempling of the divine Presence.

In pre-Consummation earth history the heavenly Glory-Presence has appeared occasionally in localized symbolic fashion in the form of the theophanic Glory-cloud. This earthly projection is identified in the Bible as the Spirit,[14] and accordingly the heavenly reality, while a trinitarian manifestation, is more particularly identified with the Spirit.

There is then an eternally continuing Glory-embodiment of God's Spirit-Presence in creation, shaping creation and constituting it a temple. The primal creation event that brought this Glory-Spirit epiphany into existence (Gen 1:1) may be called the endoxation of the Spirit. It is comparable to the incarnation of the Son. Incarnate Son and endoxate

Spirit are alike epiphanic embodiments of the God of Glory.

Each of these manifestations of the divine Presence is also the temple of God, and since the temple is God's dwelling place, each is a divine tabernacling among us. Each is an Immanuel (God-with-us) Presence. Not for the first time does the immanuel principle come to expression in redemptive history. In the original act of creation God manifested this divine eagerness to welcome his creatures into his dwelling place, to gather them as children to his bosom. Creation was as much an exhibition of God's tender, condescending love as of his wisdom and power. When, after the Fall, God yet so loved the world that he sent his Son, incarnate Immanuel, it was to restore the intimate family fellowship of God with his people for which the endoxation of the Spirit was originally designed. The incarnation of the Son subserves the original creational purpose, redemptively enhancing the manifestation of the divine love present from the beginning in the endoxate Spirit.

Exaltation to the heavenly temple, filled and formed by the Glory of the endoxate Spirit, was the reward of the incarnate Son. That Glory-Spirit temple was the Glory of the Father's own self, to which the Son returned. It was in the midst of the temple throne that the priest-king Branch took his place as God's "fellow" (Zech 13:7) at the right hand of the Father.

Jesus' followers witnessed his exaltation to the Glory-Spirit realm in his ascension (Luke 24:51; Acts 1:2,9,10). They beheld him transported above on the ascension cloud—the theophanic cloud which was the projection of the Glory-Spirit into the field of mortal vision.[15] The mode of the Lord's departure into heaven thus afforded an anticipatory glimpse of the Glory of the invisible Spirit-temple into which he was being taken up. It was also a token preview of the Glory of the Father in which he will reappear at his Parousia (Acts 1:11).

C. God's Covenant Oath (Psalm 110). "The counsel ($^c\bar{e}s\hat{a}$) of peace will be between the two of them" (Zech. 6:13e). As usually interpreted, the idea is that the object of the consultation is to promote a state of peace for God's people. Certainly the effect of Messiah's heavenly reign is such a peaceful condition of prosperity and righteousness in his kingdom (cf., e.g., Ps 72:3,7; Ezek 34:25; 37:26). But "between them" suggests that this peace refers to the personal relationship between the two enthroned persons. And it is in keeping with attested usage of the terms "counsel" and "peace" to understand the relationship affirmed here between the Branch and Yahweh as covenantal. Thus in Ps 83:5 (6) taking counsel together ($y^c s$)

with one consent and making a covenant form a parallel pair. Also, "peace" often defines covenants and characterizes covenant relationships (cf., e.g., Josh 9:15; Isa 54:10; Ezek 34:25; 37:26; Zech 9:10; Mal 2:5). What Zech 6:13e is declaring in particular is that the exaltation of the Branch to fellowship and joint reign with Yahweh on his throne is the outworking of previous covenantal commitments of the two to one another.

The covenant transaction alluded to in Zech 6:13e is expressly cited in Psalm 110. The strong affinities of Zech 6:12,13 with this earlier revelation to David are plain. Featured in the psalm is Messiah's dual office of priest and king, central in Zech 6:13. Messiah is addressed in the psalm as the king who triumphs in judgment over his enemies, but he is also identified as "priest forever." This priesthood is described as "after the order of Melchizedek," a priest-king (Gen 14:18; Heb 7:1-3). Also prominent in Psalm 110 is Yahweh's appointment of David's messianic scion and Lord to a place at his right hand and the remarkable collaboration of the two who share the heavenly throne in judicial action For the meaning of Zech 6:13e it is highly significant that this psalm which is recapitulated in Zech 6:13 presents the exaltation of the Messiah to his royal-priestly glory on the throne of heaven as that which was guaranteed by Yahweh's oath: "Yahweh hath sworn and will not repent" (Ps 110:4a). Such oath-sanctioned commitment is constitutive of covenant. Psalm 110 thus confirms the covenantal interpretation of Zech 6:13e. And like the revelation of the Davidic covenant in 2 Sam 7:5-16, the revelation in this prophetic psalm of David points behind the historical, earthly unfolding of redemption in its successive covenant administrations to their foundation in the eternal intratrinitarian covenant. It directs us to the divine oath commitments that find their fulfillment at the end of the ages in the mission of the incarnate Son, the two-stage mission of humiliation and exaltation.

III. COSMIC HERITAGE (6:9-11,14,15)

After serving its key role in the coronation of Joshua, the crown was to be deposited in the temple of Yahweh (Zech 6:14). There it was to serve as a memorial of the group of exiles who had come from Babylon with their silver and gold to participate in the restoration of the cultus. In coming days the crown would recall this past event in order to point to the future. For what the returned exiles had done was a sign, prophetic of a later universal return of God's people from far off to take part in the building of the eschatological temple.[16] We shall examine the particulars of the typical episode and then look into the significance of its antitypical counterpart in relation to Christ's reception of his covenanted exaltation.

A. *Typological Requisitioning.* The role of the individuals named in Zech 6:10 and (with some modifications) in v. 14 has been construed in different ways. It is plain enough, however, that they (at least, the first three) have come from the Babylonian captivity with a donation of precious metals. As the prophetic significance of their action indicates (cf. v. 15), their contribution was intended to support the restoration of the temple cultus in Jerusalem. Crucial for our understanding of the essential character of the episode described in CH is the role of the fourth member of the group, Josiah ben Zephaniah. That is clarified by two kinds of evidence: the genre of Zech 6:9-11 and the designation of Josiah in v. 14.

Exhibited in Zech 6:9-11 are the distinctive elements and technical terms that characterize requisition dockets. We may illustrate from a group of ostraca (sherds inscribed in ink) found at Arad in the northern Negeb, dating from the end of the Israelite monarchy.[17] At that time Arad was a royal citadel and administrative center. In the archives of Eliashib ben Eshyahu, an offical there in charge of supplies, taxes, and tithes, were requisition documents authorizing the bearers to obtain specified provisions stored at the fortress. These ostraca-slips were then kept by Eliashib as evidence of the transaction. One such text addressed to a certain Nahum reads: "To Nahum, and now: Come to the house of Eliashib ben Eshyahu and take from him 1 (jar of) oil and send (it) to me quickly and seal it with your seal." On the back of the ostracon Eliashib recorded the date of delivery as a kind of receipt: "On the 24th of the month gave Nahum oil by the hand of the Kitti, 1 (jar)."

Zech 6:9-11 matches the pattern of this requisition form in these particulars: (1) The address to the bearer of the requisition, Zechariah (v. 9). (2) The command sequence: "come ... take from." (3) The reference to the "house" of the steward and his name with his patronymic, ben Zephaniah. (4) The objects to be taken: silver and gold. (5) The disposition of the requisitioned articles: to be made into a crown. (6) Temporal reference: "that day," i.e., the day of the exiles' arrival at the "house"—the last clause of v. 10 may be translated "where they have come from Babylon" but also "when they have come (there) from Babylon." (7) The receipt for supplying the requisitioned objects—the "memorial" in Zech 6:14.

The genre of Zech 6:9-11 is clearly that of a requisition docket and Josiah ben Zephaniah emerges in this context as a treasury steward. Confirming this identification of his role is the designation for him in v. 14. In place of the name Josiah is *leḥēn*. The *l*- is usually taken as the preposition "for," which is prefixed to each of the other three names. It should, however, be taken together with the *ḥn* and this *lḥn* has been shown to be an Akkadian loanword, the Neo-Assyrian *laḫḫinu* (also attested in the Aramaic *lĕḥēn*), used as a title for a court or temple official, a steward of precious commodities.[18]

Josiah was then a temple official. Such an office was occupied in the days of Hezekiah by Kore ben Imnah, who was set over the storage and distribution of the offerings (2 Chr 31:14). Josiah's "house" does not refer to his residence but to the storage or treasury room(s) connected with the temple, over which he was in charge.[19] It was naturally to this "house" of Josiah that the returning exiles brought their treasures for the temple. And it would have been at that (treasury) house that Zechariah received through Josiah's offices the exiles' donation as requisitioned by the Lord.

It has been shown to be possible that Josiah ben Zephaniah was the great grandson of Zephaniah, a priest at the time of the destruction of Jerusalem, the "second priest" next to Seraiah, the chief priest (2 Kgs 25:18ff.). Josiah's relationship to Joshua the high priest might then have been similar to that of his great grandfather to Seraiah. Such a priestly identity of Josiah and the location of his treasury office in the temple precincts would have proven convenient in arranging for the ceremonial coronation of Joshua.

The divine prerogative of requisition, operative throughout the history of God's relationship to Israel, was the expression of the Lord's claims as covenant suzerain. Through authorized agents, like Moses or the high priest (cf. Exod 25:2ff.; Num 7:5; 31:51-54; 2 Kgs 12:4ff. [5ff.]), he required of his vassal people due tribute in the form of both regular and special offerings. Thus, at the inaugurating of the old covenant, the Lord through the covenant mediator requisitioned from the people an offering of precious materials to be used for constructing the tabernacle, site of his earthly throne and replica of his heavenly palace (Exod 25:2-9; 35:4-36:7). Beyond their possessions, the Lord claimed the covenant people themselves for the ministry of his holy palace. An application of this was the obligation that all the first-born males, representing the nation, be consecrated to the service of Yahweh in his sanctuary. In this connection, requisition took the form of a redemption tax exacted for the number of the first-born of Israel in excess of the number of the Levites, who were substituted for the first-born to perform the cultic ministry (Num 3:11ff.). Requisitioning the people themselves was actually another instance of requisitioning the materials for the building of God's royal sanctuary, for God makes his sanctified people to be a holy, living temple for his Presence in the Spirit.

Such is the requisition pattern that we find again in the CH episode. Through his representative, the prophet Zechariah, Yahweh takes tribute of gold and silver from the covenant people. As we have seen, the priestly "house" of Josiah is simply the administrative agency for storage and distribution. Though Zechariah obtains the silver and gold directly from Josiah, he is also said to take it from the three from Babylon, who represent the far off people of the Lord (vv. 10,11).[20] The praiseworthy participation of all four of them is underscored by the statement in v. 14 that the crown made from their donation was to be kept in the temple as a memorial (*zikkārôn*) to them, each of the four being named. This memorial function of the tributary crown corresponds, as observed above, to the receipt-notice appended to the requisition docket kept in the storage "house."[21] Further, in keeping with the use to which Israel's requisitioned offerings were regularly put, the tribute in Zech 6:9-15 was devoted to the cultic program, specifically, to the special ceremonial crowning of Joshua, the high priest.

The antitypical, messianic dimension of this requisition event must not be missed. Joshua, recipient of the tribute-crown, was a type of the Branch, the coming messianic priest-king. In effect, therefore, these returning exiles were by faith bringing tribute to Christ. Their mission from afar was akin to that of the wise men who came to Jerusalem from the east with their treasures to worship the one born king of the Jews (Matt 2:1-11). They were participating in advance in the eschatological crowning of the Lamb upon the throne with many crowns.

That such an antitypical perspective is present in this episode is corroborated by Zech 6:15a. There, the tributary pilgrimage of the exiles from Babylon as memorialized in the crown in the temple is said to be prophetic of an eschatological coming of those far off to help build the temple of the Lord. It is to the fulfillment of that prophecy that we shall now turn, focusing on the sovereign requisitioning activity of Christ as an aspect of his exaltation.

B. ***Christ, the Temple Requisitioner.*** The requisitioner in the Zech 6:9-15 episode is the Angel of the Lord, for (as is indicated, for one thing, by the validation formula in v. 15b) he is the divine speaker who commissions Zechariah to take the tribute from the house of Josiah. In this typological event the pre-incarnate Christ is claiming from the men returned from Babylon the tributary honor due to him, the royal crown to which he is entitled. And in connection with this he prophesies of the later antitypical requisitioning he would engage in as the incarnate Christ on a world-wide scale (v. 15a).[22]

The Gospels picture Jesus as a sovereign requisitioner even during the days of his earthly ministry. A particularly interesting instance is his commandeering of the covenant-ratifying donkey for his royal procession into Jerusalem. Simply say: "The Lord has need of it" (Mark 11:3). And a fundamental form of the Lord's requisitioning was his calling the disciples one by one to leave all and give their lives to him.

Jesus is also portrayed as a requisitioner on the larger canvas of covenant history, in relation to old covenant Israel and to the new Israel, the church of the new covenant.

In the vineyard parable of Matt 21:33-41, God's requisitioning of the covenant nation through the prophets generation after generation is depicted under the image of the lord of the vineyard requiring of the stewards the fruit in its season. He presents his claims through a succession of servants and finally through his son. The son presents the requisition demand both as representative of the father and as the heir. Such was the mission of Jesus to Israel in his first advent: he came calling upon the covenant nation to submit to him, their Lord. Israel's rebellious response is prophesied in the parable. It also announces God's subsequent taking of the vineyard-kingdom from Israel, an execution of the curse by which the old covenant had been sanctioned.

In Zechariah 11, the hinge passage in the second part of the book, the prophet foretold this future tragic confrontation of Jesus and Israel. As in CH, here again in Zechariah 11 the prophet is told to enact the role of Messiah the Requisitioner. After performing his services as shepherd-ruler of the flock he demands his wages and is given as his kingly tribute a scornful thirty pieces of silver (v. 12). Again, as in the vineyard parable, the sequel to the rejection of the divine requisitioner is covenant judgment. What Israel refuses to give is taken away from them as an act of judicial dispossession (vv. 13ff.).

But there is another chapter in the history of covenant requisitioning. The kingdom taken from the old Israel is given by the Lord and heir of the vineyard to another people (Matt 21:43) in a new covenant, a covenant of grace replacing the old covenant of works which was broken (Jer 31:31-34; Heb 8:7-13; 10:9). When promulgating the new covenant (Matt 28:18-20) Jesus declared that absolute authority was given him in heaven and earth (v. 18). Thereby he claimed to be Lord of the covenant with the divine right of sovereign requisition. Then he gave his disciples the commission of global requisitioning in his name (v. 19a). Zechariah had prophesied that Jerusalem's king, who would come riding on the requisitioned donkey and whose dominion would be to the ends of the earth (cf. Ps 72:8), would "speak peace unto the nations" (Zech 9:9,10). And the apostle Paul declared of Christ that "he came and preached peace to you that were far off and peace to them that were nigh" (Eph 2:17). Out of all the nations Christ summons those alienated from God to find peace with God through the Cross (Eph 2:16), as they submit in faith to his sovereign claims on their lives and consign themselves by baptismal oath under his covenant lordship (Matt 28:19b,20a). It is by the mouth of his commissioned representatives, the gospel witnesses, that Jesus speaks peace to the nations, requisitioning those far and near for the praise of his glory. Requisitioning the world for Christ—that is the kerygmatic mission of the church.

As those whom God effectually calls by his Spirit obey this requisition summons, the prophecy of Zech 6:15a is fulfilled: "Those who are far off shall come and help build the temple of Yahweh." From fallen mankind, exiled from God's presence and paradise as the aftermath of Adam's transgression, from the diaspora of the Gentiles augmented by the diaspora of the Jews (cf. Rom 11:30-32), from far off they come to Christ, God's temple (John 2:18-21; Eph 2:12,13). They come and participate in the building of the extended temple, the church-body of which Christ is the head, the temple of which he is the chief cornerstone and his apostles and prophets the foundation. They contribute to the raising up of this church-temple by giving themselves when they hear Christ issue his requisition demand that they become living stones in that holy edifice (1 Cor. 3:16,17; 2 Cor 6:16; Eph 2:20-22; 1 Pet 2:5,6; Heb 3:6).

"And you will know that Yahweh of hosts has sent me unto you" (Zech 6:15b). Here, as in the previous appearances of this formula (2:9,11 [13,15]), it is the sovereign constructing of the world-wide temple of God through the power of the Spirit that is declared to be a convincing validation of the divine origin of the messianic mission.[23] Beyond the notion of inward comprehension, the verb "know" (yd^c) may signify public acknowledgment. That is, v. 15b might be taken as part of the prophecy of v. 15a, foretelling that confession of Jesus as the Christ of God, the Lord, will resound far and wide—the confession of the mouth, which, accompanied by faith in the heart that God raised him from the dead, is "unto salvation" (Rom 10:9,10).

Christ's success in requisitioning a vast company from all nations to come and build God's temple, the validation of the heavenly origin of his mission, also witnesses to the fact that the outcome of his mission has been his exaltation to the heavenly throne. For Christ's efficacious gathering of God's elect is accomplished through the power of the Spirit whom he bestowed on his disciples at Pentecost, and this descent of the Spirit testifies to the prior ascent of the Son to receive the Spirit from the Father. Psalms 72 and 110 make this connection between Christ's effective requisitioning and his exaltation. In Psalm 72 it is the one invested with the prerogative of divine judgment (v. 1) and exercising universal dominion (vv. 8,9) of whom it is said that the kings of Tarshish, Sheba, and Seba shall render to him his requisitioned tribute (v. 10) and, indeed, that "all nations shall serve him" (v. 11). And in Psalm 110 it is in the context of Messiah's session on God's throne as a priest-king forever (vv. 1,4,5) that the word of the Lord declares: "Your people will offer themselves willingly ... in holy splendor" (v. 3a). On the day of battle (cf. vv. 2,5,6), when Messiah musters his priestly army for the holy war (cf. Rev 19:14), the host of volunteers that rally to his banner will be like the abundance of dew that covers the earth at dawn (v. 3b; cf. 2 Sam 17:12).

Christ's requisitioned people not only attest to but constitute a major component of his exaltation. For they are themselves the promised inheritance awarded to the messianic heir of the Father. Participating in the building of God's temple (Zech 6:15a) signifies that those who come from far off have been received into the holy company of God's people and God's covenant people are his own personal treasure, his chosen possession (sĕgullâ),[24] redeemed from Egypt "to be unto him a people of inheritance" (naḥălâ),[25] his "portion" (ḥēleq).[26] This identification of the covenant community as God's chosen inheritance is prominent in the visions of Zechariah that CH is recapitulating. The first vision contains the assurance that Yahweh will again choose Jerusalem as his own, the site of his temple (1:17). In the fourth vision God's election of Jerusalem is appealed to by the Angel of the Lord in his rebuke of Satan (3:2). And in the third vision (2:1-13 [5-17]) the divine choosing of Jerusalem is explained in inheritance terms: "Yahweh will inherit (nḥl) Judah as his portion (ḥēleq); for his sanctuary ground he will choose Jerusalem" (2:12 [16]). This is the more significant for our recognition of the divine inheritance concept in CH because of other correspondences of vision three to CH. As in CH, Messiah speaks as universal Lord (2:13 [17]), and immediately associated with the inheritance theme in 2:12 [16] are the two elements of 6:15a,b, namely: a prophecy that those from far off will enter into covenant with the Lord and his people (2:11a [15a]) and, second, the attestation formula (2:11b [15b]).

For the idea of the people of God as the inheritance of the Messiah in particular, we turn to Psalm 2, where we discover much the same complex of concepts that we have found in CH and in vision three, which CH echoes. In Psalm 2, right after God's assertion that he has set his Anointed (cf. v. 2) as king on Zion (v. 6), Messiah cites the decree of Yahweh on the occasion of the coronation: "You are my Son, this day have I begotten you. Ask of me and I will give you the nations for your inheritance (*naḥălâ*) and the uttermost parts of the earth for your possession" (vv. 7, 8). This decree was proclaimed in confrontation with the nations conspiring against the suzerainty of the Lord and his Anointed (vv. 1-3). God derisively rebukes the folly of their rebellious counsel (vv. 4-6) and asserts that the dominion of his king over them will be enforced in a shattering eruption of his wrath (v. 9; cf. v. 12b). But along with this threat, a directive is given to earth's kings to exchange the folly of revolt for the wisdom of allegiance to the Son (vv. 10,11,12a), and blessing instead of curse is promised to those who commit themselves under his protectorate (v. 12c). The prospect emerges here of a remnant from the nations, battle spoils as it were,[27] who accept Messiah's overtures of mercy as he speaks peace to the nations. Messiah thus receives the nations as his possession in the sense that a chosen company from the ends of the earth become his own covenant people, his precious inheritance (v. 8).[28]

In the light of the passages closely related to CH, those who are described in Zech 6:15a as coming from afar to take part in the temple building are seen to be Messiah's chosen portion, the inheritance which he, as exalted Lord, appropriates through world-wide gospel requisitioning.

C. *God's Covenant Decree (Psalm 2)*. In dealing with each aspect of Christ's exaltation we have traced it to a covenant transaction—his throne rights as royal scion and temple builder to the Davidic covenant (2 Samuel 7) and his heavenly enthronement as priest-king to the covenant oath of Psalm 110. We have already traced Messiah's requisitioning of his universal inheritance to the decree (*ḥōq*) of Ps 2:7,8 and shall now examine the covenantal character of that decree.

Ḥōq, "decree," is paralleled by *běrît*, "covenant," in several passages. For example, with reference to God's covenant with the patriarchs, Ps 105:8-10 (cf. 1 Chr 16:15-17) observes: "(v. 8) He (Yahweh) remembers forever his covenant (*běrît*) ... (v. 9) which he made with Abraham, even his sworn promise to Isaac, (v. 10) which he confirmed unto Jacob as a decree (*ḥōq*), to Israel as an everlasting covenant (*běrît*)."[29] This corresponds closely with Ps 2:7,8, where the covenantal *ḥōq* again concerns an inheritance. In fact, the land of Canaan promised to the patriarchs is the prototype of the global inheritance granted to the Messiah in Psalm 2.

The Father's covenantal decree cited by the Son beforehand in Ps 2:7,8 was issued at the exaltation of Jesus. It was an enthronement declaration.[30] But that assigning of a global inheritance to Christ at his exaltation was not the beginning of the matter. In issuing that decree at the enthronement of the Lord Jesus, the Father was fulfilling his commitment made in the eternal covenant of grant, promising the Son cosmic dominion, with a people from all nations as his inheritance. Old Testament prophecies like Psalm 2 unveil heaven and reveal that the covenant constituting commitments between the Father and the Son have already been made long before Messiah's earthly mission.

The exaltation of the Messiah in view in the Ps 2:7,8 decree (and thus in the Zech 6:15 prophecy) is traced back to the divine predetermination in eternity by the apostle Paul in Ephesians 1-3, a context in which he treats the whole range of themes found in Zech 6:9-15 and the related passages. Included among these shared themes are: the cosmic dominion of the exalted Christ (1:10,20-23); Christ's requisitioning of the Gentiles as he speaks peace to those far off (2:17; 3:8), a process involving the despoiling of Satan (2:2ff.); the reception of Gentiles into the covenant as the people of God (2:11-22; 3:6-9,15) and as the heritage of Christ (1:11); the building of God's temple (2:20-22). And all of this Paul declares to be the carrying out of God's eternal purpose and predestinating will (1:4,5,11; 3:11).

Eph 1:11 is of special interest because it contains the divine inheritance concept and so reflects the general Old Testament notion of Israel as the Lord's chosen portion and the more specific idea of the Messiah's inheritance found in Ps 2:8. In that verse Paul particularizes the idea presented in the immediately preceding context. The apostle has been developing the thought that all creation finds its unity in Christ, all things are summed up in him as his (1:10), and then, focusing on Christ's people in particular, he states that "we were made a heritage, being predestined ... that we should be to the praise of his glory" (1:11,12). Or, as it is put in 1:22,23, the church is Christ's own body, the fullness that belongs to him. Also in 1:14 believers are called "(God's) own possession," which he will redeem to the praise of his glory. And similarly in 1:18 Paul exults in "the riches of the glory of his (God's) inheritance in the saints." Surely the interpretation of the heritage in 1:11 as the inheritance that belongs to Christ is preferable to the common opinion that the reference is to the inheritance believers will receive. And the fact that the apostle explicitly locates Christ's claim to the church as his inheritance in the divine counsels before the foundation of the world substantiates the theological construct of the intratrinitarian covenant and, more specifically, the conclusion that Christ's exaltation finds its ultimate determination in that eternal arrangement.

Prerequisite to the Son's reception of the inheritance appointed to him in the eternal covenant was his winning of the Father's approbation in his earthly mission. By the ordering of God, the Sabbath Consummation of the kingdom is secured by way of probation, as a reward to be earned. We are confronted by this principle in the closing statement of CH: "This shall come to pass if you [plural] diligently obey the voice of Yahweh, your God" (Zech 6:15c). There is an ethical prerequisite for dwelling in fellowship with God, a spiritual quality of faith and holiness in conformity with divine stipulation (cf. Deut 30:11-14; Rom 10:6-10; Heb 12:14).[31] But that is not what is referred to in Zech 6:15c as a condition for the realization of the messianic kingdom of glory. The condition in view is rather the obedient performance of a special probationary assignment. That accomplishment, that one act of righteousness, constitutes the legal, meritorious ground for receiving the heavenly reward.

Zechariah casts his prophecy of Christ and the church in the prophetic idiom, employing the old typological order to depict the new covenant realities. And according to the covenantal constitution for that old order, corporate Israel must earn the continuing enjoyment of the typological kingdom inheritance by their obedience. This works principle is a conspicuous feature of the sanctions section of the Mosaic treaties.[32] Expressing things in old covenant terms, Zechariah therefore says that God's kingdom of glory is the reward for the probationary obedience of the elect corporately. In the light of the total Scriptural revelation, we understand, however, that this act of probationary obedience is performed not by them but by Christ their federal representative—by the one for the many. It is a righteousness of God imputed to the elect by grace through faith.

In Zechariah's fourth vision the Messiah's role as the individual representative probationer is revealed more explicitly. There again the attainment of heaven is made the reward for the obedient discharge of a specific duty, the guarding of God's sanctuary (Zech 3:7), and it is Christ, the Servant-Branch, as typically portrayed by the individual figure of Joshua the high priest, who must fulfill this probationary priestly mission. What we have then in Zech 6:15c is the pre-incarnate Christ directing his people in faith to himself as their vicarious probationer, who secures for them God's approbation and so puts them beyond probation.

The function of probationer that Christ assumed as the true Israel-Servant was more basically his in terms of his identity as second Adam (Rom 5:14; 1 Cor 15:45-47).[33] The covenant with the first Adam was a works-probation arrangement.[34] Hence, for the Son to covenant with the Father to become a second Adam meant he must win the promised messianic exaltation (which he shares with his own) as the reward for a victory of obedience in a probationary mission. This is implicit in CH in the Branch's role of building the temple of the Lord (Zech 6:12c,13a), for, as we have seen, the prelude to and qualification for temple construction was regularly the faithful waging of the Lord's battle against his enemies. Messiah's temple building presupposes his victorious warfare against Satan. That was the specific probationary task whose accomplishment established his right to requisition the materials and build God's temple, and indeed to take his place on the divine throne in the holy of holies.

As advertised by his birth under the Torah covenant of works (Gal 4:4), Christ came to earth as one under the intratrinitarian covenant of works. It was by fulfilling the probation of that supernal works covenant that he became the mediator of the Covenant of Grace, the covenant in which his people become by faith joint-heirs with their Lord of the eternal kingdom of glory (Heb 9:14; Rom 8:17). Law is thus foundational to gospel; gospel-grace honors the demands of divine justice as definitively expressed in law covenant. In Rom 3:31 Paul makes this point forcefully: "Do we then make the law of none effect through faith? God forbid; nay we establish the law." The apostle is not concerned here with the normative nature of the Mosaic laws but with the law as a covenant governed by the principle of works in contrast to the gospel with its principle of grace. And even though he is arguing that we are justified not by works but by grace through faith, he insists emphatically on the continuing validity of the works principle as foundational to the gospel order. It is by the obedience of the one that the many are made righteous (Rom 5:19).

Messiah's exaltation would follow humiliation. The way to the Sabbath throne on Har Magedon led through the abyss of Gehenna. As stipulated in his covenant with the Father, the Son must become incarnate in human likeness and be obedient unto the death of the Cross (Phil 2:5-11). It would be because of his obedience as the suffering Servant of the Lord that he was lifted up very high (Isa 52:13-53:12). In CH, Messiah's descent prior to his ascent is intimated by the designating of him as the Branch who comes forth from the human line of David (Zech 6:12a,b; cf. Isa 53:2), the Branch who is the suffering Servant (Zech 3:8).

Sharpening the point that Christ earns his exaltation as a due reward is the identification of his inheritance possession as something he has purchased. "Jesus Christ, who gave himself for us that he might redeem us from all iniquity and purify for himself a people for his own possession" (Titus 2:13,14; cf. Eph 1:14). Giving the redeemed to him as his allotted portion is an act of justice, pure and simple. They belong to him by virtue of his paying the purchase price as stipulated in the supernal covenant of grant.

And the purchase price itself tells us again of the humiliation and suffering that was the appointed way to Christ's ultimate exaltation. "You were redeemed ... with the precious blood of Christ as of a lamb without blemish or spot" (1 Pet 1:18,19; cf. Eph 1:7; Heb 9:12). It was "with his own blood" that the Lord acquired the church, his bride (Acts 20:28; cf. Rev 7:14; 19:7,8; 21:2,9). This note sounds forever in the music of heaven acclaiming the exalted Redeemer: "You are worthy to take the book and to open its seals;[35] for you were slain and have purchased to God by your blood (a throng) from every tribe and tongue and people and nation" (Rev 5:9). "Worthy is the Lamb that was slain to receive power and riches and wisdom and might and honor and glory and blessing" (Rev 5:12).

---

1 CH (central hinge) will be used below as an alternative designation for Zech 6:9-15.

2 On the introductory formula in v. 9, cf. Zech 1:1,7; 4:8; 7:4; 8:1,18. From Zech 6:15b it appears that the word of the Lord that comes to Zechariah in CH is a speaking of the preincarnate Word. The same phenomenon is found in Zech 4:8,9. It will be seen below that v. 9 also functions as an element in a particular genre we shall identify.

3 In this respect CH is similar to vision five.

4 Cf. our introductory comments on vision four.

5 Because of the resumptive nature of much of the content of CH, our treatment of some matters will be cursory. For further discussion of such points consult appropriate commentary on the visions above.

6 For $h\hat{o}d$ as glorious raiment, cf. Job 40:10 and Ps 104:1. Note also the use of the verb $n\acute{s}^\circ$ for wearing the ephod (1 Sam 2:28; 14:3; 22:18).

7 The specific terminology of covenant and oath is applied to this arrangement in Pss 89:3,28,34 (4,29,35); 132:11,12. At the coronation of Joash, bestowal of the crown was accompanied by presentation of a covenant witness document, which would identify the kingship as authorized and regulated by the Lord (2 Kgs 11:12). Note also the parallelism of crown and God's covenant with the king in Ps 89:39 (40).

8 Variously designated by covenant theologians, we may refer to it as the eternal or supernal covenant in distinction from temporal, earthly covenants made with men.

9 The Covenant of Grace is to be distinguished from the eternal intratrinitarian covenant of works, for it differs from it in fundamental respects, including: the parties to the covenant, the role of the Son, and the principle of inheritance.

10 On the translation of the preposition ʿal, see below.

11 The preposition ʿal must then mean "on" in v. 13c, and so too in v. 13d, for ʿal kisĕʾô is to be rendered the same way in these paired clauses.

12 Cf., e.g., Ps 110:1; Acts 2:33,34; 7:55,56; Rom 8:34; Eph 1:20; Heb 1:3; 8:1; 12:2; Rev 3:21; 12:5 (which speaks of the Messiah being caught up "to God and to his throne").

13 This interpretation is anciently attested in the church.

14 Cf. my Images of the Spirit, 13ff.

15 Note in Acts 1:10 the customary association of angelic beings with the Glory-cloud.

16 This episode in CH provides a transition to the introduction to the second half of the book (Zechariah 7 and 8). There again we read of the visit of a delegation of Israelites to the Jerusalem temple which becomes the occasion to foretell how peoples of all nations would one day make their way to Jerusalem to seek Yahweh (8:18-23). Like CH these introductory chapters open and close with sections that refer directly to the delegation and their activity.

17 On these ostraca cf. Y. Aharoni, "Arad: Its Inscriptions and Temple," Biblical Archaeologist 31.1 (1968) 2-32, esp. 13-15.

18 For the evidence see A. Demsky, "The Temple Steward Josiah ben Zephaniah," Israel Exploration Journal 31 (1981) 100-102. Our identification of the requisition genre of Zech 6:9-11 confirms in turn this interpretation of lḥn in v. 14.

19 For this use of bayit, cf., e.g., 1 Chr 28:11; Neh 10:38 (39); Mal 3:10.

20 On contributions of those in exile to the postexilic restoration of the temple, cf. 2 Chr 36:22,23; Ezra 1:1-6; 2:68,69.

21 The poll-tax atonement money taken from the Israelites and used for the service of the tabernacle, God's royal court, is also said to serve as a memorial, reminding the Lord that the ransom had been paid for them (Exod 30:16; cf. Col 2:14). Numbers 31 records an episode with similar requisition features. Moses and Eleazar are commanded to take for the Lord a specified portion of the victory spoils from the battle against the Midianites (cf. Gen 14:16-20). A special tribute of gold presented by the military leaders was deposited in the tent of meeting as a memorial of the Israelites before the Lord (v. 54).

22 The themes of CH and the third vision (2:1-13 [5-17]) correspond closely. Christ is presented in both passages as the sovereign summoning his people from all the earth, in the third vision under the model of the kerux, and in CH, of the requisitioner.

23 For exaltation as evidence of the messianic identity of Jesus, cf. Matt 26:64.

24 See Exod 19:5; Deut 7:6; 14:2; 26:18; Ps 135:4; Mal 3:17; cf. Titus 2:14.

25 Cf. Deut 4:20; 9:29.

26 Cf. Deut 32:9. On this passage, see my Kingdom Prologue, 177,178.

27 Similarly in Zechariah's third vision the hostile nations are threatened with judgment (2:9 [13]), in the midst of which there will, however, be a conversion of Gentiles, a redemptive spoiling of the nations. By this despoiling which is a discipling many are brought into covenant with the Lord as his people, his chosen inheritance (2:11,12 [15,16]).

28 In Hebrews 1, where Ps 2:7 is quoted (v. 5) in an exposition of the exaltation of the Son, he is described as "the heir of all things" (v. 2).

29 See also 2 Kgs 17:15; Ps 50:16; Isa 24:5.

30 It is so interpreted when quoted in Acts 13:33; Heb 1:5; 5:5; cf. Acts 4:25.

31 A state of indefectible holiness is the necessary precondition of entering into the eternally secure felicity of the Sabbath-Glory (cf. 1 Pet 1:4). Thus, under the original covenant in Eden divine approbation upon successful probation would have been accompanied by transformation to the prerequisite state of confirmed righteousness.

32 Cf. e.g., Lev 18:5; Deut 28:1,9,13,15; 30:15-20. As Paul's appeal to Lev 18:5 shows (Rom 10:5; Gal 3:12), a legal principle of meritorious works was operating in the Torah covenant opposite to the gospel principle of grace.

33 In Gal 4:4, "born under the law" identifies Christ as the second Israel, under the Torah covenant. "Born of a woman" brings out his humanity and so suggests his second Adam status.

34 Though the covenant produced by creation displayed God's goodness and love, it was not a grace transaction, for none of its benefits, whether original or proferred, had been or would have been bestowed on people who had forfeited them by sin. The divine benevolence *complemented* the principle of simple justice governing this works covenant; it did *not qualify* that justice.

It is God's covenantal word that defines divine justice. Analysis of God's covenant with Adam has been plagued with a tendency to judge the terms stipulated in this covenant by some extraneous standard and to pronounce the value of the award offered disproportionate to the value of the service. Thereby any "merit" still attributed to the performance of the stipulated duty in this arrangement (confusingly dubbed "gracious") is radically qualified, the law-gospel contrast is changed into a continuum, the absoluteness of God's justice is relativized, and the foundation of the gospel is destroyed.

35 The imagery of the seven-sealed book evokes the legal sphere of testament and inheritance.

Appendix

THE STRUCTURE OF THE BOOK OF ZECHARIAH

Canonical Zechariah falls into several fairly distinct divisions: (1) an oracular exhortation (Zech 1:1-6); (2) a series of visions with oracles interlaced (1:7-6:8); (3) a symbolic action performed by the prophet (6:9-15); (4) oracular instruction (chaps. 7-8); (5) a pair of "burdens" (chaps. 9-14; cf. *maśśāʾ*, 9:1; 12:1).

Our treatment of 6:9-15 as a separate major section calls for comment. The section is set off from 1:7-6:8 by its own introductory formula (6:9; cf. 4:8; 7:4; 8:1,18) and by the fact that it is not a vision like the preceding material. It is also distinguished from what follows in chaps. 7-8 by the date formula in 7:1, which, like those in 1:1 and 1:7, clearly marks a new division. Addressing the question of the precise role of 6:9-15 in the composition of Zechariah will take us to the heart of our proposal concerning the overall structure of the work.

I. THE THREE-HINGE FRAMEWORK

A key structural device of the book emerges with the recognition that 6:9-15 shares with two other passages (3:1-10; 11:1-17) a peculiar set of formal and thematic characteristics. Common to these passages and to them alone in Zechariah is the formal feature of symbolic action in which the prophet personally participates and specific historical individuals are involved.[1] Further, these three passages are thematically unified: in each the prophet participates in a coronation, an investiture to theocratic office. Indeed, all three portray Messiah's commissioning to his royal-priestly task. Moreover, in addition to sharing exclusively this striking set of features, each of these passages occupies a central position either in the book as a whole or in one of its two main blocks of material.

Before showing more particularly how each of the three passages in turn exhibits the distinctive characteristics mentioned above, I would like to state at once the hypothesis at which I arrive, following the direction pointed to by these data. My proposal is that the book of Zechariah is a diptych with 6:9-15 as its primary hinge or central spine and that the main part of each side panel of this diptych is itself a diptych formation with 3:1-10 and 11:1-17 as the hinges of the night visions and the burdens respectively.

1. *Zech 3:1-10.* Located in the middle of the night visions, 3:1-10 stands apart from the formulary scheme that provides a framework for the preceding and following visions.[2] So distinctive is this passage in style and substance that some exclude it from the numbered sequence of visions and assign it a separate status within the structure of Zechariah 1-6.[3] In my proposal, that special status of 3:1-10, the fourth vision in my numbering, consists in its function as one of the trio of hinges in the macrostructure of the book.

Unlike the visions before and after it, 3:1-9 does not introduce imaginary objects to symbolize the earthly realities but presents actual living persons (Joshua and his priestly colleagues). Though historical people— like the oppressor nations, the Israelites in exile, and so forth—are referred to in the other visions in the oracular interpretation of symbolism, they are not seen as figures in the vision. This is true even of the reference to Zerubbabel in Zechariah 4.[4] The other visions do include in their visual content heavenly persons, divine and angelic. Some of these are represented symbolically (e.g. the horsemen of Zechariah 1), but the divine angel appears in these visions, as in Zechariah 3, in the form he assumed elsewhere in nonvisionary theophany. Nevertheless Zechariah 3 remains distinctive in its inclusion of actual earthly persons in the visual action.

Closely related to this is the other formal point of similarity between Zech 3:1-10 and the other main hinge sections. Elsewhere in the night visions Zechariah's role does not go beyond the reception of revelation and inquiring into the meaning of the symbolism.[5] But in 3:1-10 the prophet plays an active role in forwarding the dramatic action. When the angel of the Lord orders the reclothing of the redeemed high priest in his official vestments, Zechariah speaks out urging on the climactic coronation act of setting the miter on Joshua's head (v. 5).

This motif of donning royal-priestly regalia and acquiring the accouterments of office is itself one of the features peculiar to the three main hinges. In the case of Joshua in Zechariah 3, the replacement of his soiled attire with garments of holy glory signified his reinstatement as Israel's high priest (vv. 3-5; cf. Exodus 28-29). Thus invested anew with authority for governance, set over the council of priests for judicial oversight of God's courts (Zech 3:7-8a), Joshua was declared a sign of "my servant the Branch" (v. 8b). Joshua typified the coming Messiah in his twofold office, the suffering servant who undergoes extreme humiliation to accomplish a priestly sacrifice for sin and then experiences the highest exaltation as the royal Branch of David (cf. Isa 52:13-53:12; Jer 23:5; 33:15). Special attention is directed to the miter bearing the golden gemstone badge of royal-priestly dignity (Zech 3:9a; cf. Exod 28:36-38; 29:6; Lev 8:9), the item for which Zechariah had expressed particular interest (Zech 3:5). Crowned with this, Joshua prefigured Christ, the priestly remover of iniquity (v. 9b) and the royal restorer of paradise and of man as God's glory-image (vv. 9b-10). Such portrayal of Messiah in his priest-king mission is also found in the other two hinge passages.

2. *Zech 6:9-15.* In our examination of this primary hinge passage we will note first the formal marks that distinguish the three hinges. Going beyond his role in 3:5, the prophet here is himself the main actor in the symbolic drama. He receives the offertory materials (vv. 10-11a),[6] he takes part in the preparation of the crown (v. 11b)[7] and possibly its later disposition (v. 14), and he is the agent in the coronation (v. 11c), whose typological meaning he expounds (vv. 12-13). As for the participation of other actual persons, there are several returned exiles, cited by name, who provide precious metals for the crown, and Josiah son of Zephaniah (vv. 10,14). Also, Joshua is again recipient of the crown (v. 11c).[8]

Clearly evident from the above comments is the presence in 6:9-15 of the thematic distinctive of the hinge sections, the coronation investiture of a messianic prototype. This motif, obvious in the crowning act in v. 11c, may also be alluded to in the statement: "He shall bear the glory" (v. 13b). This may refer to investiture with the total regalia of office, imagery that is prominent in Zechariah 3, because *hôd*, the term used for the "glory" to be "borne" (*nś'*), is at times a majesty in which somebody is clothed (cf. e.g. Job 40:10; Ps 104:1), and *nś'* is used in the sense of wearing the ephod, which is similarly a vestment signifying authority (cf. 1 Sam 2:28; 14:3; 22:18).

Moreover, the coronation is the commissioning of one who typifies Christ. As in Zech 3:8, Joshua's experience is interpreted as a foreshadowing of the messianic Branch (v. 12). Also, the role of the returned exiles in contributing to the restoration of the Jerusalem cultus is interpreted as prefigurative of analogous developments in the messianic age (vv. 14-15).

Emphasized in the 6:9-15 treatment of the typological commissioning of the Messiah is the union in him of the royal and priestly offices. The addition of the kingly dimension to the priestly is expressed in the designating of the one prefigured by Joshua the high priest as the Branch, a title associated (as noted above) with the Davidic dynasty. Also the term for the crown (ʿṭrh) is ordinarily used for royal rather than priestly insignia.

Further, the prefigured Branch (re)builds the temple, an enterprise associated with the legitimation of kingship in the ancient Near East and certainly a royal function in the biblical tradition. The succession of Solomon to David's throne as recorded in 1 Chronicles 29 (which itself combines the themes of temple building and validation of succession) provides the more specific background of the declaration in Zech 6:13 that the Branch, the builder of the temple of Yahweh, "will bear the glory (hôd) and sit and rule by his throne." 1 Chron 29:25 refers to the majesty (hôd) God bestowed on Solomon as he magnified him in Israel. And in 29:23 the throne occupied by Solomon, anointed successor of David, is called the "throne of Yahweh." Echoing this background Zech 6:13 affirms that the majestic priest who "shall build the temple of Yahweh … shall sit and rule by his [Yahweh's] throne (ʿl-ksʾw) and shall be a priest by his [Yahweh's] throne (ʿl-ksʾw)."[9]

In the Israelite theocracy, David's throne was an earthly representative of God's heavenly throne, and the throne in the Holy of Holies, to which the high priest had access, was also a typological replica thereof. In the ultimate heavenly reality Yahweh's temple and palace thrones are one, and that throne is the place of Christ's session at the right hand of God. Zech 6:13 refers to this throne of Yahweh and this session of the messianic priest-king. The last clause in that verse, "the counsel of peace shall be between them both," is not to be taken as a personification of the two separate offices of the priest-king. It refers to two persons; the second is Yahweh himself. The royal one who builds the temple of Yahweh, site of the throne of Yahweh, sits as a priest at the right hand of Yahweh,[10] and these two reign together in perfect accord to accomplish the šālôm of God's kingdom (cf. Pss 45:6-7; 110:1; Heb 1:3,13; Rev 5:6).[11]

This reception of Messiah into the presence of the throne of God is another theme common to Zech 3:1-9 and 6:9-15. In the former the equivalent idea is expressed in the promise to the messianic prototype that he would be accorded access among the attendant throne angels of the heavenly court (3:7). The presidency of Joshua over his colleagues referred to in 3:8 was an earthly replica of the heavenly reality of Messiah in the midst of the angelic council.

The Zecharian prophetic portrayal of the coming Christ, the priest-king, reaches its zenith here—appropriately, for this passage is structurally the central hinge of his work.

3. *Zech 11:1-17.* In this third major hinge section the personal involvement of the prophet in the symbolic action is the most intense of all. That action, again an investiture commissioning to royal-priestly office, is not simply urged on by the prophet or even performed by him on somebody else. He is here called upon to be himself the one so commissioned. He is instructed to play the part of the messianic priest-king, specifically the good shepherd sent on mission to the flock—"shepherd" being a familar image of kingship.[12] In keeping with the shepherd motif, the imagery of coronation and royal investiture found in 3:1-10; 6:9-15 is translated into that of donning the outfit and taking accouterments suited to tending flocks. The shepherd's staff (11:7,10) replaces the scepter, but the basic theme of official investiture is present again in this passage.[13] So too is the other formal feature of the involvement of actual individuals, whether contemporary or future (cf. vv. 5,6,8,12,13). These features are not found in the burdens before or after 11:1-17 but are peculiar to the three hinges.

Various other correspondences supplement this formal thematic evidence of the interrelationship of 11:1-17 with 3:1-10; 6:9-15. Critical action transpires in the house of the Lord in the third section (11:13) as in the first (3:7) and second (6:12-14). Access to the divine council, noted above as linking the first two hinge sections, is experienced by Zechariah in 11:1-17 as recipient of the direct communication assigning his symbolic role. The royal role, common to all three hinges, takes the particular form of judicial functioning in the courts of God's house in the first (3:7) and here in the third, where the good shepherd enters into judgment against the false shepherds (11:8; cf. v. 17).[14] Also characteristic of the hinge passages are judgments evaluating the royal-priestly figure in terms of gold and silver. In the first the Lord's judgment of Joshua culminates in the bestowal of the golden crown, the "stone" on his priestly turban, engraved by the Lord himself (3:9; cf. v. 5). In the second the crown that honors the Lord's anointed is composed of both silver and gold, tributary gifts of the grateful worshipers restored form exile (6:11). In the third the judicial assessment is made by rejecters of the good shepherd, who set his value at thirty pieces of silver (11:12-13), which, like the crown in 6:14, ends up in the temple (11:13). This hostile assessment of the messianic figure in Zechariah 11 (prophetic of the betrayal of the Lord by Judas when Satan entered into him) matches the malicious accusation of the satanic adversary against Joshua in 3:1. And corresponding to the Lord's rebuke of Satan in 3:2 is the divine judgment of the despisers of the good shepherd portended by his repudiation of the despicable wages (11:13). In short, significant topical correspondences are discovered that weave 11:1-17 together with 3:1-10 and 6:9-15 in their identity as a special trio in structuring the Zecharian composition.[15]

II. PARALLELISM OF THE SIDE PANELS

We shall now explore the two panels flanking the central hinge (6:9-15), noting how they match each other in formal structure and thematic patterns. Such balancing of the structure around 6:9-15 supports the analysis of Zechariah as a diptych hinged on that passage.

1. *Formal correspondence of 1:1-6:8 and 7:1-14:21.* Each of these main side panels consists of an introduction (1:1-6 and chaps. 7-8) and an extended block of stylistically homogenous materials: visions in 1:7-6:8, burdens in chaps. 9-14. The introductions require particular discussion here; the other sections will be dealt with further below.

Similarities between the two passages identified as introductions include the following:[16] an opening date formula for the revelation to Zechariah (1:1 and 7:1,4); recollection of lessons from past covenant history, accented by references to the lawsuit complaint of earlier prophets and the exile punishment (1:2-6 and 7:7-14; cf. 8:14); exhortation to fulfill present duty (1:3-4 and 8:16-17); promise to the repentant of new evidences of the Lord's favor, replacing curses with blessings (1:3 and 8:2-15, 18-23).

Zechariah 7:1-8:23, though patently similar to the 1:16 introduction, is not usually viewed as another introduction (to chaps. 9-14), certainly not by those who attribute the latter to a different author.[17] But if we accept the integrity of the canonical composition and recognize the nature and role of the hinge sections in the total work, then the location of chaps. 7-8 right after the central hinge and immediately before the burdens, plus its observed similarity to 1:1-6, argue for regarding it as introductory to the material that follows it.

As for the stylistic difference between chaps. 7-8 and the burdens, this is akin to that between the 1:1-6 introduction and the visions. Moreover there are shared features of various sorts that connect chaps. 7-8 with what follows. Significantly, ties are particularly strong with the opening and closing portions of chaps. 9-14. The theme of festival and fast days, which opens and closes chaps. 7-8, is resumed in the prophecy of the eschatological celebration of Tabernacles at the climactic conclusion of Zechariah (cf. 14:16). The inclusio thus formed by chaps. 7-8 and the conclusion of the burdens orients the former toward chaps. 9-14. Similarly, the promises that Zion will be the "holy mountain" in 8:3 and that total holiness will characterize God's house in Jerusalem in 14:20-21 form another such inclusio bond.[18] With respect to the prophetic prospects of God's people, chaps. 7-8 and the chapters that follow are alike in giving attention to aspects like the following: (1) ultimate divine judgment of the nations—including, however, a remarkable conversion of a remnant of the Gentiles, who henceforth come to Jerusalem to worship the Lord of Hosts[19] (8:20-23 and 9:1-8, esp. v. 7; 10:11; 12:2-8; 14:13ff., esp. v. 16); (2) God's strengthening presence with his people in the conflict, resulting in their deliverance and universal worship of Yahweh (8:23 and 9:8,15; 10:8-12; 12:8 14:4); (3) regathering of the exiles from far countries for happy reinstatement in their heritage (8:7-8 and 9:12; 10:8-10); (4) Jerusalem become the ideal city at last, fully inhabited, the delight of young and old (8:3-5 and 12:6; 14:11). A telling point in the area of diction is the phrase "so that no one passed through or returned," which is found in identical Hebrew form in 7:14 and 9:8 and nowhere else in the OT. Divine blessing and curse are expressed in terms of agricultural success and failure (8:12 and 9:17; 10:1; 14:8,17-19). The use of *hwšyᶜ* for God's work of salvation appears first within Zechariah in 8:7,13 and is then resumed in the burdens in 9:16; 10:6; 12:7 (cf. 9:9). Moreover the associated terms and ideas are similar in these contexts. Connected to the saving is the strengthening of the saved (8:9,13 and 9:13-15; 10:6; 12:8). In 8:7,13 the object of this saving and strengthening is God's "people," "the house of Judah," "the house of Israel." Similarly in 9:16 it is God's "people," in 10:6 "the house of Joseph and the house of Judah," and in 12:7 "the tents of Judah." The *hwšyᶜ* usage in the burdens is clearly a development of its introductory appearance in 8:7,13.

I conclude that the panel following the 6:9-15 hinge, like the panel before it, contains an introduction and a main unit. The balanced nature of these two panels will be further evidenced as we examine the relationship of the contents of the visions unit (1:7-6:8) to the burdens unit (chaps. 9-14).

2. *The diptych structure of the visions and burdens.* Repeating the overall structure of the book on a secondary level, both the visions and burdens assume a diptych form centering respectively on 3:1-10 and 11:1-17, the passages whose striking correspondences to the 6:9-15 hinge have been detailed above. Such a remarkable structural parallelism in the major units on either side of 6:9-15 demonstrates again the identity of the latter as the primary central hinge of the entire work. Our examination of these secondary diptych forms will disclose that their panels also match each other formally and thematically, so supporting our identification of 3:1-10 and 11:1-17 as secondary hinges.

The visions (1:7-6:8) exhibit a balanced diptych form. Examination of the scheme of introductory formulae indicates conclusively that there are seven visions with 3:1-10 as the fourth, standing between two triads. These formulae are located at 1:7-8; 2:1; 2:5; 3:1; 4:1-2; 5:1; 6:1. The patterns of the two triads match. The first members describe the revelatory setting in terms of a night or sleeping situation (1:8 and 4:1).[20] The second and third members of each triad have identical introductions. Moreover, the second pair (5:1 and 6:1) is the same as the first (2:1 and 2:5), except for the addition of "again" (*w⁾šwb*), which characterizes the entire second triad (cf. *wyšb* in 4:1). Observe also that all six visions of the two triads include the phrase "I saw, and behold" but that this is absent at 5:5 where many would begin a second vision within chap. 5 and so set the total count at eight.[21] If we are not to disregard the scheme of the introductory formulae with their pattern of parallel triads, we will see Zechariah 5 as a compound vision of the flying scroll and flying ephah.[22] There are then seven, not eight, visions, with two triads flanking the central fourth, whose distinctive opening phrase is one of the things that set it apart from the visions before and after it.

An inner coherence further marks each of the triads as a distinct subset within the seven visions. So, for example, the two elements in the divine declaration at the climax of vision 1 are treated in the rest of the first triad, the Lord's displeasure with the oppressor nations (1:15) in vision 2 and his determination that Jerusalem be prospered as his chosen temple site (1:16-17) in vision 3. Unifying the second triad is the use of imagery derived from the temple, its architecture and furnishings. Also, the guaranteed completion of the program of the kingdom house of the Judge of all the earth (vision 5) is carried out in his judicial advance through the covenant land (vision 6) and then on to the world center (vision 7).[23]

A concentric (ABA') arrangement of the visions in each triad underscores its coherence as a discrete subset of the night visions and constitutes a formal point of correspondence between the two triads. Upon examination this correspondence is found to entail parallels in topic and idea.

Formally, all the A-sections (visions 1,3,5,7) include direct divine oracles that interpret and make application of the visions in which they are inserted. The B-sections (visions 2,6), as noted above, are both compound visions. Topically the A-sections all portray the divine presence, whether in the messianic Angel or the Glory-Spirit theophany, while the B-sections present symbols of secondary agents of the divine action. When we trace out this topical pattern somewhat further, parallel developments emerge in the two triads. The first vision in each triad (1,5) contains the elements of divine presence in the midst of paradisiacal trees of life (the Angel in the midst of the myrtles and the Spirit over the měnôrâ, "lampstand"), with allusion to re-creation in the image of God.[24] The second visions (2,6) concern the removal of aliens and apostates from the covenant land through instruments of divine judgment (cf. esp. 2:4; 5:4,9-11). The third visions (3,7) prophesy a mission of the Glory-Spirit to the hostile nations (cf. esp. 2:12; 6:8), particularly to the land of the north (2:10; 6:6,8), which results in the establishment of God's holy sovereignty from Zion to Babylon.

The balance of the triads flanking the fourth vision is also exhibited in a concentric (ABCDC'B'A') pattern, the contents of visions 1-3 being reflected in visions 5-7, but now in reverse order. This chiasm is signalized by the clear correspondence of the first (A) and the last (A') visions, both of which portray a world mission of the Lord of Hosts under the imagery of variously colored horses. In both, hthlk in its judicial sense is used to describe the world-traversing of the heavenly horsemen (1:10; 6:7). Answering to the vision 1 situation where nations insensible of Yahweh's sovereign claims are at rest (1:11), is the vision 7 picture of God's Spirit now at rest, for his sovereignty has been enforced in judgment on those nations.

Picking up the trail thus disclosed by the outside visions and following it toward the center, we observe that the focus or range moves from the world in visions 1 and 7 to the land of Judah-Israel in 2 and 6 (cf. 2:2,4; 5:3,6)[25] and to Zion, the very heart of the theocracy, in 3 and 5.[26] This progressive inward movement of the thematic focus as we move inward in the literary structure of the visions reaches its climax in the Holy of Holies in the central fourth vision, where we behold the Lord himself at his throne site, accompanied by his angelic court and dispensing judgment. Zech 3:1-10, the hinge passage of the visions, is the central point of their chiastic pattern.

As for the B-B' pair of visions (2,6) in this chiasm, we have already mentioned certain correspondences: their composite nature, the absence of an oracular element, focus on the holy land and concern with the removal of unholy elements from it. Observe also the motif of lifting up and casting or setting down in this pair (cf. 2:4; 5:4,7-11).

In the case of the C-C' pair (visions 3,5) divine presence, focus on the center of the theocracy, and oracular proclamation have been noted above as parallel features. In addition both set forth the presence of God as the glory and power of his kingdom people (2:9-10,14-16; 4:6). Prominent in both is the theme of judicial reversal: the spoilers of God's people become a spoil to them (2:12-13), and the haughty world mountain becomes a lowly plain (4:7). Both have building imagery: in C the messianic figure holds a measuring line (2:5), and in C' Zerubbabel—a messianic prototype—holds a plummet line (4:10). Both stress the consummating of God's program, whether in the completion of Jerusalem (2:8-9,14-16) or the temple (4:7-8). In both, this triumph of redemptive judgment and restoration is cited in validation of the divine authorization of Messiah's mission: "You will know that the Lord of Hosts hath sent me" (2:13,15; 4:9).

As with the visions, the burdens (9:1-14:21) also exhibit a balanced diptych form. The headings in 9:1 and 12:1 identify the materials in chaps. 9-10 and 12-14 as two burdens.[27] Attesting the inner coherence of each burden are the concentric pattern of its contents and the chiastic arrangement that is evidenced when the two burdens are taken together, along with their central hinge (11:1-17)—the same remarkable complex of literary patterns observed in 1:7-6:8.

Though the more obvious kind of formal evidence that demarcates the visions is not available for determining the precise bounds of the units within each burden, there is a clear enough broad ordering of major themes into the patterns just mentioned. Genre analysis also helps.

In the first burden Hanson identifies 9:1-17 and 10:3-12 as divine-warrior hymns set in the conflict-myth scheme.[28] The intervening verses he identifies as a *rîb* against the unfaithful shepherds.[29] In the second burden Hanson again identifies two extended passages (12:1-13:1; 14:1-21) that draw upon the ancient ritual pattern of the conflict myth. Concerning the material between them he suggests that 13:2-6 may not be an original part of the composition beginning at 12:1 and that 13:7-9 belongs with 11:4-17, as its original conclusion or perhaps an early addition.[30]

Genre analysis thus discloses a matching concentric triadic structure (ABA′) in each of the burdens. This conclusion is corroborated by other patterns discernible in Zechariah 9-14. Of special interest is the relation of the two B-units (10:1-4; 13:2-9) to the central hinge of the burdens (11:1-17). Like the latter they contain the shepherd-flock motif[31] and develop it in terms of the conflict of the true (messianic) and false shepherds, the suffering of the former and condemnation of the latter, the sustaining of those of the flock identified with the messianic shepherd and the dispersion of the others associated with the false shepherds. It thus appears that these three passages, one the hinge between the two burdens and the other two the middle units in each burden, closely reproduce within Zechariah 9-14 the main structural feature we have identified in the book as a whole—namely, the three hinge sections, all dealing with the messianic coronation and commissioning, and functioning together as the framework for a diptych with concentric side panels. The repetition of this extraordinary overall structure of Zechariah within the second half of the prophecy argues for one mind behind the whole. It would be difficult to take seriously the assumption that a later author-redactor wrote chaps. 9-14 and attached it to the materials of chaps. 1-8 that he found at hand, so producing as redactor this remarkable scheme in the compound work overall as well as in the half that he authored.

Certainly also the concentric pattern of each of the two burdens is evidenced by this distinctive character of their middle (or B) members. Moreover the A and A′ members within each burden exhibit the correspondence appropriate to such a pattern.

In the first burden, both A (9:1-17) and A′ (10:5-12) foretell subjugation of hostile nations and, correlative thereto, the restoration of God's people to Zion as a divine protectorate. More specific correspondence is seen in a cluster of elements in both 9:4-6 and 10:11. Included are God's smiting the sea, loss of king/scepter, and humiliation of the proud. Conspicuous in both A and A′ (and forming an inclusio for A′) is the imagery of the military strengthening of the faithful: they become mighty warriors and weapons.

Found only here in Zechariah is *gbwr*, "mighty warrior" (9:13; 10:5,7; cf. *hgbyr* in 10:6,12). Both A and A′ speak of the Lord's favor resulting in joy, expressed by the verb *gyl* (9:9; 10:7), not used elsewhere in Zechariah. Other terms used in both these passages and only in them in this book are *nwgś*, "oppressor" (9:8; 10:4); *qšt mlḥmh*, "battle bow" (9:10; 10:4); *ṭyṭ ḥwṣwt*, "mire of the streets" (9:3; 10:5); *kmw-yyn*, "as through wine" (9:15; 10:7). Note too the similar references to the domain of Yahweh, with the double use of *ym*, "sea," and the north-south boundaries, in 9:10 and 10:11.

The correspondences between 12:1-13:1 and 14:1-21, the A and A′ members of the second burden, are obvious. Both deal with the final gathering of the world forces against Jerusalem. The term *ʾsp*, "gather," that describes the siege in 12:3 and 14:2 (cf. v. 14) is used only here in Zechariah. In both passages there is a sustained emphasis on the universal scale of the assault, expressed as "all the nations" (12:9; 14:2,16), "all the peoples" (12:3; 14:12), "all the peoples around" (12:2,6) and "all the nations around" (14:14), "all the nations of the earth" (12:3) and "the families of the earth" (14:17). Also common to both are the following: Judah is identified with Jerusalem in the siege (12:2,5; 14:14); God is present and fights for his people, defending Jerusalem, his protectorate (esp. 12:4,9; 14:3); confrontation with the divine warrior strikes panic into the enemy ranks (12:4; 14:13); animals are afflicted along with men in the judgment (12:4; 14:12,15); God's judgment issues in the destruction of the gathered nations and the secure settlement of Jerusalem (12:6; 14:11).

Formally balanced by their common ABA′ structure, the two burdens also manifest thematic parallelism. Their B-members, as observed above, both contain the sphepherd-flock theme (present in the 11:1-17 hinge also). The A- and A′-members of both burdens all portray the Lord's judgment of the world powers as he restores Zion, establishing it forever as the place of his presence and favor. More specific parallels like the following are also found: the motif of God's opening his eyes upon the distress of the faithful as a prelude to their judicial vindication and deliverance (in the two A-members, at 9:8 and 12:4); the imagery of an escape passage produced by the divine act of dividing, whether of sea or mountain (in the two A′-members, at 10:11 and 14:4).

Further important evidence of the balanced diptych form of Zechariah 9-14 and of the hinge role of 11:1-17 between the two burdens is an ABCDC′B′A′ scheme, with 11:1-17 as the central (D) member of the chiasm.

The correspondences between the A and A′ pair (9:1-17 and 14:1-21) are conspicuous. In each there is a dramatic advent of the Lord as King (9:9; 14:3-4). His rule extends to the ends of the earth (9:10; 14:9). He engages in military judgment against the nations that would occupy the covenant heritage (9:1ff.; 14:3ff.). The defeated foe loses its amassed wealth, its silver and gold becoming a spoil for God's people (9:3; 14:1,14). Out of the ranks of the enemy nations a converted Gentile remnant is incorporated into the redemptive covenant, observing its cultic stipulations (9:7; 14:16). Preserved by the Lord's encompassing guardianship, his protectorate at last dwells safe from affliction (9:8; 14:9-11).

The B and B′ pair (10:1-4 and 13:2-9) in this chiasm were also the two B members of the ABA′ formations on either side of the 11:1-17 hinge, and their notable correspondences have already been detailed above.

The chiastic nature of Zechariah 9-14 is thus firmly established by the manifest parallelism that marks the A-A′ and B-B′ pairings, as well as the clear role of 11:1-17 as the central point, and comparison of the passages that remain (10:5-12; 12:1-13:1) indicates that they qualify as the matching C-C′ pair that fills out this inverse parallelism. Beyond their general similarity in theme—namely, the Lord's restoration and defense of his people and the humbling of their foes—are specific parallels in topic and terminology. The Lord's afflicted people strengthen themselves in him

(10:6,12; 12:5) and are thereby made like great heroes in battle (10:7; 12:8). In the enemy army, the riders of horses are confounded (10:5; 12:4) as the Lord acts to save the house of Israel (10:6; 12:7).

3. *Parallelism between the visions chiasm and burdens chiasm.* We have seen that the visions and burdens are both arranged in seven-unit chiasms. It remains to observe that the corresponding units of these two chiasms parallel each other topically. This evidence adds weighty support both to the case for the unitary character of the book of Zechariah and to our particular analysis of this work as a diptych with 6:9-15 as its central hinge.

The centerpieces (D-units) of the two ABCDC'B'A' schemes (3:1-10; 11:1-17) are, of course, the hinges in the middle of the diptych side panels of the overall diptych. We are already well acquainted with their remarkable similarities.

Each of the A-units of the two chiasms (1:7-17; 9:1-17) presents a mounted[32] Messiah figure: the Lord of angels on the red horse (1:8), and the king of Israel on the donkey of covenant ratification (9:9). He is the ruler over all the nations (1:11; 9:10). The Lord engages in a worldwide surveillance through heavenly agents known as his eyes (1:8-11; 9:8) and threatens to overthrow the nations arrogantly secure in their strongholds, indifferent to the God of Israel (1:15; 9:2-6). Military imagery makes allusion to the history of the conquest of Canaan (1:8 [cf. Josh 5:13]; 9:1-6). The Lord refers to "my house," promising to restore and defend it (1:16-17; 9:8).[33] Proclamation of good and joyful tidings to Jerusalem is commanded and performed (1:13-14; 9:9).

That the opening unit of the burdens chiasm exhibits such numerous and notable parallels to the corresponding A-unit in the visions chiasm gives an unmistakable signal of the author's intention to conduct us again along the same route traversed in the earlier part of his work. The second half of the overall diptych turns out to be an apocalyptic recasting of the prophetic visions in the first half.[34]

The B-unit of the chiasms under review (2:1-4; 10:1-4) is each relatively brief. Topically they match, both speaking of the dispersal of Judah (cf. 2:2,4; 10:2) and the Lord's judgment on those responsible for that, whether the foreign powers without or the false prophets within.

In both the C-units (2:5-17; 10:5-12) a divine summons to return to the homeland is issued to those in distant exile (cf. 2:10-11; 10:8-11). This return, accomplished through divine intervention, is depicted as being a new exodus (cf. 2:12-13; 10:5,8-11). Emphasis falls on the astounding expansion of the covenant people (2:8,10,15; 10:8-10). By reason of the multitudes Jerusalem will be like an unwalled city (2:8), and the land will not be sufficient for them (10:10). This restoration will register anew the covenantal election (2:12,16; 10:6) and will be an occasion of joy and song (2:14; 10:7).

Continuing the comparison of the chiastic units into the triad beyond the central D-hinge, we observe that both C'-units (4:1-14; 12:1-13:1) present the Lord as the power source for the victory over the world and the completion of the temple-kingdom (esp. 4:6; 12:5,8). By his might the world power is brought low (4:7), its attack on Jerusalem resulting in its own destruction (12:3,9). Salvation is attributed specifically to the Spirit (4:6; 12:10) and involves a spiritual work of grace, a display of divine favor (4:7; 12:10).[35] The Spirit transforms God's people into the likeness of his own fiery Glory theophany; they are likened to burning lamps (4:2) and flaming torches or firepans (12:6; cf. 12:8; Gen 15:17). Messiah, mediator of the Spirit and salvation, is portrayed under the figure of representatives of the royal house of David: Zerubbabel in Zech 4:7-10, David himself in 12:8. A shared motif is the Lord's eyes looking with fostering favor on his servants in their kingdom struggles (4:10; 12:4).

The common message of the B'-units (5:1-11; 13:2-9) is judgment within the covenant realm, referred to in both as "all the land" (5:3,6; 13:8). Apostates are cut off from their place in the holy land (5:4,9-11; 13:8). Associated with this removal is the motif of uncleanness, the unclean stork (5:9) and the unclean spirit (13:2). Prominent in the indictment is swearing or speaking lies in the name of the Lord (5:4; 13:3).

Establishment of God's universal eschatological reign is the subject of the A'-units (6:1-8; 14:1-21). Revelation of the divine sovereignty in universal judgment (6:5; 14:2,9,14) is a *parousia* event, a day of the Lord, an advent with the heavenly hosts (6:5,8; 14:1,3-5).[36] All the points of the compass are referred to in depicting the fulfillment of the kingdom sanctions (6:6-8; 14:4,8). A shared image is the two mountains identified with the site of the Lord's *parousia* (6:1; 14:4-5).

CONCLUSION

The latter portion of canonical Zechariah, to which fashionable higher criticism would assign a different provenance than the first eight chapters, is found to be structurally interlocked with those earlier chapters by means of an intricate triple-hinge mechanism. Within this framework the two parts alleged to be of different origins constitute the finely balanced side panels flanking the central hinge. Such a curious overall structuring is rather clearly to be attributed to an original master plan for the whole work, not to a secondary redactional development, particularly since the central hinge is located in the supposedly earlier part.

Something beyond the interests of literary artistry was involved in this compositional creation. At all the key hinge points in this arrangement the theme of the messianic priest-king is not only present but dominant. The formal structure was evidently designed to highlight the figure of the coming Christ, ordained to priestly sacrifice and subsequent highest royal glory, the one who is the central hinge and focus of prophetic revelation.

---

1 In 6:9-15 the symbolic action is apparently a real external transaction, while it is performed within a vision in 3:1-10 and 11:1-17.

2 For details see below.

3 See e.g. C.L. Meyers and E.M. Meyers, *Haggai, Zechariah* 1-8 (AB 25B; New York: Doubleday, 1987) lv-lvii, 179,213ff. We will be interacting particularly with this work because it gives considerable attention to compositional questions.

4 Underestimating the significance of this difference in the treatment of Joshua (Zechariah 3) and Zerubbabel (Zechariah 4), Meyers takes these two visions together as a centerpiece of the night visions (cf. *Haggai* liv ff.). That, however, conflicts with Meyers' own inclusion of Zechariah 4 in the count of the visions, thereby associating it with those visions over against Zechariah 3, not so included.

5 Assisting is an interpreting angel, present in each of the other visions but significantly absent from 3:1-10 (and the other two hinges).

6 Reception of voluntary silver and gold contributions from individual leaders for cultic objectives by someone not a Levitical priest is attested in Exod 25:2ff. (cf. 35:5); Num 31:51-54; 2 Kgs 12:3-17. A close literary parallel to Zech 6:10-11 is Num 3:45-47 (the ʾt in v. 46 being equivalent to the mʾt in vv. 49,50). The genre is a kind of divine requisition adapted from commercial dockets.

7 We cannot here discuss the notion that two crowns are in view. I assume there was a single crown, probably one composed of separate circlets of gold and silver. See further the next note.

8 I regard reconstructions of the text that would substitute or add the figure of Zerubbabel as unwarranted conjecture. But even if such a view were adopted, the observations we are making about the formal and thematic characteristics shared by 6:9-15 in common with the other two hinge sections would still hold true.

9 The repetition of ʿ*l-ks*ᵓ*w* demands that it is a single figure, a priest-king who is depicted here as sitting by Yahweh's throne.

10 The LXX rendering of the second ʿ*l-ks*ᵓ*w* of MT, as if reading ʿ*l-ymynw*, possibly suggests the interpretation of the throne as Yahweh's.

11 In 1 Chronicles 29, the background passage, the peace of Solomon's reign is described, a time of prosperity and loyalty (v. 23). Note too that conjoined to the statement of Solomon's anointing as king is that of Zadok's appointment as priest (v. 22).

12 Before his visionary experience is concluded, Zechariah is also obliged to impersonate the false shepherd (11:15-17).

13 P.F. Hanson, *The Dawn of the Apocalyptic* (Philadelphia: Fortress, 1975) 337, entitles this section, to which he attaches 13:7-9, "A Commissioning Narrative Transformed into a Prophecy of Doom." On the distinctiveness of this section within Zechariah 9-14 see P.L. Redditt, "Israel's Shepherds: Hope and Pessimism in Zechariah 9-14," *CBQ* 51/4 (1989) 634.

14 This becomes more explicit in the resumption of the theme of the afflicted shepherd in 13:7.

15 Some of the parallels are particularly between the two side hinges. Also, the first and third passages are visionary in nature, whereas the central hinge is nonvisionary. A concentric pattern is thus exhibited by the hinge sections.

16 See Meyers, *Haggai* lii, for a chart of some of the terminological and topical correspondences.

17 They, however, face the redactional problem that 7:1-8:23 was hardly intended as the conclusion of a work restricted to chaps. 1-6 apart from chaps. 9-14.

18 R.A. Mason notes several ways in which Zechariah 8 and 14 give prominence to Zion, suggesting that "proto-Zechariah" has influenced the formulation of "deutero-Zechariah"; cf. "The Relation of Zechariah 9-14 to Proto-Zechariah," *ZAW* 88 (1976) 227-231.

19 Cf. ibid. 234.

20 In view of this relationship, "by night" (1:8) is not a symbolic detail in vision 1 but refers to the prophet's experience in reception of all seven visions. Likewise the date in 1:7 belongs to the entire series.

21 A phrase akin to that found in 5:5a is found elsewhere in the middle, not beginning, of a vision (cf. 2:7). The language of lifting up the eyes and seeing is in 5:5b, but (unlike 2:1; 2:5; 5:1; 6:1) in the form of an imperative (cf. 6:8).

22 This is, in fact, another feature in the parallelism, for 2:1-4, the corresponding second vision of the first triad, is also a compound vision (cf. the four horns and the four craftsmen).

23 Because of space restrictions we are obliged here and throughout this essay to limit ourselves to a partial account of supportive data. We will simply try to give enough of the evidence to establish our analysis as an attractive working hypothesis for further testing, elaboration and, hopefully, corroboration.

24 Cf. M.G. Kline, "The Rider of the Red Horse," *Kerux* 5/2 (1990) 2-20; 5/3 (1990) 9-28; *Images of the Spirit* (Grand Rapids: Baker, 1980) 86-90.

25 In 5:3,6 ᵓ*rṣ* refers to the holy land, from which covenant breakers are being removed and banished to Babylon.

26 Vision 3 pictures the rebuilding-perfecting of Jerusalem, the temple-city, and vision 5 takes us into the temple with its lampstand symbolism expounded in terms of a rebuilding and completing of God's house.

27 On the recognition of the distinctiveness of 11:1-17, see above.

28 Hanson, *Dawn* 292ff.,325ff. Hanson's form-critical observations are of value but cannot sustain his speculations on the development of apocalyptic eschatology and its sociological setting. Moreover, his genre history is warped by misdating of important blocks of biblical evidence.

29 Relevant to the question of the exact bounds of this middle-section are considerations like the presence of the flock motif in 9:16 and the continuation of the theme of the Lord as the true shepherd-provider (10:1) to 10:4. This unit is here taken as 10:1-4, but see also n. 31 below.

30 Hanson, *Dawn* 338,354ff., 371ff. I regard 13:2-9 as a unit (within the integral Zecharian whole) but cite Hanson in support of the basic point of the tripartite form of the second burden.

31 The key term $ṣ^ʾn$, "flock," is found in Zechariah only in these three passages (10:2; 11:4,7,11,17; 13:7) plus the transitional 9:16. Note also the three appearances of $ḥrb$, "sword," in Zechariah in 9:13; 11:17; 13:7. Do these data suggest that the beginning of the B-unit of the first burden might better be put earlier? Cf. Redditt, "Israel's Shepherds" 634.

32 In both cases *rōkēb* is used.

33 In both passages ^ʿôd, "yet," occurs; cf. Mason, "Relation" 229.

34 In addition to the correspondences in the successive individual units we may note the structural parallelism between the ABC group in each of the chiasms—that is, between the first three visions and the first of the burdens. We observed above that the two themes of the oracle that closes the first vision are developed in turn in the following two visions. Similarly in the tripartite burden of 9:1-10:12 the second unit (10:1-4) resumes the shepherd-flock motif introduced in the closing divine proclamation of the first (cf. 9:16-17), while the third (10:5,12) develops the theme of the Lord's strengthening his people for battle, central to that same proclamation (cf. 9:13-15).

35 Here are the only two appearances of $ḥn$, "grace" in Zechariah.

36 Both use $yṣ^ʾ$, "go forth," for the advent; cf. 6:1,5,6,7; 14:3.

INDEX OF BIBLICAL REFERENCES

282